Irish Diplomacy at the United Nations, 1945–1965

Irish Diplomacy at the United Nations, 1945–1965

National Interests and the International Order

Joseph Morrison Skelly

IRISH ACADEMIC PRESS

This book was set in 10.5 on 12 point Ehrhardt
by Carrigboy Typesetting Services, Co. Cork for
IRISH ACADEMIC PRESS
44, Northumberland Road, Ballsbridge, Dublin 4, Ireland
and in North America for
IRISH ACADEMIC PRESS
5804 NE Hassalo St, Portland, Oregon 97213.

A catalogue record for this title
is available from the British Library.

ISBN 0–7165–2574–7

This book is printed on an acid-free and a wood-free paper.

Printed in Great Britain
by Redwood Books, Trowbridge, Wiltshire

Foreword

This book is thorough, well researched and documented, and a welcome addition to the study of Irish diplomacy and, indeed, to the study of modern Irish history. Its inevitable denseness is accommodated without loss of readability.

The work is about the development and evolution of Ireland's political foreign policy at the UN which, in the circumstances of the period covered, necessarily revolved around issues arising in the General Assembly, and so the focus is on this body to the virtual exclusion of every other forum (including the Security Council, even for the year when Ireland was a member). Examination of a wider scope of activities would have diluted the treatment of the work's basic theme.

Dr Skelly puts the role played by Ireland at the UN into proper perspective. Firstly, he demonstrates that at all times Ireland's policy was inspired by national interest, even if often interest in a broad sense that was likely to be shared with several other countries. The differences in policies pursued in the successive phases owed their origin to nuances of perception of national interest and of how it should be pursued, as held by successive Governments.

Indeed, the book identifies three phases of different policy approaches during 1955–65, corresponding mainly to the terms in office of different Taoisigh: 1955–57, 1957–59, 1959–65. The author argues, with convincing support from the evidence of events, that in all three phases the Taoisigh, Costello, de Valera and Lemass, were not only fully cognisant of Ireland's UN policy, but also influenced it, to an extent not generally appreciated.

Policies over the whole period roughly progressed from a line, in the first phase, that was pro-christian values, pro-Western and anti-communist, through a more independent and pro-active line, in the second phase, aimed at reducing international tensions, to a return, in the third phase, to a pro-Western stance, influenced by anxiety to promote closer relations with Western, particularly the US and European Economic Community members, for mainly economic reasons.

Secondly, he assesses realistically the importance of Ireland's role. It was, in theatrical terms, a supporting role in contrast to a leading role on the one hand or a walk-on part on the other. Ireland was never remotely close to exerting influence like that exerted by a great power. Indeed its proposals were successful only when they enjoyed the support of a great power (usually the US) – which is not to say that all of its unsuccessful initiatives were without influence, especially in the longer term. The role played was facilitated by the importance of the General Assembly as a forum at the time and the usefulness of 'middle powers' which could come up with compromise solutions.

The relative importance of Ireland's role, as assessed by the author, emerges from the detail of his account of events. This account traces Ireland's contribution towards mitigating Cold War tensions, promoting decolonisation in Africa and Asia, opposing apartheid in South Africa, defending human rights in Tibet and mediating disputes in Kashmir, Somaliland and South Tyrol. Of particular interest is the Irish initiative under Frank Aiken, Minister for External Affairs, on a series of resolutions on nuclear non-proliferation which led to the Nuclear Non-Proliferation Treaty in 1968. This period also marks the genesis of Ireland's UN peacekeeping tradition with the contribution of several thousand troops to the UN's operations in the Congo, the Sinai and in Cyprus.

Ireland's overall contribution was recognised in the leadership positions taken up by its diplomats in the UN: Frederick Boland as President of the General Assembly in 1960, Conor Cruise O'Brien as Dag Hammerskjold's personal representative in the Congo in 1961 and General Sean McKeown as Military Commander of the UN's mission in the Congo.

Dr Skelly avails of newly released materials from the Department of Foreign Affairs and the Department of the Taoiseach deposited in the Irish National Archives, and the publication by Irish Academic Press is timely following the 50th anniversary of the founding of the UN and the 40th anniversary of Ireland's membership.

MARY ROBINSON
President of Ireland,
February 1997

Preface

John Millington Synge once said that 'all art is collaboration'. So too is the writing of history. I am thus indebted to many people.

I am most honored by the contribution of a Foreword from President Mary Robinson, whose own noteworthy efforts in the field of international relations mirror those of the first Irish diplomats at the United Nations.

I wish to thank the staff of the National Archives, Dublin for their invaluable assistance. Aideen Ireland, Catriona Crowe, Eamon Mulally, Paddy Sarsfield, Lorcan Farrell and all of their colleagues facilitated my research from beginning to end. Likewise, I wish to express my sincere appreciation to several members of the Department of History, University College Dublin: Professor Mary Daly, Professor Ronan Fanning, and Dr David Doyle guided, and inspired, my postgraduate studies; Mr James McGuire and Dr Maurice Bric offered timely advice and support. Throughout the past several years Dr Gerald Straka, of the University of Delaware, encouraged my endeavors.

The staff of several other institutions sustained my work. In Ireland, Commandant Victor Laing at the Military Archives, Cathal Brugha Barracks; Fran Carroll, Jim O'Shea, and their associates at the National Library; Seamus Helferty, University College Dublin Archives; Bernadette Chambers, Archivist in Iveagh House; and the Manuscript Department, Trinity College, were all extremely helpful. So were many in the United States, including Christine Killingbeck in the Photo Library and Ms M. Guptil in Archives Department at the United Nations; the Rare Books Room, Butler Library, Columbia University; the Seely G. Mudd Manuscript Library, Princeton University; the John F. Kennedy Presidential Library; the Massachusetts Historical Society.

I appreciate the insights of several Irish and UN officials: Mr Liam Cosgrave, Mr Noel Dorr, Ambassador Eamon Kennedy, Ambassador James Kirwan, Ambassador Robert McDonagh, Mrs Máire MacEntee O'Brien, Dr Conor Cruise O'Brien, Ambassador Tadhg O'Sullivan, Sir Brian Urquhart, and Ambassador Charles Whelan. A debt of gratitude is owed to several family members of past diplomats: Frank and Eileen Aiken, Fergal and Yvonne Boland. I am grateful to Michael Adams, Martin Healy, Martin Fanning, and Ronan Gallagher of Irish Academic Press for their initial interest, professional input, and recent guidance in preparing this manuscript for publication.

Thanks are also due to Clara Acton, John and Colleen Aulenti, SFC Douglas E. Bell (US Army, Ret.), Eoin Burke-Kennedy, Carl and Sharen Butrum, Ger Cagney, Joe Calvi, Mike Cantwell, Martin and Catherine Davis, Fionnula Downey, Richard and Maxine English, Sean and Jessica Faughnan, Michael and Dorothy Forde, Mariya Fridman, Mike and Ann Hayes, Pat Henry, Bob Gill, Mikhail and Irina Iogman, Barry and Vera Keane, Michael Kennedy, Deirdre McMahon, Pat McPherron, Senan Murphy, Lisa O'Halloran, Tom and Celia O'Neill, Meg O'Sullivan, Moira Palumbo, Dave and Nicola Peden, Lou Potter, Bob 'Duke' Schneider, Chris Spain and Anita Borgenicht, Sean and Tammy Sullivan. Most important, I thank my entire family for their unstinting support, including my late uncle, Ron Morrison, and especially my parents, to whom this book is dedicated.

For my Mother and Father

Contents

Illustrations

1 The General Assembly of the United Nations in Plenary session

2 Members of the Irish delegation to the Eleventh Session in 1956

3 Frank Aiken (left) and Frederick H. Boland review documents prior to the Twelfth Assembly's General Debate in September 1957

4 Members of the Irish delegation to the Thirteenth Assembly in 1958

5 Freddy Boland, Chairman of the Trusteeship Committee

6 General Sean McKeown, Commander of the United Nations peace-keeping operation in the Congo (ONUC)

7 Frederick H. Boland, President of the General Assembly, and Secretary General Dag Hammarskjold

8 Cornelius Cremin, who replaced Frederick H. Boland as Ireland's Ambassador to the United Nations in January 1964

Abbreviations

CAB	Cabinet Minutes, National Archives, Dublin
DD	*Dáil Éireann, Parliamentary Debates, 1922–69*
DFA	Department of Foreign Affairs, Central Registry Files, National Archives, Dublin
DFA CM	Department of Foreign Affairs, Common Market Series, National Archives, Dublin
DFA PMUN	Department of Foreign Affairs, Permanent Mission of Ireland to the United Nations Series, National Archives, Dublin
DFA P	Department of Foreign Affairs, Secretary's Files, P Series, National Archives, Dublin
DFA PS	Department of Foreign Affairs, Secretary's Files, PS Series, National Archives, Dublin
DFA S	Department of Foreign Affairs, Secretary's Files, S Series, National Archives, Dublin
EEC	European Economic Community
FLN	National Liberation Front, Algeria
GA/RES	General Assembly Resolution
GC	Government Minutes, National Archives, Dublin
NATO	North Atlantic Treaty Organization
OECD	Organization for Economic Cooperation and Development.
OEEC	Organization for European Economic Development
ONUC	*Force de l'Organisation des Nations Unis en Congo* (UN Peacekeeping Force in the Congo)
S	Department of the Taoiseach, Secretariat Files, National Archives, Dublin
SC/RES	Security Council Resolution
TD	Teachta Dala (member of the Irish parliament)
UN	The United Nations
UNEF	United Nations Emergency Force (Sinai)

Introduction

Ireland first applied for membership in the United Nations in the autumn of 1946, but the Soviet Union vetoed its bid in the Security Council. The ostensible reason for its action was the absence of diplomatic relations between the two countries, but the USSR actually feared that a pro-western Ireland would dilute its standing in the General Assembly. After anxiously seeking entry for nine years, Ireland finally gained admission in December 1955 as part of a sixteen-nation deal sealed during a brief thaw in Soviet-American relations.[1]

Ireland thus entered the Organization when two forces had rent the international system: the Cold War had divided the world into east and west; anticolonialism in Africa and Asia had riven the globe into north and south. These dynamics dominated the General Assembly's heated debates over Hungary and the Suez in 1956, the Middle East in 1958, the representation of China, Tibet, disarmament, the Franco-Algerian conflict, apartheid in South Africa, the Congo, West New Guinea, and countless other questions.

These international forces and Assembly issues also presented Ireland with unique dilemmas. With regard to the Cold War, Ireland was militarily neutral, yet a western democracy not indifferent to its outcome. With respect to decolonization, Ireland was a European state with close ties to the European colonial powers, but concurrently a nation that had experienced a long period of foreign rule and its own recent struggle for independence.

The ensuing diplomatic resolution of these conflicts inaugurated one of the most compelling chapters in the history of the state's foreign policy. From the mid-1950s until the mid-1960s the Irish delegation, led by an extraordinary team of talented, dedicated diplomats, occupied a prominent place in the General Assembly.

Previous commentators, however, have misinterpreted this intriguing era. In seeking an analytical model, several have over-relied upon the three principles Liam Cosgrave enumerated in his 1956 Dáil address.[2] Some have

---

1 For a review of this nine-year period, see Joseph Morrison Skelly, 'Ireland, the Department of External Affairs, and the United Nations, 1946–55: a New Look', in *Irish Studies in International Affairs*, Vol. 7 (1996).
2 Cf. Conor Cruise O'Brien, 'Ireland in International Affairs', in Owen Dudley Edwards (ed.), *Conor Cruise O'Brien Introduces Ireland* (Dublin, 1969), pp. 128–9; Norman

uncritically accepted Ireland's high profile, refusing to ponder the veracity of contemporary reports of the formation of an 'Afro-Irish bloc' in New York, or claims that due to its Assembly endeavors Ireland bestrode 'the world stage like a Colossus'.[3] By the same token, scholars have worn out the mantra that Ireland's influence was 'out of all proportion' to her size.[4]

Conversely, others have too zealously deflated Ireland's well-deserved reputation. They have inaccurately asserted that it was manufactured: 'Skillful public relations by Irish officials contributed to a national and international perception of the distinctiveness and importance of their contribution, particularly in areas of anticolonialism, disarmament, and peacekeeping.'[5] A few have devalued Irish policy by claiming that it was merely 'declaratory'.[6] Likewise, one observer erroneously contends that Ireland acted as an 'International Good Citizen' solely to enhance its prestige.[7]

These limitations demand redress. So do two others. For the most part, Irish surveys have paid little attention to Ireland's foreign policy; subsequently, the canon of Irish historiography has neglected Ireland's role at the United Nations.[8] So have histories of the Organization. Irish peacekeeping and Conor O'Brien's service as Dag Hammarskjold's representative in Katanga are well-known. The broader narrative, however, has overshadowed the Irish delegation's place in UN diplomacy.[9]

MacQueen, 'Ireland's Entry into the United Nations, 1946–56', in Thomas Gallagher and James O'Connell (eds.), *Irish Contemporary Studies* (Manchester, 1983), pp. 72–5; Trevor Salmon, *Unneutral Ireland* (Oxford, 1989), p. 226.

3   Cf. Brian O'Connor, *Ireland and the United Nations*, Tuairim pamphlet (Dublin, 1961), p. 1; F.S.L. Lyons, *Ireland since the Famine* (London, 1973), p. 594. The laudatory references to the Irish delegation appeared in separate issues of the *Economist* (19 December 1959, 31 December 1960). The author of both pieces, Andrew Boyd, was on excellent terms with several members of the Irish delegation, which accounts, in part, for his effusive tone: Donald Harman Akenson, *Conor: A Biography of Conor Cruise O'Brien*, Vol. I (Montreal, 1994), p. 159, n. 21, p. 166.

4   T.D. Williams, 'Irish Foreign Policy, 1949–69', in Joseph Lee (ed.), *Ireland, 1945–70* (Dublin, 1979), p. 139. In many other respects this essay is interesting and reliable. The author's contacts in the Department of External Affairs, particularly his correspondence with Conor O'Brien, account for his accurate insights: Joseph Lee, *Ireland, 1912–85: Politics and Society* (Cambridge, 1989), p. 633; DFA 417/167, 7 July 1957; DFA 417/205, 15 September 1958.

5   Lee, *Ireland*, p. 370.

6   Cf. Patrick Keatinge, 'The Europeanization of Irish Foreign Policy', in P.J. Drudy and Dermot McAleese (eds.), *Ireland and the European Community* (Cambridge, 1983), p. 34; Paul Sharp, *Irish Foreign Policy and the European Community* (Aldershot, 1990), pp. 44, 49.

7   Sharp, *Irish Foreign Policy*, pp. 44–66, 236–8.

8   Cf. Roy Foster, *Modern Ireland, 1600–1972* (London, 1988), pp. 570, 581; Lee, *Ireland*, pp. 369–71. Dermot Keogh's *Twentieth-Century Ireland: Nation and State* (Dublin, 1994) is the only general history of Ireland that analyzes foreign policy in detail.

9   Cf. Brian Urquhart, *Hammarskjold* (New York, 1972), p. 257; Evan Luard, *A History of the United Nations* (London, 1982 & 1989).

Thus, the full story of Ireland's participation in the General Assembly remains untold. The time is ripe for scholarly investigation; this study responds to that opportunity. A timely one in the wake of the fiftieth anniversary of the founding of the Organization and the fortieth anniversary of Ireland's entry, it provides a balanced, complete, historical assessment of the first decade of Irish diplomacy at the United Nations.

A propitious development has facilitated this task: the opening of the Irish National Archives.[10] The significance of this moment cannot be overstated. For too long the unavailability of official sources has handicapped the writing of the history of independent Ireland; now the systematic study of the state is underway. Indeed, a new era of Irish historiography has commenced. By mining the records of Irish government departments, researchers are over-turning popular assumptions, confirming certain conclusions, and generating new insights.[11] As a result, Irish citizens are learning how their nation has been governed. This knowledge will enhance the interpretation of Ireland's performance in the twentieth century as it prepares for the twenty-first.

The foregoing is especially true with regard to the analysis of Irish foreign policy, which represents a microcosm of the wider historiographical milieu. Despite the scarcity of official sources, scholars in this field have done an admirable job. Many of the publications that have appeared to date are excel-lent; more so, they have served as a vital starting point for the study of Irish foreign policy.[12] Nevertheless, because writers were denied complete access to Irish sources they focused on broad, accessible issues – neutrality, partition, Anglo-Irish relations – at the expense of other areas of investigation: European bilateral relations, international organizations, post-war economic policy. Also, their findings are sometimes inconclusive. The study of Irish foreign policy, therefore, stands to benefit immensely from the opening of the government archives, as the most recent publications in this discipline prove.[13]

Like these latest volumes, this one is based upon a thorough analysis of the files of the Irish Department of Foreign Affairs – the records of those who actually formulated and conducted Irish diplomacy at the UN. Other primary sources have been consulted. The archives of the Department of the Taoiseach have proved invaluable. So have private collections and selected

10 The National Archives, established by the National Archives Act (1986), opened in Dublin in 1991.
11 Cf. Keogh, *Ireland*; Mary Daly, *Industrial Development and Irish National Identity, 1922–39* (Dublin, 1992); Donal Ó Drisceoil, *Censorship in Ireland, 1939–45: Neutrality, Politics and Society* (Cork, 1996).
12 Cf. Patrick Keatinge, *The Formulation of Irish Foreign Policy* (Dublin, 1973); Patrick Keatinge, *A Place Among the Nations: Issues of Irish Foreign Policy* (Dublin, 1978); Denis Maher, *The Tortuous Path: The Course of Ireland's Entry into the EEC, 1948–73* (Dublin, 1986); Salmon, *Ireland*.
13 Cf. Dermot Keogh, *Ireland and the Vatican: Politics and Diplomacy of Church-State Relations, 1922–60* (Cork, 1995); Michael Kennedy, *Ireland and the League of Nations, 1919–46: International Relations, Diplomacy and Politics* (Dublin, 1996).

United States government documents. The use of United Nations public manuscripts, Irish, American, and European newspapers, Dáil debates, government publications, and personal interviews has rounded out this study.

Still, a significant, but paradoxical, point must be stressed: Irish policy at the UN cannot be fully elucidated unless the broad canvass that has heretofore obscured it is taken into account. Elements of it, like the status of the international system, are considered. So too is the institutional nature of the United Nations, whose smooth functioning during the Cold War depended upon committed members like Ireland. The effects of Ireland's domestic priorities and its wider foreign policy are also weighed.

* * *

Two themes underpin this study: national interests and the international order. With regard to the former, Irish statecraft at the United Nations is best analyzed within the framework of the steady pursuit of Irish national interests. This proposition is certainly not new in an international sense; it is axiomatic that states predicate their foreign policy on their own interests.[14] Yet too few historians have applied this concept to Irish foreign policy generally. They have been reluctant to accept that *raisons d'état* have motivated Ireland, just like all other nations. Instead, they have posited that Ireland is *sui generis* – somehow set apart from the rest of the international community.[15]

There have been some astute exceptions to this trend, most notably with regard to inter-war diplomacy and neutrality during World War II.[16] But no one has applied this principle to Ireland's posture in the General Assembly. Until now. Indeed, this investigation relies on national interests as the primary conceptual apparatus for interpreting Irish diplomacy at the UN, as must all future studies of Irish foreign policy. To do otherwise flies in the face of convention, wisdom, and reality. Ireland is not *sui generis*.

A full explanation of this thesis requires the delineation of its two interconnected strands. First, throughout the 1950s and 1960s three distinct phases are discernible, during each of which three successive Irish governments assigned priority to one of the several national interests they pursued at the UN. Preferences shifted when new governments took charge in 1957 and in 1959; these internal changes in Dublin precipitated external policy transformations in New York. Moreover, because the primary interest during each stage coincided with the sitting Taoiseach's predilections, the periods are defined by these men.

14 Cf. Henry Kissinger, *Diplomacy* (New York, 1994), *passim*.
15 Cf. Salmon, *Ireland*, p. 8.
16 Cf. Ronan Fanning, 'Irish Neutrality – an Historical Perspective', *Irish Studies in International Affairs*, Vol. 1, No. 3 (1982); Lee, *Ireland*, p. 263. Michael Kennedy's new, groundbreaking study of Irish policy at the League of Nations astutely incorporates, in part, the pursuit of national interests: Kennedy, *League*, p. 16.

The first phase is thus labeled the Costello era, in recognition of the leader of the second Inter-Party government, which held power from 1954 until 1957. This stage comprised only the Eleventh General Assembly in 1956. The principal national interest pursued at the UN was western success in the Cold War. The means by which Ireland advanced this objective was to act as a staunch ally of the United States and western Europe in the Assembly.

The de Valera period lasted from March 1957, when Fianna Fáil's election victory ousted the Inter-Party government, until June 1959, and encompassed the Twelfth Assembly in 1957 and the Thirteenth Session in 1958. During this second phase the cardinal aim was the amelioration of international tension generated by the Cold War, movements for self-determination in Africa and Asia, and the interaction of the two. To promote this goal the Irish delegation adopted an independent, activist identity in the Assembly. (But it never assumed a neutralist stance like the leaders of the Non-Aligned Movement: India, Indonesia, Ghana.)

The Lemass phase began in June 1959. The paramount interest during this stage was the promotion of a stable international system, delimited by Sean Lemass' own pro-western proclivities and the newly-anointed national priority: economic development. Ireland, therefore, stressed its commitment to the United Nations Charter rather than its own standing as an independent actor.

The prioritization of interests at the United Nations underscores three noteworthy features of Irish diplomacy there. The UN was certainly a vital focal point of Irish foreign policy. When Ireland was admitted into the Organization in 1955 it had formal relations with only twenty countries,[17] so the UN became a clearing house for diplomatic contacts with other countries and a forum wherein it responded to every international issue. Nonetheless, the UN constituted just one dimension of Irish foreign policy; other aspects of it were equally important. So were domestic economic priorities, especially after 1959. Irish officials pursued other interests – at home and abroad, in bilateral relationships and in other international organizations – so events in Dublin, London, Brussels, Paris, and Washington often acted upon decisions taken in New York.[18]

Next, two centers of influence existed within the Department of External Affairs[19] and the UN delegation. A pro-western nucleus comprised John Costello, Liam Cosgrave, the Inter-Party government's Minister for External Affairs, Freddy Boland, Ireland's Ambassador to the United Nations, Eamon Kennedy, Counsellor at the Permanent Mission in New York, and Con Cremin, Secretary of the Department from 1958 until 1963. An independent locus

17 Keatinge, *A Place*, Appendix II.
18 In many cases these aspects of Irish foreign policy – bilateral relationships, other international organizations, trade issues – await their author.
19 Throughout this book the appellation Department of External Affairs is employed; only in 1971 was it renamed the Department of Foreign Affairs.

coalesced around Eamon de Valera, Frank Aiken, Fianna Fáil's Minister for External Affairs from 1957 until 1969, and Conor Cruise O'Brien, Counsellor in the International Organizations Section. Their authority shifted throughout the three phases of UN policy outlined herein; the government in power determined which focal point was ascendant. The Boland axis predominated during the Costello period; the Aiken-O'Brien axis prevailed during the de Valera stage; Freddy Boland's influence reemerged in the Lemass era. Tension sometimes surfaced between these two groups when issues were being discussed, but the professional settling of differences always strengthened Ireland's final stand. And, despite lingering discord between certain officials, which received public expression in the late 1960s,[20] cooperation, not competition, was the overriding ethos in Iveagh House.

Finally, shifting objectives and the foregoing personal dispositions mirrored the divergent modes of reconciling Ireland's military neutrality with its UN profile. Since strict military neutrality never arose as a separate item in the Assembly, it did not figure prominently in the Irish delegation's rhetoric, nor in its confidential communications with Dublin, and never alone determined a vote. Yet neutrality did exert a secondary influence. Both Fine Gael and Fianna Fáil interpreted it as meaning that Ireland would stand apart from formal blocs in the Assembly. There the similarities ended. Fine Gael further construed it as a reason to adopt a line sympathetic to the west. For example, during a verbal bout with Fianna Fáil in 1959, Liam Cosgrave said that 'Military neutrality imposes on us a greater obligation in the political field to show our support for the western democracies and to help them in the United Nations Organization as far as we can.'[21]

De Valera, Aiken, and Lemass held different perspectives. For the first two, neutrality equaled opportunity: Ireland was free to propose solutions to international problems that the great powers could not, to undertake initiatives, even risks, in the Assembly.[22] On the other hand, in the light of his European aspirations Lemass viewed neutrality as somewhat of a challenge, although he never abandoned it wholesale.

* * *

The second strand of the pursuit of Irish national interests at the UN complements the first. It is true that separate governments accorded primacy to distinct goals, but, simultaneously, all three consistently acted upon shared Irish concerns. In short, the ordering of objectives did not overshadow a genuine community of interests.

20 Cf. *Irish Times*, 3, 4 June 1968.
21 Quoted in Norman MacQueen, 'Frank Aiken and Irish Activism at the United Nations', *International History Review*, Vol. 6, No. 2 (May, 1984), p. 229.
22 Cf. MacQueen, 'Aiken', pp. 227–8, 230.

For instance, Irish statesmen regularly interjected an element of morality into international affairs. This exercise took three forms: Irish spokesmen depicted Ireland as a moral actor in the international system; in Wilsonian fashion they stressed the moral force of decisions taken by the General Assembly;[23] a combination of the first two elements sustained the notion that Ireland had a unique role to play in the Assembly, if not in world affairs. This inclination, though, does not mean that Ireland set out to follow a moral policy, nor that its stand was a *moral* one. In the light of Ireland's small state status and the lack of military and economic levers at its disposal it must be viewed as an attempt to influence the behavior of larger nations.

The limits to Irish power and its small state status informed three additional interests. First, Irish delegates advocated the rule of law in international relations. In 1960 Frank Aiken reminded the Assembly that the 'supreme interest of small powers is to reduce violence and to extend the principle of peaceful settlement'.[24]

Because nations did not always observe this principle successive governments acknowledged that Ireland's security was enhanced by membership in an effective, competent United Nations. As Sean Lemass once said:

> If national self-interest is the fundamental motive force in international affairs, it is most assuredly, in the case of the small nations, that national self-interest and the interests of the United Nations as a whole, as defined in the United Nations Charter and the Universal Declaration of Human Rights, are most closely aligned.[25]

Third, Ireland ardently defended small nations ruthlessly invaded by their powerful neighbors: Egypt, Hungary, Tibet, Tunisia. This latter interest and yet another – the delegation championed self-determination in Africa and Asia – were by-products of an Irish historical consciousness that permeated the Department of External Affairs and Irish public opinion generally. Frank Aiken captured the essence of these two convictions in a speech before the Assembly in October 1960. Ireland was a sovereign, independent state, yet its people retained 'a historical memory' of the years when it too was dominated by a foreign power:

23 In February 1919 Woodrow Wilson reminded the Versailles Peace Conference that the effectiveness of the proposed League of Nations depended 'primarily and chiefly upon one great force, and that is the moral force of the public opinion of the world': quoted in Kissinger, *Diplomacy*, p. 235.
24 Frank Aiken, *Ireland and the United Nations* (Dublin, 1960), p. 16. The Department of External Affairs annually published Aiken's UN speeches in booklet form.
25 Sean Lemass, 'Small States in International Organizations', in A. Schou and A.O. Brundtland (eds.), *Small States in International Relations* (Uppsala, 1971), p. 115–16. This essay was based on Lemass' speech to the Cambridge University Liberal Club on 31 January 1960, which can be found in *Eire-Ireland: Bulletin of the Department of*

a memory which gives us a sense of brotherhood with the newly emerging peoples of today, a memory which makes it impossible for any representative of Ireland to withhold support for racial, religious, national or economic rights in any part of the world, in South Africa or Tibet, in Algeria or Korea, in [Egypt] or Hungary. We stand unequivocally for the swift and orderly ending of colonial rule and other forms of foreign domination.[26]

Last, consecutive Irish governments were sensitive to partition, but in a sharp departure from the disastrous 'sore thumb' strategy at the Council of Europe in the late 1940s, they never formally raised it in the Assembly.[27] Like their predecessors at the League of Nations,[28] Irish diplomats correctly grasped that the UN was an inappropriate forum for airing this grievance. Still, in several cases – Cyprus, Korea, Vietnam, Germany, West New Guinea, Algeria – Ireland argued against partition as an expedient for resolving political conflicts. With Ulster nationalists in mind, the delegation defended the rights of minorities in Tibet and South Tyrol. And, Ireland adopted a liberal interpretation of Article 2.7 of the Charter (which precluded UN interference in the domestic affairs of Member States) so as not to undermine any future, although unlikely, move to introduce partition.[29]

* * *

The second overarching theme of this study complements the first. In his book, *Ireland, 1912–85: Politics and Society*, Joe Lee throws down the gauntlet to historians of independent Ireland. He asserts that their 'main function ... is

External Affairs, No. 468 (1 February 1960). Freddy Boland wrote the speech for Lemass: DFA 417/29/II, 27 May 1970.

26 Aiken, *Ireland* (1960), p. 15. Likewise, one writer has noted that 'An instinctive sympathy for other "small states" – occasionally amounting to a belief that "smallness" (usually undefined) is a guarantee of virtue – can be found in many public policy debates through the history of the state': Keatinge, *A Place*, p. 172.

27 Due to the pressures of de Valera's anti-partition campaign the first Inter-Party government repeatedly raised partition in the Council of Europe, but without effect: Conor Cruise O'Brien, *To Katanga and Back: a UN Case Study* (London, 1962), p. 14. This same writer speculates that had Ireland been a member of the UN at this time, 'internal pressures combining with the Cold War in the Assembly would have constrained the Irish delegation to give an "anti-British-but-anti-communist" exhibition, which would have made the delegation an object of general aversion and even ridicule': O'Brien, 'Ireland', p. 128, n. 1.

28 Cf. Kennedy, *League*, pp. 254–5.

29 Article 2.7 of the UN Charter reads: 'Nothing contained in the present Charter shall authorize the United Nations to intervene in matters which are essentially within the domestic jurisdiction of any state or shall require the Members to submit such matters to settlement under the present Charter; but this principle shall not prejudice the application of enforcement measures under Chapter VII.'

to evaluate the performance of a sovereign people'.[30] This implied challenge is valid, but Lee overlooks Irish diplomacy at the United Nations. He devotes only two out of close to seven hundred pages to it, ending his brief review with the pithy observation that 'There was, inevitably, a certain amount of posturing for good and against evil. But there was also much solid work.'[31] This is an unintentional, but clear, underestimation. The history of Ireland's participation at the UN is nothing less than a chronicle of contributions to the international order. It is an Irish success story.

It is important, of course, not to transform Professor Lee's omission into an overestimation. Ireland's influence in world affairs was modest; it was always a member of the supporting cast, never a major player. Similarly, in terms of real power the United Nations in the late 1950s and early 1960s was far less influential than the United States, the Soviet Union, and the respective military alliances they anchored: NATO and the Warsaw Pact. Hence, resolutions carried in the Assembly did not necessarily alter the global environment. Nor did influence inside of the UN, which Ireland possessed to a limited extent, automatically transmute into hard coin in the international arena. Further, Ireland was not altruistic: strengthening the international system was in its own national interest, which Irish statesmen explicitly recognized.

Nonetheless, in the United Nations Ireland was not found wanting. For example, the delegation mediated disputes over South Tyrol, Somaliland, Kashmir, and other contentious issues that threatened regional peace. Ireland cosponsored numerous resolutions on decolonization. It was one of the first European nations to champion human rights in South Africa. It stridently condemned the invasions of Hungary, Egypt, and Tibet. Ireland's nuclear non-proliferation initiative paved the way for the 1968 Nuclear Non-Proliferation Treaty, which was indefinitely extended in the spring of 1995. The Irish delegation defended the United Nations when the Soviet Union assailed it in 1960. Ireland's participation in the Congo peacekeeping operation established a tradition that thrives to this day.

Ireland's peers in the Assembly recognized its invaluable contribution by electing it to important UN bodies: the Committee on South West Africa, the Congo Advisory Committee, the Security Council. Likewise, Irish representatives assumed prominent UN leadership roles at a rapid rate. In 1958 Freddy Boland was named Chairman of the Fourth, or Trusteeship, Committee; two years later he was elected President of the Fifteenth General Assembly. In 1959 Eamon Kennedy was appointed rapporteur of the Committee on South West Africa, which undoubtedly reflected the excellent reputation he had earned as Ireland's representative on the Fourth Committee the previous two years. In the spring of 1961 Dag Hammarskjold chose Conor O'Brien as his personal representative in Katanga. General Sean McKeown commanded the

---

30 Lee, *Ireland*, p. xiii.
31 Ibid., pp. 369–71.

UN peacekeeping force in the Congo (ONUC) from January 1961 until March 1962.

This record was no small achievement. The Irish delegation was under-staffed, underfunded, and overworked. Yet guided by sound principles, committed diplomats, and a desire for peace it interjected a sense of progress into foreign affairs. By working through the United Nations, Ireland fortified the international order.

CHAPTER I

An Ally of the West: The Inter-Party Government at the Eleventh General Assembly, 1956

INTRODUCTION

On 14 December 1955 the Tenth General Assembly ratified a Security Council deal admitting sixteen nations, including Ireland, into the UN.[1] Upon learning of this auspicious development, Liam Cosgrave, the Minister for External Affairs, instructed John Conway, Counsel General at the Irish Consulate in New York, to take up Ireland's seat, which was later blessed by Father D'Souza of the Indian delegation.[2]

No weighty issues arose in the few remaining days of the Assembly session, so the Irish delegation cast no substantive votes. Still, others at home and abroad assumed that Ireland would play an energetic role at the Eleventh Assembly when it convened in the autumn of 1956. John Conway alluded to this prospect in a report forwarded to Sean Murphy, the Secretary of the Department of External Affairs, describing the close of the Tenth Session:

> The first and strongest impression I received was that most of the members, and particularly the Arab and Asian and the Latin American groups, expected us to play an important part in the activities of the United Nations, and they welcomed us warmly on that account.[3]

This was certainly good news: despite Ireland's ten-year absence the Organization's more experienced members respected it. This fact, combined with an impartial approach to foreign affairs, boded well for Ireland. Freddy Boland highlighted these circumstances when he said during an interview that:

---

1 GA/RES 995 (X). The nations comprised Albania, Jordan, Ireland, Portugal, Hungary, Italy, Austria, Romania, Bulgaria, Finland, Ceylon, Nepal, Libya, Cambodia, Laos, Spain. See also Inis L. Claude, *Swords into Plowshares: The Problems and Progress of International Organizations* (London, 1965), pp. 83–6; United Nations Yearbook, 1955, pp. 22–9.
2 DFA 417/129, 24 December 1955.
3 Ibid., 20 December 1955.

as a member of the UN Ireland is in a rather unique position. There can be few members of the Organization in such an independent position as we are. We have no alliances ... we have no ambition in the external sphere, and no claims. We have traditional friendships which reach out to every quarter of the globe.[4]

Nonetheless, participation in the UN posed serious challenges. For instance, would Ireland be able to sustain its international friendships in a forum where votes were cast, stands taken, and speeches delivered on divisive issues? Moreover, how would the delegation resolve conflicts arising from several competing interests: Irish neutrality versus the Inter-Party government's strident anti-communism; or, Ireland's close relations with European colonial powers and its natural sympathy for independence movements in Africa and Asia?

The Inter-Party government's task in the spring of 1956, therefore, was to define in precise terms the parameters of its UN policy. External presumptions had surfaced with Ireland's entry. In his report to Murphy, Conway noted the perception among other delegations 'that Ireland will follow an independent line, and will not be attached to the Anglo-American bloc or to the neutralists. It is assumed, of course, that we will be quite definitely anti-communist.'[5] Yet after the cabinet had completed its work, in July 1956, this statement was only partially correct. It had concluded that a resolute, pro-western line best served the nation's interests. By its very nature this decision located the Irish delegation closer to the Anglo-American constellation, thus limiting its scope for independent action; an anti-communist posture and an autonomous identity were incompatible in the strained atmosphere of the Cold War. The Irish delegation did endorse the principle of self-determination in Asia and Africa in its speeches, but not in the more essential manner of voting when the demands of western solidarity overruled it.

The foreign policy predisposition of Fine Gael, the Inter-Party government's senior partner, foreshadowed Ireland's stance, expressed during debates over Hungary, Suez, China, Algeria, and several decolonization questions. Concurrently, the government was faithful to a long-standing Irish tradition of support for international organizations, but this was unsurprising since elements of the coalition had contributed as much to this bipartisan policy as had Fianna Fáil.

POLICY ORIGINS

Fine Gael boasted a legacy of international activism dating back to Ireland's independence. One observer has noted that the Free State's first government –

4   *Irish Times*, 14 January 1957.
5   DFA 417/129, 20 December 1955.

led by Cumann na nGaedheal, the forerunner to Fine Gael – 'made it possible for the country to play a part in international affairs.'[6] In 1923 they piloted Ireland into the League of Nations. Originally, Cumann na nGaedheal exploited membership to validate the country's newly-won statehood; hence the registration of the Anglo-Irish Treaty with the League Secretariat in 1924. Throughout the 1920s and early 1930s, though, the Saorstát greatly expanded its horizons by addressing universal issues: fair election procedures to the League Council, the codification of international law, disarmament, the invasion of Manchuria. From 1930–3 Ireland was a member of the Council, and Sean Lester, its Permanent Representative, later served as High Commissioner in Danzig and as the League's last Secretary General.[7] Ireland's priorities in Geneva thus anticipated, in some respects, its policy in New York several decades later.

As a reluctant member of the Commonwealth, the Free State established close relations with Australia, New Zealand, Canada, and South Africa, another country at odds with the suffocating air of the British Empire. At the Commonwealth Conference in 1931 Irish diplomats worked closely with this delegation to pass the Statute of Westminster, which liberalized Dominion status.[8] Concurrently, the Saorstát joined several world-wide technical and trade bodies: the International Labor Organization, the International Transport Union, the Universal Postal Union.[9]

Fine Gael remained committed to internationalism after World War II. During a July 1946 Dáil debate over a government motion seeking authorization to apply for admission into the newly-created United Nations, Fine Gael TDs, who were 'optimistic about Ireland's prospects' there, unanimously backed the proposal.[10] Before the vote Patrick McGilligan, the Free State's Minister for External Affairs from 1927 to 1932, came out 'strongly in favor of having [Ireland] a member of the United Nations Organization'.[11] Likewise, both the first Inter-Party government (in power from 1948 to 1951) and the second (1954–7) resisted vociferous public demands for the withdrawal of Ireland's stalled bid.[12] Under the first Inter-Party administration Ireland was a founding member of the Council of Europe and, because membership in the General Assembly was not a prerequisite, joined several UN specialized agencies,

6 O'Brien, 'Ireland', p. 111.
7 For a full review of the Free State's policy, see Kennedy, *League, passim.*
8 Keogh, *Ireland*, p. 51. For a detailed study of Ireland's membership in the British Commonwealth in the 1920s and 1930s, see David Harkness, *The Restless Dominion* (London, 1969).
9 DFA 417/129, (nd) 1955, departmental memorandum: 'Ireland's Membership in International Organizations.'
10 MacQueen, 'Entry', p. 67.
11 DD, Volume 102, Column 1421, 24 July 1946.
12 Cf. *Irish Independent*, 23 September 1953; DD 116, 865, 21 June 1949; DD 117, 886, 13 July 1949; DD 121, 157, 17 May 1950.

including the World Meteorological Organization and the Food and Agricultural Organization.

* * *

Other Cumann na nGaedheal and Fine Gael proclivities presaged the Inter-Party government's western, Christian, anti-communist UN posture. Joining the remnants of Cumman na nGaedheal to form Fine Gael in September 1933 were the Centre Party (previously the Farmer's Party) and General Eoin O'Duffy's National Guard, formerly the Army Comrades Association and better known as the Blueshirts, Ireland's own neo-fascist movement.[13] The party named O'Duffy its first president; they appointed William Cosgrave, the head of Cumann na nGaedheal, its leader in the Dáil. On a few occasions during the mid-1930s Fine Gael deputies unjustly accused the Fianna Fáil government of leftist sympathies.[14] In 1934 Patrick McGilligan went so far as to depict recent criticisms of Hitler as scare-mongering.[15] In 1935 Fine Gael TDs reluctantly backed sanctions imposed by the League of Nations against Italy after its invasion of Ethiopia,[16] but there was strong support within the party for Franco's forces fighting in the Spanish Civil War. Fianna Fáil maintained diplomatic relations with the Republican government in Spain until the end of the fighting, but in 1936 the Fine Gael opposition tabled an unsuccessful motion urging the recognition of Generalissimo Franco's regime.[17]

In a show of national unity Fine Gael endorsed Irish neutrality throughout World War II, but once hostilities ended the party's traditional bias resurfaced. During the Dáil's July 1946 debate on UN membership, its potential erosion of neutrality preoccupied several deputies, but not Fine Gael's John Costello. This ardent anti-communist, who later served as Taoiseach in both Inter-Party coalitions, opposed neutrality while the specter of Soviet domination haunted Europe. It should be obvious, he said, 'that whether or not we were neutral in the last war, there can never be any question again of this country being neutral in any future war'.[18]

In 1949, however, the first Inter-Party government declined an American invitation to join NATO, the west's security alliance, on the grounds that Ireland could not participate in a military treaty with Great Britain while partition remained in force. Some observers have suggested that de Valera maneuvered the government into this position through the anti-partition

---

13 Lee, *Ireland*, p. 179.
14 O'Brien, 'Ireland', p. 113.
15 DD 53, 255, 13 June 1934.
16 Cf. Keogh, *Ireland*, pp. 57–61.
17 DD 64, 1194–1228, 27 November 1936. General O'Duffy later led a brigade of Irishmen to fight in Spain alongside Franco's forces: Keogh, *Ireland*, p. 95.
18 DD 102, 1374, 24 July 1946.

campaign,[19] but partition was already high on the agenda of Sean MacBride, Minister for External Affairs and leader of Clann na Poblachta, the junior partner in the coalition, who used it to sway the cabinet.[20] MacBride, a fierce anti-communist, unsuccessfully pursued instead (with the government's blessing) a bilateral arrangement with the United States. Nevertheless, one observer has accurately described the original NATO decision as 'at best dubiously consonant with the traditions of Fine Gael'.[21]

More consistent with Fine Gael policy was the decision taken by the first Inter-Party government, at its opening cabinet meeting, to dispatch a cable to the Vatican reminding Pope Pius XII of:

> our filial loyalty and of our devotion to your August Person, as well as our firm resolve to be guided in all our work by the teaching of Christ, and to strive for the attainment of a social order in Ireland based on Christian principles.[22]

Within months the Inter-Party government demonstrated the sincerity of this message when a communist-socialist electoral alliance in Italy suddenly threatened the Vatican. The government backed a Church fundraising drive in Ireland that collected over £60,000 for the Christian Democratic Party, which handily won the election.[23]

POLICY FORMULATION

The rationale for bypassing NATO did not preclude membership in the United Nations, and following Ireland's entry John Costello spelled out the second Inter-Party government's foreign policy during a tour of the United States in March 1956. The catalyst for the journey was Yale University's bestowal of a Chubb Fellowship upon the Taoiseach, but the trip included huge welcomes in New Haven and New York on Saint Patrick's Day, a stopover in Philadelphia, and a meeting with President Eisenhower in Washington. Costello infused his public speeches in these cities with familiar

---

19 Cf. Keatinge, *A Place*, p. 92; Salmon, *Ireland*, pp. 180–5.
20 Keogh, *Ireland*, p. 193.
21 O'Brien, 'Ireland', p. 127. O'Brien also asserted in the same essay that 'a Fine Gael government, with a safe majority of its own, would have taken a strong Cold War line, and would eventually have committed itself to NATO' (p. 124). Another commentator believes that Ireland's reasons for staying out of NATO were more complicated and not due solely to partition: Raymond J. Raymond, 'Ireland's 1949 NATO Decision: A Reassessment', *Eire-Ireland*, Vol. 20, No. 3 (1985), *passim*.
22 Quoted in Keogh, *Ireland*, p. 187. For a review of Costello's attempt to achieve just such a domestic Christian social order, see Lee, *Ireland*, pp. 314–19.
23 Cf. Keogh, *Ireland and the Vatican*, pp. 230–49.

Fine Gael and Irish themes: anti-communism; Christianity; support for west-ern civilization; the Irish diaspora; Ireland's moral influence in world affairs; its support for the rule of law; its willingness to play an active role in the UN; a brief nod to the issue of partition (qualified by the assertion that Ireland's parochial interests would not compromise western unity). It is true that Costello was acutely sensitive to his audience, an American public unnerved by the Cold War, but, as later documents and decisions reveal, his proclamations were genuine; they also foretold Ireland's UN disposition.

On 15 March Costello informed the National Press Club that Ireland, as an 'almost exclusively Christian' nation, promoted 'the spirit of justice, Christian charity and goodwill on which the hope of peace must ultimately depend'.[24] Another vital interest, the 'preservation of the rule of law in international affairs', mirrored the Irish constitution.[25] The next day, at Georgetown University, Costello delineated the unique nature of Irish neutrality – it was more like Austria's than Sweden's or Switzerland's – and added: Ireland was 'not an "uncommitted" country in the sense in which that phrase is used. In the battle of ideas we are firmly committed.'[26] Likewise, he told the House of Representatives: 'communism, in our view, is a creed which confronts the established order of society with the most uncompromising challenge in his-tory, a creed to which we are implacably opposed'.[27]

The Taoiseach echoed these themes at Yale, where he attributed growing American interest in Irish foreign policy to its recent admission into the UN.[28] He deemed one assertion – Ireland would never 'subtract from the rel-ative power' of the west – 'a touchstone' of its United Nations policy. Ireland, therefore, could intervene only 'in disputes where no compromise to its own fundamental principles' were involved. Specifically, it could not mediate between the free world and the communist bloc. Due to the presence of a thriving Irish American community, however, Ireland could act as 'a bridge between Europe and America'.

* * *

24 S 16021/A, 15 March 1956.
25 Article 29 of the Irish Constitution states: '(1) Ireland affirms its devotion to the ideal of peace and friendly cooperation amongst nations founded on international justice and morality; (2) Ireland affirms its adherence to the principle of the pacific settlement of international disputes by international arbitration or judicial determination; (3) Ireland accepts the general recognized principles of international law as its rule of conduct in its relations with other States.'
26 S 16021/A, 16 March 1956. Costello said that 'Neutrality in the world today is a varied thing. In Europe alone there are three degrees of neutrality: the absolute neutrality of Switzerland, which refuses any alliances yet is in the OEEC; the military neutrality of Sweden, which does not preclude cooperation in the OEEC and the Council of Europe; and a stage half-way between the two, the present position of Austria. Ireland falls into the middle category.'
27 Quoted in Keogh, *Ireland*, p. 232.
28 S 13750/C, 21 March 1956.

When Costello landed at Collinstown Airport he promised to furnish the government with a summary of his journey that would 'prove of great benefit in formulating our national policy in connection with the United Nations Organization'.[29] He duly submitted a memorandum, completed on 30 April,[30] to the cabinet on 18 May.[31] This seminal document merits close scrutiny. It limns Costello's approach to international relations, represents the genesis of the Inter-Party government's UN policy, and, in its unequivocal pro-western tone, resounds the Taoiseach's remarks in the United States.

Costello first affirmed that Ireland was not 'a small, unimportant island', but rather 'a country which has made a very large impact on the world and has contributed very much to shaping the most important power in the modern world: America'.[32] Several episodes had convinced him of this: the Saint Patrick's Day parade in New York, which he called a 'fillip to national self-confidence'; his 'extraordinary welcome' in Philadelphia; and a 'lively and enthusiastic reception' at Yale University. He had noticed, in comparison to earlier visits, the 'increased popularity of Ireland, and ... an increase in its prestige'. One likely cause was the 1948 Republic of Ireland Act, which had encouraged the American government to bestow 'honors [upon] me as representative of the Irish people'.[33] A more 'fundamental reason' was that Irish Americans had 'grown in prosperity and moved up on the social scale'; they had become 'immensely significant' in industry, commerce, the professions, and politics.

Concurrently, the Taoiseach had detected a 'new interest' in Ireland on the part the State Department, Vice President Nixon, and President Eisenhower; the latter two had spoken 'in terms which might suggest they were concerned to flatter me'. The Taoiseach attributed this to several causes: the Chubb Fellowship; the 'conciliatory attitude' he had adopted in his speeches, particularly with regard to partition; and, Ireland's recent entry into the United Nations.

With this last reference Costello launched into his central theme: due to 'the importance of the United Nations as a means of impressing other countries

29 *Irish Times*, 2 April 1956.
30 S 13750/C, 30 April 1956. Costello received assistance in drafting the report from his aide and son-in-law, Alexis Fitzgerald, who had accompanied him to the United States: S 16021/1, 28 April 1956.
31 CAB 2/17, 18 May 1956.
32 Costello had made this same point several years earlier in Montreal, Canada on 1 September 1948. He said of Ireland: 'Though a small nation it wields an influence in the world far in excess of what its mere physical size and the smallness of its population warrants. We are sometimes accused of acting as if we were a big nation. In fact we are. Our exiles who have gone to practically every part of the world have created for their motherland a spiritual dominion which more than compensates for her lack of material wealth': John A. Costello, *Ireland in International Affairs* (Dublin, 1948).
33 Costello was being somewhat self-serving here since this act was passed while he headed the first Inter-Party government.

with an appreciation of Ireland's sense of responsibility and value in world affairs', it was imperative that the country's 'foreign policy in all its aspects should be formulated in principle and, so far as possible, in detail, and without delay'. He had tried to do so in his American speeches, but it had been impossible to offer 'an exhaustive or comprehensive dissertation on the subject'. Nevertheless, 'the general lines of policy to which I referred' there would facilitate 'the more detailed and considered formulation of policy which is now essential'.

Costello then made several points. First and foremost: 'It is the thesis of this memorandum, and one on which all my speeches on our foreign policy was based that, while we cannot muster big battalions, our moral influence is, or at least could be, considerable.' Accordingly, it was vital to wield this authority 'so as to strengthen the Christian civilization of which Ireland is a part'.

Next, the country's foreign policy should 'be framed in relation to the United States of America, Great Britain, the United Nations, and the European countries'. Ireland could not 'take any action which by subtracting from the power of America and Britain would relatively strengthen the power of Russia'. In contrast to the first Inter-Party government's policy in the Council of Europe, Ireland should 'not be merely anti-British, or else we will come to be completely discounted'. Costello highlighted 'the necessity for the closest possible relations with Canada', which had always expressed its 'friendship' for Ireland.[34] Finally, as a 'small nation' Ireland was required to 'do everything in her power to uphold' the United Nations; it offered the means 'for small nations to exert some influence on world affairs and for the maintenance of peace, and [for] securing some [recourse] to justice'.

The United Nations provided another opportunity. Having eschewed formal alliances, Ireland depended upon close bilateral relationships to further its interests, and the UN was an organization that could be 'readily utilized to make such friends'. It was also a place to consolidate old alliances, like the one between Ireland and the United States, which Costello elevated into 'a cardinal point of our policy'. That relationship, combined with other actions – 'keeping in close touch with and guiding the opinion of Irish Americans', maintaining an independent posture at the UN, pursuing a policy there rooted in 'Christian morality' – would make Ireland 'a significant force ... and secure national' influence.

Ireland could then achieve several foreign policy goals. If it acquitted itself 'well and intelligently at the United Nations ... we may hope gradually to create conditions in which, through the influence of our friends, partition may be brought to an end'. Costello warned, however, that 'friendship cannot be

34 Just after Ireland was admitted to the UN in December 1955 Liam Cosgrave held a brief, but congenial, meeting with Lester Pearson, the Canadian Foreign Minister, who was passing through Shannon Airport. They agreed to cooperate closely at the United Nations: DFA 417/129, 19 December 1955.

won by an entirely selfish policy'. Ireland's best chance of convincing the United States and others to adopt 'a more favorable attitude on the issue of partition' was to demonstrate in the UN, 'by its influence on former colonial countries and elsewhere in the world, how useful, helpful, and constructive it can be in the interests of Europe generally against Russia'.

The country might also attract 'the interest of prospective investors. If Ireland makes good at the United Nations I believe it will help us in the securing of American investment in Ireland.' Moreover, the interest expressed by 'countries other than the United States' since Ireland had entered the UN underscored the potential for its presence there to act as a magnet for foreign capital. Last, through the UN the government could assist 'Irish missionaries and, indeed, all Catholic missionaries everywhere', particularly in Africa and India, where there was 'great affection for Ireland because of her long struggle for freedom'.

Following this extended presentation Costello outlined the 'practical measures' required to implement this policy. He reminded the cabinet that 'these steps will inevitably involve what to us must be regarded as rather heavy expenditure'. Nevertheless, the outlay would 'pay large dividends': it would generate assistance 'that we would not otherwise get to end partition'; and, it would encourage 'investors to invest their money in Ireland'. Further, if the government did not:

> act properly in every way and live up to the expectations that now exist in our regard it would be better to forget that the Irish spent seven hundred years of toil and struggle to become a nation and just sink into the position of being an unimportant province – and recognize Ireland to be what the late George Bernard Shaw once described her, a cabbage patch thrown into the Atlantic Ocean.

Swayed by these arguments, the cabinet sanctioned Costello's numerous recommendations.[35] The first decision affirmed that 'Ireland must play a prominent role in the United Nations Organization and that everything must be done to ensure that our contribution is effective and likely to bring credit and distinction to the country.' The second averred that 'steps be taken forthwith to formulate the principles and, so far as possible, the details of the different aspects of our foreign policy, having regard to matters outlined in the memorandum', and that the Minister for External Affairs 'should prepare a draft statement of those principles and details for early consideration by the government'.[36]

---

35 CAB 2/17, 18 May 1956. The cabinet approved eleven major decisions; several included sub-recommendations, so the total was seventeen.

36 The call to outline the 'details' of Ireland's UN policy proved to be over-zealous. On 29 May Sean Murphy, Secretary of the Department of External Affairs, forwarded a

Several decisions pertained to Irish–American relations. The Consulates at Boston, Chicago, and San Francisco were 'raised to the status of Consulates-General'. One requested the Ministers for External Affairs and Finance to investigate 'the adequacy of the existing representation allowances' paid to Irish diplomats in the United States. Another asked the Minister for External Affairs to examine several items: 'the question of maintaining close and continuous contact with Irish Americans and Irish American organizations'; the appointment of 'a press officer to one of the Consulates-General – preferably in New York'; the 'establishment of Honorary Consulates in Baltimore and in other places in the United States'. The Minister for Industry and Commerce was invited to organize a 'plan for following up the efforts that have been made to secure the investment of American capital in Irish industry, and for keeping in close touch with well-disposed groups and persons' in the United States.

Costello's memorandum was quite significant in several respects, but it also exhibited shortcomings; both aspects require further attention. It was, first of all, the definitive foreign policy statement of the second Inter-Party government. It delineated an anti-communist, western, Christian interpretation of international affairs. It placed Ireland solidly in NATO's political orbit, and left no doubt as to where the government stood *vis-à-vis* the Cold War. It contained brief references to Ireland's independence of blocs, but this meant only that Ireland would not be a party to any *military* alliance (read NATO), still a sensitive issue in domestic Irish politics.[37]

Most significant, the memorandum made the United Nations a pillar of Irish foreign policy. The government correctly grasped that the Organization provided an effective platform for a small power like Ireland to participate in international affairs. Costello deserves credit for this, and for realizing that Ireland could contribute to the world body in return. Still, it is important to recall once again that the UN did not constitute the totality of Irish foreign policy; other foreign commitments, not to mention the pull of domestic priorities, acted on the nation's UN posture.

In his memorandum Costello resurrected a recurrent theme of Irish foreign policy: Ireland's supposed moral influence in the international system.[38]

---

minute to Liam Cosgrave noting that the general principles of Ireland's policy, as 'stated by the Taoiseach in his speeches in the United States', were easily summarized, but he found 'it difficult to see how we can go into details'. Cases likely to arise at the UN, such as Algeria, were in a state of flux, and 'while we should endeavor to apply the principles which the Taoiseach has already formulated, nevertheless, we should not detail what our line will be until we are confronted with the facts and consequences of each situation'. Cosgrave accepted this prudent advice, for he penciled on Murphy's minute: 'Secretary, I agree with the general outline of policy as set out above': DFA 422/11/29, 29 May, 7 June 1956.

37 This memorandum is most likely the one that Conor Cruise O'Brien suggested was 'designed to place Ireland "squarely into the NATO bloc … without ever mentioning NATO"': Sharp, *Irish Foreign Policy*, p. 47, n. 8.

38 For an overview of the moral dynamic in Irish foreign policy, see Keatinge, *A Place*,

This unique perspective blended several currents of thought. One was the conviction that due to its historical experience Ireland's voice was a singular one within the western world. It reflected a Catholic ethos that surfaced periodically in Irish foreign policy and lingered on until the early 1960s, when it slowly evaporated.[39] More so, it was an attempt to compensate for Ireland's insignificant military strength in an unstable post-war world: Ireland promoted a code of moral conduct to modify the behavior of the great powers. Nonetheless, Costello's one-sided world view undermined his call for the interjection of morality into foreign affairs: he did not subject the west to the same rigorous standards as the communist bloc.

The memorandum's proposition that influence accrued at the United Nations might be translated into foreign investment in Ireland is important in a historiographical context. It undermines claims that post-war Irish governments pursued unconnected foreign and economic policies.[40] Scholars have assumed that this long-standing practice continued well into the 1960s, but Costello's objectives show that by the mid-1950s, if not before, Irish policy makers were conscious of the interrelationship between foreign and economic policy. They became even more sensitive to it by the end of the decade.

Costello's foreign investment premise, however, was flawed on two counts. First, it rested upon inflated perceptions of American, and Irish American, interest in Ireland. The friendliness exhibited by United States officials, including President Eisenhower,[41] during Costello's visit must be viewed in the context of the upcoming autumn presidential election and the Republican Party's desire to capture Irish American votes. Remarkably, Costello had recognized this possibility in his memorandum, but then discounted it: with a touch of naiveté he said that the United States government's enthusiasm could not 'be explained simply by reference to the fact that this was a presidential election year'.

The Taoiseach's depiction of Irish American ardor for Ireland was also over-blown. It was the by-product of being surrounded in New York, New Haven, Philadelphia, Baltimore, and even Washington, DC by successful Irish Americans celebrating Saint Patrick's Day, their great ethno-religious holiday. Costello erred in assuming that Irish Americans sustained this high

pp. 171–90. One observer has detected it in Irish interpretations of neutrality during World War II: 'Common sense was not enough [of a reason to be neutral] for a people fed on fantasies of their unique moral stature. Neutrality therefore had to be crowned with a halo, and exalted to a level that would allow those who, very sensibly, looked in the first instance to their own safety, like everyone else, to pose as paragons of virtue ... it was this apparent need of the Irish mind to feel a sense of moral superiority that mainly explains Irish touchiness about neutrality': Lee, *Ireland*, pp. 262–5.

39 For a discussion of this trend in Irish policy, see Keatinge, *A Place*, pp. 176–9.

40 Cf. Keatinge, *Formulation*, pp. 32–5; Salmon, *Ireland*, pp. 228–9; Sharp, *Irish Foreign Policy*, pp. 67–8, 236–7.

41 Costello read an amicable letter he had received from Eisenhower, dated 16 March, at Collinstown airport upon his return to Ireland: *Irish Times*, 2 April 1956.

level of interest in Ireland all year long. They did not. By the mid 1950s Irish
Americans had moved into the mainstream of American life – their growing
support for the Republican Party being but one example of this – and their
primary concerns were American ones.[42] Nothing demonstrated this more
clearly than the visceral reaction of the Irish American press to Ireland's 1957
UN vote in favor of a discussion of the representation of China, which is
explored in the proceeding chapter.

Further undermining Costello's contention that Ireland's UN policy might
promote foreign investment was his over-simplification of business decisions.
These, naturally, depend upon a sophisticated analysis of economic opportunities, not a prospective country's diplomatic reputation. Ireland's UN performance did heighten its international profile, and even promoted a sense of
goodwill towards the country, but among governments, not corporations. By
the same token, the high level of foreign investment in Ireland in the late
1950s and 1960s was the result of successful government policies (some
implemented by the Inter-Party coalition) that transformed Ireland into an
attractive, profitable site for outsiders – not its UN policy, however commendable.

Costello's assertion that laudable behavior at the United Nations might
generate a solution to partition was also faulty. Somewhat remarkably, he
overlooked Northern Ireland's strategic role in the defense of the north
Atlantic and NATO's unwillingness, in the midst of the Cold War, to compromise on this point.[43] Moreover, under no circumstances would the United
States have supported an Irish initiative on partition, no matter how adroitly
pursued, because the Soviet Union would have seized upon it to drive a
diplomatic wedge between the USA and its close ally, the United Kingdom.
To America, the UN was a front in the Cold War where western solidarity
overrode secondary relationships. Fortunately, seasoned Irish diplomats recognized this and later abandoned all thoughts of raising partition in the
General Assembly.

Costello's exaggeration of Irish influence in America and his overestimation
of the UN as a means to end partition or generate investment recall a minor
feature of Irish foreign policy before the late 1950s: Irish spokesmen sometimes adopted an unrealistic view of relations between states. Several factors
accounted for this inclination: Ireland's small size; its disengagement from the
destructive collisions of larger nations; its recent experience of neutrality during
World War II; and, the subtle understanding that the country, while not a
member of NATO, was shielded by its military umbrella. Costello's world
view, for example, did not resonate in the rhetoric of smaller European states
– Belgium, the Netherlands, Denmark, Czechoslovakia, Austria, Poland –

42 Cf. William Shannon, *The American Irish* (Amherst, 1966), pp. 410–13.
43 Cf. Ronan Fanning, 'The United States and Irish Participation in NATO: The
Debate of 1950', *Irish Studies in International Affairs*, Vol. 1, No. 1 (1979), *passim*.

recently trampled by belligerent neighbors or presently living in their shadows. Contrariwise, this trend was never the dominant characteristic of Irish foreign policy and it faded with the ascendancy of Sean Lemass in 1959.

LIAM COSGRAVE'S DÁIL ADDRESS

Costello's memorandum initiated a private review of Ireland's posture at the United Nations; Liam Cosgrave's signature speech to the Dáil on 3 July 1956 during the Department of External Affairs' Estimates debate, extensively recounted elsewhere yet still demanding attention, launched a similar discussion on a public level.[44] In his best-known contribution to UN affairs, Cosgrave outlined three principles for directing Ireland's activities. The Inter-Party government's Minister for External Affairs considered their affirmation 'a very important decision of national policy', involving 'nothing less than the basic principles on which our policy towards the outside world and its problems is to be based'.

The first guideline proclaimed Ireland's unequivocal support for the United Nations Charter and for the 'application of its provisions in any situation to which it is intended to apply'.

Second, Ireland 'should try to maintain a position of independence, judging the various questions on which we have to adopt an attitude or cast a vote strictly on their merits in a just and disinterested way'. Accordingly, the Irish delegation should avoid 'becoming associated with particular blocs or groups so far as possible'. The disadvantages of this approach would be outweighed by the 'respect and influence' gained by leaving 'our hands free to pursue what may come to be generally recognized as a fair, helpful, and constructive role'.

The third principle declared that:

> It must be our constant concern – indeed our moral responsibility – to do whatever we can as a member of the United Nations to preserve the Christian civilization of which we are a part, and with that end in view to support wherever possible those powers principally responsible for the defense of the free world in their resistance to the spread of communist power and influence ...

Cosgrave added that 'In the great ideological conflict which divides the world today our attitude is clear, by geographical position, culture, tradition, and national interest.' Ireland belonged 'to the great community' of nations comprising the United States, Canada, and those of western Europe, and it was in Ireland's 'national interest that this group of states should remain strong and united ... '

44 DD 159, 137–146, 3 July 1956. See also Keatinge, *A Place*, p. 173; Ronan Fanning, *Independent Ireland* (Dublin, 1983), pp. 202–3; Keogh, *Ireland*, p. 234.

The salient feature of Cosgrave's speech, and the one noted most often by scholars, was the intrinsic tension between the second and third principles.[45] Frank Aiken alluded to this when he reminded Cosgrave that the third principle 'departed to some extent from the first and second'; the Minister was 'rather tying himself up in his third point of policy'.[46] Unlike Aiken, some viewed the dynamic between the second and third principles as one of the speech's strong points: 'If the weakness of Cosgrave's three principles lay in their inherent contradictions, their strength, similarly, was in their broad political appeal.'[47]

Yet the placement of Cosgrave's address within a broader context reveals that the Inter-Party government perceived no inconsistency whatsoever between the second and third guidelines; they regarded the pro-western, anti-communist, Christian proposition as the core of the speech. This insight, of course, has important consequences. It resolves the tension between the last two principles. It means that the speech no longer serves as the primary point of departure when assessing Irish policy; only the concept of national interests can do so. And, it demonstrates that Cosgrave's principles did not constitute a permanent guide to UN affairs; their relevance is limited to the Inter-Party government's stewardship in 1956.

The first component of the wider milieu in which Cosgrave's speech must be evaluated is the foreign policy tradition that Fine Gael carried into the second Inter-Party government. Past practice does not necessarily determine contemporary policy, but common themes – anti-communism, Catholicism, democratic capitalism – linked Cumman na nGaedheal and the first Inter-Party coalition with Fine Gael. These priorities were clearly evident in the second element of this broader milieu: John Costello's speeches in the United States. Admittedly, they were addressed to an American audience, but this alone does not account for the unswerving support Costello professed for the west; his sentiments were not merely rhetorical, but personal and, more so, representative of his government.

The pro-western, anti-communist tone of Costello's memorandum, with its express purpose of outlining Ireland's policy at the UN, further reinforces this new interpretation of Cosgrave's three principles. Costello was freer to express his views in the privacy of a cabinet meeting than in a public forum; the memorandum's replication of his American speeches underscores the conclusion that Cosgrave's third principle was the bedrock of Ireland's policy. In fact, the memorandum can be considered the origin, or an earlier draft, of Cosgrave's speech; it was hardly altered before delivery.[48]

45 Keatinge, *A Place*, p. 173; Fanning, *Ireland*, p. 202; MacQueen, 'Entry', p. 74.
46 DD 159, 147–8, 3 July 1956.
47 MacQueen, 'Entry', p. 74.
48 Considering that the relationship between Costello and Cosgrave was 'one in which a
    superior retained the final decisions on questions of policy', it is not at all surprising

Similarly, John Costello concurred with the thrust of his Minister's remarks. One week later he told his Dáil colleagues that Irish independence at the UN had its place, but the 'primary consideration for us must be to see that the forces of atheistic communism are repelled, and that we do not allow ourselves to become tools to serve communist imperialist interests, no matter how carefully they may be camouflaged'.[49] The following day John McQuaid, the Archbishop of Dublin, wrote to Costello, with whom he was on excellent terms, to 'congratulate you warmly on your statement concerning atheistic communism. The statement in its rightness and firmness is excellent ... '[50] In his reply one week later the Taoiseach told McQuaid that 'we have a great opportunity of putting the Catholic point of view in the deliberations of the UN ... '[51] He added that it might be possible to secure 'much influence for Ireland', but if this opportunity was forsaken the nation's 'influence and prestige will be seriously damaged', so 'we ought not to fail'. True, Costello was speaking to a Catholic archbishop, but he sincerely believed that a Christian policy was in Ireland's best interests.

Later developments fully explored below, such as Ireland's anti-communist posture at the General Assembly in 1956 and Fine Gael's trenchant criticism of Fianna Fáil's 1957 UN voting record, which they branded a betrayal of the west, round out the heretofore unrecognized setting within which Cosgrave's speech must be assessed. Doing so reveals the essence of his three guidelines. His first principle, support of the UN Charter, was a sincere expression of policy and echoed a universal Irish commitment to international organizations and international law. Cosgrave's second principle, emphasizing Ireland's independence, demands closer scrutiny. At best it was 'a gesture against the whole notion of accepting polarization as an inherent characteristic of international organizations ... '[52] Conversely, it was no more than a nod to Irish neutrality, simply a statement of fact. It was intended primarily for domestic consumption, not external policy. This latter purpose, however, accounted for Cosgrave's third, pro-western guideline. It was the foundation upon which the Inter-Party government built its UN posture. In practice it overshadowed the first two principles and was designed to do so.

that Cosgrave's speech so closely mirrored Costello's memorandum: Keatinge, *Formulation*, p. 96.

49 DD 159, 621, 11 July 1956.
50 S 16021/D, 12 July 1956. For a description of Costello's friendship with McQuaid, see Keogh, *Ireland*, p. 208.
51 S 16021/D, 19 July 1956. Liam Cosgrave confirmed this approach during a visit to the Holy See in March 1956. In a meeting with Monsignor Tardini, the Vatican Pro-Secretary of State, the Monsignor remarked that at the UN Ireland could 'do much there to ensure the observance of Christian principles in international life'; Cosgrave replied that Ireland's policy 'will certainly be applied to that end': DFA 417/129, 20 March 1956.
52 MacQueen, 'Entry', p. 73.

ADMINISTRATIVE PREPARATIONS

While the foregoing general lines of policy were being drawn, the Department
of External Affairs addressed several practical items. Sean MacBride's reor-
ganization and increased staffing of the Department had readied it, in part,
for the added duties engendered by UN membership,[53] but budget cutbacks
in 1953 and 1954 slowed this momentum.[54] Hence, a lack of manpower handicapped early preparations for the 1956 autumn Assembly. A spring 1956 report,
arguing no doubt for greater resources, noted that 'It is impossible, owing to
shortage of staff, to attend to many UN matters which should by now be well
in hand.'[55] Such arguments were effective, for several of the decisions taken
by the government following its consideration of Costello's memorandum
backed a personnel and material commitment to the United Nations.

For instance, the third decision reached by the government on 18 May 1956
declared 'That a separate Permanent Mission should be accredited to the
United Nations Organization', and its fifth decision directed the Ministers for
External Affairs and Finance to 'examine forthwith the question of the staffing'
of the Mission so that it might be completed 'without delay'.[56] This latter task
sparked off a debate between the two Departments. When drawing up its
Estimates in the spring of 1956, External Affairs included provisions of £8,000
for the UN Ambassador's salary, £2,600 for additional staffing in Iveagh
House, and £1,100 for staff at the UN Mission, but these figures were cut by
Gerard Sweetman, the Minister for Finance, who woefully contended that the
proposed sums could 'be saved merely by requiring existing officers of the
Department to perform the UN work in question as a side-line in their spare
time'.[57] External Affairs challenged this move, arguing in an internal memorandum that the reply to the Minister for Finance:

> must simply be that the UN work, on which the Department must now
> embark (because of the decision of the government and the Dáil that
> Ireland should join the UN), far from being a side-line, will probably
> be the largest, most onerous and, in some ways, most important 'block
> of work' to be dealt with by the Department for the future: as regards
> spare time, a number of Ministers at last year's meeting of the Cabinet

---

53 Cf. Keatinge, *Formulation*, pp. 112–14; Ronan Fanning, *Irish Department of Finance*
(Dublin, 1978), pp. 407–8.

54 Cf. Keatinge, *Formulation*, Appendix (Figure I); Lee, *Ireland*, pp. 321–6.

55 DFA 422/11/26/1, memorandum (nd, most likely March or April 1956): 'International
Organizations Section.'

56 CAB 2/17, 18 May 1956. In his memorandum Costello had said that the decision to
establish a separate UN mission, rather than assign the work to a Consulate or Embassy
in the United States, was based upon advice he had received from Dag Hammarskjold,
the Secretary General of the UN, after meeting him in New York.

57 DFA 422/11/26/2 (nd).

sub-committee on Estimates testified to the fact that our offices abroad, in general, are very much over-worked (and, incidentally, under-paid): as regards the staff at Headquarters, it has been our constant theme throughout the past year that the drastic economies of 1953–54, having cut the Department to the bone, no further staff economies could be achieved at Headquarters with out eliminating some vital part of the Department's work.[58]

The large sum for UN-related expenses later sanctioned by the Dáil shows that Iveagh House won this inter-departmental debate.[59] The unequivocal stand that Costello took in his April memorandum was decisive; the government had adjudged the UN a priority. Nevertheless, later reports revealed that the resources allocated, although substantial by Irish standards, were insufficient according to international ones, and this impinged slightly upon the effectiveness of the Irish delegation in New York.[60]

* * *

In his memorandum Costello stated that the ambassador accredited to the United Nations 'should be one of our most experienced diplomats, a good debater, and entirely Irish in character';[61] the fourth decision reached by the government on 18 May 1956 declared that the envoy so designated 'should be the best qualified and most suitable person that can be secured for the post'.[62] Freddy Boland, named to the office in June, certainly fitted the bill. The son of H.P. Boland, a high-level Department of Finance official, he graduated from Trinity College in 1925 with a classics degree, earned an LL.B. in 1926, and then spent two years in the United States as a Rockefeller Research Fellow. Boland entered the Irish diplomatic corps in 1929 and three years later was appointed First Secretary in Paris. The outstanding quality of his political reports from France, noted by his superiors in Dublin, presaged the high standard of his dispatches from the UN. In 1934 he returned to Iveagh

---

58 Ibid. (nd).

59 The Dáil voted close to £80,000 for UN affairs. This amount represented 18% of External Affairs' total expenditure for 1956 (£457,000), which had increased by 15% over the previous year. The Department's expenditures as a percentage of total government spending also showed a sharp increase in 1956: DD 159, 127–9, 3 July 1956; Keatinge, *Formulation*, Appendix (Figure I).

60 In this context, Ireland allocated a great deal less money to its foreign ministry over-all relative to other European nations of the same size. In a speech to the Dublin Chamber of Commerce on 1 November 1956 Liam Cosgrave reported that Denmark and Norway, with population levels close to Ireland's, spent four times the amount of money on their External Affairs budgets as did Ireland. By arguing that Ireland received 'good value for its money' he was refuting popular, albeit erroneous, suggestions that the nation did not need a foreign service: DFA 305/210/I, 1 November 1956.

61 S 13750/C, 30 April 1956.

House to head the League of Nations Section; the experience and contacts garnered during this posting served him well at the United Nations. After being seconded to the Department of Industry and Commerce (1936–8), he was named Assistant Secretary and then, in 1946, Secretary of the Department of External Affairs. In 1950 he became Ambassador to the Court of Saint James, where he remained until the UN beckoned.[63]

Boland was eminently suited for the New York post. One of Ireland's most talented diplomats, he was witty, well-spoken, and 'combined – as few do – common sense and immense intellectual ability ... ' He was a committed internationalist, especially while Secretary of External Affairs just after World War II. Under his direction the Department 'acquired new confidence and vigor and ... extended the scope of Ireland's diplomatic activity'. He coordinated the country's participation in the Marshall Plan, realizing that 'international economic cooperation of this kind afforded Ireland an opportunity to reenter the mainstream of European diplomatic life and to rehabilitate her international image without abandoning neutrality'.[64]

Still, he was pro-western by nature. During World War II he successfully argued for accommodation with the Allies 'and so helped to counteract the Anglophobia of Joseph Walshe, the Permanent Head of the Department'. He penned Liam Cosgrave's three-principles Dáil speech, with its Christian, anti-communist slant. At the UN he sympathized with the emerging nations of Africa and Asia, but not at the expense of 'the close ties ... between Ireland and certain western countries, notably Britain and the United States ... ' Boland was also even-tempered. A colleague once described him as 'a man who could make his own the words of the aged Duke of Newcastle's rebuke to the young Gladstone: "I confess, young man, I have a great notion of the horrors of enthusiasm".'[65]

Concurrently, Boland was deeply proud of his generation's record of service to Ireland, including his peers in the Irish hierarchy. In a February 1957 letter to him, Father Dermot O'Doherty, an unknown and unreasonable Irish priest stationed in Minnesota, excoriated the Irish mission for not pressing partition in the General Assembly.[66] It was 'an irritation to find you pressing the rights of Hungary with more vigor than the rights of Ireland.' The British had dominated Ireland for over three hundred years, yet 'your remarks thus far upon this bitter grievance have been couched in language so conciliatory as to insure continued indifference among the nations'. He irrationally claimed that

62 CAB 2/17, 18 May 1956
63 *Irish Times*, 6 December 1985; Dermot Keogh, *Ireland and Europe, 1919–48* (Dublin, 1988), p. 52; Ambassador Eamon Kennedy, Personal Interview, 11 March 1993.
64 Raymond, 'Ireland's 1949 NATO Decision', pp. 24–5; Raymond J. Raymond, 'The Marshall Plan and Ireland', in P.J. Drudy (ed.), *The Irish in America: Emigration, Assimilation and Impact* (Cambridge, 1985), pp. 302–3; *The Times*, 6 December 1985.
65 O'Brien, *Katanga*, p. 35; *The Times*, 6 December 1985; Akenson, *Conor*, p. 154.
66 DFA 313/36, 8 February 1957.

if the Irish delegation took no action to defend the minority in Northern Ireland 'suspicion will be confirmed that the present Irish government (to which we might join the Irish Bishops) is as zealous a defender of British interests as the British themselves. Woe to such a government; woe to such a treason.'

Boland delivered a stinging riposte. He told O'Doherty that 'Although I normally try to give all my correspondents a considered and courteous reply to their enquiries', he struggled in this case because O'Doherty's final sentence was 'an imputation against the Irish government and the Irish hierarchy which, as a Catholic and an official of the Irish government, I cannot over-look'.[67] Boland was unaware what knowledge or experience of Irish affairs O'Doherty possessed that allowed him:

> to pass judgment on the elected representatives of the Irish people. I, however, have served all the governments there have been in Ireland since 1929. I have known not only the members of those governments, but their records. I know that they have all included men who have devoted their whole careers to the service of Ireland, often at great personal sacrifice, and who have risked their lives in her cause. Their claim to be the leaders of the Irish nation has been endorsed by the people of free Ireland at successive elections. I must tell you emphatically, Reverend Father, that, for you, or any other Irishman, to charge the men to whom I refer with being defenders of British interests seems to me quite outrageous, and I fail to understand how, in common sense or Christian charity, you could permit yourself to lend your voice to such an aspersion.

Boland was equally incensed by O'Doherty's reference 'to a similar "suspicion" as regards the Irish Bishops', several of whom he counted 'among my personal friends'. He could:

> only say – and I am sure that as a Catholic priest, you will, on reflection, admit the soundness of my view – that I am quite certain in my own mind that, in all they do and say, the Irish Bishops are actuated solely by one motive – namely, the spiritual welfare of their flocks. The mere repetition of what you call the 'suspicion' that they are 'defenders of British interests' seems to me gravely scandalous.

Boland then sent a copy of both letters to Sean Murphy, Secretary of External Affairs. In an explanatory note he said that 'Frankly, I cannot feel that it would be reasonable or consistent with duty to overlook the kind of imputations made in Father O'Doherty's letter.'[68] Murphy concurred. He humorously wrote to Boland: 'Hearty congratulations on your masterly not to

67 Ibid., 20 February 1957.
68 Ibid.

say devastating reply which will probably make the Reverend Father a Trappist even if he does not join the Cistercian Order.'[69]

The Department of External Affairs was fortunate to have many other resourceful officials like Freddy Boland within its ranks and it tapped this pool of talented diplomats to form Ireland's delegation to the Eleventh Session. Boland and Liam Cosgrave headed the contingent. The gifted Dr Conor Cruise O'Brien, recalled from Paris to supervise the newly-created International Organizations Section in Iveagh House, joined them;[70] as later events proved, bringing him into the UN fold was an inspired decision. Likewise the appointment of Eamon Kennedy to the post of Counsellor in the Permanent Mission to the UN; he became an indispensable member of the delegation. Sheila Murphy, Counsellor in the Political Section, Sean Morrissey, the Department's legal advisor, Paul Keating, Second Secretary in the Permanent Mission, and two officials from the Washington Embassy – Ambassador John J. Hearne and Joseph Shields, Counsellor – rounded out the Irish team.[71] Their maiden Assembly did not permit a gradual adjustment to the nuances of UN diplomacy or the heady atmosphere of New York because two serious crises, the Russian invasion of Hungary and the Anglo-French seizure of the Suez Canal, broke upon the world stage in the autumn of 1956.[72] But Ireland's representatives were not overwhelmed. Instead, they responded with aplomb and contributed significantly to the Assembly's deliberations.

THE SOVIET INVASION OF HUNGARY

In late October 1956 the Soviet Union invaded Hungary in order to quash the nationalist uprising that had accompanied Imre Nagy's recent ascent to power. The ensuing response of the west is well-known. Having encouraged eastern Europeans to rise up against their Soviet oppressors, the United States, deciding that the risk was too great, did nothing of substance. Instead, it dropped the entire matter in the UN's lap, fully aware that it, too, was powerless in this situation.[73]

Reactions within the Irish delegation were mixed. Conor O'Brien 'was stunned by what he perceived as the cynicism of the US government'.[74] Freddy

69 Ibid., 5 March 1957.
70 O'Brien, *Katanga*, p.13. In his memorandum to the government Costello said that it 'will not be possible to formulate successfully and maintain well a good foreign policy unless more of our stronger men are at home'; this observation may have prompted O'Brien's relocation to Dublin.
71 Cf. Appendix 3.
72 For a description of the UN and New York in 1956 from an Irish perspective, see Akenson, *Conor*, pp. 154–60.
73 Cf. Kissinger, *Diplomacy*, p. 548.
74 Akenson, *Conor*, p. 155.

Boland, who undoubtedly recognized the transparency of verbal attacks from New York, nevertheless took the UN proceedings very seriously. Welcoming an opportunity to chastise the communists, he harnessed Ireland to the west's condemnation of the USSR and served as the delegation's spokesman on this issue. On the morning of 28 October the United States, Great Britain, and France requested an urgent meeting of the Security Council, which convened at 4:00 p.m. that afternoon. At the close of the session the Security Council President announced that several nations had notified the Secretary General of their support for the initiative. Ireland was one of them; at 8:30 p.m. Boland had handed a letter to Dag Hammarskjold informing him, 'In accordance with official instructions', that Ireland endorsed 'the proposal ... that the Security Council should concern itself urgently with the situation which has arisen in Hungary'.[75]

Boland's letter was somewhat disingenuous; he had acted independently after unsuccessfully trying to contact Cosgrave in Dublin. In a follow-up report to Murphy, he explained that he had done so in the light of the Minister's recent speech to the Dublin Rotary Club and the formidable array of nations – Italy, Spain, Austria, Turkey, the Philippines, Argentina – backing the motion.[76] Boland 'felt that, in view of his general policy, the Minister would wish me to act on my own initiative and associate Ireland formally with the three-power proposal'. Establishing a precedent that later evolved into standard practice, Murphy and Cosgrave welcomed Boland's autonomous move to support the west.[77] So too did the United States and Britain. Henry Cabot Lodge, the American Ambassador to the UN, told Boland that the greater the number of countries that backed the proposal the stronger was its moral effect on the Hungarian people.[78] Sir Pearson Dixon, Great Britain's Permanent Representative, concurred, adding that wide-spread support increased the chances of effective action.

---

75 DFA PMUN X/51, 28 October 1956.
76 DFA 313/36, 29 October 1956. The theme of Cosgrave's address, delivered on 22 October, was Ireland's UN policy. He said that the 'task of the United Nations was to set up certain basic rules of international conduct, particularly in matters likely to affect the peace of the world, and to secure the acceptance and observance of those rules by all the states of the world without distinction. It was because we believed that the successful performance of that task was essential for the preservation of world peace and the establishment of the rule of law in international relations that we had become members, and intended to do our best to uphold its authority to secure the proper observance of the provisions of the Charter': *Irish Times*, 23 October 1956.
77 External Affairs sent a cable to the Irish Mission the next day reading: 'Action approved and official statement therein released today': DFA 305/210/I, 30 October 1956. The leeway granted to Boland on several important occasions stemmed from the trust placed in him by John Costello, who shared Boland's outlook and realized that his vast experience outweighed even that of his Minister for External Affairs, Liam Cosgrave: private source.
78 DFA 313/36, 29 October 1956.

On 4 November a Soviet veto shut down the Security Council. The western powers then convened an Emergency Session of the General Assembly, which immediately adopted, by a vote of 50 (including Ireland) to 8, with 15 abstentions, a United States-sponsored resolution condemning the invasion.[79] In addition to the expected Soviet bloc opposition, several Afro-Asian nations abstained on the suspect grounds that the west was intentionally neglecting the Suez crisis in favor of Hungary. The Assembly motion also called for a withdrawal of all foreign troops from Hungary; requested the Secretary General to investigate the situation directly through his appointed representatives and report back to the Assembly with recommendations for ending the strife; and demanded that observers and humanitarian aid be permitted into Hungary.

Four days later Boland elucidated Ireland's vote in brief remarks to the Assembly; he would return often to the concepts that imbued this speech: anti-communism; the national character of the Hungarian rebellion; Irish empathy for small nations callously invaded by powerful neighbors; the moral influence of the United Nations. He asserted that the Hungarian uprising had been a 'popular revolt embracing all sections of the community'. The Russian onslaught, which constituted 'one of the blackest chapters in the history of our times' and 'a challenge to all the values' the UN represented, was 'an outrage to the national pride of the Hungarian people'; the Irish delegation's vote reflected 'the deep indignation and the intense grief' it had provoked in Ireland.[80] Boland hoped that the UN would continue to use its 'moral authority ... to assert the indefeasible rights of the Hungarian nation and to safeguard the principles of the Charter'. In the light of their actions in Hungary, he berated Soviet efforts to portray themselves as 'champions of the right of national self-determination' during UN deliberations. Any future attempt to do so would evoke in the minds of the Irish, and 'the peoples of many other of the smaller nations ... the name of Hungary'.

After Russia spurned the Emergency Assembly's first resolution, it passed a second one on 9 November by a vote of 48 to 11, with 16 Afro-Asians still abstaining. Cosponsored by Ireland, Cuba, Italy, Pakistan, and Peru, it called once more for the withdrawal of Soviet forces, supported free elections under UN auspices, and reaffirmed its earlier request that the Secretary General investigate the situation.[81] Predictably, the Soviets ignored this motion too, but its easy passage illumines an important feature of UN diplomacy in the mid-1950s: the United States could muster a majority on any Assembly vote deemed vital to its interests. In fact, America enjoyed a preponderant role in the Organization notwithstanding the Soviet Union's veto in the Security

79 GA/RES 1004 (ES–II).
80 DFA 417/130/5, 8 November 1956. The BBC's UN correspondent singled out the speech in a news telecast that day: DFA 305/210/I, 9 November 1956.
81 GA/RES 1005 (ES–II). Ireland also voted for two resolutions regarding humanitarian assistance for Hungary: GA/RES 1006 (ES–II); GA/RES 1007 (ES–II).

Council. So, despite its decision not to intervene militarily in Hungary, the USA flexed its diplomatic muscle in New York. This was not remarkable, simply inevitable considering the Cold War nature of this issue and the propaganda value at stake.

* * *

The Eleventh Session convened on 12 November. Disturbed by reports that the puppet regime in Budapest was deporting its own citizens to Siberia, the Assembly carried a measure on 21 November urging 'prompt compliance' with its two previous resolutions, calling for an immediate end to forced deportations, and requesting the Secretary General to keep the Assembly informed of compliance with these demands.[82] Ireland voted for the resolution. Liam Cosgrave, who had recently arrived in New York, told the Assembly that 'mass deportation – or transportation as it was called in the dark phases of my own country's history – is one of the cruelest forms of political inhumanity'.[83] Not only did it 'plunge individuals into the anguish of exile', it destroyed families and filled 'the whole nation with a sense of agonizing loss. This barbarous expedient is the *ultima oratio* of tyranny.'

Interestingly, but unsurprisingly, a few days before this vote Freddy Boland had sought to square Ireland's Hungarian policy with the official Catholic line. On 17 November he cabled Sean Murphy and asked him to:

> Please ascertain urgently from [our] Ambassador at [the] Holy See Vatican thinking on [the] present utility of UN resolutions concerning Russian action in Hungary. [It is] suggested in some quarters here that such resolutions do more harm than good by hindering or reversing anti-Stalinist evolution [in] Poland and elsewhere.[84]

Murphy, who had been thinking along the same lines, had already requested an update from Leo McCauley, Ireland's Ambassador to the Vatican, and had received several dispatches from Rome.[85] On 21 November he informed Boland that the Vatican considered the Hungarian resolutions 'useful, and not doing more harm than good because they form principles of justice and freedom which are [the] cornerstone of peace, which is the purpose of the UN'.[86] Likewise, during a meeting the next day Monsignor Angelo Dell' Acqua, Secretary of the Ordinary Affairs Section in the Curia, told McCauley (who immediately passed the information on to Murphy) that 'he was pleased with the action' of the Irish delegation, whose outspoken stand 'was necessary at

82 GA/RES 407 (XI). The vote was 55 to 10, with 14 abstentions.
83 *Irish Press*, 21 November 1956.
84 DFA PMUN X/51, 17 November 1956.
85 DFA 305/210/I, 8, 11 November 1956.
86 DFA PMUN X/51, 21 November 1956.

the time'.[87] Dell' Acqua 'added that he considered the Hungarian situation as the great test of the effectiveness and future value of the United Nations'.

Iveagh House was no doubt heartened to learn that this view obtained at the highest level of the Vatican; in mid-December Dell'Acqua informed McCauley that Pope Pius XII 'had noted the line taken by our delegation, had mentioned it to him, and was pleased by it'.[88] Official Irish concern with the Holy See's outlook on this question was consistent with the spirit of Costello's memorandum. It did not, however, become standard practice; the government did not seek the Vatican's opinion on other issues. In this case Irish diplomats were especially sensitive to Rome's response because the Hungarian crisis constituted an immediate threat to Christian Europe; plus, the Hungarian prelate, Cardinal Josef Mindszenty, was in protective custody in the American Embassy in Budapest. More important, this episode demonstrated that Costello, Cosgrave, Murphy, and Boland were thinking in concert.

* * *

By early December the Hungarian situation had not improved, so the Assembly opened a debate on a fourteen-power draft resolution; like its antecedents, this latest measure called for the withdrawal of all foreign troops, called for an end to deportations, demanded that UN observers be permitted into the country, and set a date of 7 December for compliance with these terms.[89] The Irish delegation cosponsored the motion, and Boland spoke briefly in favor of it on 4 December.[90] Later that day the Assembly approved it by a wide margin.[91] Before the vote the Secretary General and the Hungarian authorities had apparently agreed on a date for Hammarskjold to visit Hungary, but the Hungarian government immediately reversed itself.[92]

On 6 December the fourteen sponsors of the resolution met to discuss possible action once the deadline of 7 December had passed.[93] They considered two options: a motion censuring the Soviet Union; or, an American measure barring the Hungarian delegation from the proceedings of the Assembly.

---

87 Ibid., 22 November 1956.
88 DFA 305/210/I, 13 December 1956.
89 Ibid., 4, 5 December 1956. The sponsors were Argentina, Australia, Belgium, Cuba, Denmark, El Salvador, Ireland, Italy, Netherlands, Norway, Pakistan, Sweden, Thailand, and the United States
90 During his remarks to the Assembly, Boland averred that the only conclusion to be drawn from Soviet recalcitrance was 'that the Hungarian authorities and their Russian masters are still intent on disregarding the voice of this Assembly'. He labeled the new regime in Budapest 'a counter-revolutionary government which could not remain in power for five minutes without the support of the Soviet aggressors': DFA 417/130/5, 4 December 1956.
91 GA/RES 413 (XI).
92 DFA 305/210/I, 5 December 1956.
93 Ibid., 9 December 1956.

The sponsors raised doubts about each draft: the first might indirectly harm the Hungarian people by provoking a diplomatic break with the USSR; the second might require Security Council approval because it involved sanctions. A legal wrangle ensued, and the meeting adjourned. According to a report that Boland forwarded to Murphy, the Irish delegation had taken a hard line. They had 'supported the American proposal throughout the entire discussion, emphasizing that a resolution merely condemning or censuring Soviet Russia would be a very lame outcome' of the Assembly's deliberations.

The sponsors hammered out a final compromise formula and on 10 December they introduced a resolution into the Assembly censuring 'the violation of the Charter by the government of the Union of Soviet Socialist Republics in depriving Hungary of its liberty and independence and the Hungarian people of the exercise of their fundamental rights', but not expelling Hungary.[94] The United States asked Ireland to speak in support of it, and Boland agreed.[95] When he referred to the representatives of Hungary as 'impostors' and said that other members should refuse to listen to them, the Hungarian delegate rose from his seat and left the Assembly. The *Daily Mail*'s UN correspondent wrote that it was the 'universal opinion in the press gallery' that Boland's hint of a boycott had provoked the walkout;[96] the American delegation agreed and was pleased with the speech.[97] Several other newspapers in London picked it up; it was, the Irish Embassy noted, 'the first substantial coverage yet received in the English press for any of our interventions at the UN'.[98]

After Boland had spoken Krishna Menon, the Foreign Minister of India, criticized the joint resolution as a return to the Cold War and representative of 'bloc' politics.[99] His delegation, joined by Ceylon, Burma, and Indonesia, then proposed an alternative resolution. The sponsors of the western motion discussed it at a meeting later that day. They viewed it, and the several amendments to their own that Menon had also suggested, in an unfavorable light. Boland challenged Menon's speech, claiming that the issues were not those of the Cold War, but matters of right and wrong, and told Murphy that he had played 'a leading part in persuading the group to have nothing whatever to do with the draft resolution proposed by India and the other three powers'.[100] His 'point of view seemed to commend itself to the group as a whole', and the caucus decided that its members should either vote against the Indian resolution or abstain.

94 *Irish Times*, 11 December 1956.
95 DFA 305/210/I, 10 December 1956.
96 DFA 313/36, 18 December 1956.
97 DFA 305/210/I, 10 December 1956.
98 Ibid., 11 December 1956.
99 Ibid., 10 December 1956.
100 Ibid., 11 December 1956.

During the debate on 11 December Boland noticed that India's interpretation had not won over many Afro-Asian countries and a strong current of resentment toward the Soviet Union had coalesced within the group. When the western caucus met that evening the Afro-Asian shift was 'noted with satisfaction'.[101] Sir Pearson Dixon, the British Permanent Representative, then suggested that in order to win over India, Ceylon, Burma, and Indonesia the group should add a paragraph to the joint resolution instructing the Secretary General to undertake any feasible initiative with a view to securing a solution of the Hungarian problem in accordance with the Charter and previous resolutions. The group consented to this move, and on 12 December the Assembly adopted the final draft, now sponsored by 20 powers, by a margin of 55 to 8, with 9 abstentions.[102] Those abstaining included several Arab states, plus Greece, Egypt, and Finland. India withdrew its resolution, which Boland described as a blow to Menon.[103]

* * *

Hungary still commanded the attention of the Assembly after its Christmas recess, and Ireland continued to play an active role. In early January Hammarskjold circulated the report of an informal investigative group that he had appointed in November to advise him on the situation, but because its members had been denied access to vital information the report was of little value.[104] The Secretary General then suggested that the Assembly establish, 'as a mark of its active and continued concern with the Hungarian situation', its own *ad hoc* investigative committee. The American delegation drew up a working resolution. On 8 January they requested Ireland to act as one of the twenty-four cosponsors and asked Boland to speak first in the debate.[105]

When introducing the resolution on 9 January Boland said that the Irish delegation had consented to serve as one of its twenty-four sponsors 'because we believe it to be of vital importance that the truth should be established as fully as possible regarding this great and tragic chapter in human history'.[106] In a private update forwarded to Murphy he was more realistic, but endorsed the formation of the committee nonetheless: there was 'no great expectation' that it would 'achieve much more than the informal group of three set up by the Secretary General'; it was 'more a gesture symbolizing the determination of the United Nations to continue to interest itself in the fate of Hungary'.[107] On 10 January the Assembly adopted the resolution by a vote of 59 to 8, with

101 Ibid.
102 DFA 313/36, 13 December 1956; GA/RES 1131 (XI).
103 DFA 313/36, 13 December 1956.
104 Ibid., 9 January 1957.
105 Ibid.
106 DFA 417/130/5, 9 January 1957.
107 DFA 313/36, 9 January 1957.

10 abstentions; Australia, Ceylon, Denmark, Tunisia, and Uruguay were named to the Special Committee.[108]

Boland did not report extensively on the matter again until 7 March. On 27 February the *ad hoc* committee had released its interim report, but Boland said it contained little of interest.[109] On 6 March the twenty-four nations that had sponsored the resolution establishing the committee met to review further action. Boland argued against any new steps on the grounds that certain circles regarded Hungary as a UN failure and it would be better to avoid inconclusive action that might reinforce this view. The United States proposed a draft resolution similar to earlier ones that Boland termed 'unimaginative'. The Irish delegation believed that if a resolution were to be introduced at all it should not address another appeal to the Soviet Union, but should 'bring out in clear and condemnatory language the fact that the USSR had obdurately refused to comply with Assembly resolutions, thereby drawing the sharp distinction between her conduct and that of France, Britain, and Israel in relation' to the Suez crisis. Denmark, Spain, Belgium, Italy, and New Zealand supported this interpretation, but the United States, Great Britain, and Peru still wanted a debate.

At the meeting Boland backed Ambassador Lequerica of Spain, who opposed delaying an impending discussion on the Middle East because doing so might play into the hands of Afro-Asian delegations, who had claimed that the west had used the Hungarian issue as a smokescreen to avoid Arab-Israeli questions. The United States eventually acceded to this argument, but only after the group accepted a compromise resolution that suspended, rather than adjourned, the Eleventh General Assembly so that it could be reconvened when the Special Committee completed its report. The American delegation once again asked Boland to speak in favor of this motion and suggested that he stress that the failure to consider the Special Committee's interim report did not signal a weakening of UN concern over Hungary.[110] Boland readily agreed and resolutely condemned the Soviet Union on 8 March 1957.[111] The Assembly then adopted the measure and recessed.[112]

In retrospect, and despite all of the foregoing diplomatic deliberations, Assembly resolutions, and veiled threats, the lack of any *real* action with regard to Hungary reinforces the popular notion that in this case the UN failed. Contrariwise, this episode highlights one of the UN's vital functions in the international system. Once the United States determined that it was too risky to intervene in Hungary, it shifted responsibility for the calamity to the

108 GA/RES 1132 (XI); DFA 313/36, 10 January 1957; DFA 305/210/4/I, 11 January 1957.
109 DFA 305/210/I, 7 March 1957.
110 Ibid., 12 March 1957.
111 DFA 313/36, 8 March 1957.
112 GA/RES 1119 (XI).

UN, *knowing* that it would not succeed. This tactic thus deflected public dissatisfaction onto the UN, thereby relieving western leaders of pressure to act,
which would have had serious and unforeseen consequences. As a former
member of the Irish delegation has astutely pointed out:

> the main thing that endears the United Nations to member governments,
> and so enables it to survive, is its proven capacity to fail, and to be seen to
> fail. If there is something you are expected to do, but don't want to do,
> or even have done for you, you can safely appeal to the UN, in the com-
> fortable certainty that it will let you down. This capacity is useful for
> the selfish purposes of the governments concerned, but it also helps, in
> its own rather sordid way, to make the world slightly less dangerous.[113]

In the 1990s this phenomenon has transpired in Bosnia, Rwanda, Somalia,
and elsewhere. The United States, Russia, and the European Union, who
were all reluctant to get involved, let the United Nations take over, muddle
through, and shoulder the blame for the tragedies in these and other regions
until the odds of success on the ground had improved, at which point the
great powers entered the picture.

THE SUEZ CRISIS

A second major crisis confronted the United Nations in the autumn of 1956:
the Anglo-French invasion of Egypt.[114] On 29 October Israel sent troops
streaming across the Sinai Peninsula and into the Gaza Strip. Two days later,
in accordance with secretly designed plans, French and British forces, using
the Israeli-Egyptian hostilities as a pretext, opened a bombing campaign against
Egyptian military targets and threatened to seize control of the Suez Canal,
which Gamal Abdel Nasser, the president of Egypt, had nationalized in July
1956. In concert with world opinion – including that of the United States,
which would not support this neocolonial action by its Cold War allies – Ireland
condemned the invasion even though two of the perpetrators were western
European nations with whom it had close ties. There was hope, however, that
this naked act of aggression might be reversed by prompt, determined effort
at the United Nations, so international attention focused on New York.

At 6:00 p.m. on the evening of 31 October Boland sought instructions on
how to respond to calls for an Emergency Session of the Assembly, a move
necessitated by French and British intransigence in the Security Council and
backed by the United States.[115] This request proved to be unnecessary because

---

113 Conor Cruise O'Brien, 'UN Theater', *New Republic*, 4 November 1985, reprinted in
    Akenson, *Conor*, Vol. II, pp. 280–4.
114 Cf. Keith Kyle, *Suez* (New York, 1991), *passim*.
115 DFA 305/173/II, 31 October 1956.

within hours the Security Council reversed itself and voted to convene an Emergency Session at 5:00 p.m. (New York time) the following day.[116]

Nonetheless, at noon on 1 November Iveagh House wired Boland, advising him that 'For your guidance ... please see [the] immediately following telegram containing [a] statement to be included' by Liam Cosgrave in an address to the Dublin Chamber of Commerce that evening.[117] The text, a reaffirmation of Irish principles, condemned Israel, Great Britain, and France for violating the UN Charter by using force to settle their dispute with Egypt. Cosgrave asserted that:

> a small country like our own can only exist if international obligations are respected, including the vital obligation to seek a peaceful solution of differences. It is therefore in my view the duty of an Irish Minister for External Affairs to speak out when these obligations are flouted and when countries – even countries with which we have many ties – resort to war as an instrument of policy.[118]

Later that same day Murphy, Cosgrave, Maurice Moynihan, Secretary of the Department of the Taoiseach, and John Costello met to fine tune the position Ireland should adopt at the Emergency Session of the Assembly. At 6:30 p.m. Murphy informed Boland by cable that he:

> should support whatever Assembly resolution is likely to meet with general acceptance and will be directed towards cessation of hostilities and withdrawal of troops from Egyptian territory. Without interfering with your discretion it is felt that you might support [the] line taken by America and Canada. If [a] statement is called for you should strongly urge cessation of hostilities and [a] return to peaceful negotiation.[119]

Meanwhile, Boland had been considering the appropriate course of action, and he sent a dispatch to Dublin in response to the first, mid-day communication from Iveagh House that crossed the second, 6:30 p.m. wire. He recommended that the delegation should:

> First, avoid [a] prominent role in [the] condemnation [of] Britain [and] France; second, uphold [the] principles of the Charter in voting; third,

---

116 Ibid., 31 October 1956.
117 Ibid., 1 November 1956.
118 Ibid. Cosgrave added: 'It may be said – indeed it is often said – that since a country in our position cannot have any military influence over the course of events, it is in vain for us to declare our views. I do not share that opinion. The very existence of the UN and its Charter is a testimony to the moral force of public opinion.'
119 DFA 305/173/II, 1 November 1956.

only speak if necessary and if so insist in moderate terms that principles of Charter must prevail. [The] foregoing assumes [that the] lead will be given by [the] Americans, not [the] Russians. If otherwise [we] would seek fresh instructions. Please cable views.[120]

Murphy concurred with Boland's assessment, for in a minute to Moynihan the following day regarding the two crossed cables he said: 'you will see that the instruction to Boland replies generally to his enquiry'.[121] Boland and top officials in Dublin, thinking along the same lines, had arrived at similar conclusions concerning Ireland's response to the crisis: Ireland would take a backseat to any American initiative; call for a speedy end to hostilities; and stress its support for the principles of the UN Charter. Irish condemnation of the invasion was firm, but decidedly less trenchant than its censure of the Soviet Union's assault on Hungary. On this occasion Irish thinking and rhetoric focused on the regrettable *action* taken by two close allies; it thus differed in an important respect from Ireland's full-scale rebuke of the intrinsic *nature* of the Soviet Union following its invasion of Hungary.

On 2 November the Emergency Session passed, by a vote of 64 to 5 with 6 abstentions, a United States-sponsored resolution calling for an immediate cease-fire, urging a withdrawal of all forces behind the lines delineated by the 1949 Israeli-Egyptian General Armistice Agreement, and recommending that all Member States 'refrain from introducing military goods in the area'.[122] The motion further urged that once a cease-fire was in effect steps be taken to reopen the Suez Canal and requested the Secretary General to monitor compliance with the resolution and report back to the Security Council and General Assembly with any additional recommendations. Ireland voted for the resolution without speaking; Australia and New Zealand joined with Great Britain, France and Israel to oppose it; Canada, Belgium, the Netherlands, Portugal, South Africa, and Laos abstained. Afterwards, Boland informed Murphy that UN members were pessimistic about resolving the crisis.[123]

But the tide soon changed. In the face of world-wide disdain, not to mention abandonment by their closest allies, Great Britain and France sought a dignified retreat. Subsequently, on 3 November the Canadian delegation introduced a motion requesting the Secretary General to organize a UN force 'to secure and supervise the cessation of hostilities in accordance with all the terms' of the previous day's resolution.[124] This was actually 'a token move to facilitate British and French withdrawal, since United Nations forces are never kept on the soil of a sovereign country against its wishes, and Nasser

120 Ibid., 1 November 1956.
121 S 16113/A, 2 November 1956.
122 GA/RES 997 (ES–I).
123 DFA 305/173/II, 2 November 1956.
124 GA/RES 998 (ES–I).

was certain to demand their removal' at a later date.[125] The Emergency Session approved the Canadian draft by a vote of 57 (including Ireland) to 0, with 19 abstentions, and within days Hammarskjold had established the United Nations Emergency Force (UNEF). Boland soon detected a lessening of tensions and an increasingly positive reaction to the UN's mediation.[126] Hammarskjold's announcement on 6 November that France, Great Britain, Egypt, and Israel had agreed to a cease-fire confirmed these assumptions.[127] The crisis had passed.

That same day the French Ambassador to Ireland, Jacques de Blesson, who was acting on instructions from his government, called on Murphy to explain the Anglo-French action in the Middle East.[128] It had been undertaken, he lamely contended, to prevent the outbreak of war between Egypt and Israel. Recent Soviet arms shipments to Egypt had disrupted the balance of power in the Middle East and had increased the likelihood of such a conflict; in the prevailing circumstances, awaiting UN approval would have proved costly. In a report of the meeting forwarded to Cosgrave, Murphy was rightly skeptical of the Ambassador's rationalizations.[129] The argument regarding Soviet arms sales was specious, and de Blesson never mentioned the fundamental reason for France's action: the threat Nasser's control of the Canal posed to its commercial and colonial interests in the region.

The withdrawal of British and French forces from the Suez Canal, completed on 22 December 1956, and the introduction of UNEF eased the strain in the Middle East, although it took months of intense negotiations to secure Israel's retreat from the Sinai.[130] Interestingly, the Suez affair, according to Conor O'Brien, reveals another of the UN's international roles. Once France and the UK realized that their Suez strategy had backfired, they wanted nothing more than to extricate themselves from the debacle. Hence, after initially rejecting outside interference, 'they called upon the UN to shoulder the

---

125 Kissinger, *Diplomacy*, p. 542.
126 DFA 305/173/II, 5 November 1956.
127 The Emergency Session also passed two more resolutions regarding UNEF and two Afro-Asian resolutions calling for the withdrawal of all foreign troops from Egyptian territory: GA/RES 999 (ES-I); GA/RES 1000 (ES-I); GA/RES 1001 (ES-I); GA/RES 1002 (ES-I).
128 DFA 305/173/II, 6 November 1956.
129 Ibid.
130 Ireland readily agreed to pay its share of the cost of UNEF, but it did not provide troops: CAB 2/17, 4 December 1956; DFA PMUN J/5, 4 December 1956. Concurrently, Ireland did not contribute to the cost of clearing the Suez Canal; the government believed that the aggressors should pay: GA/RES 1121 (XI); DFA 305/173/2, 12 January 1957. For a detailed review of the Eleventh General Assembly's further deliberations on the Middle East, including Hammarskjold's mediation of the Arab-Israeli dispute, see Andrew Cordier and Wilder Foote (eds.), *Public Papers of the Secretaries-General of the United Nations*, Vol. III (New York, 1973), *passim*.

burden' of their mistakes through the introduction of a peacekeeping force.[131] They could then put a positive spin on the outcome by claiming, for example, that 'by its principled intervention, in the interests of international peace and security, Britain [and France] had finally induced the United Nations to act' against threats to the Suez Canal. In essence, the UN allowed them (and still permits other governments) to back down while saving face at home and abroad.

LIAM COSGRAVE AND THE GENERAL ASSEMBLY

Liam Cosgrave amplified Ireland's reaction to the Suez and Hungarian crises in his General Debate speech on 30 November 1956. It was Cosgrave's most significant contribution to the Eleventh Assembly. Preparations began in New York in October,[132] and Conor O'Brien completed the final draft.[133] Freddy Boland's comment several months after the close of the Eleventh Session – 'Our general policy and our attitude towards the principal political problems before the Eleventh Assembly were outlined by the Minister in his speech in the General Debate', and 'subsequent interventions were based on the principles and viewpoints expressed therein' – underscores its relevance to Ireland's posture in 1956.[134]

Cosgrave opened by referring to the 'two great currents' then shaping international relations: 'the movement for freedom which is stirring peoples everywhere throughout the old overseas empires'; and, 'the movement for freedom among the peoples which endure the twentieth century form of imperialism under various forms of Soviet domination'.[135] O'Brien's input most likely prompted a critique of colonialism so early in the speech; the stricture of communist Russia was closer to Cosgrave's heart. His reminder that 'In both cases, the common interest of us all, the preservation of world peace, enjoins policies of prudence and forbearance', and later references to the moral authority of the UN, were concerns shared by the entire delegation.

Cosgrave located the Suez crisis within the context of these two major forces. So far the Irish delegation had walked a fine line: it had condemned the French and British *action*, but had not excoriated, in sweeping terms, its western European neighbors. Cosgrave followed this same course. The invasion of Egypt was 'tragic'; Ireland 'deplored and condemned the Anglo-French attack both as a violation of the Charter of the United Nations and as a grave political blunder'.[136]

---

131 O'Brien, 'UN Theater', pp. 280–4.
132 DFA 417/130, 31 October 1956.
133 DFA 313/36, 8 April 1957.
134 Ibid.
135 DFA 417/130/5, 30 November 1956.
136 In early December John J. Hearne, the Irish Ambassador in Washington, reported that in a recent conversation Herve Alphand, the French Ambassador to the United

But Cosgrave also warned against creeping Soviet intervention in the Middle East. Because Egypt had 'come to rely on Soviet arms and Soviet aid' he counseled it to 'draw back from this dangerous involvement'; its 'new-found friends may be more dangerous to its freedom than were its recent foes'.[137] He asked the Egyptian delegation to heed 'the feelings on this matter of a traditionally friendly and firmly anti-imperialist country'.

Later, Cosgrave recalled Ireland's experience as 'a western country which has undergone foreign rule' when he appealed further to France, Great Britain, and the nations of the Middle East to resolve their differences 'by rational negotiation in a spirit of Christian charity', an interesting request considering that Arabs and Israelis were not of this faith.[138] He pressed for a quick settlement to the Arab-Israeli dispute and encouraged Britain and France to 'implement the General Assembly's resolutions by withdrawing as promptly as possible' from the region. Their presence had supplied 'the Soviet propaganda machine with excellent and sorely needed ammunition' and weakened 'the understanding and the unity which should prevail among the western powers in the face of the common and constant threat'.

The Soviet invasion of Hungary starkly demonstrated that threat. Unlike France and Great Britain, the Soviet Union had 'paid no attention at all to the resolutions' of the Assembly. 'Far from accepting a cease-fire, it used its enormous military power with absolute ruthlessness to crush the Hungarian people.' In a warning to Arab, Asian, and African countries tempted by the Soviet siren call, Costello termed their actions 'an instance of the colonial method and outlook in its most arrogant and ruthless phase'.

Cosgrave's oration provoked a positive reaction in New York and in Ireland. Within hours Boland informed Iveagh House that it had been 'Very favorably received by delegates and the press.'[139] The *Irish Times* said the address was 'packed tight with good sense'.[140] The Minister 'has inaugurated our career in the General Assembly with a wise speech – wise because it was animated by the spirit of moderation for which it appealed', it looked to the future, and 'it summed up the peaceful aspirations which are the object of passionate hopes of so many people in so many lands'.

States, regretted that in his speech Cosgrave had 'criticized the French occupation of the Suez Canal Zone as a reversion to French colonial policy'. Hearne correctly replied that he thought the 'Minister's condemnation of the Anglo-French attack on Egypt was based on the ground that it was a violation of the Charter and a grave political blunder': DFA 305/173/II, 7 December 1956.

137 Cosgrave then offered a relevant example from Irish history: Diarmuid's invitation to Strongbow to assist him in Ireland.

138 A slight was not intended; Cosgrave believed that his reference to Christian principles would go down well in Ireland: Conor Cruise O'Brien, Personal Interview, 5 August 1993; Akenson, *Conor*, p. 155.

139 DFA 417/130, 30 November 1956.

140 *Irish Times*, 1 December 1956.

Three days later Boland reported that 'we continue to hear compliments paid to the Minister's speech in [the] Assembly'; Paul Hoffman, a member of the American delegation, and the Israeli Ambassador to the UN had praised the address, no doubt because of its empathy for their countries.[141] A Guatemalan delegate termed it 'impeccable'.[142] Conor O'Brien, who was responsible for a great deal of it, but not in agreement with its entire contents, later said that Cosgrave 'delivered a dignified and felicitous statement which considerably impressed the Assembly'.[143] While Cosgrave's condemnations of communism and the Soviet invasion of Hungary were unequivocal, the essence of the speech – Ireland's world view – accounts for its positive reception. Its equable tone, correctly noted by the *Irish Times*, was significant; O'Brien deserves credit for tempering the vehement anti-communist rhetoric that might have otherwise surfaced. Ireland's historical experience lent credibility to its appeals to Egypt to avoid entanglements with the Soviet bloc and its counsel to the European powers to hasten their withdrawal from Asia and Africa (which is explored below).

BOLAND'S INTERIM REPORT

The General Assembly's Christmas recess presented Boland with 'an opportunity for reviewing the work of the session to date and placing on record some of the conclusions which we in the delegation have formed as a result of our first contact with the United Nations'.[144] His report, sent to Sean Murphy on 26 December, merits close attention for its insights into the delegation's early experiences and Boland's interpretation of Ireland's role.

So far the Assembly had been 'completely overshadowed by the twin problems of Suez and Hungary'. The Afro-Asian bloc had welcomed the UN's 'relatively prompt and successful action' in the Middle East after initially suspecting the west of paying too much attention to Hungary. Boland, ever the resolute anti-communist, applauded the concentration on eastern Europe. He claimed, with some exaggeration, that:

> it is now generally realized that the events in Hungary, far from being merely isolated disorders, are the outward expression of a deep-rooted spirit of revolt which threatens the whole fabric of communist totalitarianism, not only in the satellites, but even in Soviet Russia itself.

141 DFA 305/210, 4 December 1956.
142 DFA 417/130, 28 December 1956.
143 O'Brien, *Katanga*, p. 15. In a letter to Boland, Ambassador Hearne noted that 'We were all delighted here to read of the phenomenal success of the Minister's splendid speech ... Heartiest congratulations to you all on the delegation on this historic re-entry of our country into the Society of Nations': DFA PMUN X/65, 6 December 1956.
144 DFA 417/130, 26 December 1956.

In this same over-blown vein he added: 'The general view, indeed, is that Hungary is likely to prove a major turning point in world history.'

In early December Boland had forwarded an interesting report to Iveagh House. He said that the delegation was 'so tied up with this Hungarian question at the moment that we find it difficult to keep track of other things'.[145] Nevertheless, since it was 'by far the biggest question before the Assembly' he recommended that he and his colleagues 'continue to concentrate our attention on it rather than dissipate our efforts on matters of lesser importance'. According to Boland's interim report, the delegation adhered to this plan: Ireland had 'played as large a part as any other delegation in insisting, from the very beginning, on the vital issues involved in the Hungarian situation' and in keeping the attention of the Assembly focused on the question.[146] More so, this energetic approach had paid dividends:

> Although it may sound callous to say so in the context of such an immense and appalling tragedy, the Hungarian crisis afforded us, as a new member participating in the work of the Assembly for the first time, just the kind of opportunity we needed. It gave us at once an issue on which we could, if not play a leading role, at least display some degree of initiative and leadership. It also helped us to establish, much more quickly than we could have otherwise done, close and confident relations with the delegations here who have the same sort of ideals as we have ourselves and who think as we do. Thanks to this, and to the development to which I am about to refer, I think it can fairly be claimed that Ireland already enjoys in the United Nations an unusual amount of goodwill and prestige for so small a country and for so recent an entrant into the Organization.

The 'development' Boland alluded to was Liam Cosgrave's General Debate speech. He said that from the delegation's perspective it was, 'by far and away, the most important' event to date. Emilio Nunez-Portuondo of Cuba called it 'the best speech he had heard in the Assembly in ten years'; another 'described it as being "*d'une transcendence phenomenale*"'. Boland's enthusiasm, however, was over-heated. It was a fine speech, but the pre-Castro Cuban delegate admired Ireland's anti-communist posture and recognized an ally when he saw one.[147]

---

145 Ibid., 10 December 1956.
146 To illustrate this claim Boland cited specific evidence: the New York Times' declaration that Ireland's 28 October letter to the Secretary General was an 'unprecedented step'; the 'prominent part' Ireland played in the drafting of the early December, twenty-power resolution condemning Hungary; the press coverage his speech on 10 December had received and the communist indignation it had inspired.
147 In January Boland was speaking with Krishna Menon, India's Foreign Minister, when the Cuban delegate's name surfaced. Menon told Boland that 'Nunez-Portuondo is

Somewhat reluctantly, Boland registered a mild complaint: 'Unpalatable as the statement must be ... it will not be possible for Ireland to participate effectively in the annual session of the Assembly with a delegation of the size we have here at the present.' He had referred to this problem earlier, and raised it again in February, noting that a shortage of staff had 'handicapped' Ireland's effectiveness on certain committees.[148] This complaint was valid, but the Department of External Affairs was undoubtedly stretched to its limit.

The report closed with a brief description of contacts with other members. Incipient relations had been established with some Afro-Asian nations – Iraq, Pakistan, Sudan, India, Thailand – and several Latin American delegations. Ireland was 'already on close terms with almost all those of the western European and Commonwealth countries, and the United States'. This development was unsurprising. Surely it was welcomed by John Costello, who probably read Boland's dispatch. There is no record of Murphy's reaction to Boland's review, but he must have discussed it with him when he traveled to New York in early January to join the Irish delegation.

THE REPRESENTATION OF CHINA

The Hungarian and Suez crises were not the only issues that came before the Eleventh General Assembly, and Ireland responded to every one that arose in the world body. As a whole, the delegation continued to pursue a pro-western, anti-communist line; the representation of China illustrates this trend. The fundamental question at stake in this case was who should represent China in the United Nations: the nationalist government on Taiwan, which still did in 1956; or, the communists in Peking, who had controlled all of mainland China since 1949? For the United States this was a matter of extreme gravity. Indeed, it was inconceivable, at the height of the Cold War, that communist China should replace Taiwan in the Assembly.

Complicating matters for the USA, however, was the fact that many non-communist delegations rejected its stand over China.[149] Leading Afro-Asians

---

really not a bad fellow at all – only that he is bitten by the anti-communist bug – like yourselves': DFA 313/36, 24 January 1957.

148 DFA 305/210/I, 9 December 1956; DFA 313/36, 18 February 1956. In a UN context Boland's point was credible: the Irish delegation, with 7 full-time members and two part-time delegates, was considerably smaller than the Swedish and Norwegian delegations, with 19 and 14 members respectively. On the other hand, the delegations of other small nations were not much larger than Ireland's (Australia, Belgium and Denmark had 11; Austria, Finland, the Netherlands, and Spain had 10), but for a small delegation the addition of one or two members would have made a huge difference: *United Nations Yearbook*, 1956, pp. 526–9.

149 Ruth B. Russell, *The United Nations and United States Security Policy* (Washington, 1968), pp. 368–76.

like India were the most vociferous, but the Nordic countries had expressed their reservations, and even some NATO members had their doubts. Great Britain, for instance, had actually recognized the communist Chinese government, fearing that it might otherwise annex Hong Kong. So if the substantive issue of which government should actually represent China in the UN ever arose in the Assembly, the UK would have had to back Peking.

To forestall this contingency the USA employed several procedural tactics. Every year the Steering Committee debated requests that various items be inscribed on the General Assembly's agenda and forwarded a list of those it had approved to the Assembly for a final vote. Since 1950 the Afro-Asian group had annually requested that the representation of China be placed on the Assembly's agenda, but the American delegation organized a majority to defeat this request – first in the Steering Committee and then in the Assembly when the Afro-Asian's tried to amend the Committee's report. The United States also sponsored a shelving resolution in the Assembly. Yet because many countries disagreed with it on this issue, the American delegation often resorted to classic diplomatic arm-twisting to raise its blocking majority. It leaned on its wavering allies and exerted heavy pressure on small and medium-sized countries dependent on the USA for economic and military aid. As a result, a full-scale debate about the representation of China never transpired, and many western delegations were spared from voting against the USA on a sensitive Cold War issue.

The United States did not have to lean on Ireland in 1956. On 15 November Liam Cosgrave explained to the General Assembly why his country would vote for the American motion shelving the China question. He admitted that a dilemma existed: eventually the international community had to decide 'whether we are going to leave the de facto government of over 500 million people without representation in the United Nations, or whether we should' compromise on the matter.[150] But in the wake of the Hungarian invasion it was inappropriate to discuss the admission of communist China, which shared 'the political philosophy which made these events possible' and had 'itself been guilty in recent years of acts and conduct which have outraged world opinion and violated the provisions of the [UN] Charter'.

The American measure passed by a vote of 47 to 24, with 8 abstentions.[151] Cosgrave's comments and Ireland's vote were entirely consistent with their overall policy supporting the west and their close cooperation with the United States; any other position on such a straight Cold War issue was unfathomable.[152] Still, it has been suggested, based on Cosgrave's hint of a compro-

150 DFA 417/130/5, 15 November 1956.
151 GA/RES 1108 (XI). The nations voting against the measure included members of the Soviet bloc, Afghanistan, Burma, Ceylon, Denmark, Egypt, Finland, India, Indonesia, Nepal, Norway, Sudan, Sweden, Syria, Yemen, and Yugoslavia.
152 In December 1956 Ireland supported the United States on another issue related to

mise, that 'his inference was clear: the issue of Chinese representation would indeed have to be addressed by the Assembly at some time'.[153] This observation is inaccurate. Cosgrave later asserted that he was simply being diplomatic; he did not think that a discussion of the question of Chinese representation would ever be suitable.[154]

* * *

Additional issues evinced the Irish delegation's anti-communism. For example, in mid-December the Soviet Union called for a debate on the United States' 'subversive activities' in eastern Europe. The American delegation, welcoming an opportunity to score a Cold War propaganda victory, agreed, and the item was assigned to the Special Political Committee, one of the General Assembly's seven main organs.[155] Ireland immediately aligned itself with the USA. In a 'Confidential' report Freddy Boland told Sean Murphy that the delegation 'will, of course, support the United States in the vote and, if necessary, in the discussion in the Special Committee'.[156]

The Committee did not take up the item until February 1957. Just beforehand, Boland apprised Murphy that Ireland would:

> take the line that what the Communist world is suffering from is not unwarranted interference by the United States or other outside countries, but its own political mistakes and the breakdown of its own philosophy as evidenced by the fact that the revolt against communism is not confined to eastern Europe ... but is becoming increasingly obvious in the communist parties outside the communist orbit, many of which, in public statements, are now blaming their difficulties on the policy decisions of the Kremlin.[157]

communist China. On 3 December Arthur Emmons, Counsellor in the American Embassy, called on Eoin MacWhite in Iveagh House to solicit an assurance that Ireland would not permit communist Chinese 'cultural' delegations to visit Ireland; the US believed that they were fronts for communist infiltration into the west. MacWhite assured Emmons that it was unlikely that Ireland would allow such a visit. Sean Murphy initialed MacWhite's report of the meeting and sent a copy to New York: DFA 305/115/A/I, 8 December 1956.

153   MacQueen, 'Aiken', p. 219.
154   Cosgrave said: 'Of course you should never say "never"', but that is what he had in mind. He added that in the light of the fact that the Chinese government has not changed in many respects, perhaps Ireland's policy was the right one: Personal Interview, 11 April 1992.
155   Cf. Appendix 2.
156   DFA 313/36, 13 December 1956.
157   Ibid., 18 February 1957.

True to his word, Boland denounced the Russian initiative. In the context of recent events in eastern Europe, he told the Committee, the Soviet complaint reminded the world:

> in a most melancholy and depressing way how wide and deep is the gulf which separates the beliefs and ideals of the free countries from those of the Soviet Union and the countries subject to her influence. Nowhere is that conflict more apparent than in our respective conceptions of the place of truth in official propaganda.[158]

Freedom of speech, the press, and political expression in the west meant that in all of their pronouncements 'our governments must constantly be prepared to meet the challenge of those who have both the means of knowing the truth and absolute freedom to express it'. But in the 'Soviet world ... the truth is a constant menace to its stability'. Why? Because the Soviet system:

> rests on a myth; and, in order to preserve that myth, the Soviet authorities are inexorably driven into the position in which they must regard zeal for the truth as treason, if it evidences itself at home, and as an unwarranted and subversive intervention in the domestic affairs of the Soviet Union, if it emanates from abroad.

The misguided Soviet measure died an ignominious death in the Committee. Cold War considerations surely motivated Boland's opposition, but it was also founded upon admirable principles – civil rights, democracy – that the Irish delegation consistently championed.

SECURITY COUNCIL ELECTIONS

Tracking the determination of Ireland's vote in the contest between Spain and Sweden for the Security Council seat being vacated by Belgium at the end of 1956, which traditionally went to European nation, further reveals its western, anti-communist, Catholic posture. On 30 May 1956 John Belton, Assistant Secretary in External Affairs, submitted an election update to Sean Murphy.[159] Folke Wennerberg, the Swedish Minister in Dublin, had recently called to discuss his country's candidacy. Knowing that Ireland's approach was 'never to give a promise in advance in such matters', he did not seek a commitment, but he did inform Belton that the United States, France, and Great Britain had declared their support for Sweden. Belton also noted that Italy might announce its candidature for the same seat; after reading the update Murphy added that so might Spain.[160]

158 DFA 417/130/5, 26 February 1957.
159 DFA 417/128/1, 30 May 1956.
160 Ibid., 31 May 1956.

As the electoral picture crystallized during July and August, the likelihood of conflict within the western European caucus loomed.[161] Sweden remained a contender, while Italy and Spain had announced their candidatures. Sweden asserted that, based on the 1946 'Gentlemen's Agreement' regarding the geographical distribution of Security Council slots, the one under discussion was traditionally held by a Scandinavian or Benelux country. Italy, claiming that the recent admission of new members had altered the basis for the allocation of the seat, wanted the European caucus to settle the matter, but Sweden rejected this proposal. In mid-July Paul Keating, Second Secretary in the International Organizations section, sought instructions on who to support; in late August he was told that no decision had yet been taken.[162]

Italy's withdrawal in late October in exchange for one of the Assembly's Vice Presidencies simplified the situation somewhat. On 1 November the International Organizations Section in Iveagh House submitted a report to Cosgrave summarizing the arguments for and against Spain and Sweden; it was unsigned, but Conor Cruise O'Brien probably penned it.[163] The reason 'in favor of voting for Spain is that Spain is a Catholic country with which Ireland has close traditional bonds of friendship and sympathy'. Likewise, Ireland had supported Spain 'throughout the period of the ban imposed by the UN on her membership of international organizations'. Conversely, there were several 'aspects of the present Spanish regime which we, as a democratic country, must deplore, e.g., denial [of] free elections, free speech, free press, to mention only a few'. Plus, 'Spain has had little experience of the working of the United Nations', since she only entered the Organization in 1955.

Sweden, though, was 'a democratic state with, like ourselves, a policy of freedom from military alliances'. It was 'an experienced member of the United Nations with an excellent record of service in the organization', and there was no doubt that 'she could make a valuable contribution to the deliberations of the Security Council'. This was the first time Sweden had sought a seat and, if Spain was not a candidate, 'she would be sure of election'. Ireland's 'best policy', therefore, 'would seem to be to vote for Sweden this year, and tell Spain that we shall be prepared to give sympathetic consideration to her candidature next year'.

161 UN delegations were divided into several geographical groups for the purposes of deliberation and discussion. In early May 1956 Iveagh House had instructed diplomats at the New York Consulate to attend the meetings of the western European caucus and they reminded the delegation of this in August. This was not a political decision; geographically, Ireland belonged in the western European caucus and was joined there by both members and non-members of NATO. Cognizant of historical ties of friendship and shared interests, Iveagh House also advised the UN mission to stay abreast of proceedings in the Commonwealth caucus, so long as this 'did not commit us to any definite association with the group': DFA 417/145, 9 May, 20 August 1956.
162 DFA 417/128/1, 4 June 1956, 16, 21 July, 4, 10, 20 August 1956.
163 Ibid., 1 November 1956.

On the following day Ambassador Wennerberg sought a commitment from Ireland.[164] John Belton replied that the matter was still being discussed; evidently O'Brien's report had not had the desired effect. Wennerberg thanked Belton for his attention, adding that the Swedish government was quietly confident that they would be elected.

Wennerberg's prediction was accurate, but initially the Irish delegation heeded neither his wish, nor O'Brien's counsel. While at the UN in November Cosgrave had informed Boland 'that he was in favor of our voting for Spain on the first ballot, but if it became obvious that Spain had no chance of getting the seat, we should then switch our vote in favor of Sweden'.[165] On 13 December Boland sought Murphy's confirmation of this line, probably because he doubted the wisdom of voting for Spain.[166] Two days later Iveagh House notified him that '[The] government has decided that Spain should be supported for the Security Council seat.'[167] Subsequently, Ireland voted for Spain on the first two ballots and, after it withdrew, voted for Sweden on the third and final ballot.[168] Ireland's initial support for Spain was telling. In the face of widespread western support for Sweden, and despite Conor O'Brien's advice, which made a great deal of sense, Ireland backed its traditional Catholic ally, thus underscoring the Christian orientation of the Inter-Party government's foreign policy.

* * *

Not only did Irish policy makers initially oppose Sweden's candidature for a Security Council seat, but they consistently rejected, in concert with John Costello's earlier disavowal of the idea, external proposals that at the UN Ireland play a 'Swedish' role – crisis negotiator and east-west mediator. Folke Sunessen Wennerberg first mooted the notion during a private meeting with Costello in April 1956.[169] He suggested a modification to the Taoiseach's remark in America that Ireland might serve as a bridge between the United States and Europe: instead – and like Sweden – Ireland could act as an 'interpreter of the west to the east' in the United Nations. To reinforce the similarities between the two countries Wennerberg referred to the success of Swedish neutrality, but Costello remained non-committal.

Swedish perceptions of common ground with Ireland surfaced again during a conversation in July between Josephine McNeill, the Irish Minister in

---

164 Ibid., 3 November 1956.
165 Ibid., 13 December 1956.
166 Ibid.
167 Ibid., 15 December 1956. No official government decision was taken; it is likely that Costello, Cosgrave, and Murphy discussed the matter amongst themselves.
168 Ibid., 20 December 1956. Interestingly enough, Ireland received one vote on the last ballot, but the delegation did not know who cast it.
169 S 13750/B, 16 April 1956.

Stockholm, and Lief Belfrage, the Secretary General of the Swedish Foreign Office.[170] The two spoke about issues likely to arise at the UN in the autumn. Belfrage told McNeill that the Foreign Office had not adopted a final position on many questions, but said that Sweden wanted to be an 'element of recon- ciliation between opposing blocs and to exert their influence as such in the interests of peace and human progress'. He hoped that Ireland 'would be inspired by the same desire of objectivity in our activities in the UN' and he believed that 'an excellent basis for cooperation would be found between the Swedish and Irish delegations'.

On at least two occasions during the Suez crisis Irish diplomats in Europe were reminded of Ireland's potential to act as an intermediary at the UN. During a meeting in late August Mr Trevedi, Counsellor at the Indian Embassy in London, inquired of Francis Biggar, Chargé d'Affaires at the Irish Embassy, 'whether Ireland was likely to take any initiative at the United Nations in regard to the Suez crisis'.[171] Trevedi hoped to see a mediating committee formed, 'consisting of, say, Ireland, Argentina, and Indonesia on the grounds that they would be disinterested parties'. Biggar replied that such a move was unlikely. Nevertheless, he told Sean Murphy that Trevedi's view might 'be of interest as another indication of the role that we may be asked to play in the UN as a western country uncommitted to any power bloc'.

In early October Michael Rynne, recently named Irish Ambassador to Spain, spoke with the Saudi Arabian Ambassador, Dr Medhart Sheikh El-Ard, who assumed that Ireland was a 'neutralist' regarding the growing tensions over the Suez Canal.[172] Rynne's reply reflected official Irish thinking. He said that Dr El-Ard was correct in the sense that because Ireland was not a 'Canal user' it 'would tend to keep out of the Canal controversy'. It was also true that the Irish people sympathized generally with nationalism whenever it was genuine and anti-imperialist. But, Rynne continued:

> the Irish people – and the government had endorsed this sentiment – could not be neutral 'against' (that is, 'in respect of') communism. I was sure that we should hate to see the Arab League resort to purely Russian aid, no matter how hard we saw them being pushed by the westerners. On the whole I felt we were mostly inclined to look to the Americans – our very dear friends and kinsmen – to save this unfortunate situation.

Hence, in 1956 Ireland could have followed an independent line at the UN. Two uncommitted countries, India and Sweden, and at least one Arab country believed that Ireland might do so. They recognized that Ireland's his- tory, sensibilities, and non-participation in military alliances suited it for such a role. Yet the Irish government did not seize this opportunity because its top

170 DFA 440/7, 6 July 1956.
171 DFA 305/311/I, 27 August 1956.
172 Ibid., 10 October 1956.

policy makers – Costello, Cosgrave, Murphy, Boland – imagined that such a course would distance Ireland from the western orbit and provoke doubts about its support for the free world. Dr Rynne's remarks in Madrid highlight these fears. Not until the Twelfth Session in 1957 would Ireland embrace the Swedish mantle.

DECOLONIZATION

Peacefully dismantling the European colonial system and guiding new African and Asian states to independence was one of the most crucial challenges confronting the United Nations in the late 1950s; it evolved into one of its most ambitious undertakings. It was not a voluntary mission, however. The UN Charter explicitly assigned this responsibility to the Organization and established the apparatus to perform the task: the International Trusteeship System, the Trusteeship Council, and its counterpart in the General Assembly, the Fourth Committee.[173]

It has become fashionable, of late, to denounce the UN's record in this field, especially in the wake of ongoing turmoil throughout much of Africa and parts of Asia. Yet this trend neglects significant realities of the 1950s and 1960s. It underestimates the unquenchable desire for self-rule that swept across the southern hemisphere (which often expressed itself in armed revolt) and the popular support independence movements enjoyed in North America and Europe. It ignores the Afro-Asian conviction that the United Nations had a fundamental role to play in the decolonization process – indeed, that it was their closest ally.[174] More so, this view slights the UN's notable, numerous achievements throughout Africa and Asia over the past several decades, not simply with regard to ending colonialism and its vestiges (in the Cameroons, Togoland, Angola, Namibia, and South Africa, for example), but in other crucial areas as well: health care, disease eradication, economic development, public administration, literacy.[175] In short, present-day difficulties cannot obscure past UN accomplishments.

173 Cf. Chapters XII, XIII of the United Nations Charter.
174 African states, according to one scholar, viewed the UN and its Charter as 'an instrument through which colonialism [could] be eliminated. The UN Charter ... has over the years become the testament of faith and a documentary confirmation of the legitimacy of African nationalist aspirations'. Even with the complete dismantling of colonialism the Afro-Asian world has not lessened its commitment to the United Nations. Membership provides these states not only 'with a forum through which they can participate in world diplomacy, but also enables them to bring to the attention of other member states their problems of racism, economic development, and the amicable resolution of international conflicts': Wellington W. Nyangoni, *Africa in the United Nations System* (Rutherford, 1985), p. 21.
175 For a detailed discussion of the UN and decolonization, including its successes, see A. Rigo Sureda, *The Evolution of the Right to Self-Determination: A Study of United Nations Practice* (Leiden, 1973).

These achievements were often the result of cooperation between the Afro-Asian group and likeminded states. For instance, during Ireland's brief stint at the Tenth Assembly in December 1955 the Permanent Representative of Syria, Rafik Asha, informed John Conway that several Afro-Asian delegations anticipated that 'Ireland would have a lot in common with them, and they with us'. Asha even proposed that:

> Ireland could, and should, accept a leading and active position among the anti-colonial small powers since Ireland, although a western European country, is not a western European colonial power and is considered, because of her history, to be sympathetic to claims for self-determination.[176]

But would Ireland build on this common ground? At least twice Liam Cosgrave highlighted Ireland's anti-colonial credentials. Following his three-principles address to the Dáil he referred to 'the sympathy we naturally feel for other nations justly struggling to be free ... '[177] During his General Debate speech he urged colonial powers to 'come to prompt and reasonable terms with legitimate, national independence movements' through 'free and responsible negotiation'.[178] In the Dáil, however, he qualified Ireland's support: it would not apply to communist movements masked as independence struggles.[179] Likewise, he couched his General Debate delivery in strident Cold War rhetoric; he called for talks so as to 'defeat communism' in Africa and Asia.[180] Ireland's relationships with several European colonial powers further delimited its options, and the Irish delegation had to balance all of these considerations. If doubts arose about the proper course of action the Inter-Party government's pro-western, anti-communist predilections overrode its compassion for colonized peoples. At the Eleventh Assembly Irish support for self-determination was not *carte blanche*. The Franco-Algerian conflict demonstrates this fact.

ALGERIA

The Algerian rebellion, spearheaded by the National Liberation Front (FLN), flared up in November 1954.[181] When several Afro-Asian delegations raised

---

176 DFA 417/129, 20 December 1955.
177 DD 159, 145, 3 July 1956.
178 DFA 417/130, 30 November 1956. Cosgrave then held up Ireland as an example of a nation which had achieved independence through such methods.
179 DD 159, 145, 3 July 1956.
180 DFA 417/130, 30 November 1956.
181 Cf. Alistair Horne, *A Savage War of Peace: Algeria, 1954–62* (London, 1977); John Talbott, *The War Without a Name: France in Algeria, 1954–62* (Boston, 1980). For an

the matter at the Tenth General Assembly in 1955 the French delegation walked out, claiming that this violated Article 2.7 of the Charter, which prohibited interference in the domestic affairs of Member States. Soon thereafter, the Assembly postponed discussion of the conflict when France tentatively agreed to negotiate with the leaders of the Algerian independence movement. The subsequent failure of these talks ensured that the issue would arise at the Eleventh General Assembly.

Diplomatic maneuvers commenced in late May 1956 when Jacques de Blesson, the French Ambassador in Dublin, called on Sean Murphy to discuss an Afro-Asian move underfoot to convene a Special Session of the Assembly in the near future. He hoped that the Irish government 'would not agree to such a proposal'.[182] Murphy allayed the French envoy's apprehensions: Ireland would not. De Blesson also said that there would be a strong push to place the Algerian question on the Eleventh Assembly's agenda and he trusted that Ireland would oppose this action, 'in view of the fact that the Algerian question was clearly a domestic one within Article 2.7 of the Charter'. On this point Murphy was diplomatic. He told de Blesson that he 'could not commit the government to anything', but promised to refer the matter to the Minister for External Affairs immediately. He did so; Cosgrave noted Murphy's report, but did not comment on it.[183]

Murphy's hesitation to accede to de Blesson's second request was significant; Irish empathy with Algerian claims to self-determination, in principle, over-ruled the disavowal of a discussion of the issue at the UN. Simultaneously, in the light of Ireland's close relations with France, Murphy and Cosgrave were opposed to the volatile Afro-Asian call for a Special Session of the Assembly. They were trying to reconcile two competing Irish sensibilities; Freddy Boland would soon have to do the same at the UN.

William Fay, the Irish Ambassador in Paris, kept the Department of External Affairs apprised of how the Algerian crisis was unfolding in France. After briefly referring to the matter in August 1955,[184] he submitted a comprehensive twenty page report in mid-June 1956.[185] In a follow-up minute sent to Murphy two weeks later Fay contended that his lengthy narration

---

interesting comparative perspective, see Ian S. Lustick, *Unsettled States, Disputed Lands: Britain and Ireland, France and Algeria, Israel and the West Bank-Gaza* (Ithaca, 1993).

182 DFA 440/11, 22 May 1956. Murphy was familiar with the nuances of French diplomacy. He had served as the Irish envoy to Vichy France and remained in Paris as Ireland's representative until 1950: Keogh, *Ireland and Europe*, pp. 182–91; Ronan Fanning, 'Charles de Gaulle, 1946–58 – From Resignation to Return: The Irish Diplomatic Perspective', in Pierre Joannon (ed.), *De Gaulle and Ireland* (Dublin, 1991), pp. 70–1.

183 DFA 440/11, 22 May 1956, 23 May 1956.

184 DFA 313/4/C, 10 August 1955.

185 DFA 440/10, 15 June 1956.

was completely factual – he had 'endeavored to remain on the plane of pure analysis' – but the tone of the report implied a pro-French bias.[186] More so, the 'conclusions' that Fay included in his follow-up to Murphy demonstrated that he 'was personally much more sympathetic to the French government and much more hostile to the Algerian campaign for independence'.[187]

Fay's first judgment was that the Algerian revolt was not 'the expression of a specific Algerian nationality, so much as a mixture of local elements with a vague conception of the Maghreb, much influenced, controlled, trained, and equipped by pan-Arabic influences in Egypt'. In addition, 'the movement enjoys the unconditional support of Soviet Russia and of the French and Algerian Communist parties'. Therefore, France would 'seem to be morally and juridically entitled to resist the armed rising', but the odds did not favor the successful pursuit of such a policy. With regard to the autumn General Assembly, Fay recommended that, subject to a consideration of the impact that 'the thesis that Algeria is an internal French affair' might have on future plans to raise the question of partition, the Irish delegation should 'adopt an attitude generally favorable to France on the question of substance'.

In his reply Murphy thanked Fay for his report and referred to de Blesson's recent visit to Iveagh House seeking Irish support for France's position at the UN.[188] He said that Cosgrave would make no 'definite decision' until Boland had settled in New York and 'had an opportunity of expressing his views'. He added that it was 'extremely unlikely' Ireland 'would vote against France on the Algerian question'. Murphy did admit that 'we must, as you say yourself, examine very carefully the implications of voting for a country which is invoking Article 2.7'. (This detail, however, did not persuade the Irish delegation to oppose France in the Assembly; rhetorically refuting the notion resolved their dilemma.) One does not detect in this minute Fay's ardor for the French establishment's point of view, and in this sense Murphy's elusive response to Fay mirrored his reply to de Blesson's second request. Although he was pro-French, Murphy was more sensitive than Fay to Algerian claims for independence.

* * *

Diplomatic initiatives remained on hold until the autumn, when fifteen Afro-Asian nations requested that the question of Algeria be placed on the General Assembly's agenda.[189] On 16 November Murphy sent a cable to the Irish

186 Ibid., 28 June 1956.
187 Fanning, 'Charles de Gaulle', p. 75.
188 DFA 440/11, 11 July 1956.
189 DFA 440/10, 1 October 1956. The fifteen countries were Afghanistan, Burma, Ceylon, Egypt, Indonesia, Iran, Iraq, Jordan, Lebanon, Libya, Pakistan, Philippines, Saudi Arabia, Syria, and Yemen.

Mission detailing another meeting with de Blesson.[190] France had acceded to demands that Algeria be discussed, but wanted the item placed as low as possible on the schedule of debates because secret negotiations then in progress might soon produce a cease-fire. The United States backed this move. So did John Costello: Murphy informed the delegation that the Taoiseach had agreed that the 'French request be supported by us' unless Cosgrave, who was in New York, held 'strong views to the contrary'.

Simultaneous with this development, William Fay had forwarded another long dispatch to Dublin. This report detailed the latest events in the Algerian crisis and exhibited the same pro-French proclivities that had colored his previous efforts. Once again, Fay argued that 'on the issue of substance we should support France' in the Assembly.[191] The recent appeal by the new French Premier, Guy Mollet, to halt the fighting, 'with a formal promise of free elections', was significant, especially since there was no reason why France 'should accept the self-constituted leaders of the revolt as necessarily being "valid spokesmen" of Algerian national aspirations'.

With Murphy's consent, 'and in particular with an eye to the coming debate in [the] UN', Fay sent a copy of his report directly to Boland in New York, accompanied by a handwritten covering minute. In the minute Fay asserted, in regard to his suggestion in the report, that 'I am quite clear on the recommendation – I think Mollet's attitude is reasonable (even if he hasn't made enough concession to national sentiment perhaps) ... '[192] This was certainly a bald attempt by Fay to influence Ireland's policy at the United Nations. As later developments demonstrated, it was only partially effective; Murphy, Cosgrave, and particularly Boland, agreed with the letter, but not the spirit, of Fay's recommendation.[193]

In mid-January, with a debate imminent, Boland met with Louis de Guiringaud, France's Permanent Representative to the UN, Jean Soustelle, his colleague on the French delegation, the Permanent Representative of Sweden, and the Secretary General of the French administration in Algeria. After the French had presented their point of view Boland explained the Irish position, namely, that 'in our circumstances, it was impossible for us not to sympathize with the demands of the Algerian people for self-determination and the recognition of their nationality'.[194] Boland then drew the attention of his luncheon companions to Cosgrave's General Debate call for negotiations to resolve colonial conflicts. He did add the qualification that 'debates and resolutions of this Assembly may prepare the way' for talks, but the UN was not

190 DFA PMUN X/65, 16 November 1956.
191 Ibid., 15 November 1956.
192 DFA PMUN X/65, 17 November 1956.
193 William Fay sent three additional reports from Paris on 18, 25 and 31 January 1957 covering the Algerian conflict. Neither contained any further recommendations: DFA 440/11, 18, 25, 31 January 1957.
194 DFA 313/36, 14 January 1957.

'a super-state. We should not expect it to be a kind of "god from the machine" which can resolve all problems.' Based on this view Boland told the French diplomats that the Irish delegation believed:

> that the best solution of the problem was an agreement freely negotiated between the French government and the people of Algeria, and we did not think that any action which the United Nations could take could supply as satisfactory a solution as an agreement of that kind.

More so, Ireland was likely to follow this 'line if we intervened in the discussion on the Algerian problem' in the Assembly.

This very important conversation illumined Irish perceptions of the Algerian revolt. Boland's rejoinder to the French delegates that Ireland sympathized, in principle, with Algerian demands echoed Murphy's hesitant responses to de Blesson and Fay; Boland thereby distanced himself from Fay's uncritical acceptance of the French government's thesis. More important, Boland's declaration, welcomed by his French companions, that the Irish government discounted the UN as the final arbiter of the conflict, and favored direct negotiations instead, satisfied French wishes that the UN not involve itself too intimately in the crisis. This position meant that the Irish delegation would support France on the matter of substance – voting. In addition, Boland's emphasis on direct negotiations, as opposed to a free-for-all-debate at the United Nations, was a call for a moderate, reasoned, responsible handling of this explosive situation, an approach that mirrored his personal style.

Cosgrave, who was keeping abreast of unfolding events, cooperated with Murphy and Boland to formulate Ireland's final position. On 1 February External Affairs sent a cable to the latter two in New York stating that '[The] Minister would like your views soonest on [the] line to be taken on the Algerian question.'[195] This wire underscores the wide latitude granted to Boland and demonstrates that the three men worked well together, primarily because they held similar views on most matters.

Boland did not have time to respond to Cosgrave's query, but four days later he elucidated Ireland's perspective in an address to the First Committee. The speech, drafted by Conor O'Brien and infused with his thinking,[196] sought to reconcile conflicting Irish sympathies. It was crucial, Boland asserted, that the Assembly's deliberations did not 'inflame passions still further, and leave the problem more intractable than before'.[197] He did not mean 'to imply that the problem is not proper to be debated here at all'; the Irish delegation, for example, rejected the French thesis that the Algerian crisis was a matter 'excluded from our competence by Article 2.7 of the Charter'. Nevertheless,

195 DFA 440/11, 1 February 1957.
196 DFA 417/130, 8 April 1956.
197 DFA 417/130/5, 5 February 1957.

'To say that this problem can suitably be discussed in this Assembly is not to say ... that it can be solved here.' That was best achieved by negotiations 'leading to an agreement between responsible French leaders and the leaders of the Algerian national movement', which Ireland considered a legitimate force. To soften the blow of support for Algerian national aspirations, Boland heaped lavish praise upon France. He then concluded with an apology for speaking 'at some length on this matter', but said it was because the Irish delegation felt:

> particularly deeply about it – and that, for three reasons: because of our natural sympathy with peoples struggling to be free; because of our traditional friendship and admiration for France; and because of our anxiety lest this grim and protracted struggle should serve to promote the expansion of Soviet influence in this critical area of the world.

Boland reported that the speech 'was well received by the Committee as a whole'.[198] Ferhat Abbas, the FLN's unofficial UN representative, thanked Boland 'most cordially'.[199] A Canadian diplomat said that it was the 'speech they would have made if not partners of France in NATO'; the British delegation admired it greatly.[200] In essence, Boland had tried to temper the discussion by pursuing a middle course between the competing camps. His speech contained something for everyone; he alluded to this when he noted that other speakers had 'expressed agreement with our views – each of them, of course, picking out the passages in the speech which happened the best to fit in with his own particular standpoint'.[201] Concurrently, it satisfied neither group; it did not support hard-line Algerian demands, but trod, ever so softly, on French sensibilities by backing Algerian claims to self-determination. Boland attempted to resolve this conflict when he told Murphy that 'Although what we said seemed to be particularly popular with the Afro-Asian delegations ... it was not unpalatable to the French.'[202] Members of the French delegation felt:

> that we went rather far in expressing sympathy with Algerian nationalism, but they appreciated the tributes we paid to France's position in the free world and, above all, they were gratified for the view we expressed that the UN should not attempt to adopt any resolution purporting to impose, or suggest the lines of, an Algerian settlement.

In the same vein, although he did not agree with everything in the speech, the French Foreign Minister, Christian Pineau, appreciated Boland's 'courtesy',

198 DFA 313/36, 6 February 1957.
199 DFA 440/11, 7 February 1957.
200 DFA 313/36, 7 February 1957.
201 Ibid.
202 Ibid., 18 February 1957.

and recognized that Ireland supported France 'on the point on which they were principally concerned' – that the matter lay outside the competence of the United Nations.[203]

Boland later noted that several Afro-Asian delegations had 'construed our speech in the sense that we were prepared to support their point of view against that of the French government'.[204] Subsequently, members of the Irish delegation went to great lengths in conversations with African and Asian diplomats 'to correct this impression ... making it clear that we would not be able to vote for any resolution if the French delegation decided to vote against it'. Boland insisted that this position was 'consistent with the line we took in [my] speech ... '

* * *

The Irish delegation's dilemma presaged the difficult task the First Committee faced in drawing up a resolution that would, according to Boland, 'command a majority in the Committee and satisfy France's opposition to the adoption of any resolution at all'.[205] Eighteen hard-line Afro-Asian delegations proposed a strident measure that requested 'France to respond to the desire of the people of Algeria to exercise their fundamental right of self-determination' by entering into immediate negotiations presided over by the Secretary General.[206] This motion was unlikely to pass. A Latin American and Italian resolution sympathetic to France stood a better chance. It simply noted the UN's discussion of the Algerian question and expressed 'the hope that a peaceful and democratic solution' would be found. Three moderate Afro-Asian nations – Japan, Thailand, and the Philippines – offered a compromise formula requesting that, 'in conformity with the principles of the Charter ... the Algerian people would endeavor, through appropriate negotiations, to bring about the end of bloodshed and the peaceful settlement of the present difficulties'.

On 13 February the Committee moved to a vote on the three measures; Ireland's middle course would now be put to the test. One week earlier Boland had informed Murphy that, 'Consistent with the line taken in our speech', the Irish delegation had associated itself with European and American opposition to any measure likely to provoke 'a breach between France and the United Nations'.[207] Hence, it 'would not be in favor of any resolution if France decided to vote against it'. They 'would support any resolution, however, which France was prepared to accept, or on which she abstained'. The delegation, therefore, voted against the Afro-Asian measure, supported the

203 Ibid., 6 February 1957.
204 Ibid., 18 February 1957.
205 Ibid., 7 February 1957.
206 *United Nations Yearbook, 1956*, p. 119.
207 DFA 313/36, 7 February 1957.

resolution amenable to France, and abstained on the compromise motion; the Committee adopted the latter two.[208] Paris welcomed the Irish votes. On 14 February Murphy cabled Boland with the news that:

> [the] French Prime Minister has expressed through [our] Paris Embassy appreciation of our support for [the] South American resolution on Algeria, and has requested that on the next occasion the Japanese-Philippines-Thailand resolution comes up for voting we might vote against rather than abstain as on the last occasion.[209]

Murphy added that Liam Cosgrave was 'agreeable to [a] negative vote unless you see strong reasons to the contrary'.

Iveagh House's attitude and the delegation's ballots had thus fallen in solidly behind France. Once Ireland had expressed its support, in principle, for self-determination it felt comfortable voting with its European neighbor. The question of casting another negative ballot did not arise, however, because on 15 February the Assembly unanimously carried a new compromise resolution acceptable to France.[210]

William Fay reported that the French authorities appreciated Ireland's restraint. They knew that the Irish delegation was predisposed toward France, but also understood 'that our own revolutionary past made it impossible for us to take an entirely negative attitude towards the apparent desire of the Algerians' for independence.[211] General Ganeval, Chief of the Military Household of the French President, and M. Bourges-Maunoury, the Minister for Defense, were delighted that Ireland had supported a resolution 'most favorable to France and the one she herself was prepared to accept'. Fay concluded that this response represented 'a distinctly positive factor in our future relations with France', but his enthusiasm was more an attempt to vindicate his earlier recommendations.

In his own report Boland applauded Ireland's posture throughout the debate, but its tone and his conclusion that the outcome was a 'moral victory for the French' underline official Irish sympathies for France.[212] He had detected the feeling among the more extreme members of the Afro-Asian group 'that our attitude, when it came to the question of voting, was not entirely in line with the general tone of our statement', but refuted this argument by asserting that 'to a large extent, our position was soundly vindicated by the fact that, in the end, every delegation found itself voting for the kind of "middle

208 DFA 440/11, 14 February 1957.
209 Ibid.
210 GA/RES 1012 (XI). This anodyne motion expressed the 'hope that, in a spirit of cooperation, a peaceful, democratic, and just solution will be found, through appropriate means, in conformity with the principles of the United Nations Charter'.
211 DFA 440/11, 6 March 1957.
212 DFA 313/36, 18 February 1957.

of the road" attitude which we had advocated'. Moreover, others shared this outlook: one diplomat told Boland that his 'speech on Algeria ... is thought to have done a good deal to moderate the tone of the subsequent discussion'.[213]

* * *

The Irish response may have satisfied the French and others, but Boland was correct, and lingering doubts about Ireland's reliability persisted among the Afro-Asian and Arab blocs; their complaints sparked off a mild, but significant, exchange between Boland and Conor O'Brien in the spring of 1957 that presaged later differences. In a report forwarded to Sean Murphy, William Warnock, the Irish Minister to Germany, mentioned that several 'ex-colonials', including the Iraqi and Indonesian Ambassadors to Germany, had 'expressed to me disappointment at our attitude when the question of Algeria was being discussed at the United Nations'.[214] After coming across Warnock's aside Boland, who was 'intrigued' by it, raised it in a minute to O'Brien.[215] He did not think 'that our statement on Algeria got as chilly a reception from the anti-colonial countries as all that'. Ferhat Abbas, the FLN representative, 'could not have been more pleased and laudatory', and the delegates of Iraq and Indonesia 'went out of their way to [commend] our contribution in their speeches'. Boland concluded 'that the matter need not trouble us too much. The trouble about an attitude of moderation is that it never gives 100% satisfaction.'

O'Brien replied candidly to Boland's letter; he probably felt emboldened because Frank Aiken, who was amenable to his thinking, had become the new Minister for External Affairs following Fianna Fáil's election victory in March. O'Brien agreed that Boland's address had received 'a warm response from most of the anti-colonial countries ... '[216] Those questioning Ireland's record, however, were not thinking of the speech 'so much as of our voting, which as you remember, could be interpreted as being a good deal more "pro-French" than our statement was'. O'Brien believed 'that the *decalage* between our words and our votes on this particular question was rather wide', but admitted that he was 'regarded as something of a fanatic in this matter' due to his sympathy for the Algerian nationalists. He also distanced himself from Ambassador Fay's reports, which he claimed 'on the whole, understandably enough, tend to reflect French official and semi-official opinion'.

In a friendly rejoinder Boland defended his equable approach.[217] He did not believe that 'there was anything in our action at the last Assembly which

213 Ibid., 20 February 1957.
214 Ibid., 18 April 1957.
215 Ibid., 9 May 1957.
216 Ibid., 31 May 1957.
217 Ibid., 11 June 1957.

we need regret'. The more the Algerian conflict heated up, 'the greater the need for the application of the principles of moderation which we advanced, and the more apparent the irrelevancy of UN Assembly resolutions becomes'. He too did not share all of 'the points of view put forward in some of Ambassador Fay's reports', but was convinced that 'as long as the leadership of affairs in Algeria remains in the hands' of the extremist FLN there would be no agreement.

Boland argued for popular elections to counter the FLN's influence. Revealing his Irish sensibilities, he compared conditions in Algeria to Ireland 'if there had been no parliamentary elections at all after 1916'. Irish affairs:

> would have remained entirely in the hands of the men doing the fighting; the more moderate, democratically-minded elements in the national movement would have had no opportunity of asserting their influence; and by degree the people, deprived of effective articulate political leadership might have tended to become confused and critical of the militant elements.

Hence, if elections were held the 'moderate, far-seeing, and constructive elements in Algerian nationalism can come to the front and assert their authority over the more irresponsible and extreme elements in the national guerrilla forces'.

O'Brien obviously had reservations about Ireland's middle course, although his differences with Boland were cordially expressed and purely professional.[218] He recognized that Ireland was incapable of satisfying France and the Afro-Asian group simultaneously. In the strained atmosphere of a colonial debate at the UN the medium was the message: a delegation's vote counted, not its rhetoric. This was particularly true considering that the Afro-Asian bloc looked to the UN for assistance in breaking down the colonial system. By this standard, therefore, Ireland had backed France, regardless of the content of Boland's speech. O'Brien grasped (and endorsed) what the UN meant to Afro-Asian nations. So did Boland, but their extremism frustrated him. At the same time, future events, in Algeria and elsewhere, certainly demonstrated the wisdom of Boland's call for moderation, and his voice would often be a source of reason in the turbulent times ahead.

FRENCH TOGOLAND

On two other colonial issues, French Togoland and Portuguese Goa, Ireland not only supported its respective European neighbors, but reversed its

---

218 Later, as an olive branch, O'Brien sent Boland an extract from a report by Con Cremin noting a Tunisian diplomat's great admiration for Boland's statement in the First Committee: DFA PMUN X/65, 27 June 1957.

standard practice of not attending Fourth Committee meetings in order to do so.[219] A controversy surrounding French Togoland arose in the Fourth Committee when members of the Afro-Asian bloc criticized France for contravening UN instructions. Without proper UN supervision it had sponsored, in October 1956, a plebiscite on the Trust's future status, which produced a majority in favor of an 'autonomous republic' within the French Union.[220] Afro-Asian delegations claimed that by not offering the territory the option of independence outside of the French Union, the French authorities had intentionally impeded any move by the French Togolese to merge with the new west African state of Ghana, composed of the former Gold Coast and British Togoland.[221]

In a January 1957 dispatch to Murphy, Boland admitted that 'there appears to be some substance in this criticism of the French', but the manner 'in which this issue has been exploited by the Afro-Asian bloc, under the leadership of Krishna Menon, has created profound resentment' among the European, North American, and Commonwealth delegations.[222] Hence, a 'vigorous effort' led by the United States was underway 'to beat the Afro-Asian bloc on this issue'. Ireland had not been attending sessions of the Fourth Committee due to a lack of personnel, but they had been 'strongly pressed by the American and French delegations to come in and support them on the issue'. Despite the fact that the matter was 'not a straightforward one, and the French position does not appear to be completely above criticism', Boland argued that it was:

> a case in which we should lend the Euro-American bloc any aid we can, and we therefore propose to attend the Fourth Committee on Monday morning when the vote is taken, and to give general support to the Euro-American point of view.

Sheila Murphy represented the Irish delegation when the Fourth Committee discussed Togoland on 14 January. The debate 'turned out to be a rather half-hearted and unsuccessful attack' on France by 'Arab and certain other Afro-Asian states led by Mr Krishna Menon'.[223] As predicted, France 'was supported by practically all the European, Latin American, and Commonwealth votes', and the Committee passed a resolution sympathetic to France that

---

219 Before the Christmas recess Boland had informed Murphy that the delegation had been 'unable, with our staff resources, to follow very closely the work of the Fourth Committee, which deals with Trusteeship matters': DFA 313/36, 18 December 1956.
220 DFA 417/139, 11 January 1957.
221 Based on a plebiscite in the British trust territory the Assembly recommended, on 13 December 1956, that British Togoland be united with Ghana. The vote was 64 in favor (including Ireland), O opposed, with 9 abstentions: DFA 313/36, 12 December 1956.
222 DFA 417/139, 11 January 1957.
223 Ibid., 14 January 1957.

praised it and the Togolese people for the progress made toward self-rule, confirmed the results of the 1956 plebiscite, and appointed a UN Commission to assess the territory's readiness for autonomy.

When the Fourth Committee voted on the motion, it cast ballots on each paragraph and only narrowly passed two clauses referring to the plebiscite results and the 'Autonomous Republic of Togoland'. The Afro-Asian states were hoping to deny 'any measure of recognition' to the referendum or to the government of Togoland set up by the French after the vote.[224] The French government preferred that the General Assembly vote on the motion as a whole to avoid a lengthy debate, and on 21 January Jacques de Blesson called at Iveagh House to secure Irish support for this procedural step.[225] In a minute to Máire MacEntee, First Secretary in the International Organizations Section, Robert McDonagh, Third Secretary in the Political Section, contended that the response to the French request should be left to the discretion of Boland; his arguments illumine the Department of External Affairs' inclination to leave many decisions in Boland's hands. McDonagh opined that:

> It seems to me that this is the very type of question on which the Permanent Representative should be allowed to exercise his discretion. He must in the nature of things be better aware of the general background of the Fourth Committee debates on the subject than we could become by a hasty perusal of them, which is all that would be possible at this stage. I submit that we should simply inform the Permanent Representative by cable of the approach made by the French Ambassador and give him discretion to act as he thinks fit.[226]

John Belton and Liam Cosgrave penciled their approval on the bottom of the minute; later that day Iveagh House wired Boland with news of the French entreaty and informed him that 'The Minister leaves the matter entirely to your discretion.'[227] The next day Ireland supported the French when the General Assembly passed the Fourth Committee's resolution after voting for the measure as a whole.[228]

PORTUGUESE GOA

The Irish delegation followed the precedent it had set in the case of Togoland when a dispute broke out over Goa, a Portuguese enclave on the western

224 Ibid., 22 January 1957.
225 Ibid.
226 Ibid.
227 Ibid.
228 DFA 313/36, 24 January 1957; GA/RES 1046 (XI).

coast of India. The disagreement arose when Portugal irked Indian and Afro-Asian sensibilities by refusing to comply with the provisions of Article 73.e of the UN Charter, which required colonial powers to transmit information concerning their trust (or Non-Self-Governing) territories to the Trusteeship Council on a regular basis.[229] Portugal, however, refused in the case of Goa and its other overseas territories (Angola, Mozambique, the Cape Verde Islands, San Tome and Principe, Portuguese Timor, Macao), claiming instead that they were an integral part of Portugal.

In early January 1957 Vasco Garvin, Portugal's UN Representative, requested Ireland's backing 'against the attacks being made in the Fourth Committee' by India against the Portuguese doctrine relative to Goa and its overseas possessions.[230] Boland told Murphy that the principle was 'one we would probably find it hard to endorse, even if we were in a position to do so', but no Irish delegate had been sitting in on Fourth Committee sessions, 'and it would probably be a mistake for us to suddenly appear at it merely for the purpose of helping Portugal on this matter'.

On 1 February External Affairs informed Boland that Cosgrave had recently spoken with Amilcar Franco, the Portuguese Chargé d'Affaires in Dublin, about the impending debate over Goa.[231] After outlining the Portuguese case Franco asked for Ireland's support, but 'No promise was given' to him. Cosgrave preferred to delegate his authority to Boland, who was instructed that 'The Minister leaves the matter entirely to your discretion.' Boland received the same instructions a few days later after Franco once more sought an assurance from Cosgrave that Ireland would support Portugal in the Committee and Assembly deliberations, which had just opened.[232]

Boland overcame his earlier reservations, and the 'grave doubts' the delegation had about Portugal's position, and on 5 February voted against an Indian-sponsored resolution in the Fourth Committee.[233] The motion did not specifically mention Portugal, yet by its reference to 'new members' of the United Nations, and its call for the establishment of an *ad hoc* committee to

229 Article 73.e of the UN Charter reads: 'Members of the United Nations which have or assume responsibilities for the administration of territories whose peoples have not yet attained a full measure of self-government recognize the principle that the interests of the inhabitants of these territories are paramount, and accept as a sacred trust the obligation to promote to the utmost, within the system of international peace and security established by the present Charter, the well-being of the inhabitants of these territories, and, to this end, will transmit regularly to the Secretary General for information purposes, subject to such limitation as security and constitutional considerations may require, statistical and other information of a technical nature relating to economic, social and educational conditions in the territories for which they are respectively responsible other than those territories to which Chapters XII and XIII apply.'

230 DFA 313/36, 9 January 1957.
231 DFA PMUN X/17, 1 February 1957.
232 Ibid., 6 February 1957.
233 DFA 313/36, 7 February 1957.

study the question of the 'Transmission of Information from Non-Self-Governing Territories' and report back to the Assembly, it was directly aimed at that country. In explaining his ballot to Sean Murphy, Boland noted that he had been swayed by the recalcitrance of the Afro-Asian bloc, whose drive against colonialism had become 'so irrational, immoderate, and indiscriminating that at the present stage probably more harm than good is done by lending it encouragement on points of this kind'. Citing the example of West Irian, he said that the bloc had shown no regard for the principles on which they based their attacks on the colonial powers when their own interests were at stake.

The Indian-sponsored measure actually passed in the Committee, but it did not receive the necessary two-thirds majority in the General Assembly, where Ireland opposed it once more.[234] Ireland also voted with Portugal against an Afro-Asian-sponsored procedural motion declaring that the 'Transmission of Information from Non-Self-Governing Territories' was not an 'important' question requiring a two-thirds vote, but one requiring only a simple majority.[235] Portugal appreciated this support. Vasco Garvin sent effusive letters to Boland after the vote in the Fourth Committee and the debate in the General Assembly.[236]

During the deliberations over French Togoland and Portuguese Goa the Irish delegation pursued a policy consistent with the line taken during the Algerian debate: on the matter of substance – voting – Ireland supported its European allies. The delegation even went out of its way to do so by attending meetings of the Fourth Committee. This medium undoubtedly sent a message to both the colonial nations and the Afro-Asian delegations. Boland's claim that Ireland was under-represented on the Fourth Committee due to a lack of manpower was correct; with its limited personnel the delegation simply could not attend every meeting during the Assembly session. Nevertheless, the delegation freely chose how to allocate its resources and its decision not to regularly attend the Fourth Committee implied that decolonization was not a priority. Perhaps this was because the intemperate members of the Afro-Asian bloc had alienated Boland. More relevant, Costello, Cosgrave, Murphy, and Boland had concluded, in the context of Irelands pro-western policy, that the delegation's efforts should be directed to more immediate issues: Hungary, the Middle East, and the political implications of the Algerian revolt.

234 DFA PMUN X/17, 26 February 1957.
235 Article 18.2 of the Charter defines what questions are 'important' and therefore require a two-thirds majority for passage in the Assembly. Article 18.3 asserts that the General Assembly can decide, by a simple majority, if issues not defined in Article 18.2 require a two-thirds majority for passage.
236 DFA PMUN X/17, 7, 26 February 1957.

CONCLUSION

One month after the Eleventh Assembly's March recess Boland forwarded a lengthy final report to Murphy recounting the delegation's activities through-out the Session.[237] In a covering minute Boland highlighted its informal nature, noted that it was based on 'personal views and impressions', and added that its conclusions were 'personal to myself and are, of course, open to objection and argument'. He may have stressed this dimension because he was unsure how Frank Aiken, the new Minister for External Affairs, would interpret the report. He did suggest that Aiken might want to circulate it to the government, but this was 'entirely a matter for his discretion'. Aiken eventually did so, but for the cabinet's 'information' only.[238]

Boland first noted the 'thirty more or less formal statements' made by members of the delegation and highlighted its active contribution to 'western European caucus meetings about Hungary and the Egyptian situation'. He then outlined the principles that had guided Ireland's policy; he stressed that Cosgrave had elucidated them in his General Debate speech. They included:

> (a) support for the principles of the UN Charter; (b) opposition to Soviet imperialism; (c) support for policies designed to check the spread of com-munist influence; (d) opposition to policies calculated to impair the unity and cohesion of the free world; (e) support and sympathy for dependent peoples struggling to achieve their freedom; (f) unity of action, so far as possible, with powers with outlooks similar to our own (e.g. the USA and European Catholic countries such as Spain, Portugal and Italy); and, (g) support, wherever possible, for the European-American-Commonwealth point of view against the more neutralist and "fellow-traveling" attitudes of the Afro-Asian bloc.

Boland admitted that at certain times, 'such as the question of Algeria for example, these considerations came into conflict and had to be balanced against one another'. In these circumstances, the delegation's:

> general line was to take fair and frank account of the merits and demer-its on each side of the case and the conflicts of principle, if any, to which they seemed to us to give rise, and, by so doing, to present our final attitude as the result of a reasonable and just assessment of the issues involved.

237 DFA 417/130, 8 April 1957.
238 S 16051/A, 18 June 1957. In October 1957 copies of the report were circulated to all Irish missions abroad: DFA 417/130, 3 October 1957.

He (naturally) was convinced that this type of 'moderate, balanced, dispassionate approach will always assure us more influence and sympathy in the Assembly' than the 'one-sided and indiscriminate vehemence' that typified many interventions. Despite these qualifications, however, Boland's guidelines are significant: they place Ireland squarely in the west's orbit during the Eleventh Session. Indeed, Boland echoed themes limned on several previous occasions and completed the policy process John Costello initiated with his April 1956 memorandum.[239]

In his memorandum Costello had suggested that Ireland's role at the United Nations might indirectly lead to an end to partition. Yet the Irish delegation never considered raising the issue; in his final report Boland acknowledged the limitations of the UN in this respect. It was true that the delegation 'missed no opportunity of keeping the problem of partition before the minds of the delegates', but he was now apprehensive about bringing the matter 'formally before the United Nations. The question whether any such action should be taken requires the most careful consideration.' Boland added that on the two occasions when radio correspondents had asked him if the Irish government intended to raise the topic, he replied that it 'would be guided solely and exclusively by the consideration [of] whether the fact of bringing the question before the United Nations would help to bring the end of partition nearer or not'. Boland thus exhibited more realism than Costello. (He also aimed his radio comments at Irish Americans who were pestering him about partition.)

Boland's colleagues won high marks. The Irish delegation was 'exceptionally fortunate in the choice of the personnel' assigned to New York. Sean Morrissey, Sheila Murphy, Eamon Kennedy, and the delegation's secretary, Miss Mooney, were singled out for commendation. Boland reserved his most glowing praise for Conor O'Brien. 'Undoubtedly, one of our greatest assets ... was Dr Cruise O'Brien's skill in formulating political ideas and expressing them in eloquent and forceful language'; he composed the delegation's major addresses, including its one on Algeria and Cosgrave's during the General Debate. 'Whatever credit and prestige the Irish delegation gained for itself at the recent session', Boland insisted, 'was very largely the result of these two speeches.'

* * *

239 Ireland's shared interests with the west and Boland's suspicions of the Afro-Asian bloc also surfaced in the final reports of Ireland's representatives on the Second and Fifth Committees. For example, in his summary of the activities of the Second Committee, which was responsible for economic and financial matters, Eamon Kennedy said that 'Although Ireland is not, of course, a member of a bloc, the Irish delegate often found himself sharing an approach to the economic problems before the Committee with the delegates of the United States, Canada, Britain, Italy, the Netherlands, Norway, Belgium, Denmark, New Zealand, and Australia': DFA 417/130/8, 30 March, 27 April 1957.

Previous assessments of Ireland's participation at the Eleventh Assembly have paralleled other misguided evaluations of Ireland's UN policy during the broader period from 1956 until the early 1960s: they have interpreted Ireland's posture in 1956 in terms of Cosgrave's three principles, particularly how the delegation resolved the inherent tension between the second, independent guideline and the third, western principle. One commentator has said that it is 'hard to assess' the performance of the Irish delegation because the vital issues of 1956 – Suez, Hungary – 'did not cause the Irish government much heart-searching, since they were all questions where outright condemnation was comparatively easy for an uncommitted small state'; indeed, there was 'no difficulty in interpreting Mr Cosgrave's three principles of UN policy on these issues'.[240] In precisely the same terms, another observer has remarked that in 1956 'the right positions were also the popular ones', and when these responses 'were also advocated by the United States, no inward struggle was required in order to know what to do'.[241]

Yet Costello, Cosgrave, Murphy, and Boland were not concerned with resolving the tension between the last two principles because they perceived no conflict whatsoever. It was clear well before the Eleventh Assembly convened that Ireland's policy would be animated by the third, 'western' principle. What remains then is to consider Ireland's policy in 1956 on its own terms. It was geared toward supporting the west, reinforcing Christianity, and opposing communism whenever possible. The Inter-Party government pursued this posture because they deemed it to be in Ireland's national interest. It was not a haphazard approach, but a well-planned policy set out in Costello's April memorandum, amplified by Cosgrave's Dáil speech, and successfully implemented at the United Nations by the Irish delegation. Irish officials thus deserve credit for devising a policy and following it through to completion.

One of the most noteworthy aspects of Ireland's first encounter at the UN, and that which assured its success, was the active, interested contribution made by those who developed and carried out Ireland's plans. John Costello first recognized Ireland's opportunity at the United Nations, and his memorandum, despite its analytical shortcomings, placed the UN at the center of Irish foreign policy. Liam Cosgrave eloquently outlined Ireland's policy before the Dáil and General Assembly, and worked closely with Sean Murphy and Freddy Boland to guide Ireland through the diplomatic rapids at the UN.

Costello's and Cosgrave's wisest moves were to appoint Boland as Ambassador to the United Nations and grant him the freedom to direct day-to-day affairs. The trust placed in Boland was based on his ability and judgment. It also paid off. He stamped his own enthusiastic, professional qualities on Ireland's identity. Owing to his guidance, the Irish delegation experienced

240 Keatinge, *Formulation*, p. 83.
241 O'Brien, *Katanga*, p. 15. O'Brien asserted elsewhere that the Irish delegation 'did nothing to disappoint' the expectations of the United States: O'Brien, 'Ireland', p. 129.

no real difficulties in coping with the complexities of UN diplomacy, and his energetic approach accounted for the remarkably active role the delegation assumed from a standing start. His skills were readily noticed by his colleagues, both in the Department of External Affairs and at the UN.[242] Joseph Shields, a member of the Irish delegation, recalled a conversation he had in December 1956 with Ambassador Hood, the Australian representative to the International Atomic Energy Agency and an advisor to their UN team, who 'expressed his great admiration for the part Ambassador Boland was playing in the deliberations of the Assembly'.[243] Boland was well-respected and had 'become one of the great personalities of the present session'.

As Boland stressed himself, the talented Irish diplomats that had accompanied him to New York fostered Ireland's ready engagement in the Assembly's deliberations.[244] Their accomplishments were all the more noteworthy considering that they were working with limited resources. Several commentators appreciated the delegation's contribution. In December S.M. Finger, an American delegate, 'stressed the fact that Ireland's part in the proceedings to date had won [the delegation] much goodwill from many different sources'.[245] T.K. Whitaker, Secretary of the Department of Finance, said that during a trip to Washington the Vice President of the World Bank 'went out of his way to speak in highly appreciative terms of Mr Kennedy's statements in the Second Committee', which were 'admirable, both in matter and manner'.[246] A former Prime Minister and member of the Iraqi contingent, Mohammed Jamali, who had attended every Session since 1945, 'rated the Irish delegation to the 1956 General Assembly as among the best in his experience'.[247] A Guatemalan envoy remarked that the Irish delegation 'presented themselves very well ... '[248]

Of course, the foregoing praise emanated primarily from western, Christian countries, rather than communist or Afro-Asian delegations. The nations Ireland had deliberately set out to support had noted and had appreciated its activities. The Inter-Party government thus achieved its policy goals. But those countries that assumed the Irish delegation could be counted on as a dependable ally were in for a surprise. After taking office Eamon de Valera and Frank Aiken did not embrace all of the objectives of their predecessors. Determined to pursue a different fundamental interest, they charted a new course.

242 Boland's Irish associates confirmed his leadership: Liam Cosgrave, Personal Interview, 11 April 1992; Eamon Kennedy, Personal Interview, 11 March 1993.
243 DFA 417/130, 11 December 1956. This view was also voiced to Shields by an American diplomat and Wellington Long, the representative of the Scripps-Howard news service.
244 Liam Cosgrave also noted the strength of the delegation: Personal Interview, 11 April 1992.
245 DFA 417/130, 11 December 1956.
246 DFA 313/36, 27 February 1957.
247 Ibid., 18 April 1957.
248 DFA 417/130, 28 December 1956.

CHAPTER 2

An Independent Agent: Fianna Fáil at the Twelfth General Assembly, 1957

INTRODUCTION

Fianna Fáil's election victory in March 1957 not only ushered in a new government, it precipitated the first shift in Ireland's UN policy. In breaking with its predecessor, the Fianna Fáil administration concluded that the Organization provided 'scope for independent action in regard to matters arising in the world' and 'a shield behind which some initiatives might be taken without undue risk of undesirable conflict with other nations'.[1] This judgment immediately voided the pro-western posture of the Inter-Party coalition and heralded a fresh approach to UN affairs. Subsequently, at the Twelfth Assembly, which convened in September 1957, the Irish delegation pursued an autonomous, activist stance more commonly associated with the Organization's Scandinavian members.

This new, independent policy inaugurated the most well-known period of Ireland's participation at the UN and marked it as a distinctive force in the Assembly. The Fianna Fáil government did not introduce it to achieve fame, however, but because they believed it served Ireland's national interests. Eamon de Valera and Frank Aiken determined that the pursuit of an unfettered line at the UN would allow them to further what they had adjudged the paramount objective of a small nation in an unstable, nuclear world: the alleviation of international tension arising out of the Cold War, growing movements for self-determination in Asia and Africa, and the collision of the two.[2]

Ireland thus fostered 'the cause of international peace through the exercise of independent judgment on the issues' that arose in the Assembly.[3] To ameliorate the strain between the world's opposing blocs, the Irish delegation

---

1   Lemass, 'Small States', p. 115.
2   Frank Aiken realized all too well, as he reminded the Assembly in 1959, that the actions of larger states directly affected the smaller nations: 'When great powers agree, as when they fail to agree, all our peoples will undoubtedly be touched by the consequences, for good or ill': Aiken, *Ireland* (1959), p. 17.
3   O'Brien, 'Ireland', p. 130.

acted as a dynamic agent at the UN. In this spirit they cast bold votes on controversial issues (China), mediated disputes (South Tyrol, Somaliland, Kashmir), sponsored surprising initiatives (troop withdrawal from central Europe), and contributed to UN peacekeeping forces.

This change of direction recalled Ireland's activism while a member of the British Commonwealth and the League of Nations during the 1920s and 1930s and its neutrality during World War II. But in one important respect Ireland's role at the UN in the late 1950s differed from its foreign policy before and during the war. In the earlier period one of the primary motives (but not the only one) of Ireland's enterprising involvement in the international arena was the assertion of the nation's sovereignty and its identity as an independent state.[4] By the late 1950s Ireland's place in the international community was secure, and the same intent, contrary to what is claimed elsewhere, did not inform the country's autonomous approach at the UN.[5]

The same high level of professionalism and dedication that the Irish delegation displayed at the Eleventh Session facilitated the implementation of Fianna Fáil's policy. Freddy Boland was initially taken aback by Aiken's forthright proposals and tried – sometimes subtly, other times directly – to rein in his Minister's enthusiasm. Nevertheless, he developed an honest, productive working relationship with Aiken. He was an indefatigable diplomat who remained the delegation's greatest asset; his growing reputation attested to his talent and underscored his commitment to the execution of Ireland's foreign policy.

Conor Cruise O'Brien assumed a more visible role, primarily because he shared the outlook of his new superiors and was capable of translating their views into effective action. Correspondingly, the Twelfth Assembly witnessed the ascent of the Aiken-O'Brien axis within the Irish delegation.[6] By no means, however, were other delegates excluded from the policy making process. Aiken solicited views from everyone, and many important decisions were taken following consultations at delegation meetings, which were often chaired

---

4 Cf. Fanning, 'Irish Neutrality', p. 30; Kennedy, *League, passim.*
5 One observer mistakenly contends that due to problems of credibility as a sovereign state Ireland acted as an 'International Good Citizen' at the United Nations primarily to enhance its prestige. He erroneously describes 'Aiken's activities at the UN as the last, fairly wild, fling in the story of the achievement of an Irish independence which was based upon little real contact with the outside world': Sharp, *Irish Foreign Policy*, pp. 44–66, 236–8. For a similar misinterpretation, see MacQueen, 'Aiken', p. 229. Countering these inaccurate views, Conor O'Brien has noted that the delay in Ireland's admission into the UN 'was fortunate for Ireland's international repute and also for her self-esteem. By this time Ireland's [international] status was no longer a matter of internal controversy; neutrality was common ground among the parties; anti-partition had lost its momentum. A domestic consensus existed, adequate to allow Ireland to play a modest but serious part in the United Nations': O'Brien, 'Ireland', pp. 127–8.
6 O'Brien often served as Aiken's advisor at meetings of the First Committee, one of the UN's most important committees: O'Brien, *Katanga*, p. 27.

by the Minister himself, who was always courteous.[7] This cohesiveness served the delegation well in the face of the sometimes testy reaction to its ground-breaking policy.

The consistency of the delegation's high level of performance from 1956 to 1957 highlights the significant point that the new direction pursued at the Twelfth Session did not induce a complete break with Ireland's policy at the Eleventh. For example, the Irish team maintained close contact with its European neighbors and the United States, even though its new motives were not always understood, nor appreciated. Likewise, Ireland opposed aggression wherever it occurred, backed small nations threatened by larger neighbors, upheld the principle of self-determination, supported humanitarian causes, and subscribed to the view that the United Nations represented a vital force in international relations.

THE ORIGINS OF FIANNA FÁIL POLICY

Frank Aiken may have consulted his colleagues on the Irish delegation before making important decisions, but he did not follow Liam Cosgrave's precedent and delineate, in a major speech to the Dáil, the principles of Fianna Fáil's UN policy. Nor did Eamon de Valera initiate a wide-ranging, cabinet-level discussion by submitting a comprehensive memorandum to his ministerial colleagues like John Costello did on 18 May 1956.

A late May 1957 communication O'Brien forwarded to John Belton, consisting of a draft of the United Nations section of Aiken's Estimates speech and a covering minute, sheds light on the government's reluctance to sponsor a full-scale Dáil debate about its intentions.[8] At just over two pages, the UN portion was very brief. It first recalled the Irish delegation's responses to the major issues at the Eleventh Session. It also noted that because 'a considerable volume of goodwill towards Ireland appears to exist among members of the Assembly, including many of those countries, principally in Asia, which have themselves only recently achieved sovereignty', there were 'good grounds for believing that Ireland may be able to play an influential and useful part in the United Nations'.

In his explanatory minute O'Brien drew Belton's attention to two 'deliberate' omissions in the draft. There was no reference to the International Organization Section's 'work which is concerned with partition and allied political matters'. Nor was there 'mention of any positive initiatives in the

---

7 O'Brien, *Katanga*, p. 27; Conor Cruise O'Brien, Personal Interview, 5 August 1993. In like manner, O'Brien once said that in 'his relationship with the people that worked in the Department [Aiken] was very considerate and friendly ... He was good company, unpompous': *Irish Times*, 19 May 1983.

8 DFA 417/130, 30 May 1957.

United Nations in relation to partition'. The reason for both omissions was 'the same, viz., that there does not seem to be much point in provoking a discussion on partition in the Dáil at present'. It was 'undesirable' in Aiken's speech:

> *either* [*sic*] to give the impression that anything which could be done in the United Nations could bring the ending of partition appreciably nearer, *or* to tie ourselves in advance as to whether we will raise the matter there at all and, if so, in what form.

Like its Inter-Party predecessor, the Fianna Fáil government had wisely rejected the prospect of airing Ireland's partition grievance at the UN; any discussion of the matter in the Dáil would therefore have been superfluous.

A second factor, according to O'Brien, accounted for the brevity of the draft: Aiken might wish to be 'very brief indeed on the subject' of the UN in the light of a report on the Eleventh Session being prepared in Iveagh House for presentation to the Dáil.[9] Conversely, 'in view of the importance of the period under review in the history' of the Department of External Affairs, O'Brien hinted that the Minister might consider saying 'at least a few words about the major issues which confronted Ireland's first delegation at the UN'.

Aiken ignored this last bit of advice. He omitted any reference to the delegation's work at the Eleventh Session because he embraced the spirit of O'Brien's minute to Belton (without any prodding) and delivered a remarkably succinct statement. Aiken's entire Estimates speech, delivered in Irish, was barely longer than O'Brien's UN section alone.[10] It did not even include a UN section. He said absolutely nothing about the government's foreign policy, nor the principles that would guide it. He simply announced that External Affairs sought £498,130 for the coming fiscal year and explained how and where it would be spent.

The address dismayed the opposition. John Costello strenuously objected to its lack of substance: 'There was no indication of foreign policy' whatsoever.[11] He was flabbergasted that Aiken said nothing about the United Nations, especially in contrast to Liam Cosgrave's address the previous year, and regretted that Aiken had not a word to say about partition. Cosgrave, for his part, asserted that Ireland's UN policy in 1956 was 'sound' and should be maintained.[12] Deputies Esmonde and O'Higgins reinforced these views, and the latter lamented Aiken's failure to praise Cosgrave for his fine work at the Eleventh Session.[13]

9 No report, however, was ever submitted to the Dáil.
10 DD 163, 578–581, 3 July 1957.
11 DD 163, 596–605, 3 July 1957.
12 DD 163, 605–10, 3 July 1957.
13 DD 163, 610–17, 3 July 1957.

In reply to this criticism, Aiken simply said that there was no need, 'after the long years of the people's experience of Fianna Fáil policy, to labor the obvious'.[14] It was not the first time that the Dáil had debated foreign affairs, and 'the Deputies and the country know the policy upon which Fianna Fáil has acted in relation to external affairs, and that is the policy upon which we propose to continue to operate'. Aiken was reticent in response to a specific query about the government's partition policy. His only comment was that Britain could send a message to the Soviet Union about the reunification of Germany by agreeing to a plebiscite on partition in all of Ireland.[15]

The desire to avoid a prolonged debate on partition does not totally account for the brief Estimates speech. The concise remarks were wholly consistent with de Valera's and Aiken's well-established tradition of silence regarding the motives of Irish foreign policy. De Valera inaugurated this trend while he was both Taoiseach and Minister for External Affairs during the 1930s and 1940s. He made most foreign policy decisions himself, rarely seeking the counsel of his Ministers, who 'were not encouraged to volunteer advice in this area'.[16] In the Dáil 'he gave little away',[17] and outside of it he 'never encouraged public discussion of foreign affairs'.[18]

Frank Aiken agreed with de Valera. The salient trait of Aiken's 'parliamentary style was a certain reticence which was particularly noticeable in the way he conducted debates on foreign policy'.[19] Sean MacBride described him in 1953 as the only Minister for External Affairs in 'the world who can get up here and introduce his Estimate without even mentioning that there is an international situation in the world, or mentioning that we have any policy'.[20] Aiken defended himself in 1960, advising the Dáil that:

14 DD 163, 617–620, 3 July 1957.
15 In the autumn of 1957 the government asserted publicly, on two occasions, that it would not irresponsibly raise the issue of partition in the General Assembly. In October it defeated a motion introduced into the Dáil by Jack McQuillan of the National Progressive Democratic Party, demanding that Ireland's UN delegation 'be instructed to seek in the Assembly of that body' the dispatch of UN observers to Northern Ireland and a UN supervised 'national plebiscite of the whole people of Ireland on the question of Partition'. Frank Aiken argued that such a motion usurped the government's prerogative: 'it must be left to the government to decide on matters of this kind and on the content and timing of any motions that are put before either the United Nations or any other assembly in which the government represents the country': DD 164, 146–164, 23 October 1957. In November Eamon de Valera delivered the same message to his party at the Fianna Fáil *Ard Fheis: Eire-Ireland: Bulletin of the Department of External Affairs*, 2 December 1957 (No. 388).
16 Keogh, *Ireland and Europe*, p. 61.
17 Keatinge, *Formulation*, p. 57. One observer has attributed this silence to the 'Civil War legacy in Irish politics', which had made 'bipartisanship in the area of foreign policy virtually impossible': Keogh, *Ireland and Europe*, p. 61.
18 T.D. Williams, *Leader*, 31 January 1951.
19 Keatinge, *Formulation*, p. 88.
20 DD 138, 779, 24 April 1953.

I do not think that it is any sort of valuable exercise to debate general principles stated in general terms. It is much better to test the general policy of the Minister by examining in detail the actions he took. I am prepared to be judged and the government are prepared to be judged by our acts or lack of action in any international matters in which we should have acted. We are not bound to comment on every incident in international affairs. We have the freedom to remain silent as well as the freedom to speak and sometimes it is valuable to keep silent just as on other occasions one must be prepared to speak one's mind and to represent clearly and definitely where one's country stands.[21]

DE VALERA'S FOREIGN POLICY LEGACY

Although a formal statement outlining its UN policy was not forthcoming from the Fianna Fáil government, the experiences, records, achievements, and philosophies of de Valera, Aiken, and O'Brien presaged the autonomous role Ireland carved out for itself in the Organization. This background also demonstrates that the new period inaugurated in 1957 was consistent with an earlier Irish foreign policy tradition.

Eamon de Valera's approach to the League of Nations was significant. After becoming Taoiseach he advocated 'the concept of a strong League which would unhesitatingly attempt to settle disputes by means of some form of international justice and not just with expedience in mind'.[22] He often 'went to great pains to stress the importance of the smaller states playing a positive role in the League, independent of the pressures from the great powers'. During the uncertain 1930s he asserted that 'the act of participation of the smaller states is more important than ever ... because they constitute the strongest element in making for peace'.[23]

De Valera then transformed Ireland into a model of the activist state the League required. During a candid address to the League Assembly in September 1932, when he happened to be President of the League Council, he lectured 'the assembled statesmen and diplomats on their shortcomings, particularly on their failure to use the League machinery in good faith'.[24] In 1934 the Irish delegation voted in favor of the Soviet Union's successful application for admission into the League of Nations. De Valera justified this controversial move by invoking the principle of the universality of member-

---

21 DD 182, 800, 8 June 1960. In defense of Aiken, it has been suggested that most TDs were uninterested in foreign policy debates: Keatinge, *Formulation*, p. 216.

22 Keatinge, *Formulation*, p. 23.

23 Quoted in Patrick Keatinge, 'Ireland and the League of Nations', *Studies*, Vol. 59 (1970). p. 141.

24 Ibid., p. 142.

ship. Ireland's record during the Manchurian crisis and the Italian invasion of Ethiopia showed it to be one of the League's most consistent supporters of international law and the rights of small nations. In 1938 de Valera was elected President of the League Assembly.[25]

As a result of his policies de Valera has been called 'assertive at Geneva',[26] and has been described as 'one of League's uncomfortable consciences ... '[27] He thus forged a role for Ireland that portended its involvement at the UN. An Irish paper linked him with the two bodies after the adjournment of the Twelfth General Assembly. Ireland, along with Canada, Norway, and Italy had stood out:

> in the UN for influence far beyond their size or power. To many diplomats schooled in unhappy experiments in international struggles for peace, Ireland has a special place as a "third force" in the UN. For their memories are still vivid of Ireland's historic League of Nations fight for the rights of small nations, and if any individual is regarded today as a bridge between the League and the UN, it is Eamon de Valera.[28]

FRANK AIKEN AND THE IRISH DELEGATION

As Minister for External Affairs, Frank Aiken established an Irish identity at the United Nations that equaled the autonomous, activist posture the country had assumed under de Valera's leadership at the League of Nations. He insisted that Ireland maintain its 'independence and not become part of any tied group, bound by agreements to support one another, no matter what the subject matter for discussion'.[29] As one of the members of the Irish delegation described him, Aiken 'required little, if any, advice from us, his juniors and subordinates, on ... the virtues of a "Swedish" position, of resisting pressure, and so on'.[30]

A striking dimension of Aiken's independent policy was his penchant for making bold proposals designed to 'relieve international tension ... to negotiate real peace, and [to] prevent a suicidal [nuclear] war'.[31] He believed, in

---

25 Kennedy, *League, passim.*

26 Dermot Keogh, *Ireland and Europe, 1919–48* (Dublin, 1988), p. 41.

27 Patrick Keatinge, 'Ireland and the League of Nations', *Studies*, p. 142.

28 *Irish Press*, 10 April 1958. The glowing tone of this passage is partly attributable to its appearance in the semi–official press organ of Fianna Fáil. Still, Freddy Boland once reported from the UN that 'many diplomats remember [de Valera] from the League of Nations and others, who were not there, know him as a world figure': DFA 313/36 25 April 1958.

29 DD 159, 147, 3 July 1956.

30 O'Brien, *Katanga*, p. 15.

31 DD 164, 1205, 28 November 1957.

fact, that this was 'what the role of the Irish delegation should be within the United Nations'.[32] Over several years he thus unveiled a troop withdrawal scheme for central Europe, a comprehensive Middle East settlement, his Areas of Law formula, a peace plan for Algeria, and a nuclear non-proliferation initiative. The salient feature of these proposals was the high profile reserved for the UN. Aiken believed that the Organization could act as an assertive, impartial intermediary in troubled regions around the globe. In this respect, he was far ahead of his time. Indeed, the groundbreaking nature of his proposals, and the fact that the great powers did not always embrace them, reinforced Ireland's independent identity in the Assembly.

But Aiken was unruffled when others did not welcome his ideas. Why? He truly believed that small, neutral nations had a crucial role to play in UN diplomacy. How so? Whereas it was difficult for a member of a great power bloc 'to take an initiative', an independent delegation could, whenever it saw 'that something should be done, propose that it should be done in the UN'.[33] In this sense, he believed that Irish neutrality 'provided an opportunity rather than imposed a constraint'.[34] Anthony Hartley, writing in the *Spectator*, described this outlook as 'positive neutrality'.[35] Aiken once put it in stronger terms:

> We have, owing to the accident of history or whatever way you like to put it, been independent, untied, neutral in the accepted sense of the term, in the military sense of the term. It was our duty as a delegation at the United Nations to take full advantage of that position, in order to promote the peace, to try to make propositions which countries tied to blocs could not make without committing their bloc.[36]

Policy cannot always be separated from personality, especially in a small delegation like Ireland's, and Aiken's past experiences illumine his pursuit of an independent UN identity. During Ireland's War of Independence he rose to the position of Commandant of the Fourth Northern Division of the IRA. He was the last Chief of Staff of the Irregulars during the Civil War, but was a reluctant member of the Anti-Treaty forces.[37] He entered the Dáil in 1927

---

32 DD 176, 693, 7 July 1959.
33 DFA 305/384/2/IX, 21 December 1964. This quote is from the transcript of an interview given by Aiken to Yugoslav correspondent, Mr Bozidar Pahor.
34 MacQueen, 'Aiken', p. 230.
35 Quoted in *Eire-Ireland: Bulletin of the Department of External Affairs*, No. 398 (24 November 1957).
36 DD 191, 675, 11 July 1961.
37 Aiken was born in Camlough, Co. Armagh in 1898. At an early age he became active in the Gaelic League and GAA. He joined a Volunteer Company in 1913 and rose to the rank of lieutenant before it disbanded following the Redmond split. He first worked with Eamon de Valera during his victorious Clare by-election campaign in 1917. In February 1918 Aiken organized the Camlough Company of Volunteers, which

as a Fianna Fáil TD from Louth. Being 'widely regarded as a leading member of [de Valera's] political "old guard", he occupied a prominent position in Fianna Fáil from its parliamentary beginnings'.[38] Following the party's electoral victory in 1932, he received the Department of Defense portfolio, the first of many ministerial assignments. During World War II he headed the Ministry for the Coordination of Defensive Measures. From 1945 to 1948 he served as Minister for Finance. When Fianna Fáil regained control of the government in 1951 de Valera named Aiken Minister for External Affairs and reappointed him to this position in 1957.

Aiken's revolutionary background had a long-lasting impact that surfaced occasionally at the UN. Having confronted British military, might one could hardly imagine Aiken being intimidated by a UN member offended by an unexpected Irish vote or initiative, particularly if it was the United Kingdom.[39] The nature of the Irish military campaign, with its reliance on guerrilla tactics, fostered patience and persistence. For instance, during negotiations he would slowly wear someone down until they acceded to his point of view.[40] He has even been called 'a hard hitter' and 'obstinate'; equally, 'anything in the nature of compromise on fundamental issues, he detests by instinct'.[41]

Others made the connection between this man's past and the policy he pursued at the UN: it was thought 'wholly in character that Aiken, an old revolutionary, should carve out an independent role for Ireland'.[42] So did Aiken himself. A 1958 article entitled 'Man of Peace Who Killed Forty' (a reference to his masterminding of the derailment of a British troop train returning to Dublin after the opening of the Northern Ireland Parliament by George V in June 1921) placed his UN initiatives in the context of his revolutionary experience. In it Aiken observed that 'A revolutionary background puts a responsibility on you. It makes one alert to problems. You're up against different situations and you have to improvise to make do.'[43] That is precisely what he did in New York.

elected him captain. In June 1918 he was appointed Commandant of Camlough Battalion. Throughout the War of Independence Aiken was very active in the region. During the Civil War he negotiated the failed de Valera-Collins pact. Free State Forces jailed him in Dundalk, but he managed an ingenious escape: Liam C. Skinner, *Politicians by Accident* (Dublin, 1946), pp. 153–9.

38 MacQueen, 'Aiken', p. 211.
39 Some commentators have detected an anti-British streak in Aiken: Ronan Fanning, 'Irish Neutrality', in Bo Huldt and Atis Lejins(eds.), *Neutrals in Europe: Ireland* (Stockholm, 1990), p. 9; Sean Cronin, *Washington's Irish Policy, 1916–1986: Independence, Partition, and Neutrality* (Dublin, 1987), p. 255.
40 Frank Aiken, Jr., Personal Interview, 17 April 1992.
41 Skinner, *Politicians by Accident*, p. 152.
42 *The Times*, 20 May 1983.
43 *Kansas City Star*, 22 October 1958.

Aiken's experience in several ministerial positions also sheds light on his UN posture. An episode while Minister for Coordination of Defensive Measures left a deep impression on him. Faced with dwindling supplies in war-time Ireland, he traveled to the United States in March 1941 seeking foodstuffs and armaments from the American government. He stridently defended Irish neutrality during a heated exchange with Franklin Roosevelt, who was doing all he could to keep the British war effort alive. His efforts to persuade Irish Americans to back Irish neutrality angered the State Department, which almost asked him to leave the country. After three months he departed with only two shiploads of food, $500,000 from the American Red Cross, no weapons, and an unfavorable view of the United States. According to one commentator, it was 'unlikely that the experience made Aiken less hostile to the English or less sympathetic to the Axis. It is likely that it helped make him anti-American.'[44]

This trip did not compel Aiken to pursue an anti-American line at the UN, for by the late 1950s he had shed any lingering feelings of ill-will.[45] Still, it does underscore his determination not to cave in to American pressure. As he said in November 1957 in response to charges that his policy had offended the United States: Ireland 'could afford from time to time to have disputes with them on policy, as we had during the last war, but we cannot afford to lose their respect'.[46] His sentiments and revolutionary background also account for his view that the west was not blameless in the Cold War. During the debate that followed Cosgrave's July 1956 Dáil speech Aiken asserted that in some places communists succeeded because 'the non-communist nations have not behaved as they should. There are sins that are common both to the communistic states and to non-communistic states.'[47]

In addition to being obdurate, Aiken was also conciliatory. His service with the Irregulars during the Civil War, and the uncertainties surrounding Fianna Fáil's assumption of civil authority in 1932, meant that his first posting, as Minister for Defense, would require skill, tact and poise. His subsequent performance demonstrated that he possessed all three in abundance. An informed observer has noted that de Valera's nomination:

44 Joseph L. Rosenberg, 'The 1941 Mission of Frank Aiken to the United States: An American Perspective', *Irish Historical Studies*, Vol. 22 (1980), pp. 163–74. The official reception in 1941 reinforced Aiken's indifferent view of America, formed during two trips to the United States in the 1920s to raise money for Fianna Fáil and the *Irish Press*: Frank Aiken, Jr., Personal Interview, 17 April 1992.
45 Máire MacEntee O'Brien, Personal Interview, 7 June 1996.
46 DD 164, 1222, 28 November 1957.
47 DD 159, 147, 3 July 1956. Aiken added that 'Our acid test for all nations, no matter on which side of the Iron Curtain they may be, should be the test ... that it is what is done that counts and not what is said.'

proved an inspired choice. Aiken had been the last military commander of the anti-Treaty forces in 1923, but his heart was not in the Civil War and he had no blood lust. He was probably more acceptable to the Free State officers than any other possible appointment. He soon reconciled the army to the new regime.[48]

If on this occasion he was able to persuade old enemies to cooperate, he pulled off an even greater achievement during World War II by getting old friends to do the same. Despite obstacles and animosities he 'surprised many people by influencing republican veterans to cooperate with the government's defense effort'.[49] This diplomatic touch was later put to excellent use in the sometimes volatile atmosphere of the General Assembly.

By the 1950s Aiken 'was probably the closest person in the cabinet to de Valera'.[50] The latter's decision to hand Aiken a portfolio that he had personally held underlined their affinity. When named Minister for External Affairs Aiken had been 'as near to the sources of Irish foreign policy from 1932 to 1948 as it was possible for any member of de Valera's cabinet to be'.[51] Hence, it was unsurprising that he 'aspired to play a similar part in the United Nations to Mr de Valera's in the League'.[52] His UN policy was certainly original, but there were 'parallels in Ireland's League performance of the 1930s when small power activism on a range of issues' had characterized de Valera's stance.[53]

CONOR CRUISE O'BRIEN AND THE UNITED NATIONS

Because he assumed a more prominent role at the Twelfth Assembly, Conor Cruise O'Brien's experiences, world view, and conception of the United Nations demand a closer look. In 1942 he entered the Department of Finance and two years later transferred to Iveagh House. Sean MacBride promoted him to the rank of Counsellor and in 1949 named him managing director of the Irish News Agency, ostensibly an international news service, but actually a propaganda mouthpiece for the government's anti-partition campaign.[54] Here O'Brien honed his public relations skills and developed wide press contacts, which later helped him ensure ample media coverage of Ireland's UN activities.

48 Lee, *Ireland*, p. 176.
49 Rosenberg, 'Aiken', p. 165.
50 Lee, *Ireland*, p. 239.
51 Keatinge, *Formulation*, p. 85.
52 O'Brien, 'Ireland', p. 129.
53 MacQueen, 'Aiken', pp. 228–9.
54 Akenson, *Conor*, p. 135.

In 1954 O'Brien was transferred to the Paris Embassy. His indifference towards the French establishment and his strident anticolonialism, briefly revealed in the previous chapter, took shape during this posting. Not being close to the Irish envoy, William Fay, to begin with, he was further put off by the right-wing 'stance implicit in Fay's social preferences' – government officials, local luminaries, church representatives.[55] At the same time, exposure to the vicious early stages of the Franco-Algerian War broadened O'Brien's 'definition of colonialism, from a characteristic of the British to something inherent in western cultures'.[56] His contacts with French colonialists and Algerian refugees alike made him realize 'that imperialism is a set of behaviors that can emerge' anywhere.

After being recalled to Dublin in the spring of 1956, as part of the Department's preparations for the General Assembly, O'Brien stamped his personality on the International Organizations Section. It was 'known for having "dash", a sense of style and exuberance that went beyond the muted tones and hairline smiles' of his Iveagh House colleagues, most of whom had spent 'their formative years with the Jesuits. Diplomacy, if you were working under Conor, was fun.'[57] One year later he took control of the Political Section, which had assumed responsibility for UN affairs. Throughout his years in Paris and Dublin O'Brien also embarked on an intellectual career, which later made him world-famous. Under the *nom de plume* Donat O'Donnell he wrote incisive articles, essays, reviews, and in 1952 a book – *Maria Cross*, an analysis of several European Catholic authors. In 1954 he completed a doctorate in History at Trinity College; his groundbreaking thesis resulted in another volume, *Parnell and his Party, 1880–90*.

O'Brien wrote often about the role and responsibilities of the United Nations. In the early 1960s he contended that the Assembly, 'as a forum for mankind, has a most precious function, and the world would be in much more danger if it were removed': it was, due to its moral force, 'the conscience of mankind'.[58] O'Brien made the same point in an unpublished speech entitled 'The United Nations Today: Seen from the Viewpoint of a Delegate of one of the Smaller Nations' (which Aedan O'Beirne, a delegate to the Twelfth Session, actually delivered in San Francisco in December 1957 when O'Brien could not make the trip). Owing to its near universality of membership, the UN could 'bring to bear ... a far greater moral pressure, than, say, the League [of Nations] was able to do'.[59] While the League represented 'the haves of the world against the have-nots', the underdeveloped countries had 'a voice – a voice indeed which is increasingly important' – in the United Nations.

---

55 Ibid., p. 149.
56 Ibid., p. 151.
57 Ibid., p. 153.
58 O'Brien, *Katanga*, pp. 12–13.
59 DFA 417/156, 23 December 1957.

The efficacy of the UN, according to O'Brien, depended upon the commitment of its independent members, or the 'bloody mavericks'.[60] They played an essential role in 'the politics of the Assembly'. They were 'more sought after than the "safe" votes as sponsors of resolutions' and were often 'involved in those compromise efforts which mark the closing stages of the consideration of any important question in the Assembly'. In short, they were 'in the thick of things … '

The Swedish delegation was his preferred model. We have already seen how he argued in favor of Sweden over Spain in the Security Council elections at the Eleventh Session. Likewise, for himself and several External Affairs associates, 'the ideal of what constituted good international behavior was exemplified at this time by Sweden', whose 'action in the international field was, as we saw it, independent, disinterested, and honorable'.[61] The Swedes 'did not spend much time in proclaiming lofty moral principles, but they usually acted as men would do who were in fact animated by such principles'. Their UN voting record 'was more eloquent than their speeches. It seemed to contain few or no votes against conscience … '[62]

O'Brien and some of his colleagues 'hoped that Ireland would become one of the very small (and mostly Scandinavian) group of delegations at the United Nations whose chief concern it was to safeguard' the institution's moral authority; 'an independent "Swedish" line was what we hoped for'.[63] In his speech delivered by O'Beirne, O'Brien averred that Ireland was well-suited for this role. Its limited, but real, influence flowed from the 'enduring characteristics which govern her approach to every problem': independence; a commitment to equality; and, the 'degree of moral authority which she derives from her history' as 'both a western European country and a country which has undergone colonization'. Concurrently, the Irish delegation would not depend solely upon its past, but would exercise its 'own judgment' in each case that arose in the Assembly.

THE INSTITUTIONAL CONTEXT

In the late 1950s the UN was a particularly suitable platform for a small nation dedicated to reducing international discord. Earlier in the decade 'the political center of gravity' within the United Nations system itself had shifted when the United States and its western allies, frustrated by the Soviet

60 O'Brien, *Katanga*, p. 25.
61 Ibid., pp. 14–15.
62 This positive view of Sweden's role at the UN surfaced in yet another report, most likely written by O'Brien in the spring of 1956, entitled 'Note on Sweden's Record at the UN': DFA 417/128/1 (nd).
63 O'Brien, *Katanga*, p. 15.

Union's excessive use of its Security Council veto, focused their attention instead on the General Assembly, where they could easily muster a majority on any important vote.[64] Consequently, the General Assembly became an important center of world diplomacy. It also became a front in the Cold War. Who, for instance, can forget Nikita Khrushchev banging his shoe on the rostrum and Freddy Boland, the President of the Assembly, breaking his gavel when calling him to order? But unlike the Security Council, the USSR could not stifle this body; in fact, the Assembly's identity as a proxy battlefield in the Cold War further heightened its international profile.

The ascendancy of the General Assembly offered Ireland an invaluable opportunity. Whereas the great powers controlled the Security Council, 'the vote of each state was of equal value' in the Assembly.[65] By definition, therefore, the smaller and middle-sized nations carried more weight. Plus, 'the great powers had to resort to the practice of a type of parliamentary diplomacy in attempting to secure maximum support in the Assembly for their respective points of view', which induced greater respect for all other delegations. These dynamics produced a 'situation in which the smaller powers had a much more important voice in the operations of the United Nations than was originally contemplated'. Accordingly, those nations (like Ireland) that took advantage of this new opportunity often found themselves at the forefront of UN diplomacy and even in the international spotlight.

One of the most significant responsibilities of the smaller delegations was working with the UN to reduce international tension. For example, beginning with the Suez crisis in 1956 Dag Hammarskjold and his assistants in the United Nations Secretariat superseded the failed concept of collective security with a new approach to conflict resolution: preventive diplomacy. As its name suggests, preventive diplomacy sought to head off conflicts before they flared up or, in cases where hostilities had broken out, tried to dampen them by the quick arrangement of a cease-fire and the interposition of neutral troops between warring parties. In its operative form preventive diplomacy became synonymous with United Nations peacekeeping.

As the Cold War intensified Hammarskjold deemed it vital that preventive diplomacy gain currency in international relations. Although 'the risks were considerable', and the great powers were skeptical about interference in their traditional spheres of influence, he was willing to stake his reputation on its success.[66] He considered it:

> a very natural function for the Secretary General to keep problems as much as possible outside the Cold War orbit and, on the other hand, of course, to lift problems out of the Cold War orbit to all the extent he

64 Lemass, 'Small States', p. 116.
65 Ibid., p. 117.
66 Urquhart, *Hammarskjold*, pp. 257–8.

can. That is for many reasons ... It is one way, so to say, if not to thaw the Cold War, at least to limit its impact on international life.

Over time Hammarskjold became closely wedded to the concept of preventive diplomacy, even as its exact nature became blurred. In 1959 he said that 'the UN simply must respond to those demands which may be put to it'.[67] He rejected the claim that certain tasks exceeded the UN's abilities 'because I do not know the exact capacity of this machine. It did take the very steep hill of Suez; it may take other and even steeper hills ... ' With satisfaction he added Gaza, Lebanon, Jordan, Laos, and the Congo (prematurely) to the list of successful UN peacekeeping operations in his 1960 Annual Report.

Committed, disinterested UN members willing to work with the Secretariat were essential to the smooth functioning of preventive diplomacy. A constellation in the center of the Assembly assumed these duties. These delegations became known as the middle powers. They included the Nordic countries – Sweden, Norway, Denmark, Iceland, Finland – low-profile NATO members (Canada, the Netherlands), and moderate Afro-Asian states like Tunisia and Malaysia who were not at that time part of neutralist camp headed by India and Ghana. (The middle powers, therefore, were unattached to the Non-Aligned Movement.[68])

The assertive, independent policy pursued by Frank Aiken, combined with Ireland's military neutrality, paved the way for the it to join these countries. Sean Lemass, who as Taoiseach oversaw Ireland's transformation into a middle power, thoroughly described this process. The uncommitted nations in the Assembly fell into two groups: the neutralist, non-aligned Afro-Asian bloc; and, 'a group of independent countries which were trying to judge all issues on their merits and cast their votes accordingly. This latter group included Ireland.'[69] The influence of this second cluster 'was of course to a large extent illusory by comparison with the realities of world power, but it had a certain effect nonetheless'. This group:

> tended to form a party of lesser powers at the center, whose position, because their help was needed by the established voting bloc, could often exercise a distinct moderating influence in the framing of resolutions and decisions on controversial issues. This middle view taken by the independent group tended usually to support the position of the United Nations Secretariat and ... so [took] on a particular United Nations flavor.

67 Ibid., pp. 255–6.
68 For a review of this force in international affairs, see Peter Willets, *The Non-Aligned Movement* (London, 1978).
69 Lemass, 'Small States', pp. 117–18.

In this context, according to Lemass, 'the small independent states most closely shared with the Secretary General the role of "conscience of the world"'. Also, as a member of this group, 'there were times when if [Ireland] sponsored a resolution on a specific item that needed to be raised', it was likely 'we could win wide acceptance for our point of view because of our recognized position of integrity in the Assembly'. As a consequence, it must now be clear that Ireland's independent policy was not an end in itself. Instead, it constituted the means by which Ireland could take on the duties of a middle power and thereby contribute to the reduction of discord in the Assembly, if not outside it.

The Secretary General appreciated Ireland's contribution. 'In carrying out both corrective and preventive peacekeeping operations, Hammarskjold turned increasingly to the middle powers and to their representatives.'[70] Lester Pearson of Canada, Hans Engen of Norway, Freddy Boland, Carl Schurmann of the Netherlands, and Mongi Slim of Tunisia 'were the type of level-headed, widely respected, able-minded, and practical men who could provide the support and understanding which alone made it possible to set up and maintain' the detailed and difficult mechanisms of peacekeeping operations.

* * *

Ireland and the other middle powers played a second important role in the General Assembly: they formed the fire brigade. This function had less to do with the Cold War and more to do with another dynamic of the international system that had penetrated the Assembly following the increase in membership in 1956: anticolonialism in Africa and Asia. When a committee considered self-determination issues the fire brigade often found itself 'engaged in drawing up, at the end of the debates, a compromise text' amenable to the European colonial powers and the Afro-Asian bloc.[71] Similarly, the fire brigade frequently devised 'a rotating device to avoid a clash' of European and Afro-Asian candidates during elections for Assembly offices. It also acted as an intermediary between Hammarskjold and the interested parties so that feasible resolutions were crafted.[72] The make-up of the fire brigade varied 'according to the fire, but at least one Scandinavian country was almost always on it', joined by delegates from Canada, Tunisia, Nigeria, Yugoslavia, Mexico, and Ireland.[73] Ireland's history, its independent reputation within the Assembly, and its outspoken support for the right to self-determination meant that it was especially suited it for membership of the fire brigade. In turn, its efforts in this regard earned it the respect of other delegations.

70 Urquhart, *Hammarskjold*, p. 257.
71 O'Brien, *Katanga*, p. 26.
72 DFA 417/220, 7 September 1970.
73 O'Brien, *Katanga*, pp. 26–7.

TROOP DISENGAGEMENT FROM CENTRAL EUROPE

On 18 June 1957 the Special Committee on Hungary, established by the Eleventh Assembly, released its final report. It unequivocally condemned the Soviet Union's 'massive armed intervention' in Hungary and labeled the subsequent revolt a 'spontaneous national uprising'.[74] The 'sufferings inflicted on the Hungarian people by the AVH', the Hungarian secret police, had 'deeply shocked' the Committee.

Freddy Boland's robust reaction echoed the staunch anti-communism he had exhibited at the Eleventh Session (and his tendency to exaggerate the demise of the USSR). He told Sean Murphy that the 'report is generally considered to be a workmanlike and effective document and constitutes a damning indictment of the Soviet government'.[75] It did not add greatly to common knowledge about the events, but it was 'well worthwhile to have got the facts of what may prove to be one of the most important political developments of the century thoroughly investigated and clearly established by an impartial international tribunal ... ' It represented 'one of the biggest propaganda reverses which Soviet Russia has ever suffered', so much so that 'communist influence outside the Soviet orbit is bound to feel its effects'.[76]

Boland was influential in determining the response to the report. When the European caucus met on 26 June two options emerged: the UN could reconvene the Eleventh Assembly immediately, or in September, just before the opening of the Twelfth Session.[77] Despite American and British preference for an instant gathering, there was 'little support' for this move. Boland favored the second alternative, arguing that if the UN allowed itself to be 'swept along by public opinion into convening an ill-attended, low-level meeting ... in mid-summer, the net result might be a disillusioning disappointment': whatever steps 'the General Assembly could take would fall short of what uninformed public opinion expects'. The next day Boland reported that his preference for an autumn Assembly was gaining ground.[78] Australia, New Zealand, and the United Kingdom still hoped for an early date, but the American Ambassador, Henry Cabot Lodge, had accepted the wisdom of a September conference attended by foreign ministers.

---

74 Urquhart, *Hammarskjold*, p. 241.
75 DFA 305/210/6, 28 June 1957.
76 One knowledgeable commentator, who did not agree with Boland's prediction about the USSR, nevertheless shared his belief in the report's inherent worth: despite the UN's inaction in 1956, the Special Committee's report 'remains to this day perhaps the most significant, in political terms, of all the thousands of documents produced by the world body, just as in human terms it is undoubtedly the most telling': Hernane Tavares de Sa, *The Play within the Play: The Inside Story of the UN* (New York, 1966), pp. 242–3.
77 DFA 305/210/6, 27 June 1957.
78 Ibid., 28 June.

During the 26 June meeting Boland revealed his abiding humanitarianism by raising another urgent topic: the allegations of wide-spread 'executions and deportations in Hungary, and the desirability of bringing pressure to bear in the meantime on the Soviet and Hungarian authorities to prevent further brutality of this type'. He wisely asserted that 'concrete achievement in this direction would be of far more use to the people of Hungary than the adoption of yet another condemnatory resolution' by a summer-time Assembly. Boland's west European and American colleagues supported this outlook. Afterwards Eamon Kennedy briefly met with James Barco, an American delegate, who said that his compatriots 'had been very favorably impressed by the soundness and cogency' of Boland's interventions.

* * *

In reality, the western delegations could do little to alleviate the suffering in Budapest,[79] but they accepted Boland's arguments about the Eleventh Assembly and did not reconvene it until 10 September. On this day, Frank Aiken delivered his famous troop withdrawal proposal, thereby confirming Ireland's new independent stance. Essential to elucidating both Aiken's plan and the reaction to it, however, is a review of the prevailing European political and security context. The salient feature of the European geopolitical landscape in 1957 was the fault line running from the Baltic to the Balkans – the Iron Curtain in Winston Churchill's memorable phrase. It split the continent into two blocs: east and west. Huge NATO and Warsaw Pact armies were massed along this divide. It was the most sensitive flash point in the Cold War; if the war turned hot, it would do so here.

Complicating matters was the unresolved question of the Second World War: the ultimate fate of Germany – presently divided, like Europe, into east and west and occupied by the victorious powers. In 1948 America, Great Britain, and France had sanctioned West Germany's rearmament and its entry into NATO in the face of the Soviet Union's refusal to withdraw its forces to its own borders and its increasingly menacing posture in central Europe. Subsequently, West Germany's membership in NATO became a cardinal pillar of the United States' policy of containment. Not only would West Germany serve as a bulwark against further Russian advances into Europe, but there were solid historical reasons for copperfastening it to the west. Since 1871 a 'strong, unified Germany in the center of the continent pursuing a purely national policy had proved incompatible with the peace of Europe', and this remained so even in the 1950s: 'It was tempting fate to turn loose a united, neutral Germany so soon after the war.'[80]

---

79 At a later meeting with Barco, Kennedy hinted that the United States might link further progress in arms reductions to proof that the hardships of the Hungarian people had eased, but they rejected this proposal because it might destabilize the London disarmament talks then in progress: DFA 305/210/4/I, 4 July 1957.

80 Kissinger, *Diplomacy*, p. 499.

The ruling Christian Democratic Party in Bonn, and its leader, Konrad Adenauer, embraced the west's policy. They had guided West Germany into NATO, endorsed its continued membership, and sought its integration into western Europe. Adenauer had 'opted unconditionally for the west, even at the price of postponing German unity'.[81] He correctly reasoned that this was in his nation's long-term interests. Still, one of his concerns, and that of other pro-NATO Europeans, was that the United States might one day cut a deal with the USSR (involving some type of neutral Germany) and abandon Europe, leaving West Germany at the mercy of the Soviet Union. He therefore repudiated all calls for the withdrawal of NATO forces from central Europe. But his domestic opponents, the Social Democrats, did not. They 'assigned a higher priority to German unification than to Atlantic relationships ... and would have gladly paid for progress on German national aims by making a commitment to neutrality'.[82] In short, a reunited, neutral Germany was more important than a divided one disposed towards the west.

Throughout the 1950s the USSR made proposals of the kind Adenauer disliked, but that appealed to the Social Democrats – those envisioning a unified, albeit neutral, Germany unoccupied by foreign troops. Its short term goal was to relieve pressure by unhinging Germany from the west; in the long run the USSR hoped to sow doubt and confusion in the western alliance. Stalin's Peace Note, circulated among western capitals in March 1952, was designed to this end. So was Nikita Khrushchev's offer – made on American television in June 1957 – to withdraw Soviet troops from eastern Europe in exchange for the total evacuation of American forces from the continent.[83] Even the Rapacki Plan (named after the Polish Foreign Minister), which called for a nuclear–free zone in Central Europe comprising Germany, Poland, and Czechoslovakia, was intended to undermine western Europe's confidence in America's nuclear guarantee because it left the Soviet Union's conventional might in place.

* * *

Against this background, the Department of External Affairs had been considering the nature of Aiken's address to the reconvened Eleventh Assembly for some time. In his June report praising the conclusions of the Special Committee on Hungary Boland had offered his own counsel: the speech's 'essence ... should be an appeal, or if you like, a summons, to Soviet Russia to withdraw her armed forces from the countries of eastern Europe completely'.[84] He conceded that it was necessary to recognize the 'legitimate secu-

81 Ibid., p. 501.
82 Ibid., p. 503.
83 This offer was part of a wider Soviet diplomatic offensive at the time: Walter L. Hixson, *George F. Kennan: Cold War Iconoclast* (New York, 1989), p. 173.
84 DFA 305/210/4, 28 June 1957.

rity preoccupations of Soviet Russia in eastern Europe'; also, the western powers should not make 'arrangements with eastern European countries that might be regarded as aimed against Soviet Russia'. Still, the Soviet Government had to accept 'that the political atmosphere which must exist in the world before peace is assured can never exist as long as international crimes, such as her attack on Hungary, are committed'. He looked forward to 'developing this point of view' when he traveled to Dublin in early August for annual consultations with the Department. What Boland never advocated, though, was the withdrawal of allied forces from central Europe; his colleagues' later suggestions to this effect would provoke his ire.

When he returned to Ireland Boland discussed the parameters of Aiken's address with Sean Murphy and Conor O'Brien.[85] The latter also met with Aiken, whom he noted was 'closely interested in this question now'.[86] Based on these talks O'Brien completed a 'Draft Intervention in Hungarian Debate at the United Nations'. On 7 August he forwarded a copy to Murphy and the original to Aiken, who 'wanted it urgently'.[87]

The draft opened with Boland's interpretation of events in Hungary: the revolt was not an incident in the Cold War, but 'plainly a national rising in the broadest and fullest sense'. The inclusion of this observation was unsurprising considering Boland's praise of the Special Committee's report (which had reached a similar conclusion), his early August meeting in Dublin with O'Brien, and his subsequent recommendations for the reconvened Assembly's final resolution.[88]

The operative section reflected Aiken's thinking, particularly his vision of a United Nations dedicated to alleviating international discord through decisive action. It began with a question: could the Assembly 'help to prepare the way for a settlement which could save Hungary and preserve peace'? Its reply surprisingly raised the offer Nikita Khrushchev had made on American television in June to withdraw Soviet troops from eastern Europe if American forces completely vacated the continent. The draft recognized that the plan had been 'scouted' by the west, who perceived it as a trap to secure Russian control of Europe. Even so, it asserted that 'we should be ready to take risks' to win the freedom of eastern Europe. It thereby explicitly endorsed Khrushchev's offer to draw down Soviet troops and implicitly called on the United States to do the same. It also added a new twist to Boland's late June call for western security guarantees in the wake of a unilateral Soviet withdrawal by assigning that task to the UN.

Communications between Iveagh House and the Permanent Mission indicate that this version was not the finished product. On 7 August, the same

85 DFA 305/210/6, 7 August 1957.
86 DFA 417/167, 8 August 1957.
87 DFA 305/210/6, 7 August 1957.
88 Cf. DFA 305/210/I, 22, 27, 29 August 1957; DFA 305/210/6, 23 August 1957; DFA PMUN X/51, 4 September 1957.

day that O'Brien had sent a copy of the draft speech to Murphy, he received a cable from the delegation in New York stating that due to an upcoming meeting of the European caucus, where action on the Special Committee's report would be discussed, they 'would be glad to have if yet available [the] main points planned for our intervention'.[89] On 8 August O'Brien informed the delegation that 'Our intervention will stress [the] character of [the] Hungarian rising as [a] national rising and not, repeat not, [an] ideological clash or [an] episode in [the] Cold War.'[90] He alerted them to the fact that 'Other points [were] under discussion here [and] no decisions [had been] reached ... ' He requested the Mission to 'Please cable me [the] main points arising out of [the] European group meeting' and added that 'Any suggestions [from] your end as to points for inclusion in the speech would also be appreciated.' O'Brien did not allude to the incorporation of Khrushchev's proposal in the draft; he knew what Boland's reaction would be and wanted to avoid a conflict at that early, unsettled stage.

Later that day Eamon Kennedy assured O'Brien 'that we will keep you abreast of any suggestions which may arise at this end as to points which might be included in the speech'.[91] The diplomatic atmosphere at the United Nations did not encourage a swift clarification of the matter. In mid-August Boland, who had returned to New York, informed Murphy that 'Official thinking here about the debate on Hungary ... is still in a very confused and inchoate state.'[92] Hence, he doubted 'whether the Minister's opening speech in the debate can be safely finalized at this stage'; it might 'prove difficult to settle its terms and substance finally [any] earlier than a week or so before the debate opens'.

One aspect was certain: Aiken hoped to be the first speaker. In early August O'Brien asked the Permanent Mission to notify UN officials of the Minister's intent, and Kennedy duly apprised the Secretariat.[93] Boland mentioned it to M. Crosthwaite and Anthony Moore of the British delegation, who expressed their reservations: the 'general feeling was that the debate should be opened by a statement by Mr Shann of Australia, the rapporteur of the Special Committee on Hungary'.[94] Boland told the British delegates that Aiken 'would have no objection' to this. Considering that he was a newcomer to the UN, Aiken's request was remarkable. It also portended his Assembly style: never would he hesitate to speak his mind or state the truth as he understood it.

Conor O'Brien continued to work on the speech throughout August. Toward the end of the month he submitted 'the fourth revision' to Murphy.[95]

89 DFA 305/210/6, 7 August 1957.
90 Ibid., 8 August 1957.
91 Ibid.
92 Ibid., 21 August 1957.
93 Ibid., 8 August 1957.
94 Ibid., 22 August 1957.
95 Ibid., 27 August 1957.

The introduction was similar to the first draft. The operative section had evolved and closely approximated to the final version. After referring to Khrushchev's offer, the speech established Ireland's impartial, if not anti-communist, credentials by asserting that it was 'a sophism to speak of "the American forces in western Europe" and "the Russian forces in eastern Europe" as if the two were on the same footing'. This fact explained why many in the west had rejected, or had even declined to consider, Mr Khrushchev's proposals.

Khrushchev's proposals did contain 'one very important feature': the declaration of Russia's 'willingness to withdraw her troops from Hungary and the other captive nations, under certain conditions'. These were, of course, 'advantageous to Russia'. Nonetheless, the chance 'of winning freedom for the captive nations should weigh heavily on the other scale'. So the speech posed a rhetorical question: did other delegations feel, as the Irish one did, 'that a 'drawing back of non-national forces on both sides is desirable, from the point of view of providing an opportunity – perhaps the only opportunity – for the peaceful liberation' of eastern Europe? Aiken answered this query with an astonishing proposition:

> What I would suggest – in the very general terms appropriate to this stage of the debate – is that this Assembly should declare itself in favor, in principle, of a drawing back of non-national armies and military personnel an equal number of kilometers from the border of Russian occupied Europe. It would necessarily take place in stages marked out in terms of geographical distances rather than selected political units. The first phase of the withdrawal might be – for example – to a depth of some hundreds of kilometers on each side, along latitudinal lines. A later phase might be to 1,000 kilometers on each side, thus taking Russian officers and troops out of Hungary and such other captive nations as are outside the present Russian border.

The draft added several qualifications to this proposal. It was not 'an ideal solution or an ultimate settlement', but was proffered 'with the sole idea of substituting a cold, impartial, mathematical formula for emotion-charged disputes over named countries and areas'. More important, 'in the widening zone of withdrawal thus created, this Organization might be able to play a very useful part'. A UN inspection unit, made up of Member States belonging to neither NATO nor the Warsaw Pact, 'could supervise the withdrawals of the foreign contingents' and 'remain in the area to see that no new military infiltration' occurred. Echoing one of Aiken's favorite themes, the speech refuted the charge that it was inappropriate for a small country to make such a suggestion: it was sometimes useful for a country 'detached from any of the great power blocks to put forward in a general way ideas which more powerful countries might for various reasons find it difficult to advance'. Finally, Ireland had proffered the plan not so the Assembly could endorse a specific

proposal, but 'to indicate one possible answer to the fundamental question before the Assembly: what can be done to help Hungary to recover her freedom'?

* * *

Ensuing correspondence between O'Brien and Boland dramatically illumines the thinking that underpinned this version of the address, Boland's discomfort with it, and the professional relationship between Boland, O'Brien, and Aiken. On 26 August O'Brien sent a duplicate of the speech to Boland.[96] His covering minute shows that the withdrawal plan was not a casual, off-the-cuff suggestion, but a well-thought-out proposal.[97] He told Boland that the enclosed address was a 'draft only. It is understood that at least the wording, and perhaps the ideas also, will require' reworking. Yet it was 'a fourth revision and the product of many discussions with the Minister who, as indeed the redraftings ... show, has been giving a good deal of thought' to it. O'Brien then stressed that Aiken intended 'to put forward concrete suggestions and not confine himself to generalities'. He told Boland, therefore, that if he had 'any such suggestions which might be offered either in addition to or in amendment or replacement of any of the ideas in the attached two drafts, I should be glad to have them'. It might prove possible 'to amend the texts considerably', but 'any major alteration of the ideas to be put forward would best be made at the present stage – before the drafts are shown to the Taoiseach or the government', which Aiken planned to do at a later date.

In a lengthy letter marked 'Urgent and Confidential' Boland immediately responded to O'Brien's solicitation for improvements to Aiken's speech; the uneasy tone of the missive evinced his alarm.[98] He feared most the erosion of Ireland's pro-western policy and the influence, small yet significant, that it had generated. It was imperative, Boland told O'Brien, that Iveagh House 'know at once how [Aiken's plan] strikes us in relation to the atmosphere and the current of ideas' circulating in New York. To commit Ireland to the troop withdrawal proposal 'will certainly involve a great – and perhaps even a dangerous – political risk. It is always a rather ticklish business for us, of course, to be caught supporting any Soviet proposal!' In the light of certain factors – ingrained American distrust of Soviet initiatives, unquestioned western adherence to the European security system – 'for us to come out and back the pro-

---

96 DFA 417/167, 26 August 1957.
97 This point is also reinforced by Department of External Affairs communications with the Department of Defense seeking latitudinal readings on the European continent: DFA 305/341, 12 August, 2 September 1957.
98 DFA 417/167, 30 August 1957. Highlighting Boland's anxiety was a cable he sent to O'Brien after mailing his letter reading: 'Urgent for Conor O'Brien from Boland. Comments on ... your letter 26th August airmailed Friday': DFA PMUN X/51, 2 September 1957.

posal made by Khrushchev during his famous TV interview will, I am afraid, be little short of a sensation'. To reinforce this point Boland recounted the visceral reaction to Senator Bill Knowland's recent suggestion that NATO withdraw its troops from Norway in exchange for a Soviet promise to evacuate Hungary: 'The American press fell on him as one man and tore him limb from limb.'

Boland feared that the Irish delegation would find 'ourselves in a similar hornets nest'. Despite an overwhelming desire to see eastern Europe freed from domination, 'no one would favor gambling the security of western Europe to achieve it'. If Ireland proposed it, we 'will be breaking new ground. We will make headlines like "IRELAND BACKS KHRUSCHCHEV PLAN" [*sic*], and the effect – not least the effect on our people here – will be hard to correct.' The country would be perceived 'as having moved from the "anti-communist" into the "neutralist" camp, the reduction of foreign bases being, as you know, a major plank in the neutralist platform'. Boland was not questioning the merits of the proposal – 'Personally, I think there is a good deal to be said for them' – but, due to the 'serious risk of misunderstanding and criticism', doubted the wisdom 'of our espousing so bluntly a Soviet initiative in a field in which American opinion, and especially Irish American opinion, is so sensitive and so suspicious of Soviet intentions ... '

Boland then made several specific suggestions. It would be more appropriate, he opined, to place the withdrawal scheme in Aiken's General Debate speech rather than in his Hungarian intervention. To announce such a major proposal, 'in effect the complete abandonment of what have been the fundamental tenets of western policy in Europe for the past ten years', in the course of 'the relatively restricted debate on Hungary would appear, I am afraid, almost casual'. In addition, to refute Khrushchev's claim that following the retreat of Soviet forces eastern Europe would remain communist, the speech should contain a demand for 'free elections under international supervision ... ' Last, if it had to be made at all, any call for troop disengagement should be divorced 'from the suggestion made by Khrushchev entirely'. Considering it 'better to approach the idea from a completely different angle', Boland outlined a new approach: make the point that 'events in Hungary have shown that there can be no freedom for the countries of eastern Europe as long as they have Russian troops stationed in their territory; link recent developments in nuclear weapons, which raise 'the question whether the stationing of foreign troops abroad really serves any useful security purpose', to the possibility that 'negotiations for the withdrawal of Soviet troops from the countries of eastern Europe ... even if it meant some withdrawal of foreign troops in western Europe in return'; and, stress that any agreement pertaining to eastern Europe must include provisions for 'free elections under international supervision'.

After admitting that his plan 'may not fit so well with the Minister's preference for concrete suggestions' Boland described his own conception of the

General Assembly; he did so to support his arguments, but his comments reveal his personal philosophy. The Assembly was not 'an executive body in any sense. It has no executive powers. It is purely and essentially an organ of world moral opinion.' Its function was not to 'provide concrete solutions'. The 'main task of the UN Assembly is to influence world opinion' by the steady 'assertion and re-assertion' of moral principles. It was 'precisely in relation to that function of the UN Assembly that Ireland is so well situated to play a leading role'. Boland regretted any divergence of views, but hoped that 'the clash of ideas will be of assistance to the Minister in arriving at his decisions'.

O'Brien quickly replied to Boland's letter, thanking him for his straight-forward comments.[99] 'Because of the great importance of the issues', he had immediately shown the letter to Aiken, who 'read it with great care and re-read several of the passages'. Aiken's two main reflections highlight his unequivocal commitment to the troop disengagement proposal and his readiness to take the heat generated by it. Realizing that his speech was likely to provoke the outcry Boland had predicted, Aiken was, according to O'Brien, 'keenly alive to the desirability of mitigating such reaction as far as may be possible, without detracting from the substance of what he has to say', and would keep 'the various suggestions made in your letter always in mind'. At the same time, because he truly felt 'that only a joint withdrawal of forces can save Hungary and diminish the danger of war (which he feels to be much greater than is commonly believed)', Aiken considered it 'his duty to make the proposal in question even if he gets a bad press for doing so'.

Aiken had not yet reached any firm conclusions about Boland's 'suggestions for toning down' the proposal. 'He made it clear, however, that he would not add any conditions to it which would make its rejection by the Russians automatic', such as a demand for internationally supervised elections in the captive nations. He also felt that 'it would seem artificial to omit all reference to Khrushchev's proposal', an association that would inevitably be 'made by the press'. Aiken's sensitivity to Russian concerns probably stemmed from his dissatisfaction with the harsh anti-communist tone of Liam Cosgrave's appearance before the Assembly in 1956; O'Brien told Boland that Aiken was 'strongly critical of the tendency of his predecessor's speech in the General Debate last year which in his view went much too far in certain respects'. Concurrently, Aiken was very thankful 'to get such a plain warning as you had given about possible reactions, as it was better to face such things square-ly from the start and not to minimize them'.

* * *

Aiken's speech was not, as he had hoped, the first address to the reconvened Eleventh Assembly, but he delivered it on the opening day of the debate,

10 September. He never formally submitted the final draft to the government, but in early September showed it to de Valera, who approved the line taken.[100] Beforehand, O'Brien ensured that the Irish media covered it. On 9 September he reminded Brendan Nolan, Third Secretary in the Political Section, of Aiken's speech, and questioned Radio Éireann's decision to air only five minutes of it, whereas ten minutes had been allotted to Cosgrave's address the previous year.[101] O'Brien had sent a similar cable to Maurice Gorham, the Director of Radio Éireann, and wanted Nolan to follow it up. After speaking with Gorham, Nolan cabled O'Brien, telling him that Radio Éireann would cover the speech in the evening news and would devote ten minutes to it afterwards.[102]

The final version of the speech was essentially the same as the fourth draft reviewed above. The operative section was virtually unchanged.[103] It implicitly acknowledged Boland's call for internationally supervised elections following the evacuation of eastern Europe,[104] but made no explicit reference because Aiken had assumed that the Russians would automatically reject this condition. None of Boland's other suggestions surfaced; this must have been a bitter pill for him to swallow.

Reaction to the speech, which the Department of External Affairs keenly monitored, as its cable to ten European missions abroad soliciting 'press comment and official reaction' reveals,[105] was decidedly mixed. During the subsequent debate on Hungary two Afro-Asian delegates spoke highly of it. The Permanent Representative of the Philippines said that Aiken's suggestion was 'well worth further consideration'.[106] Arthur Lall, representing India, called it 'constructive ... timely and most relevant'. Another positive reaction appeared closer to home; the *Irish Times* said the speech was to Aiken's 'own credit, as well as to that of his country'.[107]

The communist bloc's response was lukewarm. Vasily Kuznestov, the Soviet Deputy Foreign Minister, called the speech 'constructive in principle', but probably did so more to annoy the west rather than out of appreciation for the plan's merits.[108] In reality, the Warsaw Pact 'appeared to distrust the Irish initiative', preferring instead their own Rapacki Plan.[109]

---

100 DFA 417/167, 4 September 1957.
101 DFA PMUN X/51, 9 September 1957.
102 Ibid., 10 September 1957.
103 Aiken, *Ireland* (1957), p. 11.
104 The speech suggested that the UN inspection unit created to serve in the demilitarized zone in central Europe 'could see that the countries concerned would be left free to govern themselves in their own way without interference'.
105 DFA 305/341, 10 September 1957.
106 DFA 417/167, 14 September 1957.
107 *Irish Times*, 11 September 1957.
108 O'Connor, *Ireland*, p. 9.
109 MacQueen, 'Aiken', p. 224.

In the west Aiken's proposal 'caused some uneasiness', and was viewed as a 'bad statement' in some quarters.[110] NATO 'showed no interest in the Irish plan, either individually or collectively'.[111] On 13 September Dr Felician Prill, the West German Minister, called on John Belton at Iveagh House to express his displeasure; interestingly enough, Boland had anticipated several of the misgivings the German envoy outlined. Prill was not acting on instructions from his government, 'but felt it his duty to ask for all available information as to the background of the speech and to what extent it represented the foreign policy of the government'.[112] He predicted that the Irish proposal 'would come as an unpleasant shock to the government and people of West Germany', and said that it 'was not calculated to improve relations between Ireland' and his country. The 'maintenance of the American and British forces in West Germany was regarded by the German government as essential to its defense against Soviet aggression'. Further, a withdrawal would not 'assist the reunification of Germany, as the East Zone would retain its highly trained and equipped divisions of Germans directly under communist control'. The timing of the proposal was 'particularly unfortunate' due to several factors: '[the] forthcoming general election' in West Germany, where the pro-NATO Christian Democrats did not want to loose ground to the NATO-skeptical Social Democrats; Khrushchev's similar 'suggestions on [the] withdrawal of American troops from Germany'; and, '[the] recent failure of [the] disarmament conference' in London.

William Warnock, the Irish Minister in Bonn, confirmed Dr Prill's message to Belton. The first reaction from the West German Foreign Ministry, relayed by Warnock to External Affairs and then on to the Irish Permanent Mission at the UN, stressed 'western military distaste of [a] partial withdrawal'.[113] The Germans asserted that 'such measures must be linked with outstanding political matters'. In early October Professor Grewe, the head of the Political Division of the Foreign Ministry, told Warnock that 'at the moment' Aiken's ideas 'stood no chance of being implemented'.[114]

The British reacted similarly. Selwyn Lloyd, Minister for Foreign Affairs, labeled Aiken's address the 'speech of a fellow-traveler';[115] likewise the press officer at the British Permanent Mission, who called it 'fellow-traveling from beginning to end'.[116] On 13 September the British Ambassador to Dublin, Sir Alex Clutterbuck, met Sean Murphy 'to enquire as to the background' of the proposal.[117] Because he had been on leave when Aiken had departed for New

110 O'Brien, *Katanga*, pp. 19–21.
111 MacQueen, 'Aiken', p. 224.
112 DFA P 299 13 September 1957. West Germany, incidentally, was not a member of the UN at this time.
113 DFA 417/167, 14 September 1957.
114 Ibid., 3 October 1957.
115 *Die Welt*, 10 March 1958.
116 DFA P 299, 3 October 1957.
117 Ibid., 13 September 1957. The summary of this meeting and Belton's with Prill were

York, Murphy 'had no opportunity of discussing his speech' with the Minister, but he rightly told Clutterbuck the 'suggestion was an effort to find some peaceful solution which would alleviate the appalling sufferings of the Hungarian people'. Clutterbuck regretted that the British were 'not notified in advance of the Minister's proposal, particularly because it was taking up a Russian suggestion'. Like Dr Prill, he also considered it 'unfortunate as to timing in view of the German elections next Sunday'.

This criticism was partially due to confusion. Boland informed Aiken (after speaking with Anthony Moore, a British colleague) that the UK delegation and the Foreign Office had interpreted 'you as proposing that foreign troops should be withdrawn entirely from western Europe. Your reference to Khrushchev's proposal had been taken as meaning that you were endorsing that proposal.'[118] Moore added that this misunderstanding was 'fairly widespread' among western delegations. Wanting to exercise some damage control, Boland recommended that the American, German, French, British, and other European Ambassadors in Dublin be thoroughly briefed on the scheme by an External Affairs representative.

Aiken did not take up Boland's proposition, *per se*, but in a press interview several months later he clarified his disengagement strategy: it would not lead to the complete withdrawal of American troops from Europe, only the evacuation of foreign troops from the center of the continent. Aiken said that his critics had 'not rightly examined the map'.[119] They believed the proposal 'would drive the [Allied troops] out of Europe, but precisely the opposite is the case'. If the Russians and Americans:

> following latitudinal lines, draw back to an equal extent east and west, until the last Russian soldier was inside the Russian boundary, then certainly West Germany, Benelux and small parts of France and Italy must be evacuated by the Americans. But would that be really be too high a price for the liberation of East Germany, Poland, Hungary, Czechoslovakia, Romania and Bulgaria, when most of France, including Fountainbleau would remain open to American troops? That is the meaning of the use of latitudinal lines of withdrawal.

What, then, is one to make of Aiken's blueprint? Specifically, what of the scheme's indifferent reception and ultimate rejection? In this light, one critic has asserted that it was not 'informed by any great awareness of the realities of current great power relationships'.[120] On the face of it, this view seems credible. Aiken certainly underestimated the desire of western governments –

forwarded to Aiken in New York on de Valera's instructions: DFA P 299, 14 September 1957.
118 DFA P 299, 3 October 1957.
119 *Die Welt*, 10 March 1958.
120 MacQueen, 'Aiken', p. 225.

including the Christian Democrats in Bonn – to nurture 'a responsible national role for Germany, which had proved elusive since its unification in 1871',[121] by harnessing West Germany to the west through NATO membership, the stationing of foreign troops there, and economic integration. Aiken also overlooked the psychological impact of his plan: although he did not call explicitly for American forces to leave Europe, his speech, in referring to Khrushchev's offer, conjured up this image; thus it was doomed.

Yet Aiken's proposal must be considered in its larger context. There is no doubt, as the correspondence between Boland and O'Brien demonstrates, that Aiken deeply believed in it. His motives were sincere. As he often emphasized: 'we should never forget the fate of the oppressed peoples of eastern Europe. We must do everything we can to help to restore their freedom.'[122] The plan was also an expression of Aiken's conviction that in the Assembly the small nations had 'their own important and critical role to play by avoiding all action which would increase tension and by promoting the climate for peace between the great powers'.[123] Aiken (erroneously) believed that the Soviets were 'prepared to withdraw from the east European countries, simply because they cannot remain there permanently'.[124] Initially, though, they had to be given 'the opportunity to save their faces', which was the object of his speech. Because the great powers could not 'make such a proposal, on grounds of prestige', Aiken took it upon himself to do so.

Most important, the plan sought 'to diminish political tension in Europe and to avert the danger of war, which is all the greater as long as soldiers of opposing armies stand face to face'.[125] In short, not only was this an independent idea, it was one designed to open a space between the power blocs and thus reduce Cold War friction, which was the primary aim of Aiken's UN diplomacy. The logical progressions of troop disengagement – Aiken's blueprints for Algeria, the Middle East, and his Areas of Law concept – pursued the same end. Although the great powers overlooked these as well, they are important nonetheless. They underscore the Irish delegation's commitment to pursuing international stability through the United Nations.

THE CHINA VOTE

Aiken's troop withdrawal plan was not his last bold move at the Twelfth Session, just his opening salvo. During the General Debate on 20 September he ruffled feathers again with candid proposals for resolving the impasse in

121 Kissinger, *Diplomacy*, p. 507.
122 *Die Welt*, 10 March 1958.
123 *America*, 19 August 1961.
124 *Die Welt*, 10 March 1958.
125 Ibid.

the Middle East and the conflict in Algeria. Three days later he cast Ireland's most famous vote at the United Nations by endorsing an Indian motion seeking a discussion of the representation of China in the Assembly. At first blush, the highly-charged reaction to this vote calls Aiken's judgment into question, but a closer examination reveals the rationale behind his move.

During the Steering Committee's discussion of the Twelfth Session's slate India, on behalf of the Afro-Asian bloc, once again requested that the item 'The Representation of China in the United Nations' be inscribed on the Assembly's agenda so that they might somehow realize their goal of replacing the nationalist government on Taiwan with the communist government in Peking as China's UN representative. The United States, as always, defeated this move in the Steering Committee, which thereby made no recommendation to the Assembly regarding Chinese representation.

On 23 September the Assembly took up the Steering Committee's final report. India tried to overcome its earlier defeat by tabling an amendment to it which would inscribe the question of 'The Representation of China in the United Nations' directly onto the General Assembly's agenda. The amendment failed – 29 to 43, with 9 abstentions.[126] Astonishingly, Ireland joined India, most Afro-Asian delegations, the Soviet bloc, and the Nordic countries in voting for it. Ireland also joined this group to oppose the United States' annual shelving resolution on the China question, which the General Assembly unsurprisingly adopted.[127]

The American response to the Irish move was swift and severe. Forewarned by a personal message from Aiken two days beforehand, Henry Cabot Lodge informed the State Department that the Irish Foreign Minister was 'going nuts'.[128] John Foster Dulles, the American Secretary of State, acted quickly. Instead of instructing Lodge to approach Aiken directly, he asked Cardinal Spellman, the Archbishop of New York, to persuade the Irish delegation to alter its vote.[129] Dulles even contacted the Vatican envoy in Washington.[130] Since it 'was not in the Fianna Fáil tradition to lean on clerical authority in international affairs (whatever they did at home)', this risible form of coercion failed – utterly.[131] Rather than being cowed, Aiken was infuriated by the ham-fisted American approach.[132]

126 Aiken, *Ireland* (1957), p. 28.
127 GA/RES 1135 (XII).
128 Quoted in Keogh, *Ireland*, p. 236.
129 For a review of Spellman's approach (which borders on the comical) and the Irish delegation's resistance to it, see O'Brien, *Katanga*, pp. 21–5; Keogh, *Ireland*, p. 236; Akenson, *Conor*, p. 158. Spellman even threatened 'a boycott by Irish American Catholics of Irish Airlines and Irish Tourism': T.D. Williams, 'Irish Foreign Policy', p. 145.
130 Keogh, *Ireland*, p. 236.
131 Keatinge, *A Place*, p. 179. In this same context, the Catholic hierarchy's condemnation of the anti-Treaty forces during the Civil War and 'the threat of excommunication which accompanied it' had done little to endear Aiken to the Catholic Church:

Why this overreaction by the Americans? While Aiken's troop disengagement proposal 'was "a bad statement" (from the then prevailing western point of view)', and therefore reluctantly tolerated, it was infinitely less harmful than 'a bad vote', which was how the United States interpreted Ireland's China ballot.[133] After all, at that stage the USA had assigned a moral significance to General Assembly votes on Cold War issues. This was especially so for John Foster Dulles, the ultimate Cold Warrior, who was conducting nothing less than an anti-communist crusade.[134] His immediate fear was that Ireland's audacious stand over the representation of China was 'as an example certain to be noted by waverers' in the Assembly;[135] in the long run he was determined to keep Peking out of the world body.

The American backlash must also be considered in the light of the close relations between the two countries during the Eleventh Assembly and the United States' dashed expectations that Irish-American cooperation would continue at the Twelfth Session. In August 1957 Arthur B. Emmons, Counsellor at the US Embassy in Dublin, prematurely forwarded a report to Washington to this effect, even going so far as to insist that Ireland would again vote against the Chinese communists.[136] One month earlier, as a sign of their respect for the Irish delegation, the American mission informed Eamon Kennedy that they would support Ireland for one of the Vice Presidencies of the Twelfth Assembly – ironically, on the Steering Committee.[137] Further, Boland's cooperation with the United States delegation on the Hungarian issue throughout the summer of 1957, which culminated in the reconvened Eleventh Assembly's final resolution, cemented this friendship.[138]

Lyons, *Ireland*, p. 465. Similarly, in August 1957 Leo McCauley, the Irish Ambassador to the Vatican, offered to discuss the agenda of the Twelfth Assembly with the Curia 'in order to ascertain their attitude on individual items', but O'Brien noted that doing so was 'hardly worthwhile': DFA 417/167 13, 19 August 1957.

132 DFA P299, 2 October 1957.

133 O'Brien, *Katanga*, pp. 19–20.

134 Cf. Kissinger, *Diplomacy*, p. 534.

135 O'Brien, *Katanga*, pp. 22–3.

136 Cf. Keogh, *Ireland*, p. 235.

137 Norman Armour, an American diplomat, told Kennedy that it 'was most desirable that a strong and able Vice President should be nominated by the European group to play an active role' in the General Steering Committee and inquired if 'Ireland would be willing to act as Vice President'. Aiken, Boland, and O'Brien discussed the matter while Boland was in Dublin and regretfully decided that because the delegation was 'far too small to be able to assume such responsibilities at this stage' they would not pursue the post: DFA 417/167/1, 26 July 1957; DFA 417/156/2, 6 September.

138 Cf. DFA 305/210/I, 22, 27, 29 August 1957; DFA 305/210/6, 23 August 1957; DFA PMUN X/51, 4 September 1957. The Irish delegation served as one of the 37 cosponsors of the resolution adopted by the reconvened Eleventh Session. The motion endorsed the findings of the Special Committee on Hungary and condemned once more the Soviet Union's defiance of previous UN motions: GA/RES 1133 (XI).

Concurrently, a vocal segment of the Irish American community shared their government's dismay over Ireland's China departure. The American Catholic press was especially vehement. For example, the New York diocesan paper, the *Catholic News*, editorialized:

> How the Irish delegation could violate Irish and natural law principles of freedom and justice by such a vote is beyond our understanding. That the people of Ireland will repudiate the vote we are absolutely certain. But it will be a long, long time before American friends of Ireland – and that includes most Americans – will recover from it. It has done more harm to Ireland in a day than its worst enemies could accomplish in a decade.[139]

Likewise, Irish Americans sent numerous visceral letters to de Valera, Aiken, and the Irish mission in New York.[140]

Boland was somewhat unnerved by the criticism. Writing to Aiken in early October, he said that while some Irish Americans were upset, overall they were not too 'het up about it'.[141] He added, nonetheless, that:

> it will be well to be careful, when voting on important matters, not to appear to be putting ourselves too frequently in the neutralist or Afro-Asian camp in opposition to the west. I propose, therefore, to consult you beforehand by cable whenever we are faced with important votes which seem likely to me to involve the risk of misinterpretation.

The unusual displeasure directed at the delegation had provoked the reappearance of his pro-western predilection and anti-Afro-Asian bias.

* * *

If the response was so vitriolic, why did Ireland vote in this manner? Two reasons account for the decision, and in combination they provide a sound, coherent foundation for it. First, the China vote must be understood as the expression of a vital principle undergirding Irish policy throughout Aiken's term as Minister: a commitment to the discussion of all topics, regardless of their contentious nature. Nothing demonstrates this more potently than the minutes of the delegation's first meeting during the Twelfth Assembly.[142] After discussing the third item that day, the 'Adoption of [the] Agenda', the delegation decided that:

---

139 *Catholic News*, 5 October 1957.
140 DFA 417/156, *passim*; S 16057/A, *passim*.
141 DFA 417/167, 7 October 1957.
142 DFA PMUN J/50/57 (nd).

We will vote for inclusion, irrespective of their intrinsic nature, of the following controversial subjects: 1. West Irian; 2. Cyprus; 3. Algeria; 4. Three South African Items: (a) South West Africa, (b) Treatment of persons of Indian Origin, (c) Apartheid; 5. The representation of China in the UN.

Aiken stressed this theme when explaining Ireland's stance to the Assembly,[143] and he reiterated it in a reply to three Irish citizens who had criticized the move: 'The question at issue in the United Nations vote was the right of discussion.'[144] He held the 'unshakable conviction that the members of the United Nations should be free to discuss in a reasonable and comprehensive way situations which might touch off the destruction of everything living in the Northern Hemisphere'.

An even more pressing reason for the vote was an undeniable fact of UN diplomacy in the late 1950s: supporting a debate on the representation of China was the *sine qua non* of an independent identity in the General Assembly. How so? A delegation established its autonomous credentials 'not by speeches, but by a pressure-resistant pattern of voting';[145] in other words, by standing up to a great power, or coalition of powers, even when doing so entailed unpleasant consequences. In this respect, China 'was a subject on which the United States annually exercised heavy pressure to get a majority for its policy', despite the private disavowal of it by most UN members.[146] Therefore, to reject the American position 'demonstrated, under pressure, the sincerity of [a delegation's] independent stand ... ' It also indicated that a country was likely to vote in an independent manner 'on all other critical issues'.[147]

These nuances of UN diplomacy proved crucial to Aiken, who wanted to shift gears at the Twelfth Session and pursue an unfettered line instead of the pro-western policy of the Inter-Party government. Before the Assembly convened he revealed his intentions to Conor O'Brien, who, having attended the Eleventh Session, explained that China was the litmus test of an independent policy: Ireland would have to back a discussion of this issue. Aiken accepted this prescription. Even when warned of the nasty repercussions, according to O'Brien, he resolutely 'hitched his shoulders in a soldierly manner, which he

---

143 He said that 'If merely by refusing to discuss the question of the representation of China in the United Nations we could do anything to improve the situation in China and Korea, we would vote without hesitation in favor of that course', but the Irish delegation believed that peace and progress can best be served 'by having a full and open discussion of the question of the representation of China in this Assembly': Aiken, *Ireland* (1957), p. 28.

144 S 16057/A, 11 October 1957.

145 O'Brien, *Katanga*, p. 25.

146 O'Brien, 'Ireland', pp. 130–1.

147 Conor Cruise O'Brien, *Ireland, the United Nations and Southern Africa* (Dublin, 1967), p. 3.

used to do in moments of crisis'.[148] Thus, the observation that 'the Minister himself was in theory and in fact responsible' for the vote is correct.[149] Aiken made the decision to pursue an independent course; O'Brien provided him with the means to do so.

Aiken secured authorization for the China vote in the same way he had dealt with his troop disengagement proposal: he did not seek a formal government decision on the matter,[150] but he 'obviously acted with the full approval of the Taoiseach'.[151] De Valera was certainly sympathetic, for Aiken's vote echoed his own support for the admission of the Soviet Union into the League of Nations in 1934. On that earlier occasion de Valera had coupled his support for Russia's entry with an appeal for greater religious freedom there.[152] Aiken, too, qualified his ballot with a stinging criticism of the Chinese government.[153] But one important difference distinguished the two votes. Britain and France, the League's dominant powers, had voted for Russia's entry along with de Valera, and 'this fact lessened the impact of the criticism leveled against him by the militant Catholic, anti-communist opposition in the Dáil'.[154] Aiken did not enjoy such international company. His Irish colleagues fully backed him, however. During a delegation meeting two weeks beforehand Aiken had announced his plan, defended it, and welcomed the approval of the Irish contingent, which was prepared for the fallout.[155]

Inevitably, the vote achieved its desired effect. In the midst of the diplomatic rivalry in the Assembly generated by the Cold War and decolonization 'Ireland's support became, after the China vote, a desirable prize.'[156] During often intense deliberations Irish delegates 'on each committee and on many questions would be approached by the stalkers of the western powers and the Afro-Asians' and they would often find themselves 'a member of the fire brigade' that formulated compromise resolutions. It was accurately noted at the time that Ireland's 'vote each year on the question of the representation of China has been partly responsible for the reputation that the country has for "independence" – particularly among the Afro-Asians'.[157] Father de Souza, an Indian delegate, expressly endorsed the Irish stand.[158]

---

148 Akenson, *Conor*, pp. 157–8; Conor Cruise O'Brien, Personal Interview, 5 August 1993.
149 T.D. Williams, 'Irish Foreign Policy', p. 144.
150 GC 3/23; CAB 2/18.
151 T.D. Williams, 'Irish Foreign Policy', p. 144.
152 Cf. Kennedy, *League*, pp. 198–201.
153 Speaking from the podium, Aiken said that 'we have no sympathy whatever with the ideology of the Peking government. We condemn its aggressive policies in China itself and, particularly, its conduct in North Korea ... we reprobate the record of the Peking regime': Aiken, *Ireland* (1957), p. 28.
154 MacQueen, 'Aiken', p. 218.
155 DFA PMUN J/50/57 (nd); O'Brien, *Katanga*, p. 37.
156 O'Brien, *Katanga*, p. 26.
157 O'Connor, *Ireland*, p. 8.
158 DFA P299, 3 October 1957.

The Irish delegation certainly grasped the importance the Afro-Asian bloc attached to the China question. In his speech 'The United Nations Today: Seen from the Viewpoint of a Delegate of one of the Smaller Nations' (which Aedan O'Beirne delivered in San Francisco) Conor O'Brien placed Ireland's vote in the context of the 1955 Afro-Asian summit in Bandung, Indonesia. The conference, which 'testified to the emergence and self-consciousness of the Afro-Asian peoples', had decided 'unanimously – I repeat unanimously – to invite the Peking government, which accordingly took its place as the government of China in that historic assemblage'.[159] This judgment by the Afro-Asian bloc, O'Brien continued, which Ireland could not ignore because of its sympathy for the aspirations of colonized peoples, was worth 'bearing in mind' when assessing the Irish vote on Chinese representation.

The desire to maintain Ireland's new independent reputation, especially with the Afro-Asians, explains why Aiken distanced the Irish delegation from claims that in the event of a substantive vote on the representation of China Ireland would vote against the Peking government. If this interpretation gained currency Ireland's independent identity and sway with the Afro-Asian group would evaporate. After he had delivered O'Brien's speech in California, a local reporter asked Aedan O'Beirne the hypothetical question: 'Would Ireland favor Red China's admission if that ever comes to a vote?' When the interview appeared in print O'Beirne was quoted as saying: 'Certainly not.'[160] In a report recounting his journey O'Beirne drew O'Brien's attention to this passage. He said that the 'quotation to the effect that the vote of the Irish delegation would definitely be cast against the admission of Red China to UN membership is, of course, quite wrong'.[161] The reporter had drawn the wrong conclusion from O'Beirne's passing reference to Aiken's criticism of the Peking government in his Assembly speech.

Despite this explanation, O'Brien informed O'Beirne a month later that there had been 'some bother' in Iveagh House after other papers and news services had picked up the misquote in the *Monitor*.[162] Based on O'Beirne's report, O'Brien explained what had happened to Aiken, but the Minister still wanted 'to know as well as you can remember, what exactly you did say in answer to questions ... ' It was nothing to worry about, 'simply a matter of getting the record straight in case a "San Francisco doctrine" is introduced into any later stages of this involved controversy'. O'Beirne immediately sent a more detailed report, which Aiken found sufficient; O'Brien informed him that the Minister was 'fully satisfied on the score'.[163]

In the light of Ireland's aims at the UN, the China vote was an opportunity well-taken. It was an unequivocal declaration of autonomy; in time it

159 DFA 417/156, 23 December 1957.
160 *Monitor*, 20 December 1957.
161 DFA 417/156, 23 December 1957.
162 Ibid., 27 January 1958.
163 Ibid., 31 January 1958; 8 February 1958.

became the hallmark of Ireland's new activist, independent stance. While the vote, as intended, boosted the delegation's prestige within the Afro-Asian bloc, it did not sever ties with the free world; many western countries quietly concurred with Ireland's move, particularly the United Kingdom, which had recognized the Peking regime. Ten days after the ballot Boland revealed to Aiken that it was endorsed 'strongly, but for obvious reasons, secretly, by [the] British delegation here'.[164] A member had informed Boland 'that they were in entire agreement with what you said, but of course you were freer to say it than they were'. Likewise, the Canadian Ambassador had disclosed to Boland that he 'sympathized with and covertly, if not overtly, agreed with your vote'.

FIANNA FÁIL'S POLICY DEFENDED

The United States did not depend solely on Cardinal Spellman to express its misgivings about Ireland's new policy. On 2 October 1957 Scott McLeod, the American Ambassador in Dublin, called on de Valera and Aiken to convey in no uncertain terms his government's displeasure. Aiken's summary of the meeting is so telling that it bears close inspection.[165] Ambassador McLeod opened the conversation with some general comments. 'The gist of the points ... was that heretofore the Americans had counted on [Ireland's] automatic support in the United Nations as an anti-communist and pro-free world country' and had expected to confer 'ahead of time all points on the agenda'. But during the present session the Irish delegation, without consulting the United States, had 'voted to discuss the representation of China' and had outlined new proposals on Europe and Algeria. The US government realized that Ireland did not wish to be associated with any bloc, 'but they wanted to know where we [now] stood, and whether the understanding, as they saw it, heretofore governing our relations at the United Nations was to be abandoned'.

McLeod next turned to specifics. Aiken's troop disengagement plan was inherently flawed. In the face of the Soviet Union's massive occupation of central Europe, American troops in Germany 'vitally strengthened' many western nations, whose governments might interpret a partial withdrawal 'as a first step towards abandoning Europe altogether ... ' Eamon de Valera responded first to this charge. He stressed the dangerous nature of the current face-to-face troop deployment; argued that 'a drawing-back of even one-hundred kilometers on either side of the Iron Curtain would help'; and suggested that

---

164 DFA P299, 3 October 1957.
165 Ibid., 2 October 1957. Copies of Aiken's report were forwarded to the Irish Embassies in London, Paris, Madrid, Vatican, Ottawa and Washington, DC: DFA P299, 10, 22 October 1957. For a review of this meeting from Ambassador McLeod's viewpoint (which confirms Aiken's account), see Keogh, *Ireland*, p. 236–7.

such a small first step might later lead to a total Russian withdrawal – in which case the reunification of Germany was inevitable.

Aiken then launched into a detailed defense of his scheme, which echoed his earlier private and public comments. He added that his failure to inform the United States delegation about his speech beforehand was not intended as a slight. He had decided against it so that he could truthfully assert that it was 'put forward on my own responsibility without having consulted any other government'. It was possible that the Russians now 'thought that Stalin was foolish when he grabbed the captive countries in eastern Europe, and might be prepared to withdraw if they could save their faces while doing so'. In that case, it 'was of the utmost importance that the idea should be put to them without the least suspicion that I was doing it as a "stooge" of the American government'. Aiken's assumption about Soviet intentions was wholly unrealistic. Moreover, he still failed to grasp the political role played by American forces in West Germany: they reassured NATO of the United States' commitment to Europe; and, they fastened Germany to the west. Yet his motive for not contacting the American delegation beforehand was sound. And his steadfast justification of the plan – with de Valera's assistance – contradicts the assertion that in the face of western criticism 'the Irish government was seeking to abandon that policy as quickly as possible'.[166]

With respect to the representation of China, Ambassador McLeod (predictably) said that the American government was against a 'formal and separate debate at this time', because it would permit the Soviet bloc 'to make a great deal of propaganda and to influence some of the "non-committed nations"'.

Incensed by the United States' clumsy handling of this issue, which had made him 'determined to see Mr McLeod' upon his return to Dublin, Aiken pulled no punches. He reminded McLeod that he had given the American delegation advance notice of Ireland's China vote and, through Freddy Boland, had requested a meeting with Henry Cabot Lodge. Lodge, however, did not follow through, even though Aiken had made it his 'business at the various functions and in the lobby to give him the opportunity by going up to him and talking to him about other matters'. Instead of speaking with Aiken, a *demarche* objecting to the proposed Irish line was handed to John J. Hearne, the Irish Ambassador in Washington. Worse, and what Aiken 'resented still more deeply, was that they had attempted to use Cardinal Spellman to force us to change our vote without any discussion of the matter' or an attempt to 'take advantage of any of the opportunities' Aiken had created for discussing it. He 'resented the attempted use of pressure not from a personal point of view, but because it was the wrong way' to conduct diplomacy. He instructed McLeod 'to inform his government that was not the way to do business with an Irish representative'. One can envision Aiken's demeanor as he resolutely and appropriately vented his rage.

166 Keogh, *Ireland*, pp. 237–8.

Concerning the vote itself, Aiken 'pointed out that the question was whether we should discuss the matter affecting a quarter of the world's population, and particularly the question of Korea'. It would enhance international stability if the Chinese, in tandem with the United States, whose forces were 'an irritant to the east',[167] could be induced to withdraw from Korea. This would pave the way for free elections supervised by the United Nations and the establishment of an independent state, also guaranteed by the UN. This was a common Aiken theme, just like his final remark to McLeod: the UN should not be utilized 'merely for making set speeches', but 'in a reasonable way to endeavor to defreeze the present situation, which if it lasted would inevitably lead to war'.

* * *

Fine Gael, like the United States government, decried the shift in Ireland's UN policy. They voiced their disdain by releasing an official statement to the press in early October and by tabling a motion in the Dáil censuring the government's activities at the UN; both actions underline the divergent approaches to foreign policy pursued by Ireland's main political parties.

On 8 October the party issued a release placing on record 'its profound disagreement with certain statements and actions of the Minister for External Affairs at recent meetings of the United Nations General Assembly'.[168] They opposed 'the foreign policy of the Fianna Fáil government' on two grounds. They rejected 'the proposal that a solution to international tension is to be found in the withdrawal of United States and Russian troops from Europe'. This move would 'immeasurably strengthen international communism by breaking up the defense of the west'. The scheme also offended 'countries with close bonds of friendship with this country'. Plus, the China vote was the 'wrong one, and has harmed our prestige and influence abroad'.

Returning to a theme asserted in John Costello's April 1956 memorandum, Fine Gael bemoaned the fact that the government's activities 'have inevitably raised considerable protest from the press and public in the United States'. Ireland's vital relations and close ties with America dictated that it 'should be a cardinal aim of Irish foreign policy to strengthen those ties, and avoid unnecessary actions which give offense to our friends abroad'. Instead, according to Fine Gael, the government, by attempting to secure neutralist support, was 'playing politics in the United Nations'.

---

167 Aiken, again exhibiting an unrealistic streak, suggested that in light of the United States' refusal to fight an all-out war against China during the Korean War and the Soviet Union's possession of nuclear weapons, American forces in Korea were superfluous and were 'driving China into the arms of Russia'. They were also making Japan too dependent on America for its own defense.

168 *Irish Times*, 9 October 1957.

The lack of a thorough public review of Ireland's UN policy had irritated Fine Gael. In its press release the party unfavorably compared Aiken's sparse July 1957 Dáil statement with Cosgrave's comprehensive speech the year before. Due to Fianna Fáil's reticence, Fine Gael regarded 'the present government as failing in its duty to the Dáil'. This left the opposition party with only one option: on 28 November Fine Gael initiated its own parliamentary debate by introducing a motion declaring 'That Dáil Éireann disapproves of recent developments in the foreign policy of the government as represented by certain statements and actions of the Minister for External Affairs at recent meetings of the General Assembly of the United Nations Organization.'[169]

The motion was soundly defeated, but in a vigorous debate Fine Gael did force Fianna Fáil to account for its UN stance.[170] In the face of withering criticism, Aiken defended his troop disengagement proposal by repeating the same arguments he had made to the UN Assembly, the press, and to Scott McLeod. He also justified it by referring to recent calls for a reappraisal of American security policy in Europe by Dean Acheson, Harry Truman's Secretary of State, and George Kennan, the American diplomat, scholar, and father of 'containment'.[171]

Irritated by Fine Gael propaganda that had completely distorted his position – during a recent by-election they had circulated a partisan pamphlet containing a letter from an Irish missionary in Asia and their own press release – Aiken forcefully defended his China vote. A 'matter of such importance should be discussed', especially when it was 'so intimately and dangerously connected with world peace' and, as Liam Cosgrave pointed out to the Eleventh Assembly, 'affects the lives of about a quarter of the world's population'. Ultimately, Aiken was unfazed by the opposition's criticism. He told the Dáil that it was inconsistent with Irish interests 'to stand silently and not offer our opinion truthfully and honestly on certain matters', and his was 'the right approach for this nation to adopt to the troubles that bedevil the world'.

DECOLONIZATION

Frank Aiken's new, energetic posture naturally animated his support for decolonization in Africa and Asia, an interest that Fianna Fáil shared, in principle, with the Inter-Party government. Aiken was more impassioned than his predecessors, however. This was not only characteristic of the man, it stemmed

---

169 DD 164, 1168, 28 November 1957.
170 DD 164, 1168–1259, 1290–1306, 28 November 1957.
171 Aiken referred specifically to Kennan's recent series of Reith Lectures at Oxford University, wherein he called for the reunification of Germany; its withdrawal from NATO; American and Soviet military evacuation from central Europe; and this region's transformation into a denuclearized zone: Hixson, *George F. Kennan*, pp. 174–80.

from his intimate role in Ireland's independence struggle: as he once reminded the Assembly, the Irish 'know what imperialism is and what resistance to
it involves'.[172] Simultaneously, Aiken's decolonization strategy complemented
his overriding foreign policy goal: the relaxation of international tensions. He
not only mediated colonial conflicts, but he opposed the inexorable transformation of Africa and Asia into Cold War battlefields. He challenged the great
powers 'to halt their present acute diplomatic competition' in the southern
hemisphere and to cooperate on joint reconstruction efforts instead.[173]

Like many others, Aiken believed that the United Nations had a central
role to play in decolonization: it was 'an agent for the liquidation of imperialism in all parts of the world'.[174] Self-determination, he posited, should be 'the
great master principle' guiding the Assembly 'in its quest for a just and
peaceful world order'.[175] Perhaps going too far, Aiken even called for the UN
to underwrite 'the cost of the practical steps necessary to assist the withdrawal
of the occupying powers ... and to assist the newly enfranchised peoples to
meet the responsibilities of freedom'.

In another departure from the Inter-Party government, Fianna Fáil backed
its rhetoric by frequently supporting the Afro-Asian bloc on the substantive
question of voting, even if this sometimes irked Ireland's European allies.
The delegation thus evolved into a widely-recognized champion of decolonization, which enhanced its contribution to the Assembly's fire brigade and
bolstered its limited influence with the Afro-Asians. Still, Ireland continued
to advocate a gradual transition to self-rule wherever appropriate. Aiken
counseled certain nations 'to be patient until [independence] arrives ... and to
act forgivingly and generously thereafter'. (Yet he had repudiated the first
part of this argument out of hand when fighting for Irish statehood!) As well,
the delegation continued to reject the extremism of the Afro-Asian bloc and
was not adverse to modifying its vote when its own interests were at stake.

ALGERIA

Despite the Eleventh Assembly's resolution expressing the hope that a 'peaceful, democratic, and just solution' could be found to the conflict in Algeria,
no such outcome was in sight as the Twelfth Session neared. Instead, the
French government's intransigence had sparked an upsurge of violence in the
territory, which led, in turn, to even stronger pacification measures. The government did introduce the *loi-cadre*, a new legal framework redefining the
relationship between France and Algeria, but it fell far short of the independence movement's demands.

172 Aiken, *Ireland* (1960), p. 13.
173 Aiken, *Ireland* (1957), pp. 21–4.
174 Aiken, *Ireland* (1960), p. 16.
175 Aiken, *Ireland* (1957), pp. 21–4.

This hopeless scenario guaranteed that the Afro-Asians would press the issue at the UN in the autumn of 1957. Iveagh House tracked the unfolding events throughout the summer months. Aiken and Conor O'Brien soon grasped that for the Afro-Asian bloc Algeria (like China) was another test of a delegation's *bona fides*. This question also challenged their principles. Subsequently, they disappointed neither the Afro-Asians, nor themselves.

The starting point for Ireland's policy was a memorandum Aiken completed in mid-July entitled 'A Suggested Approach to an Algerian Settlement'.[176] This over-enthusiastic plan, indicative of Aiken's penchant for nominating the UN as a disinterested international intermediary, comprised five main points. All Algerians were 'to be guaranteed freedom of religion and education'. Arabic and French were 'to be recognized as official languages'. For fifty years, the United Nations would oversee the compensation of minorities (read French) who opted to exit Algeria. Likewise, a UN police force would guarantee their rights. Finally, the French government would 'be compensated for fixed assets' out of Algerian or UN funds; if France and Algeria could not reach an agreement, an international arbitrator would determine the amount.

Building on Aiken's sketch, O'Brien developed his own strategy for ending the Franco-Algerian War; he discussed both formulae with Freddy Boland when the latter returned to Dublin in early August.[177] O'Brien observed that 'Points one, two, three, and five of the Minister's memorandum gave a clear outline of the sort of concrete solution' that might resolve the conflict. The more pressing challenge was determining 'the auspices under which such a solution can be reached': French authority, negotiations, or internationalization.

After dismissing the first two options, O'Brien concluded 'that a solution can be reached only under international auspices'; this was truly his own judgment, but Aiken was sure to be sympathetic since it epitomized his thinking. The French, O'Brien admitted, were unprepared for internationalization at present, but he still felt they would 'be obliged at some time, and perhaps within the next two years or so, to accept a solution on these lines'. He then suggested that such an initiative should be sponsored 'by those countries who, like ourselves, can do so in moderate terms, without acrimony and without any suspicion of our having an ax to grind'. Hence, he outlined a multi-point plan that incorporated his own ideas, elements from Aiken's scheme, and Boland's call for free elections at the Eleventh Session.[178] He correctly noted that there 'was no question of imposing a solution on France'. Nonetheless, he thought that his plan should be presented in a 'friendly'

176 DFA PMUN X/65, 12 July 1957.
177 Ibid., 21 August 1957.
178 O'Brien's plan included a cease-fire called by the General Assembly; elections for an Algerian Assembly guaranteed by the UN; a UN Commission to supervise the 'handing over of civil authority' by France to an executive elected by the Algerian Assembly'; a UN peacekeeping force; the 'resettlement and compensation' of those forced to move within Algeria, those who opted to leave, and the compensation due the French government.

manner, emphasizing 'that we do so as much in the interests of France as in those of Algeria'.

It was unlikely – based on his reaction to the inclusion of concrete proposals in Aiken's troop disengagement proposal and his assertion that the Assembly's limited role was to lay down general principles – that Boland was enthusiastic about O'Brien's scheme. There is no doubt that William Fay, Ireland's envoy in Paris, opposed it. In late July O'Brien had sent copies of Aiken's memorandum and his own plan to Fay, who responded to them one month later after returning from leave. He admitted that Aiken's design was 'carefully thought out', but it was 'obviously intended to deal with a case which has not yet arisen' and was unlikely 'within the foreseeable future', namely, French readiness to withdraw from Algeria.[179] Fay doubted the efficacy of O'Brien's 'proposals for an internationalization of the question' on grounds that O'Brien himself had raised: 'there is no question of the United Nations imposing a solution on France'. More so, O'Brien had overlooked 'the vicious character of the FLN guerrilla campaign' and had not taken into account the pending announcement of the *loi-cadre*.

In a friendly, early-September rejoinder O'Brien defended his stand. He appreciated 'the force' of Fay's comments, but while agreeing with the Ambassador's contention that no solution could be imposed on France, he asserted that 'French opinion is nonetheless sensitive to the views of the Assembly; otherwise, they would hardly be making such strong efforts to influence individual members.'[180] He dismissed the *loi-cadre* because, like so many others, he could not 'take it as a seriously meant effort at a solution'; it was simply a delaying tactic. O'Brien also apprised Fay of a recent conversation between Jacques de Blesson, the French Ambassador in Dublin, and Aiken. De Blesson had 'propounded the well-known French thesis' that Algeria was an integral part of France. Aiken, who had been devoting a great deal of attention to the subject, disagreed. He contended that 'elections in Algeria, when they come, should be for a negotiating Assembly, in respect of which conditions should not be laid down in advance'; he stressed that de Valera held this same view.[181] Plus, 'Arrangements, or as they are called *statutes lois-cadres*, which begin by declaring that Algeria is and must remain an integral part of France, are doomed to be still born.' In conclusion, Aiken said, Ireland's 'interventions and our votes on the problem at the UN will be based on that general principle'.

* * *

179 DFA 440/11, 29 August 1957. Fay sent several reports to the Department of External Affairs at this time regarding the Algerian crisis which, while basically factual in nature, were, like his letter to O'Brien, pro-French in tone: DFA 440/11, 25 July 1957, 14 September 1957, 25 September 1957; DFA 417/167, 30 August 1957.
180 DFA 440/11, 5 September 1957.
181 DFA 417/167, 26 August 1957.

Aiken was true to his word. The forthright comments devoted to Algeria in his General Debate speech reflected the principles set forth during his conversation with de Blesson.[182] Boland's emphasis on internationally-supervised elections and O'Brien's desire to internationalize the issue also informed Aiken's remarks. So did Ireland's traditional friendship with France.

The French, though, ignored this last point. Instead, Aiken's call for France to concede 'absolutely and unequivocally ... the right of self-determination to Algeria at the earliest practicable date to be fixed in agreement with' the UN had dismayed them. William Fay notified the Permanent Mission in New York of the Parisian newspaper *Figaro*'s erroneous report that Aiken had 'followed his own inspiration despite advice [from] his delegation and without consulting his government'.[183] The paper regarded his proposals as 'utopian'. On Aiken's instructions, the Mission immediately requested Fay to 'Please call personally on the editor of *Figaro*' and inform him that their 'statement [was] completely unfounded': Aiken's address represented 'Irish government policy'.[184] The Mission also told Fay to ask the paper to 'publish [a] correction', and cable the results to New York. Three days later Fay informed the Irish delegation that the matter was settled; he had been 'Received most courteously ... by [the] chief protocol editor, who promised [to] publish [a] correction immediately.'[185]

One week after Aiken's address Fay reported a diplomatic slight to Murphy that he attributed to French displeasure over Aiken's speech. 'Far more serious' than the passage in *Figaro* was what he described 'as a "social" reaction'.[186] At the last minute the French *Sous-Secrétaire d'État à la Marine Marchande*, M. Fiagianelli, had canceled luncheon and dinner appointments with Erskine Childers, his counterpart in the Irish government, who was visiting Europe. Fay, who had been 'incensed', ascertained through confidential sources that 'it was not considered appropriate that a member of the French government should visit the Irish Embassy just now in view of our Minister's speech respecting Algeria'. Nevertheless, in the light of a second luncheon invitation extended to Childers upon his return to Paris, Fay concluded that the French authorities were placing 'the emphasis on the time and place', and it was more or less 'a case of allowing things to blow over'. The incident was not '*au grand tragique*', but at the same time 'it would be perhaps a mistake to underestimate its significance', which should be 'borne in mind in arriving at the line we may ultimately adopt in the debate on Algeria'.

182 Aiken, *Ireland* (1957), pp. 24–7. In early September O'Brien completed a second draft of this speech equal in principle and form to the final version: DFA 417/167, 4 September 1957.
183 DFA PMUN X/65, 21 September 1957.
184 Ibid., 22 September 1957.
185 Ibid., 25 September 1957.
186 DFA 440/11, 27 September 1957.

Aiken was unshaken by criticism of his proposals from French or any other sources. Scott McLeod raised the issue when he called on Aiken and de Valera in early October. He said that the United States government was prepared to back 'a more vigorous resolution than last year's ... urging France to make peace', but that was as far as the UN should go. Aiken was unsympathetic to this view. He recounted how he had told the French that by their 'unrealistic' policy 'they were doing a great disservice to western civilization by denying self-determination to Algeria, which would have to be ceded sooner or later'. He claimed that many Frenchmen concurred with 'the criticisms I had voiced', and it was vital to air them 'where they would be heard by the French people, whose support would be necessary to enable the French government to change its line'.

Iveagh House, conversely, was not wholly insensitive to French concerns. Acting on the instructions of his government, Jacques de Blesson called on Murphy on 18 November to dissuade the Irish government from supporting a Tunisian initiative underfoot at the UN to convene a multi-party conference on Algeria attended by France, Morocco, Tunisia, and the FLN.[187] De Blesson, believing that the Tunisians wanted to work this concept 'into the resolution on Algeria', emphasized that France could not accept the FLN 'as representatives of Algeria'. Acceding to de Blesson's entreaty, Murphy instructed the delegation to 'Make no commitments on [the] Algerian question.'[188]

* * *

In his wire Murphy also advised Boland to 'Use your judgment' about speaking when the Algerian question came up for discussion.[189] Shortly thereafter Boland explained to Murphy that 'Even before we received your telegram ... our feeling was against intervening in the Algerian debate in the First Committee unless something very special arose to make that course advisable.'[190] The delegation had concluded 'that the Minister had dealt with this subject so fully in his speech in the General Debate that there was really nothing that we could usefully add' when the topic arose in the Committee. Still adhering to his original interpretation, Boland noted that the sentiment was growing 'that the primary aim as regards Algeria ... should be to try to secure the holding of elections under outside supervision'. The FLN's claim 'to be the exclusive representatives of Algerian national sentiment in the absence of elections investing them with that capacity' was untenable.

The Afro-Asian bloc, of course, did not concur with Boland's moderate approach. In early December their representatives introduced into the First Committee a draft resolution asserting in the preamble 'that the principle of

187 Ibid., 18 November 1957.
188 DFA PMUN X/65, 18 November 1957.
189 Ibid.
190 DFA 440/11, 20 November 1957.

self-determination is applicable to the Algerian people' and containing an operative clause calling for 'negotiations for the purpose of arriving at a solution in accordance with the principles and purposes of the Charter of the United Nations'.[191]

To break an ensuing deadlock between the Afro-Asians and the west, the fire brigade swung into action; Ireland, Canada, and Norway proposed two amendments to the original draft.[192] The first substituted the reference to the principle of self-determination with a toned-down phrase recognizing 'that the people of Algeria are entitled to work out their future in a democratic way'; the second replaced the original operative clause with one proposing 'effective discussions for the purpose both of resolving the present troubled situation and of reaching a solution in accordance with the purposes and principles of the Charter of the United Nations'.

At the request of the Canadian and Norwegian delegations, Boland overcame his reluctance to intervene in the debate. He explained that the amendments were intended 'to make the draft resolution a somewhat more faithful and accurate reflection of the general sense' of the debate and 'the different shades of opinion which have been expressed during it' so that the Committee could 'arrive at something which will command the widest possible measure of acceptance ... if not unanimity'.[193] To those Afro-Asian delegations disappointed by the omission of the magical phrase 'self-determination' (a move intended to ameliorate western opinion) Boland said that the amended resolution still asserted 'the just right of the people of Algeria to work out their political future ... by democratic means', which implied the election of a representative Assembly. Once that position had been 'achieved the question of the future of Algeria will be immeasurably nearer to a solution'. The second amendment, replacing the phrases 'Calls for' and 'negotiations' with 'Proposes' and 'discussions', was 'mainly of a drafting character' meant to reflect more accurately 'the character and the limits of our role in connection with this matter'. Reiterating his favorite line, Boland said that the Assembly was 'not a compulsive power'; its function was 'to express the moral conscience of our peoples and the moral conscience of the world'. Therefore, the more 'accurate the language we use is attuned to the precise nature of the competence we possess, the more effective and the more authoritative our conclusions will be'.

The Committee approved the amendments 37 to 36 in two separate votes.[194] Due to Afro-Asian dissatisfaction, the vote on the amended resolution ended in a tie (37 to 37, with 6 abstentions) and the motion therefore failed. On 10 December, however, the Assembly unanimously adopted a 15-power (including Ireland) compromise resolution.[195] The fire brigade had

191 Ibid. (nd).
192 Ibid., 6 December 1957.
193 Ibid.
194 *Irish Press*, 7 December 1957.
195 GA/RES 1184 (XII).

finally accomplished its goal. The anodyne motion expressed 'concern over the situation in Algeria', took note of the offer of 'good offices' by the President of the Republic of Tunisia and the King of Morocco, and expressed the desire that '*pourparlés* will be entered into, and other appropriate means utilized, with a view to a solution, in conformity with the purpose and principles of the Charter of the United Nations'.

The results pleased the French, who had successfully avoided a strong rebuke. Christian Pineau, the French Foreign Minister, described the outcome as 'very satisfactory, and said that France would willingly engage in talks aimed at a cease-fire in Algeria'.[196] In late December John Belton informed Boland, at Aiken's behest, that Jacques de Blesson had recently conveyed 'to the Irish government the thanks of the French government for the attitude taken by the Permanent Delegation of Ireland to the United Nations in the matter of Algeria'.[197]

The indignation in Paris, provoked by Aiken's September remarks, had obviously eased. A March 1958 exchange between Eoin MacWhite, First Secretary in the Political Section, and Boland partially explains why and further illumines Boland's stand on the Algerian conflict. In the January 1958 issue of a minor information bulletin published by the Japanese Embassy in the Hague, a review of the Algerian debate at the UN claimed that Ireland, Canada, and Norway had 'proposed an amendment weakening the expression' of the Afro-Asian bloc's call for self-determination in their draft resolution.[198] After the passage was brought to his attention Dr MacWhite forwarded a copy of it to Boland, calling it 'a rather biased reference'.[199]

Boland was not at all bothered. He told MacWhite that the remark was not 'too biased. As a comment it is fair enough.'[200] More important, he explained that since the end of the Twelfth Assembly the feeling had grown at the UN 'that the Afro-Asian group made one of its biggest tactical blunders in voting against the amendments' and the amended motion in the First Committee because doing so prevented 'the otherwise certain adoption of a resolution asserting the right of the people of Algeria to work out their political future by democratic means'. The adoption of a resolution on these terms 'would have undermined the entire French position and would have attacked at its

---

196 *Irish Independent*, 11 December 1957.
197 DFA PMUN X/65, 31 December 1957.
198 Ibid., 1 January 1958.
199 DFA 440/11, 3 March 1957. Máire MacEntee, who passed the Japanese comment on to Dr MacWhite, suggested to him that 'it might be no harm if the [Irish] Legation in the Hague wrote to them, politely pointing out that it is biased and inaccurate. If they are making a bid for the leadership of the non-committed they shouldn't be allowed to get away with belittling our disinterested efforts to bring about a compromise of some real value': DFA 440/11, 6 February 1957. This suggestion was not followed up.
200 DFA 440/11, 3 March 1958.

root the basic principle of the *loi-cadre*' – that Algeria 'is an integral part of France and that the people of Algeria must work out their political future as part of the French nation as a whole'.

Concurrently, Boland averred that the bulletin erred 'in giving the Japanese Ambassador credit for drawing up the feeble compromise resolution on which agreement was eventually reached'. The Irish delegation had been intimately involved 'with these final discussions, and my recollection is that the part played by the Japanese representative in connection with them was relatively minor'.

The foregoing draws attention to the nuances of Boland's approach to the Algerian crisis. He supported, in principle, the right of the Algerian people to self-determination. He had clearly demonstrated this in his remarks to MacWhite above, his words before the First Committee explaining the amendments to the Afro-Asian draft resolution, and his correspondence with Conor O'Brien in the spring of 1957. Simultaneously, he rejected out of hand the extremist demands of the FLN and the Afro-Asian bloc; instead, he favored a moderate, balanced solution based on free elections and the dis-avowal of force.

This latter aspect of Boland's position had impressed the French. In par-ticular, they appreciated his support for the three-power compromise amend-ments diluting the Afro-Asian bloc's call for the recognition of the Algeria's right to self-determination and his prominent role in hammering out the ano-dyne compromise resolution that posed no threat to French interests. They interpreted his actions as pro-French (while overlooking his support for self-rule in Algeria); de Blesson had highlighted this view in late December. Boland was not as sympathetic to the French as they imagined, but neither was he as enthusiastic as Aiken and O'Brien for an immediate settlement granting inde-pendence to Algeria. The situation on the ground was too volatile, and many questions vital to the peaceful transfer of power and the country's future remained unanswered. It was likely, therefore, that Boland distanced himself from the over-optimistic, hurried proposals of Aiken and O'Brien during the private diplomatic maneuverings that produced a compromise resolution. Perhaps this explains why, in a departure from his standard practice, Boland did not send a comprehensive report to Dublin outlining his role in drawing up the final motion. His only reference to the vital part he played in resolv-ing this crucial issue was prompted by the passage in the Japanese bulletin, which was brought to his attention several months after the fact.

THE RIGHT TO SELF-DETERMINATION

Consistent with its support for Algerian independence and its more robust response to colonialism, the Irish delegation backed an Afro-Asian effort in the Third Committee to secure the passage of a conceptual motion entitled

'Recommendations Concerning International Respect for the Right of Peoples and Nations to Self-Determination'. Máire MacEntee, who represented Ireland on the Third Committee (which dealt with economic and social issues under the auspices of ECOSOC) limned Ireland's handling of the question in an early December minute to Eoin MacWhite.[201] A few weeks earlier, while Aiken was in New York, the delegation had decided that MacEntee should speak in the debate and elaborate upon two main points: the insufficient amount of time allotted to this item by the Committee; and, a reference 'to the Minister's own statement in the General Debate to the effect that self-determination should be regarded as the great master principle of the Assembly'.

Before the Committee took up the question the American delegation convened a meeting of potential cosponsors of a measure they had drafted; Ireland, Canada, Italy, Belgium, Sweden, Denmark, Austria, and the United States attended. The motion, regarded as no more than a shelving tactic, established an *ad hoc* committee to study the concept of self-determination and report back to ECOSOC and the General Assembly at a later date. 'Because of the political implications of the whole subject', according to MacEntee's report, Conor O'Brien attended the meeting on behalf of the Irish delegation. He said that 'while the American resolution was entirely acceptable to us on the face of it ... we were, unlike the other countries present, a country with a direct interest' in the matter. Consequently, Ireland did not want 'to be associated with any move which might be regarded as wishing to postpone' a debate. Instead, the Irish delegation supported an Afro-Asian resolution establishing a Good Offices Commission to examine alleged violations of self-determination brought to its attention by any ten members of the UN.

O'Brien's remarks came 'as quite a shock to the other members of the group'; Ireland, after all, had supported a similar American move at the Eleventh Session.[202] The Belgian representative, speaking for the colonial countries, regarded even the US resolution as the lesser of two evils and preferred an inconclusive debate. The Canadian delegate alleged that because the issue lay outside the jurisdiction of the Third Committee it should be dismissed. As a result of these divergent views, the United States could not secure cosponsors for its resolution and dropped it.

During the Third Committee's deliberations Afghanistan, Panama, the Philippines, Saudi Arabia, and Uruguay introduced a compromise resolution; later, both the Committee and the Assembly adopted it.[203] The motion

201 DFA 417/96/II, 2 December 1957.
202 When the item was being discussed at the Eleventh General Assembly the United States delegation suggested a resolution establishing an ad hoc committee but, as intended, the whole issue was later dropped. Boland said in report to Murphy at the time that 'We here are strongly of the view that we should support the US proposal and, indeed, we have begun preliminary steps towards trying to secure that Ireland would be one of the members of the Committee of 5 which the American resolution proposes to set up': DFA 417/96/I, 24 January 1957.
203 DFA 417/96/II, 2 December 1957; GA/RES 1188 (XII).

reaffirmed 'that it is of international importance that, in accordance with the purposes and principles' of the UN Charter, Member States 'shall, in their relations with one another, give due respect to the right of self-determination'; declared that Member States with 'responsibility for the administration of Non-Self-Governing Territories shall promote the realization and facilitate the exercise of this right by the peoples of such territories'; and, called on the Assembly to 'consider further at its Thirteenth Session the item "Recommendations Concerning International Respect for the Rights of Peoples and Nations to Self-determination"'.

On 2 December Máire MacEntee addressed the Third Committee along the lines set out while Aiken was in New York.[204] She also rejected the argument that the Third Committee was incompetent to discuss the item and closed with a nod to the positive aspects of the American and Afro-Asian proposals that had been floating around the corridors. O'Brien had suggested this last comment because he wanted to 'sound out possible reactions to a proposal which we might consider putting forward next year' combining the Afro-Asian 'Good Offices' and the American *ad hoc* resolutions.[205]

FRENCH TOGOLAND

Two of the parameters that governed Ireland's decolonization policy – self-determination and proven readiness for self-rule – inspired its response to a less-visible issue that arose once more in the Fourth Committee: the future of French Togoland. The UN Commission established to assess the territory's readiness for self-government (by the Eleventh Assembly) had issued its report. It found that great progress toward self-government had been made in Togoland, but it recommended that the Togolese vote once more for either association with France or complete independence.[206] It thus implicitly confirmed the validity of the complaints leveled by several African nations against France's supervision of a plebiscite the previous year that supposedly sanctioned a form of association – 'autonomous rule' within the French Union.

In mid November Ireland, Canada, Columbia, Denmark, and Liberia (the fire brigade) cosponsored a resolution on Togoland that the French authorities had promised to abide by.[207] Its operative section comprised three parts: all powers except defense, foreign affairs, and currency would be transferred to the Togolese government by 1958; UN-supervised elections for a Togolese Legislative Assembly would be held in 1958; the newly-elected Assembly would then decide the territory's status and transmit its decision to the Trusteeship Council, which would report to the Thirteenth Assembly.

204 DFA 417/167/8, 2 December 1957.
205 DFA 417/96/II, 2 December 1957.
206 DFA PMUN X/3 (nd).
207 Ibid., 18 November 1957.

On 19 November Eamon Kennedy explained to the Committee why Ireland backed the motion.[208] From 'the point of view of the self-determination of the Togolese people', it validated their 'freely expressed will'. The preamble echoed Ireland's 'profound conviction of the importance of good self-government as a condition precedent to eventual independence'. And, the measure recognized 'what we have often described in the past as *la présence française*', which was 'not a matter of colonial dominion or commercial exploitation, but of intellectual and moral leadership, which generations of her gifted sons have earned for the great French nation'.

The Fourth Committee adopted the resolution by the overwhelming majority of 50 to 0, with 26 abstentions.[209] The Assembly carried it by a vote of 50 to 1, with 29 abstentions.[210] Ghana opposed it; the Soviet and Arab blocs abstained. Gerard Jaquet, the Minister for Overseas France, welcomed Ireland's sponsorship of the motion and the work of Eamon Kennedy, who had 'played an active and influential role in steering it through the Committee'.[211] Freddy Boland, still sensitive to the changes in Ireland's policy, noted that 'French appreciation of our action in connection with this matter may perhaps serve to some extent to assuage their feelings about our attitude on Algeria.'

In mid-December an interesting development transpired that confirmed the Irish delegation's contribution to the Twelfth Assembly's proceedings and portended the future leadership roles Irish representatives would assume at the UN. On 10 December Boland sent a telegram to Aiken informing him that Denmark and Canada had just asked him to lead the UN Commission charged with monitoring the Togolese elections.[212] Boland, who was not thrilled with the idea because of his lack of experience in the tropics, the shortage of staff at the Irish Permanent Mission, and his claim that a 'different' type of man was needed (which was untrue) sought Aiken's opinion. The Minister concurred, and Boland declined the offer.[213] After a stalemate developed between candidates from Costa Rica and Chile, Denmark and Canada asked Boland if he would stand as a compromise candidate, but he refused a second time.[214] Max Dorsinville of Haiti was finally selected for the job, but future posts awaited Boland.

208 DFA 417/167/9, 19 November 1957.
209 DFA PMUN X/3, 2 December 1957.
210 GA/RES 1182 (XII).
211 DFA PMUN X/3, 23 November, 2 December 1957.
212 Ibid., 10 December 1957.
213 Ibid.
214 Ibid., 3 January 1958.

PORTUGUESE GOA

At the Twelfth Assembly the Irish delegation originally planned to reverse its policy of the previous year and support Afro-Asian demands that Portugal comply with Article 73.e of the Charter by submitting information concerning its Non-Self-Governing Territories (especially Goa) to the Trusteeship Council. Economic considerations, however, tempered this aim, and Ireland ultimately abstained on the issue. Still, by not backing Portugal outright the delegation maintained its standing with the Afro-Asian bloc.

Shortly before leaving for New York in early September, Conor O'Brien mentioned to Sheila Murphy, Counsellor in the Political Section, that Aiken had 'decided that the delegation should not support Portugal at this session on the Goa issue'.[215] Murphy immediately reminded O'Brien that the government had, for several months, 'been negotiating with the Portuguese about the abolition of discrimination against the Irish flag in continental Portugal, a matter that is of considerable interest to Irish Shipping, Ltd'. John Belton recounted this exchange in a mid-September dispatch to Boland and then drew Boland's attention to an attached memorandum showing 'that agreement in principle has now been reached with the Portuguese, but it may be some little time before the necessary exchange of [official] Notes can be completed'. He asked Boland 'to bring the matter to the Minister's attention' and assured him that 'We will, of course, keep you informed of developments at this end.'

The enclosed Department of External Affairs memorandum was entitled 'Trade Agreement with Portugal.'[216] It noted that in 1932 Portugal had ended discrimination against the Irish flag in its colonies, but not in continental Portugal. Recently, overtures made by the Irish Chargé d'Affaires in Lisbon on behalf of Irish Shipping, Ltd. had 'led to an offer from the Portuguese authorities to abolish such discriminations ... ' The Portuguese government had extended its offer through 'the Portuguese Chargé d'Affaires in Dublin, who expressed the view that it may have been inspired by our favorable vote [at the Eleventh Assembly] (obviously a reference to the "Goa" issue)'.

In late October, with the Fourth Committee about to take up the Goa question, Iveagh House instructed the Permanent Mission in New York to 'Abstain on Goa' and 'Vote without explaining.'[217] The Department issued these directions ostensibly because the 'Taoiseach thinks we do not know enough as to [the] actual situation to vote.' This explanation was disingenuous, of course. De Valera wanted neither to offend Portugal in the midst of sensitive trade negotiations nor undermine Ireland's reputation with the Afro-Asian bloc.

In early November the Afro-Asian group introduced a resolution into the Committee. To garner wider support its operative section – unlike the draft

215 DFA PMUN X/17, 16 September 1957.
216 Ibid., 1 September 1957.
217 DFA 305/271/1/1A, 23 October 1957.

at the Eleventh Assembly – did not single out Portugal by referring to 'new members'. It invited the Secretary General to prepare a summary of the opinions of Member States concerning Article 73.e of the Charter and proposed that a committee study the Secretary General's summary and report to the next ordinary session of the Assembly.[218] In addition to the Afro-Asians, the Arab states, the communist bloc, and a few Latin American countries planned to vote for the motion; all of western Europe (except for Greece), the United States, the old Commonwealth, and certain Latin American delegations intended to oppose it.[219] In a cable to Aiken on the morning of 5 November Boland said that the resolution resembled the one 'adopted by [a] small majority of [the] Fourth Committee [at the] last Assembly, but which did not obtain [the] necessary two-thirds majority in [the] General Assembly itself'.[220] He presumed, in the light of earlier communications, that the delegation 'should abstain' on the upcoming vote. He was correct; Aiken immediately sent Boland a wire instructing him to do so.[221]

Later that day the Fourth Committee approved the draft by a tally of 47 to 27, with 8 abstentions, including Ireland.[222] 'Like most other countries', and contrary to de Valera's wishes, Eamon Kennedy spoke briefly before the Committee. He later explained that:

> In view of the fact that the delegation's vote was vigorously canvassed by Portugal, Britain, and some members of the old Commonwealth on the one hand, and by India, Ceylon, Yugoslavia, Mexico, and Guatemala, on the other, we felt it absolutely essential to say a few words in explication of our abstention as compared with our opposition at the previous General Assembly.[223]

In tandem with this resolution the Fourth Committee passed a second Afro-Asian-sponsored motion owing to the fact that at the Eleventh Session the corresponding 'Transmission of Information From Non-Self-Governing Territories' resolution failed in the Assembly because, after being deemed an 'important' issue on a procedural vote, it did not receive the two-thirds majority 'important' questions required. This supplementary measure requested the

---

218 Ibid., 4 November 1957.
219 Ibid. (nd).
220 Ibid., 5 November 1957.
221 Ibid. Aiken's instructions to Boland reflected an informal decision taken earlier that day by the government that 'the Irish delegation should refrain from taking sides in any discussion of the dispute between Portugal and India concerning Goa that may arise in the course of the current session of the General Assembly of the United Nations': S 15741/A, 5 November 1957.
222 DFA 305/271/1/1A, 5 November 1957.
223 Ibid. (nd).

Sixth (Legal) Committee to determine if this question was an 'important' one and report its decision to the Assembly the following year.[224]

Meanwhile, the Afro-Asian bloc intended to exercise their right under the Charter, as they had unsuccessfully done the year before, to press a vote in the Assembly on whether the 'Transmission of Information from Non-Self-Governing Territories' was an 'important' matter. In a report on this convoluted, but essential, question Kennedy recommended to Sean Murphy that the delegation 'abstain on the vote as to whether a two-thirds majority is necessary in line with our previous abstentions in the Fourth Committee on votes relating' to this issue.[225] If Murphy did not agree with that suggestion, the next best alternative was 'to vote in favor of the two-thirds majority as we did in the last Assembly, and add an *explication de vote*' stating that Ireland did not wish to alter its position until the Sixth Committee had completed its legal review.

While Kennedy awaited instructions, the Portuguese canvassed hard for a sympathetic Irish vote on the procedural question. Their UN Ambassador 'made the most urgent and pressing representations' to the delegation.[226] On 9 November Amilcar Franco, the Portuguese Chargé d'Affaires in Dublin, sent a letter to Aiken along the same lines.[227] Nevertheless, two days later Aiken instructed Boland to 'Continue to abstain on [the] Goa issue.'[228] He reiterated these directions even after Franco personally called on Murphy the next day.[229]

Franco breathed a sigh of relief, however, when the Assembly decided that the 'Transmission of Information from Non-Self-Governing Territories' was an 'important' question; the final count, taken on 26 November, was 38 to 36, with 7 abstentions.[230] The subsequent vote on the Afro-Asian motion fell short of the necessary two-thirds margin. Ireland abstained on both ballots. The United States voted with Portugal; the Soviet Union with the Afro-Asian bloc.

224 DFA 417/167 (nd).
225 DFA 305/271/1/1A, 7 November 1957.
226 Ibid.
227 Ibid., 9 November 1957.
228 Ibid., 11 November 1957.
229 Ibid., 12 November 1957. Although Aiken would not change his vote, he was sensitive to the positions other delegations were taking. He requested from the Irish delegation 'an analysis of the reasons given by member countries who changed their vote in the Fourth Committee of the present Assembly as compared with the Fourth Committee of the previous Assembly'. Eamon Kennedy, who carried out the task, reported that 'It will be observed that the main trend of the voting in the Fourth Committee in this Assembly as compared with the last Assembly is away from opposition to the motion, i.e., a weakening of support for the position taken up by Portugal.' Kennedy attributed this to the fact that the current resolution was milder and more reasonable than the previous one and to growing impatience with Portugal's refusal to comply with provisions of Article 73.e: DFA PMUN X/17, 13 November 1957.
230 DFA PMUN X/17, 26 November 1957.

Portugal did not appreciate Ireland's stand. A few weeks after the vote Michael Rynne, the Irish Ambassador in Madrid, recounted how the Portuguese Ambassador to Spain had told him that Ireland was moving too close to the Afro-Asian bloc.[231] In September 1958, just before the Thirteenth General Assembly opened, Mr T.V. Commins, the Chargé d'Affaires at the Irish Mission in Lisbon, sent a summary of his recent meeting with Dr Caldiera Queiroz, the Secretary General of the Portuguese Ministry of Foreign Affairs, to Con Cremin, who had been named Secretary of the Department of External Affairs in January 1958 upon the retirement of Sean Murphy.[232] The Portuguese official recalled for Commins 'the great disappointment caused here by our vote last year' on the Goa issue.[233] He lamented that Ireland was, 'with the exception of Greece (which had voted against the Portuguese) ... the only western country to indicate, by our abstention, lack of support for Portugal in this vital matter'. This attitude, he said, 'seemed to be out of harmony both with the traditional relations of friendship between Portugal and Ireland and with a proper interpretation of the Charter'.

The Afro-Asian bloc, on the other hand, welcomed Ireland's new posture. In November 1957 an editorial in *Africa Weekly*, a publication devoted to UN affairs, recalled that on the Goa issue:

> Last year Ireland voted with the United States. This year she is abstaining. It may only be a straw in the wind, but it shows which way it is blowing. But then Ireland knows what colonialism is about – which may be one good reason for her positive and constructive approach to African affairs at the UN.[234]

WEST IRIAN

Ireland alienated Portugal by shifting gears on Goa, but it continued to back the Netherlands, another European ally, and Australia, an old Commonwealth member, on the question of West Irian, despite entreaties from Indonesia, a leading member of the Afro-Asian bloc. The Irish delegation's commitment to self-determination underpinned its stand on this issue. This was ironic, since this same principle inspired its overall decolonization policy, which so appealed to the Afro-Asians. Other factors also influenced Ireland's position: a similar vote at the Eleventh Assembly; its judgment that the native population of West Irian was not prepared for self-government; antipathy to proposals hinting at partition; discomfort with the extremist elements of the Afro-Asian bloc; and, sympathy for Australia's security interests.

231 DFA 305/271/1/1A, 9 December 1957.
232 GC 3/23, 29 November 1957.
233 DFA 305/271/1/1A, 6 September 1957.
234 *Africa Weekly*, 11 November 1957.

An autumn-1956 External Affairs memorandum laid out the background to the case.[235] West Irian (or West New Guinea), under Dutch rule since 1816, comprised the western part of the island of New Guinea. It was 'generally backward and poorly developed', with a population of 700,000 'mostly illiterate and primitive' Papuans. The status of the territory, not ceded to Indonesia when it gained independence from the Netherlands in 1949, was left to future discussions between the two parties, but the issue still remained unresolved. In short, the Netherlands rejected Indonesian claims that West Irian was an integral part of the country. Indonesia raised the item at the Tenth Session in 1955, but the General Assembly passed an innocuous resolution once Holland agreed to restart bilateral negotiations. When these talks failed, Indonesia unsuccessfully pressed its claim at the Eleventh Assembly, where Ireland sided with Holland on the grounds that New Guinea as a whole, not just the western part of the island, had the right to determine its own destiny.[236]

In August 1957, just before the opening of the Twelfth Session, the Dutch Legation in Dublin delivered an *aide-memoire* to Iveagh House noting that Indonesia once more planned to table the question of West Irian.[237] In fact, Indonesia hoped to solicit from the Assembly a statement supporting its claim to West New Guinea. The document countered Indonesia's tired arguments and then requested Ireland to oppose the inscription of the item on the agenda and to support Holland on the substantive issue.

The Irish government consented to the latter solicitation, but not the first. We have already seen how the Irish delegation had decided, as a matter of principle, to vote in favor of the discussion of several controversial items: the representation of China, Algeria, apartheid in South Africa, West Irian. Accordingly, on 20 September Ireland backed the Steering Committee's recommendation that West Irian be inscribed on the Assembly's agenda.[238] Concurrently, Aiken agreed to resist any Indonesian move on West Irian. He informed the Dutch Legation of his intentions on 23 August; one week later Dr P.A. Kasteel, the Dutch Minister in Dublin, acknowledged his support.[239]

The Indonesians made their own pitch. On 23 October Con Cremin, the Irish Ambassador in London, notified Sean Murphy that he had recently spoken with his Indonesian counterpart, Dr Sunario.[240] Sunario had appreciated Ireland's vote in favor of the inscription of West Irian on the agenda, hoped that it would back Indonesia when the item came up for debate, and wished to travel to Dublin to discuss the establishment of diplomatic relations between

235 DFA 305/144/A (nd).
236 *Irish Times*, 1 March 1957; DFA 305/144/A, 2 March 1957. Afterwards, the Dutch Ambassador in Dublin thanked Liam Cosgrave for Ireland's support.
237 DFA 305/144/A, 16 August 1957.
238 DFA 417/169 (nd). The USSR voted with Ireland; the United States voted against the recommendation.
239 DFA 305/144/A, 31 August 1957.
240 Ibid., 23 October 1957.

the two countries.[241] On 24 October Murphy instructed Cremin to inform Sunario that there was 'no change from last year in our attitude on West Irian', diplomatic relations were out of the question and, hence, 'no useful purpose could be served' by a meeting.[242] Nevertheless, it was impolitic to reject Sunario's request, so the next day Murphy told Cremin by phone that there was no objection to a visit so long his government understood Ireland's position.[243] In mid-November Sunario and his press attaché made a goodwill visit to Dublin, met with de Valera and Aiken, and probably raised the question of West Irian in a non-offensive manner.[244]

At the Twelfth Session the Australian dimension of the West Irian dispute emerged and reinforced Ireland's rejection of Indonesia's claim to the territory. According to a mid-November letter to Iveagh House from their Embassy in Dublin, Australia controlled the eastern part of the island of New Guinea (the Australian Trust Territory) and preferred that the Netherlands, a close ally, remained in control of the western half.[245] The occupation of West New Guinea by Indonesia would introduce an element of instability into the region and undermine Australia's security.

In the light of their shared interests, Australia and the Netherlands had issued a joint Declaration on 6 November; the Australian Embassy included a copy with their letter to Iveagh House. The two governments based their control of West New Guinea and the Australian Trust Territory 'on the interests and inalienable rights of their inhabitants in conformity with the provisions and spirit of the UN Charter'. Both of the trust administrations' economic, social, and educational policies recognized that the two territories were 'geographically and ethnologically related'. Each government promised to 'strengthen the cooperation at present existing between their respective administrations in the territories' until 'the inhabitants of the territories concerned will be in a position to determine their own future'.

In this international context, Freddy Boland spoke on 26 November against a motion introduced into the First Committee by nineteen Afro-Asian powers calling on the Netherlands to negotiate with Indonesia on the status of West Irian.[246] It was imperative, he asserted, that the Committee be guided by the Charter, and its relevant principle in this case – and 'all other cases involving disputes of a territorial character – is the principle of self-determination'. Boland admitted that the inhabitants of West Irian were 'politically very backward – so backward as to be incapable in present circumstances of expressing a general political will'. Ireland also empathized with Indonesia's demand that

241 Ibid., 24 October 1957.
242 Ibid.
243 Ibid., 25 October 1957.
244 Ibid., 1, 14 November 1957.
245 Ibid., 9 November 1957.
246 *Irish Times*, 27 November 1957.

Dutch colonialism be ended in West New Guinea. Still, other factors had to be weighed. The island of New Guinea happened to be 'partitioned by an artificial and arbitrarily-drawn colonial frontier'. The joint Dutch-Australian declaration, despite certain ambiguities, left the door open to the 'ultimate political unity of the island and the self-determination of its people as a whole'. When New Guinea achieved its independence it would be free to join Indonesia, 'but whatever the ultimate decision of the people of New Guinea, nothing should now be done to prejudice it, or to render more permanent the division of the island', including the incorporation of West New Guinea into Indonesia.

Despite Ireland's opposition, and that of other western European delegations, Indonesia enjoyed wide-spread Afro-Asian support, and the First Committee adopted the 19-power resolution by a vote of 42 to 28, with 11 abstentions.[247] When the Assembly voted on 29 November, however, the measure failed; having been labeled an 'important' question, it did not garner the required two-thirds majority.[248] Ireland, the Netherlands, Australia, and the western European delegations opposed it; the USSR voted for the motion; because of its close relations with both Australia and Indonesia, the United States abstained.

The Dutch and Australians welcomed Ireland's support. The Australian delegation appreciated Boland's address in the First Committee, especially since 'it came from a country which had taken up what are regarded as anti-colonialist positions on almost every other item on the agenda'.[249] Mr C.W.A. Schurman, the acting Chairman of the Netherlands delegation, sent Boland an effusive letter.[250] Eamon Kennedy suggested that a copy be forwarded to Iveagh House.[251] Boland agreed, but he advised that his recently-completed, ten-page review of the general political situation in Indonesia be sent first; the unsympathetic tone of this report echoed Boland's distaste for the extremism of Indonesia and some of its allies that flavored his dispatches to Dublin during the Eleventh Session and informed his speech to the First Committee on 26 November.[252]

An exchange between Michael Rynne, Ireland's envoy to Spain, and Con Cremin several months after the close of the Twelfth Assembly further elucidates Ireland's West Irian stand and its entire decolonization policy. In an April 1958 report Rynne described a recent conversation with his Indonesian

247 DFA 305/144/A, 30 November 1957.
248 DFA 417/169 (nd).
249 DFA 305/144/A, 6 May 1958.
250 DFA PMUN X/46, 5 December 1957.
251 Ibid., 31 December 1957.
252 Ibid., 2 January 1958. For instance, Boland criticized Indonesia's rash expulsion of Dutch residents and businesses. The prevailing view, he noted, was 'if the Indonesian government fancied that their action against Dutch interests would benefit either Indonesia or the cause of "anticolonialism", they were guilty of about as bad a miscalculation as Louis XIV of France when he revoked the Edict of Nantes'.

counterpart.[253] The Indonesian, probably bearing in mind Ireland's close relations with Madrid, had asked Rynne if he would press Indonesia's claim to West Irian with the Spanish authorities. Rynne dismissed this 'amazing proposition' out of hand. Yet because another encounter with the Indonesian was inevitable, he added that 'any briefing the Department can give me about our attitude' toward West Irian would be useful.

Cremin promptly forwarded a 'Confidential' dispatch to Rynne.[254] After delineating the delegation's approach at the Twelfth Session he told Rynne, with tremendous insight into Ireland's policies, that if the Indonesian Ambassador mooted the question of West Irian again:

> it might be well to make it clear that our attitude on this problem is governed by principle – the principle of eventual self-determination for the island of New Guinea – and not by the influence of another country or even by our ties, important though they are, with Australia. On the question of principle, we have not hesitated to vote against countries with which we have very friendly relations and traditional ties. To illustrate this you could mention our vote in the United Nations on the question of a discussion on Chinese credentials and, perhaps a more telling argument *ad hominem*, the fact that despite considerable ties of blood and historical sympathy with South Africa we sponsored the resolution censuring its apartheid policy.

TIME TABLES AND THE EEC

Ireland's disavowal of two proposals aimed directly at the European colonial powers demonstrated once more that the delegation or, more specifically, the Boland-Kennedy axis, was uneasy with the radical tendency of the Afro-Asian bloc. In December Burma, Guatemala, Haiti, India, and Syria introduced a motion into the Fourth Committee reaffirming resolutions passed by the Sixth and Eleventh Assemblies that established time-tables for the attainment of the objectives of the International Trusteeship System and criticized the administering countries for not completing this task.[255] The measure also requested the Trusteeship Council to update the Thirteenth Session on the progress toward this goal.

The western European administering countries, the old Commonwealth, and the United States opposed the resolution because they considered rigid schedules imprudent. After discussing the matter with Boland, Eamon Kennedy abstained in the Committee and in the Assembly. So did Austria, Finland,

253 DFA 305/144/A, 21 April 1958.
254 Ibid., 6 May 1957.
255 DFA 417/133 (nd).

Japan, Argentina, and others, but the Assembly approved the draft.[256] Kennedy later wrote that he abstained because the motion contained 'a censure of the administering countries for not drawing up time-tables, which they have often indicated they are not in a position to do so'. Moreover, several cases – British Togoland, Somalia – had suggested that 'the "target-date" approach is not necessarily the most realistic in existing conditions'.

* * *

The Afro-Asian group was also concerned about the impact greater European economic cooperation would have on the trust territories of those powers who were members of the EEC. According to a report composed by Kennedy, they feared that as this process gathered steam the economies of the trust territories would become even more closely intertwined with those of the administering powers, thereby rendering the achievement of independence more difficult.[257] The economies of the trust territories would also remain dependent upon agriculture, the export of raw materials, and the importation of manufactured goods from Europe, which would generate mass emigration. As well, the trusts would be open to exploitation by American and European capital.

With this bleak outlook in mind, the Afro-Asian bloc introduced a resolution into the Fourth Committee inviting administering members to transmit information about the interrelationship between their trust territories and the European Economic Community to the Secretary General. It also requested the Secretary General to submit a report to the next Assembly on developments connected with this association, taking into account possible studies undertaken in this field by other organs and agencies.

The Europeans did not share the Afro-Asians' gloomy prognosis. The French argued that the success of the European Common Market 'would strengthen the economy of the territories, increase their volume of trade, diversify their production, [and] stabilize raw material prices'. Simultaneously, 'the investment fund of the Common Market' would foster economic development in the trust territories. France opposed the resolution on the grounds that the UN was not authorized to discuss the economic policies of the administering powers and because the final nature of the EEC had not been determined. Other European delegations opposed the resolution because of its implied distrust of the Community's aims.

Ireland, a country with a vested interest in European economic cooperation, was wary of the Afro-Asian initiative. Kennedy told the Fourth Committee that 'as a member of the free community of Western Europe' and a nation 'whose economy might be greatly affected by the European Economic Community and by the Free Trade Area whose creation is envisaged', his delegation

256 GA/RES 1207 (XII).
257 DFA 305/271/1/1A (nd).

believed that the UN should 'proceed with care and caution in the examination of an issue which is still *in posse* and not yet *in esse*'.[258] The UN was entitled to study the implications of the EEC's expansion, but it would be regrettable if the Organization gave 'the impression that we are, in any sense, creating a kind of investigative apparatus which would aim to keep a critical eye on the developing European Economic Community'. Kennedy was particularly sensitive to the impact of such a resolution on public opinion and, more important, 'the tone of some of the interventions which might conceivably accompany the resolution' in the Assembly. In place of the motion, he backed an innocuous Canadian suggestion to place on the record a factual account of the Fourth Committee's debate.

Kennedy's arguments fell on deaf ears as first the Committee and then the Assembly – by a vote of 58 to 13, with 8 abstentions – passed the Afro-Asian resolution.[259] The six Common Market countries, the United States, Australia, New Zealand, Canada, Britain, Norway, and Sweden opposed the motion. The Irish delegation abstained after receiving instructions from Iveagh House; Aiken had decided that this was an acceptable compromise.[260]

CONCLUSION

During his maiden year in the General Assembly Frank Aiken was true to his nature: he pulled no punches. His bold strokes turned heads, ruffled feathers, sparked off debates, and raised the profile of the Irish delegation. Ireland's activism heralded the arrival of a new player on the diplomatic stage. Aiken's and de Valera's political instincts influenced this policy, but it was not impulsive. The record shows that it was planned far in advance, thoroughly reviewed by Irish diplomats, professionally implemented, and ardently defended. This active approach thus refutes the passive interpretation that due to developments in the international system, such as the 'move from collective security to preventive diplomacy, from enforcement to neutral intervention', an independent role 'was created *for* and not *by* Ireland ... '[261]

Aiken and de Valera pursued Ireland's interests. Their interpretation of those interests differed in some (but not all) respects from their forerunners, Liam Cosgrave and John Costello, which partially explains the variation in policies at the United Nations. Aiken considered it more important to alleviate acute tensions that might spark off a cataclysm than to join forces with the west in stemming the tide of communist expansion; this conviction accounted for his striking initiatives: the troop disengagement proposal; the China vote; his Algerian plan. As he asserted in autumn of 1957:

258 DFA 417/167/8, 28 October 1957.
259 GA/RES 1153 (XII).
260 DFA PMUN B/2/4, 12, 15 November 1957.
261 MacQueen, 'Entry', pp. 76–7.

The purpose of my actions and speeches was to suggest the introduction of some elasticity into the policies of the major powers ... Those who see the major powers making headlong for destruction, like two express trains speeding against each other on the same track, are in duty bound to put the danger signals on the rails.[261]

Likewise, one year later an Irish delegate reminded the Assembly that 'My country is one of those which have done what little we can ... to work for the relaxation of tensions and an end to the Cold War.'[263]

Ireland's sharp departure at the Twelfth Session in 1957 undermines the contention that its pro-western, Christian, anti-communist policy at the Eleventh Assembly in 1956 'cannot be explained simply by political preferences on the part of Fine Gael'.[264] It can be. The fundamental shift that took place at the Twelfth Assembly, well documented herein, demonstrates that Fine Gael and Fianna Fáil approached international affairs from different perspectives. Previous observers have downplayed this distinction. Yet much more than varying interpretations of the Anglo-Irish Treaty distinguished the two parties' foreign policies.[265]

Others readily acknowledged Ireland's new, autonomous posture. Two months after the close of the Twelfth Assembly the *Chronicle of United Nations Activities* recorded that Ireland was not affiliated with any bloc in the Assembly.[266] Walter Lippman, the American political commentator, told Josephine McNeill, recently appointed as the Irish Minister in Berne, that he 'found it interesting and significant' that Ireland followed an unexpected line at the UN.[267] Some, like the United States, were not pleased; more realistic delegations welcomed Ireland's contribution; the Afro-Asian bloc was impressed. So too was a respected British journal: due to its energetic efforts Ireland was poised 'to take its place as one of the small band of disinterested countries ... to whose good example such success as present international organizations enjoy is due'.[268] Likewise the UN Secretariat. One of its internal reports observed that the Irish delegation was 'composed of outstanding personalities who were often able to present a fresh point of view in an elegant form. In an atmosphere dulled by conventional, drab supporting speeches, they were able to stress their independent position.'[269]

262 DD 164, 1216–7, 28 November 1957.
263 DFA 305/210/4, 11 December 1958. Conor O'Brien was speaking during a debate on Hungary at the Thirteenth Session.
264 MacQueen, 'Entry', p. 77.
265 One commentator has noted that the foreign policy 'assumptions made by the two large parties, Fianna Fáil and Fine Gael, have been (the Treaty issue apart) very similar': Keatinge, *Formulation*, p. 258.
266 *Chronicle of United Nations Activities*, 17 February 1958.
267 DFA 417/167, 31 March 1958.
268 *Spectator*, 14 February 1958.
269 DFA 417/178 (nd). This report, written after the Thirteenth Session, came to the

The most significant by-product of the independent policy pursued at the Twelfth Session was not the applause it generated, but the valuable, constructive role it enabled Ireland to grasp within the Assembly. This role was not limited to Ireland's identity as a middle power, nor its participation in the fire brigade. Because others recognized the Irish delegation's integrity, its later proposals (Tibet, South Africa, non-proliferation) succeeded; it was able to rally the uncommitted states to the defense of the Secretary General in 1960; its advice and support were prized. This all transpired without damaging Ireland's relations with its European neighbors, or the United States, even though Aiken was not overly cautious for this reason. If Ireland had not adopted an independent line in 1957 it would have made an important contribution to the Assembly's deliberations in the future, as its participation at the Eleventh Session had demonstrated. Its role, however, would not have been as broad, varied, dynamic, and successful as it was under Aiken's tutelage. Hence, his policy was instrumental, and Aiken deserves immense credit for seizing the unique opportunity UN membership presented to Ireland.

Ireland's efforts at the Twelfth Assembly were not a one-man show, but a team effort; Aiken was assisted by talented, interested, and industrious colleagues. Eamon de Valera, more so than has been previously recognized, played a significant role in both the development and implementation of Ireland's policy at the Twelfth Session.[270] He followed the drafting of Aiken's troop disengagement proposal and his General Debate speech, which contained innovative proposals for the Middle East and Algeria. There is no doubt that Aiken cleared the vote on the representation of China with him. De Valera defended Ireland's policy in tandem with Aiken when Scott McLeod, the American Ambassador, lodged a protest. He also insisted that the delegation abstain on all of its votes on the question of Portuguese Goa. Overall he was 'delighted' that Aiken had 'acted as he did' at the UN.[271] Based on his own experience in international affairs, he was acutely aware that Ireland could win respect only if 'we stand on our own feet and act justly and act courageously. We will be despised if we take any other line.'

Conor O'Brien hit his stride at the Twelfth Session. His intuitive comprehension of Aiken's point of view, his empathy for the Minister's ideas, and

attention of Freddy Boland. He forwarded it to Iveagh House, where Aiken 'was naturally gratified to learn of the high opinion expressed in the Secretariat working paper of the delegation to the recent Session of the General Assembly': DFA 417/178 19 January 1959.

270 It has been inaccurately observed that in regard to Ireland's foreign policy in 1957 'de Valera took little positive action in an area which had formerly been one of his principle preoccupations; it was Frank Aiken, as Minister for External Affairs, who represented Ireland at the UN General Assembly, and Sean Lemass, as Minister for Industry and Commerce, who was principal spokesman on European affairs. This was hardly surprising in view of Mr de Valera's age: he was seventy-six when he resigned in 1959': Keatinge, *Formulation*, p. 60.

271 DD 164, 1297, 28 November 1957.

his uncanny ability to coherently express them lent even greater importance to his role as the delegation's preeminent speech writer. This duty placed O'Brien in close and frequent contact with Aiken. Because the two had such similar outlooks this arrangement suited Aiken. It also meant that O'Brien exerted a greater influence on Ireland's policy. He attended caucus meetings where resolutions were framed, represented Ireland in important Committee meetings, and assumed a more visible role in the Assembly.

Freddy Boland, who was initially taken aback by Aiken's fresh approach to UN diplomacy, remained the linchpin of the delegation. His rapid adaptation to Aiken's policies, and his invaluable assistance in implementing them, testified to his professionalism, his patriotism, and his commitment to the United Nations.[272] Boland did not wear his heart on his sleeve, but the moral outrage provoked by the Soviet invasion of Hungary was much more than an anti-communist reaction. He repeatedly asserted, most likely with Ireland's experience in mind, that the rights of small nations lay at the core of the Hungarian debacle. Boland's responses to Algeria and West Irian revealed his commitment to self-determination in Africa and Asia. True, he preferred a moderate approach, especially in Algeria, but he argued cogently and convincingly for the right of colonial territories to democratically express their desire for self-rule.

Eamon Kennedy played a more prominent role at the Twelfth Assembly. This transpired after his move from the Second to the Fourth Committee, where his diplomatic, speech writing, and speaking skills were put to excellent use deliberating Trusteeship matters of special concern to the Afro-Asian bloc. Máire MacEntee and Paul Keating, who represented Ireland on the less prominent but nonetheless important Third and Fifth Committees, made equally impressive contributions to the work of the Irish delegation.

Fired by its energetic outlook, diplomatic achievements, high profile, growing influence with the Afro-Asian bloc, and innovative reputation the Irish delegation was well poised, after the Twelfth Session, to play an increasingly active role in the Assembly. It proceeded to do so during the Thirteenth Session in 1958, and beyond.

272 Fergal Boland, Personal Interview, 12 December 1993.

CHAPTER 3

Areas of Law: Frank Aiken's Quest for Peace

INTRODUCTION

In 1958 and 1959 the reduction of international tension remained Frank Aiken's most important foreign policy objective. He fixed this priority at the Twelfth Session, as the previous chapter demonstrates, by advocating troop withdrawal from central Europe, an Algerian settlement, and decolonization in Asia and Africa. He then reinforced these designs with a Middle Eastern peace plan – presented to the General Assembly in August 1958 – and a formal Areas of Law proposal one year later. Essential to the success of these latest blueprints were three themes that Aiken had touched upon in 1957, but which he hammered home thereafter. In the place of half-measures he favored broad, comprehensive solutions that addressed the fundamental causes of regional strife. Once more Aiken sought to limit great power rivalry around the globe. And, he insisted that the United Nations serve as the primary stabilizing force in troubled zones. Ultimately, Aiken's Middle Eastern and Areas of Law proposals, which expanded upon earlier ideas and paved the way for later concepts, focused on both Irish interests and international aims. As he once eloquently reminded the Dáil:

> Everything I said at the United Nations was said ... to get the nations represented in the Assembly to realize their mortal danger, to urge them to reappraise their policies in the light of that danger, and to plead with them progressively to eliminate the causes of conflict and progressively to enlarge the areas in which disputes, including our own, would be settled on a basis of law and justice.[1]

THE MIDDLE EAST, 1957

The roots of Aiken's sweeping scheme for the Middle East first took hold at the Twelfth Session in 1957, when he briefly referred to the subject during his General Debate speech. In so doing, he confidently joined the ranks of those who had, since the Suez Crisis, outlined their own major proposals for

---

1 DD 164, 1204, 28 November 1957.

the area – like Dwight Eisenhower, who enunciated the Eisenhower Doctrine in January 1957.[2] Aiken made three points. Although the urgency of 1956 had faded, a lasting source of instability in the Middle East remained: the 'acute diplomatic competition' between the great powers for regional hegemony, a contest whose 'natural dynamics' led only to war.[2] To forestall this outcome he called for 'a mutual diplomatic drawing-back comparable to the military drawing-back' he had proposed for central Europe. It was geared toward 'the same end: the reduction of international friction in order that real progress can be made towards disarmament and peace'. Finally, Aiken proposed that a United Nations Commission be established 'for the promotion of reconciliation and economic development in the Middle East'. Funded by the industrialized world, the Commission would channel economic aid ('without political conditions') to the region.

Interestingly, and despite its praise for Aiken's European troop withdrawal plan, the *Irish Times* was rightly skeptical about this latest overture. The disengagement scheme applied to 'physical things like soldiers and tanks and aircraft' and had the 'merit of simplicity', but Aiken's Middle East initiative dealt with 'imponderables'.[4] The paper rhetorically asked: 'Is it practical?' In Aiken's 'favor', and without any ill-intent, it noted that two other men, the prominent British socialist and atomic scientist, Professor Blackett, and the Soviet Foreign Minister, Andrei Gromyko, had made similar proposals. Yet Aiken's interpretation of Middle Eastern countries as diplomatic puppets of the great powers was, 'perhaps, an over-simplification of the facts'. The industrial world's thirst for oil had exacerbated ageless regional disputes. 'Unity and forbearance' were not 'imposed so easily; nor, one must think, will the United Nations so easily be persuaded to impose them'.

Perturbed by the tone of the *Irish Times* leader, Conor O'Brien and Máire MacEntee countered it. On 24 September O'Brien wrote to Alec Newman, the paper's editor, to register a 'mild protest'.[5] There was 'no point' in commenting on Newman's opinion of Aiken's ideas, but quite unsettling was his 'linking them, without any perceptible necessity, with the names of Professor Blackett and Mr Gromyko'. O'Brien was 'quite sure it was not intentional, but the effect created was distinctly that of a smear on the lines associated with the name of the late, lamented legislator from Wisconsin' – Senator Joseph McCarthy. He realized that neither Newman, nor his colleagues, 'would resort to these methods. Unfortunately, your words may set a headline for some others, not so scrupulous.'

One day earlier Máire MacEntee had sent a letter to Erskine Childers, III, a Dublin-based authority on the Middle East whose father, Erskine Childers, Jr.,

2 Cf. Steven Z. Freiberger, *Dawn Over Suez: the Rise of American Power in the Middle East, 1953–7* (Chicago, 1992), pp. 204–8.
3 Aiken, *Ireland* (1957), pp. 17–21.
4 *Irish Times*, 21 September 1957.
5 DFA PMUN Y/3, 24 September 1957.

was the Minister for Lands, Forestry and Fisheries in the Fianna Fáil government and a future President of Ireland. Both she and O'Brien considered
the *Irish Times* editorial 'superficial and ill-informed, if not mischievous'.[6]
They were curious, since Aiken's views of the Middle East 'coincided to a
large extent with those which you yourself had expressed after your experience of that region', if Childers 'might be prepared to reply to the editorial'.
It was vital 'that someone should point out that the only hope for the survival
of Israel lies in some such implementation of the principle of non-dominion
and disinterested economic investment'. If, 'for professional reasons', Childers
was hesitant about signing such a missive, MacEntee suggested 'a reply from
a third party whom you could brief for the purpose'. Five days later the *Irish
Times* printed a letter from a Mr Ewart Milne of Essex (where Erskine Childers
had spent time in his youth) who expressed his 'firm and even enthusiastic
support' for Aiken's UN speeches, particularly the Minister's call for a 'full-
scale campaign for peace'.[7]

THE MIDDLE EAST, 1958

In July 1958 another major crisis erupted in the Middle East. After an anti-
western coup overthrew the Hashimite dynasty in Iraq, the United States sent
over 15,000 troops into Lebanon, ostensibly at the request of the Lebanese
president, Camille Chamoun, but in reality to guard its own interests in the
region. British forces, meanwhile, landed in Jordan. These foreign interventions
collided with other forces shaping the Middle East: the growing movement
for Arab unity spearheaded by Gamal Abdel Nasser of Egypt, which had
expressed itself in the temporary union his country and Syria into the United
Arab Republic; the unsettled Palestinian refugee problem, which constantly
spewed gasoline onto the political fire; and, the Soviet Union's persistent
efforts to gain a foothold in the region.

Unsettled by this latest crisis, Frank Aiken resolved to mitigate it. Following
detailed discussions with foreign diplomats (including Arab representatives)
and his Iveagh House colleagues (particularly Conor O'Brien),[8] he devised a
plan by late July. Stamped with his usual ardor, it elaborated greatly upon the
ideas he had expressed in 1957. Drawn up in the form of a draft resolution,
the first two of its ten points endorsed 'the right of any Middle East state,
whose inhabitants so desire, to unite or federate with another group of states'
so long as the 'civil and religious rights of minorities and the legitimate commercial interests of other nations' in the region were protected, and called on

6 Ibid., 23 September 1957.
7 *Irish Times*, 28 September 1957; John N. Young, *Erskine H. Childers, President of
Ireland: A Biography* (Gerrards Cross, 1985), p. 17.
8 DFA 305/173/III, 22 July 1958.

the UN to recognize this Arab aspiration towards unity, which was indeed 'a historic fact'.[9]

By the next pair of clauses UN Member States affirmed that 'the existence of the state of Israel is also a historic fact' and accepted 'the present frontiers of the state of Israel ... in exchange for a guarantee that Israel will at no time seek to expand beyond these frontiers'. These provisos, which counterbalanced the first two, were extremely provocative since no Arab state had yet recognized Israel; indeed, they all considered it a mortal enemy. Aiken, though, was adamant: one year earlier he had told several Arab diplomats at the UN 'that they had to be realistic and recognize that [the Israelis] could not now be driven into the sea'.[10]

The fifth paragraph addressed one of the most intractable issues plaguing the Middle East: the plight of the Palestinian refugees, who were expelled during the creation of Israel in 1948 and its subsequent war with the Arab states. The UN could resolve this 'tragic' dilemma by what Aiken labeled a 'new approach'. It could:

> declare its readiness, in the interests of world peace and security, to contribute financially – for example by making available the sum of $1,000 for each refugee repatriated or resettled – and to assist otherwise, in the carrying out of any scheme for the solution of this problem on which it may prove possible to secure the agreement of the Arab states and of Israel.

The resolution then called on the states of the region – 'in the interests of peace' – to sign a mutual non-aggression pact and to disavow the manufacture or use of nuclear weapons.

The seventh and eighth points affirmed that the region's communications – the Suez Canal, pipe lines, airports – and its abundant oil supplies were 'vital concerns of all member nations'; called on the states of the area to open them 'to all countries at all times on ordinary commercial terms'; and requested the UN to 'register and guarantee this undertaking'.

The final clauses pertained to the nationalization of foreign industries in the Middle East. Regional states would not 'take 'control of externally-owned resources, installations, and other assets without adequate compensation to the existing owners'; and, the United Nations would 'make the necessary capital for the transaction available on normal terms and conditions' to countries so long as they acted in good faith.

This outline was certainly ambitious, indeed unrealistic in some respects, but Aiken believed it addressed the inherent causes of instability in the Middle East. As he told two Indian diplomats during a conversation in Dublin on 22 July:

9 DFA 417/205, 25 July 1958.
10 DFA P299, 2 October 1957.

to tackle the existing problems in such a manner would be much more realistic and fruitful than to concentrate attention, as the west has tended to do, on disarmament. Armaments, after all, are only the manifestations of a lack of mutual confidence, and the real problems are political in character.[11]

It was essential, he continued, 'if peace is to be maintained and consolidated, to tackle each question by way of its political aspects'. Ironically, the recent British and American actions, while 'otherwise open to very serious objections, could give rise to good' if they paved the way for a *political* solution. Aiken insisted that his 'approach to the Middle Eastern problem could serve as a pattern for the solution of equally difficult problems elsewhere', namely in central Europe. He thus linked this most recent plan to his desire to reduce international tension across the globe, particularly through the auspices of the United Nations.

* * *

On 26 July Conor O'Brien forwarded a copy of Aiken's plan to Freddy Boland in New York, adding that it represented 'the trend of the Minister's thinking at the moment on the Middle Eastern questions'.[12] Aiken was not yet sure how he would pursue the issue, but he had several possibilities in mind: 'as the bones of his General Debate speech' at the upcoming Thirteenth Session; as the basis for an Assembly resolution; or, he might disclose it during a press interview. But before he acted, O'Brien informed Boland, the Minister wanted 'your comments both on the substance and on the best procedure for getting the ideas across'. Given the bold nature of his proposals, Aiken wanted to run them by his most savvy, experienced colleague, who was also in touch with diplomatic currents in New York.

Boland did not disappoint. He air-mailed an exhaustive, sophisticated analysis to O'Brien (later initialed by Aiken) on 30 July, flagging its pending arrival with a telegram.[13] Unsurprisingly, he was cautious. Opening with a few general observations, Boland stressed 'that there are two major political problems in the Middle East which are ultimately connected but, in present circumstances, largely separate. One is the diplomatic and political rivalry between east and west... '[14] It took the form of 'a clash between two groups of Middle Eastern governments, one supported by the west and the other by the east ... one side supporting and exploiting the claims of Arab nationalism and the other trying to keep them in check'. The second problem was 'the longstanding Arab-Israeli issue'.

11 DFA 305/173/III, 22 July 1958. Iveagh House circulated a record of this discussion to all Irish missions abroad.
12 DFA PMUN 478, 26 July 1958.
13 Ibid., 30 July 1958.
14 DFA 417/205, 30 July 1959.

Most observers, Boland continued, considered the former 'the more acute and dangerous of the two', so the primary aim 'must be – as we ourselves said last year – to put an end to the intense [great power] diplomatic competition' in the region. Yet because they had not even consented to meet, 'to suggest the details of what the major powers should talk about and what they should agree upon', as Aiken's plan did, 'would clearly be somewhat unrealistic and premature'. Nor would it help 'if the Arab-Israeli question is placed in issue at the same time'. Indeed, once the east-west rivalry ceased 'the Arab-Israeli problem, even if it continues unsolved, will certainly not constitute anything like the danger to world peace which exists at present'.

Boland then responded to each of Aiken's ten points. The first two, regarding Arab unification, were acceptable. Those apropos of Israel were problematic. He warned 'that it would be a great mistake for Ireland' to suggest that the UN recognize Israel and its present frontiers. Arab governments had stated repeatedly that 'the problem of Palestine is not merely one of reshaping the borders in this or that place, but is basically and essentially one of eliminating the state of Israel entirely ... ' To think, therefore, that they were ready 'to accept the existing position and to abandon their national claim is, in my view, entirely chimerical', no matter what guarantees Israel offered in return. And in an Irish context:

> The Arabs would no more think of accepting the existence of the state of Israel as a historic fact than we would think of accepting the existence of the six counties as a historic fact! We would be asking the Arabs to do something which we would not dream of doing ourselves; and, in my belief, if we were to put the proposal forward, the Arab spokesmen here at the United Nations (many of whom remember the Taoiseach's stout opposition to the partitioning of Palestine at Geneva) would not be slow to accuse us of this inconsistency.

Moreover, promoting the idea against Arab opposition would imply 'that the United Nations should, if necessary, ride rough-shod over Arab national sentiment' and impose its own settlement. This 'would be tantamount to marking ourselves down as challengers and opponents of Arab nationalism' – a result the Irish delegation 'should do everything we can to avoid'.

Does this resolute reply mean that Boland favored the Arab nations at the expense of Israel? Not at all. Simply put, he was a realist. In daily contact with Arab diplomats in New York, he was quite familiar with their sensibilities and knew that they would reject out of hand Aiken's explicit stand on Israel. The Minister's proposals also contradicted his view of the General Assembly's function: rather than dealing in specifics, it should only lay down broad principles. Boland was also guarding Ireland's interests at the UN: alienating the Arab bloc would terminate its role as a middle power and sponsor of independent initiatives (of course he knew that this particular argument would hold sway with Aiken, the architect of Ireland's autonomous stance). Last, Boland raised a technical issue in his report to O'Brien. If Aiken explicitly recognized the borders of Israel in his speech he would compromise Ireland's official policy of not establishing *de jure* diplomatic relations with Israel until it acceded to the internationalization of the Holy Places in Jerusalem, as requested by the General Assembly in 1948. (Ireland had already accorded *de facto* recognition to Israel.)[15]

Boland turned next to the Palestinian refugee issue, sparing no criticism. Aiken's claim that the UN's underwriting of a resettlement scheme would mark 'a new approach' was 'hardly in accordance with fact'. It had been willing to do so since the inception of Israel, even sanctioning $200,000,000 in 1951, but never utilized these funds. The reason, Boland said, was political not economic. According to Harry Labouisse, the UN's Special Representative on the Palestinian problem, the refugees 'bitterly opposed permanent settlement elsewhere and were openly supported in that attitude by most of the host governments'. They insisted instead on two other options: 'repatriation to Israel or compensation for the property they had lost and the damage they had suffered by their expulsion from that country'. Aiken's proposal, therefore, took 'insufficient account of this background and of the nature of the refugee problem'; it was based on 'assumptions which have been disproved in practice and which run counter to the opinion and advice of those most closely connected' with the situation.

With regard to Aiken's recommendation that the states of the Middle East abjure the production or possession of nuclear arms, Boland thought it wiser to promote a great power agreement not to ship atomic weapons to the region.

Aiken's call for open communications in the Middle East was 'absolutely sound'. His position on the nationalization of foreign capital (adequate compensation coupled with UN guarantees) was not. It undermined fundamental safeguards of foreign investment; it sanctioned 'the expropriation of foreign-owned assets as a more or less normal and natural proceeding', thus establishing 'an international precedent' applicable elsewhere; and, it bestowed the Assembly's endorsement upon a 'policy which the Middle Eastern oil-producing countries would probably not be very wise, from their own point of view, to adopt'. Boland realized that Aiken's aim was to reassure western investors, but favored instead a general provision requesting UN members 'to refrain from any action designed or calculated to impede or interrupt the free flow' of oil in the Middle East.

Boland closed with a few comments. The draft resolution ought to enjoin all members 'to refrain from direct or indirect interference in the internal affairs' of Middle Eastern states. It should also establish a UN development

15 Boland was essentially correct *vis-à-vis* Irish policy, but his point also underscores the Costello government's affinity with the Vatican, which had influenced Ireland's stand over Israel and the Holy Places. See DFA 305/62; DFA 305/62/1.

fund for the region similar to the one Aiken had proposed in his General
Debate speech at the Twelfth Assembly (Boland had made this same recommendation several months earlier).[16] Before Ireland sponsored any initiative it
was important to discuss the matter frankly with relevant diplomats and worthwhile 'to give some publicity to our point of view ... in the hope of eliciting
reactions and possible criticisms in advance', perhaps by floating a trial balloon
in the press.

Boland's honest response is thus one more example of his divergence from
Aiken's enthusiasm. His analysis was a product of experience, a realistic
approach to international affairs, and a limited interpretation of the UN's
role. Yet his criticisms were valid. It was also vital that Aiken hear them, particularly those regarding the nationalization of foreign industry and the likely
impact on Ireland's position in the Assembly. Ironically, though, Boland and
Aiken shared a similar goal: comprehensive peace in the Middle East. In the
wake of the Suez Crisis in 1956 Boland had passionately argued – in his private correspondence with Iveagh House – for a sweeping regional settlement
rather than piecemeal agreements,[17] just as Aiken sought one through his
detailed proposal. Boland and his Minister, however, disagreed on the diplomatic means to achieve this aim, as the former's critique of Aiken's plan
demonstrates. Likewise, their *ultimate* objectives differed. Aiken wanted reconciliation in the Middle East so as to reduce international tension overall. Boland
pursued it to block further penetration into the region by the Soviet Union
and China, whom he believed benefited from Arab-Israeli discord.

* * *

In early August Nikita Khrushchev called for an Emergency Session of the
General Assembly to discuss the Middle Eastern situation, although tensions
had eased somewhat in recent weeks. The Security Council confirmed this
request and ordered the Assembly to convene on 13 August. Aiken now had
a platform to air his views, so he decided to attend the session along with
other world leaders. Before departing for New York he submitted his plan to
the government on 8 August. Getting right to his fundamental point, he
argued, in a written memorandum, that Ireland 'should advocate that an
effort should be made to deal comprehensively with the underlying problems'
in the Middle East.[18] Indeed:

16 In a 'Confidential' report to Con Cremin in February Boland argued that the
   'Marshall Plan' concept was necessary in the Middle East: Arab nations had to work
   together much as Europe did after World War II. Yet the funding could not come
   directly from the USA because the Arabs would reject it. Instead, 'whatever funds are
   provided should be "dewesternized", to use the Secretary General's term ... by being
   channeled through some agency set up and approved by the United Nations as a
   whole': DFA PMUN R/41/4, 27 March 1958.
17 DFA 313/36, 19, 24 January 1957.
18 S 16057/B, 8 August 1958.

a comprehensive agreement should be negotiated by the Secretary General of the United Nations which would aim at the reduction of tension in the area; satisfy the legitimate aspirations of the Arab peoples; safeguard the position of Israel; provide safeguards for the legitimate interests of other countries in the region ... and thus create the conditions under which American and British troops could be withdrawn without loss of prestige.

Aiken then delineated the means to achieve these goals, which combined his ten-item draft resolution and Boland's criticisms. To halt great power rivalry in the Middle East – a concern shared by both men – Aiken added a plank to his original proposal requesting the UN to guarantee the formal neutralization of the entire area. This ambitious clause, which mirrored Austria's recently-negotiated status in Europe, harkened back to Aiken's troop withdrawal plan and anticipated his Areas of Law proposal. Other additions were the direct result of Boland's input: the internationalization of the Holy Places in Jerusalem; the establishment of a UN economic development fund; a great power agreement not to supply nuclear weapons. So too was the modification of Aiken's resettlement scheme: Palestinian refugees should be compensated for lost property and Israel should greatly expand upon its offer to readmit a few thousand refugees. Boland also engineered a significant deletion: Aiken abandoned his call for the explicit recognition of Israel and its borders.

In this case, therefore, Boland exerted substantial influence on the formulation of policy. The reasons: here he was on solid ground; his arguments were correct; and Aiken and Conor O'Brien accepted them. Still, Aiken retained several features of his original blueprint. He included the right of the Arab states to federate. He encouraged Israel and the Arabs to sign a non-aggression pact. He advocated open communications throughout the region. He implicitly endorsed the existence of Israel and entreated the Arab states to do the same. A provision for the compensation of nationalized foreign industries remained, which Boland had adamantly opposed. Aiken also called for the establishment of a UN force 'to prevent armed infiltration from one state to another, and to prevent an attack by any state in the region upon another'; in other words, he nominated the United Nations as the guarantor of regional security. This zealous addendum – the UN was wholly incapable of fulfilling such a task, notwithstanding its truce supervision duties in the Sinai Desert – underscores how impractical Aiken's scheme would have been without Boland's moderating influence. Yet the plan's form at that stage – an interesting amalgam of concepts – illustrates how the clash of ideas between Boland and his like-minded colleagues on the one hand, and Aiken and O'Brien on the other, often had a salutary effect.

The government evidently agreed, for they approved Aiken's proposal, 'subject to final consideration by the Taoiseach and the Minister'.[19] Aiken

19 CAB 2/19, 8 August 1958.

then met with de Valera several times to polish his blueprint before departing for New York on 11 August.[20] This entire episode is instructive. It demonstrates once more that Aiken, while extremely influential in determining its direction, was not always the sole arbiter of Ireland's UN stance. Iveagh House officials played an important role. On sensitive global issues with wide-ranging implications (such as the Middle East) the cabinet's sanction was necessary. So was de Valera's, who in this case, as his subsequent meetings with Aiken indicate, concerned himself not just with the broad principles of his Minister's scheme, but with its finer details as well.

* * *

The Emergency Session opened on 13 August. According to a Department of External Affairs summary, the immediate issue 'before the Assembly was what steps to take in the light of the Anglo-American action in Lebanon and Jordan'.[21] Opinions varied. The Soviet bloc and a large number of Afro-Asian delegations initially thought 'that the Assembly should condemn the Anglo-American action and call for the early withdraw of American and British forces ... ' Moderate Europeans and others considered the introduction of foreign troops regrettable, but they preferred to foster 'conditions which would permit of their withdrawal without immediately creating further disturbances'; precipitous action would only 'make a bad situation worse'. Once it became clear that neither of these approaches could secure the necessary two-thirds vote, however, the Arab bloc proposed its own compromise resolution, which the Secretary General supported and the Assembly adopted unanimously.[22]

In the midst of these diplomatic maneuvers Aiken continued to work on his speech. Conor O'Brien and Con Cremin, appointed Secretary of External Affairs several months earlier, had traveled with him from Dublin and upon arrival they discussed it further with Freddy Boland and Eamon Kennedy. Boland would have been pleased with the revisions to date since they took account of his views, but he continued to urge caution;[23] it is likely that Cremin supported him.[24] They convinced Aiken to drop several important points: the principle of fair compensation for nationalized industries; the call for a non-aggression pact between the Arabs and Israelis; the designation of the UN as the guardian of Middle Eastern security. Nothing substantial was

---

20 S 16057/B, 12 August 1958.
21 DFA 417/205, 13 September 1958.
22 GA/RES 1237 (ES–III).
23 On 7 August Boland had dispatched another report to Iveagh House reinforcing his earlier line of thinking; Aiken did not read it before he left Dublin, but Boland would have apprised him of its contents in New York: DFA 417/205, 7 August 1958.
24 Cremin approved of an original Irish role at the UN, but not at the expense of the west: Conor O'Brien has described him as being more comfortable with Liam Cosgrave's Third Principle (support for the west and Christianity): O'Brien, 'Ireland', p. 128, n. 2.

added. By 13 August the plan was complete. It was essentially the one Aiken had presented to the cabinet on 8 August, minus the latest deletions.[25] The delegation sent copies to de Valera and Iveagh House, which circulated it to Irish missions overseas.[26] Aiken then addressed the Emergency Session on its second day, 14 August.

Aiken's proposal deserves a fair assessment. On the downside, it was flawed in certain respects. To wit, the Emergency Session's final resolution, which reflected the general consensus on the Middle East, ignored many aspects of it. The resolution referred to neither the neutralization nor the denuclearization of the entire region, nor the internationalization of the Holy Places. It made no reference to the Palestinian refugees, nor suggested a new approach to this intractable issue. Unsurprisingly, since the Arabs nations sponsored it, the resolution did not recognize Israel. It foresaw no major role for the UN in the Middle East.

These omissions are significant. They reinforce the over-ambitious nature of Aiken's scheme. For instance, his cardinal aim – a comprehensive peace – was unrealistic. The Assembly resolution made no pretense about this. The eventual withdrawal of British and American forces in September, which effectively resolved the immediate crisis, did not precipitate an overall settlement. Nor did the outbreak of war in the years ahead. By the same token, what peace the Middle East now enjoys has not arrived as part of a comprehensive package, but through tortuous bilateral negotiations between Israel and her neighbors: Egypt, Jordan, the PLO, some Persian Gulf states.

Aiken completely misread the great powers. They had no intention of disengaging from one of the most strategic areas of the globe at the height of the Cold War, notwithstanding the destabilizing impact of their diplomatic competition: the stakes were too high. Aiken also overestimated the UN's capabilities. He did not assign the Organization a security function, at Boland's behest, but he still envisioned responsibilities – guaranteeing neutrality, administering a Development Fund, supervising refugee resettlement (a task Aiken brought back from his original plan) – that in sum were beyond the UN's means.

Nonetheless, as commentators at the UN and in Ireland pointed out, Aiken's proposal comprised some worthy features.[27] For instance, the final

---

25 Cf. Aiken, *Ireland* (1958), pp. 3–14.
26 DFA 417/205, 13, 15 August 1958.
27 Immediately after the speech Freddy Boland sent a cable with the news that the speech was 'favorably received on all sides' to Maurice Moynihan, Secretary of the Department of the Taoiseach, who duly informed Eamon de Valera. An External Affairs report noted that several subsequent speakers 'indicated approval, explicitly or implicitly, of the approach adopted by the Minister for External Affairs ... ' In a departure from its critique of Aiken's Middle Eastern stance the previous year, the *Irish Times* called the proposal 'sound and sensible ... a long-term policy for the Middle East'; Conor O'Brien's letter-writing offensive thus had its desired effect: S 16057/B, 14 August 1958; DFA 417/205, 13 September 1958; *Irish Times*, 16 August 1958.

resolution embodied parts of it (but not all, as we have seen). It endorsed the
Arab League's desire for closer unity. It called for an end to outside interference in the internal affairs of Arab states.[28] (An External Affairs report noted
that in doing so the measure corresponded 'quite closely with what was urged
by the Minister in his speech in the General Debate at the Twelfth Session,
as well as in the Emergency Session'.[29]) And although it excluded a primary
role for the UN in the Middle East, the resolution did entrust a limited task
to the Secretary General: to help resolve the immediate crisis and to study
the feasibility of establishing a Development Fund at a later date.

In the same vein, while Aiken's prescription for curing the Middle East of
its ills was over-zealous, his political analysis was correct to some extent. His
emphasis upon the dangers of great power diplomatic rivalry was prescient.
In fact, just before Khrushchev called for an Emergency Session, the *Irish
Times* noted that when Aiken shared his concern with the General Assembly in
1957 'there was as yet no evident cause to expect a revolution in the Lebanon
or Iraq, with resulting intervention by the United States and Great Britain; and
these events have borne witness to the soundness of his diagnosis'.[30] Freddy
Boland concurred. He told Con Cremin (doubtless trying to offset his earlier
criticism of Aiken's proposal) that he was pleased the paper 'picked out what the
Minister said about the Middle East ... last year. What is happening now is
precisely what the Minister forecast. Events have confirmed the accuracy of
his analysis and have fully justified his warnings.'[31]

Aiken was also right in the long term to stress the centrality of the Arab-
Israeli dynamic. He heeded Boland's advice and did not advocate the explic-
it recognition of Israel, yet he spoke forthrightly to the Emergency Session.
Raising a taboo subject, he said:

> I know that because of the great difficulties of this problem and the
> tremendous emotional forces involved, many delegations are tempted to
> set it aside, and to restrict their attention to the approachable and less
> forbidding aspects of the Middle Eastern question. Unfortunately, expe-
> rience suggests that this aspect cannot be ignored. Unless better rela-
> tions between Israel and her Arab neighbors are made possible there can
> be no lasting peace in the Middle East.[32]

28 The motion requested all UN members 'to act strictly in accordance with the principles of mutual respect for each other's territorial integrity and sovereignty, of non-
   aggression, of strict non-interference in each other's internal affairs, and of equal and
   mutual benefit, and to ensure that their conduct by word and deed conforms to these
   principles'.
29 DFA 417/205, 13 September 1958.
30 *Irish Times*, 6 August 1958.
31 DFA 417/205, 8 August 1958.
32 Aiken, *Ireland* (1958), p. 8.

1 The General Assembly of the United Nations in Plenary session.

2 Members of the Irish delegation to the Eleventh Session in 1956 seated at their country's desk in the General Assembly. From the left: Sheila Murphy, Conor Cruise O'Brien, Paul Keating, Frederick H. Boland, Eamon Kennedy, Liam Cosgrave.

3 Frank Aiken (left) and Frederick H. Boland review documents prior to
the Twelfth Assembly's General Debate in September 1957.

4 Members of the Irish delegation to the Thirteenth Assembly in 1958 meet in the corridor for an urgent discussion. From the left: Eoin MacWhite, Sean Ronan, Frank Aiken, Eamon Kennedy, Frederick Boland, Conor Cruise O'Brien.

5 Freddy Boland, Chairman of the Trusteeship
Committee during the Thirteenth General Assembly,
discusses South West Africa with Marian Anderson,
the world-famous opera singer and member of the
United States delegation, in October, 1958.

6   General Sean McKeown, Commander of the United Nations
peacekeeping operation in the Congo (ONUC) from January
1961 until March 1962, and Conor Cruise O'Brien, Secretary
General Dag Hammarskjold's representative in Katanga,
on the tarmac at Leopoldville airport in June 1961.

7 Frederick H. Boland, President of the General Assembly, and Secretary General Dag Hammarskjold enjoy a light moment during a General Assembly Plenary session in September 1960.

8 Cornelius Cremin, who replaced Frederick H. Boland as Ireland's
Ambassador to the United Nations in January 1964, presents his
credentials to Secretary General U Thant.

On this point one source remarked that 'where the Minister has revealed himself practical beyond the spokesmen of the big powers is in his insistence that the focal problem of Israel has still to be faced'.[33] Indeed, Aiken later informed the cabinet that because the final Arab resolution did not 'give any guarantee as regards Israel … it must be considered at best an interim settlement only'.[34]

One final, significant note: Aiken's speech was not just empty rhetoric. Ireland championed the needs of the refugees long after the close of the Emergency Session, for instance. The delegation cosponsored and voted for numerous resolutions regarding the maintenance of the UN's Relief and Works Agency for displaced Palestinians (UNRWA); the government contributed financially to it; Conor O'Brien often spoke eloquently on their behalf.[35] Likewise, Ireland fully supported the UN's peacekeeping efforts in the Middle East. The government, without hesitation, paid its full assessment for the UN force inserted into Egypt upon the withdrawal of French and British troops from the Suez Canal (UNEF) and it seconded Irish Army officers to the UN's operations along the Israeli-Egyptian border (UNTSO) and in Lebanon (UNOGIL).

AREAS OF LAW, 1959

In 1959 Frank Aiken consolidated his ideas regarding the opening of spaces between great powers into a formal proposal entitled Areas of Law. Its primary intent was to lessen Cold War friction. As such, it grew directly out of his European troop withdrawal and Middle Eastern blueprints. The strategy comprised three fundamental precepts. The great powers would draw down their military rivalry in a tense region around the globe. The states in this locale would then, *inter alia*, declare neutrality, abide by the UN Charter, maintain the rule of law, and abjure nuclear weapons. The UN would guarantee and supervise this arrangement. Consequently, regions where this scenario unfolded would be designated Areas of Law.

Aiken presented his proposal to the Fourteenth Assembly during its General Debate on 23 September 1959.[36] He welcomed the recent discussions between President Eisenhower and Nikita Khrushchev at Camp David, just outside Washington. The Irish delegation trusted that further talks would 'eventually result, not only in a clear definition of what is required to keep the peace in the short run, but also of the major steps which must be taken on the road to a stable peace'. Irish officials realized, however, 'that effectively controlled world disarmament and the universal rule of law cannot be attained in a single spectacular bound … ' Therefore:

33 *Irish Times*, 16 August 1958.
34 DFA 417/205, 13 September 1958.
35 GA/RES 1456 (XIV); S 16051/A, 7 September 1960; S 16051/B, 20 October 1960.
36 Aiken, *Ireland* (1959), pp. 8–20.

As first step and as an earnest of our good faith, Member Nations ought
to be prepared to cooperate in securing the firm application of Charter
principles in certain restricted areas, particularly in the areas where the
interests of the two great power groups are entangled and where there
is the greatest danger of stumbling into war ... What we have in mind is
a system whereby a group of nations in a defined area would be invited to
give guarantees of their intention to abide by their Charter obligations to
uphold the rule of law in their international relations in return for corresponding guarantees by the other Member Nations in relation to the
area in question.

For example, non-nuclear states in an Area of Law would agree, under UN
inspection, 'not to manufacture or acquire nuclear weapons or other weapons
of *blitzkrieg* or mass destruction'. In return, 'the nuclear powers and all the
other members of the United Nations would bind themselves in advance ...
to defend the members of the area from attack by means of a standing United
Nations force', which was a central component of Aiken's proposal. Since the
Security Council's paralysis necessitated a firmer guarantee for those nations
'invited to limit their own means of defense', he suggested that the General
Assembly itself establish and fund a UN army. By reaffirming their support
for collective security, the nuclear powers 'would give the world concrete evidence of their determination to uphold their Charter pledges and of their
determination to build a world order based on justice and law ... ' Moreover,
the sight of a UN force protecting 'an Area of Law would greatly increase the
moral authority of the United Nations. It would also free resources for other
uses by reducing tension, fostering international *esprit de corps*, and reducing
the necessity to maintain large national armies.'
Several regions were ripe for transformation; one was central Europe.
Inspired by his troop withdrawal scheme, Aiken claimed that there could be
no lasting peace on the continent 'unless a reunited Germany together with
Poland and other eastern European countries agree to become an Area of Law,
free from foreign troops, free from weapons of mass destruction, and subject
to United Nations inspection and guarantee'. In fact, 'if this heartland of
Europe were to become an Area of Law, it would be a much needed proto-
type for similar areas elsewhere, particularly for areas of great tension'. These
included, but were not limited to, countries 'which have recently been, or are
still under, some form of colonial rule'. Here Aiken was appealing to the Afro-
Asian nations, especially those that benefited from great power competition by
playing one off against the other for resources, weapons, and money.

CONCLUSION

How does one appraise this dimension of Aiken's foreign policy? It certainly
reflected Irish interests. The desire to ameliorate regional strife was a direct

by-product of Ireland's vulnerability as an unprotected small state at the height of the Cold War; this time, unlike World War II, great power conflict in Europe would surely engulf Ireland, with dire consequences. Aiken's call for the neutralization of the Middle East and newly-created Areas of Law reflected Fianna Fáil's enthusiasm for Irish neutrality. His focus on central Europe confirms that Irish statesmen missed no opportunity to rhetorically raise the partition of Ireland in the UN. In an aside during his Areas of Law speech Aiken said that the:

> problem of Berlin and the reunification of Germany is not only a heart-break for the German people, but a cause of great distress to their friends and to all who abhor the division of historic nations. If a just and lasting peace is to be made in Europe, the problem of German reunification must be settled in accordance with the will of the majority of the German people and with the right of nations to unity and independence.[37]

Concurrently, serious shortcomings marred Aiken's modus operandi. Most important, in the General Assembly Ireland earnestly debated matters relative to world peace, yet it was incapable of directly influencing events in the Middle East, or wherever the great powers clashed, because it possessed little real power in foreign affairs. By itself, Ireland could not put Aiken's eager plans into effect. Nor could it collaborate with its natural allies since it was not a member of NATO; it had no leverage with the west. In the short term Ireland could not reduce discord despite Aiken's overwhelming desire to do so. It is thus fair to say that he was overreaching.

Aiken also misinterpreted several features of the international system. He still clung to the idea of a neutral zone in central Europe despite being apprised of its inherent strategic limitations: NATO's rejection of the con-cept; the historic dangers of a united, neutral Germany in the center of the continent; the Soviet Union's aggressive posture. In addition, the United Nations was not ready to assume the duties he allocated to it – neither in the Middle East, as noted, nor elsewhere, nor as a world police force. In this regard one scholar has astutely observed that Aiken's:

> unfurling of the antique banner of collective security, involving not only formal great power commitments but a standing international force as well, was simply anachronistic in the late 1950s. The collective security ambitions of the post-war Charter makers were, after Korea, acknowl-edged as unattainable in practice and undesirable in the consequences of the attempt.[38]

---

37 Ibid., p. 16.
38 MacQueen, 'Aiken', p. 226.

Indeed, nearly forty years later, in the wake of the collapse of the Soviet Union and the demise of the Cold War, the UN still struggles to expand its role in the international system; witness its failed attempts at peace enforcement in Somalia and Bosnia.

Still, Aiken's stress on collective security grew out of his optimistic vision of the United Nations, which bears noting. Expounding upon its potential in the Dáil, he admitted that the institution was imperfect, but it was 'at least some sort of foundation for a better world order'.[39] Its progress would not be swift; instead, like 'a seed or plant' it depended upon 'organic and almost imperceptible growth', some of which was already visible. As proof, Aiken cited the UN's interventions in Korea, in the Sinai, and on the Indian subcontinent. Some mocked the UN 'as makeshift and ineffective, because it is merely able to keep the peace temporarily between smaller countries, and is ineffective in situations like Hungary', yet 'everything has to have a beginning'. Ultimately, as he told the First Committee in October 1958, Aiken believed that 'our aim must be to foster the gradual evolution of the United Nations towards a system of world government in which disputes between nations will be settled by law based on justice rather than by force'.[40] His Areas of Law proposals, therefore, were the precursors to such a system, its building blocks.

Over time Aiken remained committed to his view of a more stable international order. In March 1961 Sean Ronan, Counsellor in the Political and United Nations Section, forwarded a circular to all missions abroad summarizing Ireland's position on world-wide efforts to limit atomic and conventional weapons.[41] Irish diplomats required an update because for some time foreign officials had expressed interest in Aiken's major initiative in this field – nuclear non-proliferation. The Minister believed, according to Ronan, that it was time for a new approach to disarmament, so long discussed by the great powers without issue. In short, the aim was not how to 'achieve "general and complete disarmament" in the foreseeable future, but how best to tackle the problem of building up a system of world security that will give every nation at least the same protection as its weapons now give it'. One solution was nuclear non-proliferation. Another was the 'limited geographical Areas of Law approach'. Ronan then enumerated its principles, defined an Area of Law, and provided several examples where it might be applied: central Europe, the Middle East, sub-Saharan Africa, southeast Asia.

Aiken's diligence earned him respect. Anthony Hartley, writing in the *Spectator*, found it compelling 'that a country like Ireland, with the strongest bias against communism, should feel the need for some relaxation in international tension with such force that its diplomacy is willing to strike out on its

39 DD 164, 1215–6, 28 November 1957.
40 Aiken, *Ireland* (1958), p. 38.
41 DFA PMUN 331, 14 March 1961.

own'.[42] Another correspondent labeled the delegation's activities 'consistent, courageous, and honorable'.[43]

More significant than this praise, however, were the concrete results of Aiken's vision. It is true that his blueprint for the Middle East and his Areas of Law proposal failed in the traditional sense. Nevertheless, the overriding impulses that generated them – the desire to forestall conflict and the wish to stabilize the international order – gave rise to other Irish initiatives, many of which met with varying degrees of success: Tibet, the condemnation of apartheid in South Africa, South Tyrol, nuclear non-proliferation, peacekeeping, the defense of human rights, support for the United Nations. These accomplishments were the fruits of Aiken's entire philosophy, *including its more utopian aspects*. On one level, the idealistic dimension of Aiken's worldview was superfluous. Yet it fueled his realistic, worthwhile endeavors. We now review two of these initiatives within a shifting Irish diplomatic context.

42 Quoted in *Eire-Ireland: Bulletin of the Department of External Affairs*, No. 398 (24 November 1957).
43 *Irish Times*, 24 September 1958.

CHAPTER 4

Continuity and Transition: from de Valera to Lemass, 1958–61

INTRODUCTION

In June 1959 the de Valera epoch ended and a new era began when Sean Lemass became Taoiseach. His ascendancy coincided with a sea-change under-way in Irish economic policy: a more robust, expansionist strategy was super-seding the protectionist status quo. In 1956 the second Inter-Party government commenced negotiations with the International Monetary Fund and intro-duced tax breaks to promote exports. The Capital Investment Advisory Commission, established in the same year 'to examine especially the position with regard to public investment', recommended that 'a program for eco-nomic development be set up'.[1]

Two interconnected studies published in 1958 responded to the Commission's conclusion and heralded the unmistakable arrival of economic planning. In May T.K. Whitaker, the Secretary of the Department of Finance, completed his now-famous *Economic Development*; in November the government issued the *Programme for Economic Expansion*, the equally well-known White Paper based on Whitaker's recommendations. The proposals put forward in these 'historic documents' were profound.[2] They advocated the reorientation of the Irish economy away from one based on protection to one founded on free trade. Consonant with this realignment, the export of both agricultural prod-ucts and manufactured goods became paramount. Convinced that outside firms could generate employment, the accepted wisdom shifted 'from discourage-ment to encouragement of foreign investment in Ireland'. Both reports advo-cated Irish membership in the European Economic Community, and Ireland duly applied for admission in tandem with the United Kingdom in July 1961.

Lemass oversaw the transformation of these ground-breaking propositions into practical policy. Considered 'an instinctive expansionist', he had grown weary of protectionism during his long tenure as Minister for Industry and Commerce. By the time he became Taoiseach he was an advocate of energetic

1 Lyons, *Ireland*, p. 628.
2 Lee, *Ireland*, p. 344–59.

state intervention in the economy. This evolution represented 'a dramatic reversal of the rhetoric, and to a large extent of the practice, of all policy, but especially Fianna Fáil policy, since 1931'. Nonetheless, he astutely won over critics within his own party and marshaled a series of measures through the Dáil collectively known as the *First Programme for Economic Expansion*. F.S.L. Lyons has called this moment 'a watershed in the modern economic history of the country'.[3] Lemass, more than any other man except perhaps T.K. Whitaker, has been credited with this revolutionary departure, and his years as Taoiseach have been forever associated with it. The modest success of the *First Programme* secured his reputation as one of Ireland's foremost post-war political leaders. Its sequels – the *Second Programme*, enacted in 1963, and the less ambitious *Third Programme*, launched by Jack Lynch in 1969 – met with mixed results.[4] Less associated with these later efforts, Lemass is more remembered for promoting a new model of economic policy and progress.

Based on Lemass' public record during the late 1950s and early 1960s it has long been assumed, but never conclusively demonstrated, that the government's pursuit of an expansionist economic agenda had important implications for Ireland's foreign policy, particularly its independent posture at the UN. During the Department of External Affairs Estimates debate in July 1959, less than one month after being named Taoiseach, Lemass gave no indication that changes in Ireland's foreign policy were imminent. He ardently defended Frank Aiken's activist UN role. It had 'won increasing respect' for Ireland's views and was responsible for the growth of Irish 'influence in the United Nations Assembly, which can be of importance to us in the future'.[5]

But within a year Lemass was humming a different tune, hinting, but never explicitly stating, that Ireland's foreign relations would become more congruous with the government's economic goals. His comments on several occasions stressing Irish solidarity with the free world implied that Ireland's affairs with other nations would henceforth take account of the desire to attract foreign investment and open up export markets, especially in western Europe and the United States; they also revealed him to be a genuine Atlanticist.

In the foreign policy section of his keynote address to the Fianna Fáil *Ard Feis* on 8 November 1960, Lemass first paid homage to Ireland's well-established traditions: the government would promote 'the rule of law in international affairs' and the 'influence and power of the United Nations'.[6] Still, Ireland's absence from NATO did 'not mean that we are indifferent to the great issues which divide mankind today, much less that we are neutral in regard to them'. The Irish people were 'firmly on the side of those nations

3 Lyons, loc. cit.
4 For a comprehensive review of this period, see Fanning, *Department of Finance*, pp. 509–20; 'Lee, *Ireland*, pp. 341–59; John F. McCarthy, *Planning Ireland's Future – The Legacy of T.K. Whitaker* (Dublin, 1990), *passim*.
5 DD 176, 661, 7 July 1959.
6 *Irish Times*, 9 November 1960.

which share our belief in the true principle of democracy'. They repudiated not only colonialism in Africa and Asia, but also 'the newer more ruthless form of imperialism that has brought so many European countries unwilling- ly under the communist yoke'. Lemass reiterated this view one month later in a speech to the Solicitor's Apprentice's Debating Society in Dublin. Ireland was not 'neutral on the ideological issues that now divide' the globe. It was a member of the free world, 'and everybody, west and east, knows that is where we belong; and, come what may, we would not wish them to think otherwise'.[7]

Lemass' contemporaries interpreted his clear, albeit inconclusive, com- ments as forecasting a modification in Ireland's position in the General Assembly. Under an early September 1960 headline asking 'Change in Irish Policy at the UN?' the *Irish Times* reported that 'speculation already has begun on the possibilities of a change in Irish foreign policy' at the soon-to- open Fifteenth Session.[8] A recent speech by Lemass similar to the ones recounted above had sparked it off. Many assumed that Frank Aiken would still back proposals in favor of world peace and Ireland would 'maintain her role as a country with an independent' identity. Nonetheless:

> it is possible that there may be a change of emphasis, or direction, in Irish policy on other matters. Sharp differences of opinion on vital inter- national problems – such as the question of whether the proposal to admit China should be discussed in the General Assembly – might be avoided either by abstention or by an even more comprehensive state- ment on Ireland's general international policy.

When challenged a few months later to clarify the government's stand Lemass was evasive. Noel Browne, a National Progressive Democrat TD from Dublin and Minister for Health in the first Inter-Party government, asked Lemass whether his remarks at the Solicitor's Apprentice's Debating Society 'regarding the traditional policy of neutrality observed by this coun- try through two major World Wars represents government policy ... '[9] The Taoiseach replied that his speech 'may be taken as giving a general indication of government policy', but emphasized that he 'made no reference to the "traditional policy of neutrality observed by this country"'.[10]

One of Dr Browne's colleagues also detected a shift in the government's international position,[11] and a more recent scholar has recorded that by the

7 S 16057/F, 1 December 1960.
8 *Irish Times*, 6 September 1960.
9 DD 185, 909, 13 December 1960.
10 Ibid.
11 Declan Costello, a Fine Gael TD, noted that 'It seems to me there has been a shift in the foreign policy of the government over the past twelve months ... [as] shown in the

autumn of 1961 'new foreign policy considerations began to assert them-selves'.[12] But the definitive answer as to whether the government's new eco-nomic priorities influenced Ireland's activist role at the UN, and if so in what manner, has previously eluded the grasp of interested observers. This conun-drum can now be authoritatively resolved. Its elucidation is not a straight-forward procedure. It requires both a review of certain aspects of the foreign policy of the de Valera period and an examination of the process by which new designs in the economic sphere worked on UN issues throughout the Fourteenth, Fifteenth and Sixteenth Assemblies. More important, this exer-cise yields up a multi-dimensional response, thus highlighting the complex influence of economic expansion on Ireland's UN posture.

Dividing Lemass' oversight of UN policy into two stages facilitates the explication of the impact of economic development on Ireland's diplomacy in the General Assembly. The first period, encompassing the early Lemass years, which lasted roughly from July 1959 until April 1961, and included the Fourteenth and Fifteenth Assemblies, must be considered a transitional phase. During this interim span, when several crosscurrents collided, the impact of the new economic program was discernible, but not overwhelming. As a result, continuity defines this period: in several important respects UN policy paral-leled de Valera's autonomous, energetic approach; likewise, Lemass reaffirmed fundamental principles of Irish foreign policy.

This transitional phase is the focus of this chapter. The exploration of two important issues confirms the Irish delegation's consistency. Its Tibetan ini-tiative, first pursued at the Fourteenth Assembly under Lemass, but with its origins in de Valera's government, reveals the Irish delegation's constant readi-ness to assume a leading role on controversial matters, its on-going support for small nations invaded by their larger neighbors, and an abiding concern for human rights. This last consideration, especially when placed within the con-text of Ireland's history and its anticolonialism, informed the delegation's opposition to apartheid in South Africa at the Twelfth Session, and, moreso, its willingness to join with the Afro-Asian bloc at the Thirteenth, Fourteenth, and Fifteenth Assemblies to ensure that the item was brought up for debate.

At the same time, several qualifications circumscribed the continuity of the early Lemass period. For example, whereas previous independent proposals, such as Aiken's troop disengagement scheme, originated within the Irish del-egation but were ultimately unsuccessful because they were not embraced by the majority of other UN members, the Tibetan initiative was an American-inspired idea that succeeded precisely because a great power and other delega-tions supported it. Moreover, its quieting effect on critics of Ireland's China vote appealed to Lemass and Boland. While Ireland's condemnation of

declarations of the Taoiseach ... to the effect that in the ideological conflicts which divide the world today, we are not an uncommitted state': DD 191, 551, 11 July 1961.
12 MacQueen, 'Aiken', p. 211.

apartheid on human rights grounds was unequivocal, and more progressive than other western European delegations, its trade with South Africa determined its stand on economic sanctions; hence, the government's new economic endeavors strongly influenced this aspect of Ireland's anti-apartheid policy.

These trends foreshadowed the arrival of the second stage of Lemass' UN policy, wherein the Irish delegation abandoned its overtly activist, unfettered role in favor of one more sympathetic to its European allies and the United States. The ascendancy of economic interests over the desire to act as an independent agent propelled this shift. It took hold at the Sixteenth Assembly in 1961 and at the Seventeenth the following year. Nevertheless, just as the continuity that characterized the transitional period must be qualified, several factors delimited the pro-western transformatn of the early 1960s; these details, the exact nature of Ireland's new approach, and several issues that illustrate it are thoroughly reviewed in the following chapter.

                                    * * *

It is now possible to shed light on an important dimension of Lemass' stewardship of foreign policy: the nature of his relationship with Frank Aiken. Their inherent dispositions varied, of course. Lemass gravitated toward the west; Aiken favored an independent identity. As a result – and unlike de Valera – Aiken could not count on Lemass' support for ambitious schemes like troop disengagement from central Europe, so bold proposals like these trailed off. Sometimes Lemass even overruled Aiken outright. Nevertheless, the two men had an excellent working relationship. After all, they were once comrades-in-arms and then held portfolios in each of de Valera's governments – close to forty years of service together. Lemass respected Aiken's point of view. He granted Aiken the leeway due a cabinet minister. They professionally resolved their differences, and in several cases Lemass, despite his initial reservations, acceded to Aiken's recommendations after close consultations with him. More so, they concurred on several issues: human rights, decolonization, nuclear non-proliferation, the importance of the UN in world affairs, continued Irish support for the Organization, especially its peacekeeping duties. Indeed, Irish initiatives continued under Lemass, although they were more practical, and the tenor of Aiken's pronouncements more subdued.[13]

It is also time to clarify a glaring misconception of Lemass' conduct of foreign affairs: that he concentrated on European matters and allowed Aiken a wide berth at the United Nations. The common notion is that while 'Lemass

---

13 While no signs of serious discord between Lemass and Aiken surfaced in the available diplomatic documents, some have suggested that the Taoiseach kept his Minister for External Affairs at a distance: private source. This view, however, is specious: it has emanated from a brash faction within Fianna Fáil that at the time was locked in an internal power struggle with the party's old-guard.

increasingly thought in terms of London and Europe, Aiken preoccupied himself with issues raised in New York', and 'each of these two ministers kept out of each other's way, and as far as was possible left a free hand to the other'.[14] This 'pattern of fragmentation' supposedly fostered two competing foreign policies: one economic; the other political.[15] The first was 'operated by Lemass towards Europe and the creation of "a viable Irish society", while Aiken continued in the de Valera mold, prone to "the rhetoric of his ideals" in New York'.[16]

This interpretation is inaccurate. Aiken did not have a free rein at the UN. Lemass actively participated in the formulation of Ireland's United Nations policy. He discussed sensitive issues with Aiken personally, and his assertion that the cabinet reviewed UN matters was true.[17] Lemass stayed in close touch with deliberations in New York, particularly while the Assembly was in session. He had the final say on important votes and speeches, especially those affecting economic policy, and occasionally disregarded the advice of his delegation. Claims that Aiken did not have a strong personal interest in the EEC – and Lemass' ready acceptance of this – may have some substance, but future research in this field will most likely refute them.[18] After all, the Department of External Affairs, led by Aiken and its Secretary, Con Cremin, played a vital role in the negotiations surrounding Ireland's application for admission into the Common Market.[19]

The interaction of Lemass and Aiken did have a subtle effect on the internal dynamics of the delegation. Boland, sensing that the new Taoiseach was sympathetic to his own views, began to reassert himself, assisted by his ally in Dublin – Con Cremin. Conor O'Brien's brilliance continued to shine and he remained the delegation's most effective advocate of an activist policy, although under Lemass' shadow his influence waned. Moreover, after he was seconded to the UN Secretariat in the spring of 1961 to serve as Dag Hammarskjold's personal representative in Katanga, Aiken lost his most valuable lieutenant, the author of Ireland's independent identity, and his absence contributed to the further rise of Boland's point of view.

THE TIBETAN INITIATIVE

The Tibetan crisis originated in China's long-standing objective of superseding its internationally-recognized suzerainty over Tibet with the outright annex-

14 T.D. Williams, 'Irish Foreign Policy', p. 144.
15 Keatinge, *A Place*, p. 209.
16 Salmon, *Ireland*, p. 228.
17 DD 176, 661, 2 July 1959.
18 Cf. Keatinge, *Formulation*, pp. 86–7, 94.
19 Cf. Maher, *Path, passim*; S 16877, *passim*; DFA 305/57/363/28, *passim*.

ation of the country. Taking advantage of the transfer of Britain's quasi-protectorate role in Tibet to India, China invaded in the spring of 1950. A few months later El Salvador proposed that China's aggression be placed on the General Assembly's agenda, but the initiative collapsed when India and the United States opposed it: the former on the grounds that negotiations were underway between China and Tibet; the latter because it might lead to the admission of representatives of communist China into the Assembly.[20]

Hostilities cooled in 1951 when a Sino-Tibetan agreement was signed. The treaty granted Tibet limited autonomy, with no change in the country's religious structure, nor any modification of the position and authority of the Dalai Lama. China assumed responsibility for Tibet's external relations and garrisoned troops there. In 1956 China established the Preparatory Committee for the Tibetan Autonomous Region, a Sino-Tibetan body designed to govern the country. Resistance to this bald attempt by China to cement its hold soon broke out and intensified in March 1959. The Chinese response was, by all accounts, brutal. After refusing a Chinese request to quell the uprising, the Dalai Lama fled, fearing that the Chinese were about to arrest him. He sought and was granted asylum in northern India. His arrival exacerbated the country's strained relations with China, which had recently deteriorated due to border disputes.[21]

Freddy Boland took the lead in urging a strong Irish response to China's latest act of aggression. After telling Aiken, who had been in New York in March for the close of the Thirteenth Session, that 'it would be an excellent thing, from every point of view, if he would make an early public statement condemning Red China's attack on the autonomy of Tibet', he clarified his recommendation in an early April letter to Cremin.[22] An official announcement by the Minister was unnecessary; instead, a 'clear, positive reference to [Tibet] in a speech in his constituency or elsewhere would be enough'. Boland urged that it take 'the form of a definite condemnation of Red China's action, the text of which could be sent to us here for circulation to the news agencies'. He also stressed that Aiken, not de Valera, should deliver it. He did admit that the precise legal status of Tibet *vis-à-vis* China was uncertain, but argued that 'the constitutional niceties of the question are of secondary importance'. Irish reluctance to defend Tibet on the basis that China was 'doing no more than asserting her legitimate authority would make complete and absolute nonsense of the stands' the delegation had taken in similar cases. China was 'now forcibly depriving the Tibetan people' of their autonomy and long-standing, fervently defended tradition of 'internal freedom'. Further, as Boland admirably reminded Cremin:

20 DFA PMUN X/92, 6 April 1959.
21 For a closer review of this period, see Dalai Lama, *Freedom in Exile: The Autobiography of the Dalai Lama* (New York, 1990), pp. 123–159.
22 DFA 305/134/2, 2 April 1959. Boland forewarned Cremin by cable of the arrival of this report: DFA PMUN X/92, 2 April 1959.

From the beginning, one of the leading features of our policy as a member of the United Nations has been our outspoken defense of the rights of small peoples against the efforts of more powerful countries to impose their will on them by superior force. It was on the basis of that principle that we spoke up for Hungary against Soviet Russia, for the Algerians against France, for the Cypriots against Britain. We shall, therefore, not be striking out on any new line if we now speak up for Tibet. On the contrary, logic and consistency, as well the objectivity on world issues which we endeavor to preserve, oblige us to do so. And, in my view, a special responsibility, in the present case, reposes on independent countries like Ireland.

Boland realistically assessed the likely response of other delegations to the crisis. The United States and its allies would seek propaganda gains at the communist world's expense, thus allowing China to make the counter-claim that the revolt in Tibet was a western-inspired plot. Ireland could not expect much support from India, Ceylon, Burma, and Thailand, despite their large Buddhist populations, because their proximity to China made them hesitant to spark off its wrath. Ireland, however, enjoyed 'a freedom of speech in this instance which they don't'. Boland submitted that the government 'should use it ... and by so doing, we will greatly increase our stature in the eyes of the Asian countries most closely concerned and of the right-minded members of the United Nations'.

There is absolutely no question that Boland's concern for the rights of small nations and his unwavering devotion to the rule of law in international affairs engendered this commendable recommendation. Yet he also hoped to provoke an Irish censure of China to temper the negative reaction in the west to the delegation's China vote. That is why he stressed that Aiken should deliver the message. If the spokesman of Ireland's China policy condemned the invasion of Tibet it would send an unmistakable signal to the west as to where Ireland really stood.

On 6 April Cremin discussed the matter with Aiken, who indicated that he might refer to Tibet in a speech in Dundalk on 12 April.[23] At that juncture, however, Aiken held serious reservations. Cremin later told Boland that his reluctance was 'not due at all to any doubts he has about the propriety of castigating the Chinese action', but owed to recent commentary in Ireland.[24] On 31 March Dr Michael Browne, the Archbishop of Galway, had excoriated Ireland's China vote in a speech that subsequently received wide press coverage. Before Dr Browne's reproach, which Cremin called an 'unexpected and unfortunate complication', Aiken 'was firmly determined' to speak out; afterwards, however, he did not wish 'to appear to have spoken because of it and thus, as it were, in extenuation of his' China vote.[25] Obviously, Aiken (unlike Boland) did not want his statement on Tibet to undermine Ireland's independent position on the representation of China. So at this stage Aiken probably told Cremin that any potential declaration on Tibet must not include a reference to the UN or possible Irish initiatives there.

Cremin duly asked John Belton to supervise the drafting of a preliminary statement on Tibet. Belton, after cautioning him to avoid 'superlatives and also any reference to the United Nations', delegated the task to Conor O'Brien, who swiftly completed it.[26] Following Belton's instructions, the draft did not mention the UN.[27] In a covering minute O'Brien reminded Belton that it was likely 'that the Minister will be asked, if not at the Dundalk meeting then in subsequent press discussion or otherwise, how he relates this statement to his position on China', and he might respond with a 'reference to the fact that neither Tibet nor Peking China are members of the UN ... ' O'Brien also noted that he had included 'a sentence from Ambassador Boland's report which very neatly summarizes our traditional standpoint on the rule of law, small nations and peace'. At the same time, because he disagreed with Boland's intent to counterbalance criticism of Ireland's China policy, O'Brien drew the fine distinction that:

> In connection with Ambassador Boland's reference to Algeria and Cyprus, we have never used the language of condemnation in reference to events in these places, although we have advocated self-determination for the people of the territories concerned and have – more by implication than directly – criticized the policies being applied there.

Aiken approved the draft statement when shown to him on 10 April, but was still hesitant, even at this late stage, about including it in his Dundalk speech two days later; Cremin noted, in a letter mailed to Boland that day, that 'it is not yet certain that he will do anything'.[28] Within twenty four hours, though, Aiken had decided to act, and not only excoriated China, but directly referred to the UN.[29] He probably included this latter remark after consulting with Eamon de Valera, which highlights the fact that the roots of the Irish Tibetan initiative took hold while de Valera was still Taoiseach.[30]

25 Ibid.
26 Ibid., 9 April 1959.
27 Ibid. (nd).
28 Ibid., 10 April 1959.
29 The final text of Aiken's statement was decided on 11 April, one day after Cremin had written to Boland, and was immediately cabled to Boland: DFA 305/134/2, 11 April 1959. Cremin sent a follow-up note to Boland after Aiken's text had been cabled to New York saying that Aiken 'will now definitely speak tomorrow': DFA PMUN X/92, 11 April 1959.
30 In his speech Aiken said that the 'most recent case of a cruel injustice being inflicted

In New York Boland went to great lengths to publicize Aiken's statement, the manner of which underscores his wish to rehabilitate Ireland's reputation in anti-communist circles. He circulated it to the Irish Embassy in Washington and the Irish Consulates throughout the country. He forwarded copies to Father Donal O'Callaghan, Provincial of the Carmelite Order, several Irish American newspapers, including the *Irish Echo, Irish World*, and *Irish Advocate* (whose editors promised front page coverage), Catholic papers, a Catholic news service, Cardinals Spellman and Cushing, the UN correspondents of major American papers, and 'colleagues with whom I am in particularly close terms', including the Ambassadors of India, Burma, Ceylon, Malaysia, and Henry Cabot Lodge.[31] Boland was certain that Aiken's statement, which he 'thought an excellent one', would be 'widely welcomed by all our friends here'. Nor would the furor aroused by China's action fade away, leaving Ireland 'in the fortunate position of being able to say that our government was one of the first to give official expression to the almost worldwide reprobation the event has evoked'.

Boland's prediction that Ireland's 'friends' would appreciate Aiken's comments was correct, and his strategy paid quick dividends. Henry Cabot Lodge found Boland's gesture 'thoughtful' and said that Aiken had 'spoken out with courage and forthrightness and his statement made a very good impression here'.[32] Cardinal Spellman thanked Boland for his 'kindness in sending me the statement made by Mr Aiken in reference to Red China's recent aggression in Tibet'.[33]

* * *

Aiken not only referred to the United Nations in his statement on Tibet, but two days beforehand had passed on the message to Boland, through Con Cremin, that if moves were afoot at the UN 'to condemn the Chinese action ... you should associate yourself with it'.[34] In the light of Cremin's words to

by a powerful country against a weaker neighbor is the aggression against Tibet. This unprovoked aggression has shocked the conscience of the world, particularly that of small nations like our own which know the evils of foreign rule ... We can do little more than to hope that the people of Tibet may be sustained in their sufferings by the words of MacSweeney: "It is not they who can inflict most but they who can suffer most, will conquer". So far it has not been possible to have the Tibetan case considered by the United Nations ... but we can, however, record our condemnation of the acts of oppression wherever and by whomsoever they are perpetrated ... Without due respect by powerful states for the rights of their weaker neighbors there can be no rule of law in world affairs, and without a rule of law in world affairs there can be no peace and security': *Irish Times*, 13 April 1959.

31 DFA 305/134/2, 14 April 1959.
32 Ibid., 16 April 1959.
33 Ibid., 17 April 1959. Con Cremin sent a note to Boland thanking him for publicizing Aiken's remarks: DFA PMUN X/92 20 April 1959.
34 DFA PMUN X/92, 10 April 1959.

Boland that such action would, 'of course, be less important should the Minister have made a declaration here', Aiken may have considered it as an alternative means of expressing Irish loathing of China's aggression if he did not refer to Tibet in Dundalk. On the other hand, he and de Valera may have concluded that an Irish initiative on this question would not compromise their stand on China.

Boland reported to Cremin that there was a good deal of discussion in the corridors, but 'little or no support' among the western delegations for the only 'effective way of getting the Tibet situation before the United Nations at once': bringing it before the Security Council.[35] Nor did they favor raising the item in the Assembly in the autumn. They considered it wiser just to mention Tibet during the General Debate. Boland told O'Brien, who was also curious about the mood at the UN,[36] that he had recently taken steps to discount a rumor that Ireland was anxious to inscribe the item on the Assembly's agenda.[37] He added that should the question arise in the General Debate, considering 'the point of view expressed in the Minister's recent statement, presumably we will be one of the delegations who will have something to say on it'.

Throughout the summer sentiment at the UN remained opposed to formally raising the question of Tibet in the Assembly,[38] but on 11 September Boland reported that several Asian nations – Malaysia, Laos, Pakistan, the Philippines – were considering bringing it up 'on human rights grounds'.[39] Interestingly, hints that Ireland was cosponsoring this initiative had resurfaced. The delegation denied it, but Boland inquired whether Ireland should support the move. In a veiled argument in favor of doing so, he reminded Iveagh House that 'the Tibetan question [is] bound to be raised strongly in [the] Assembly in one form or another'.

Aiken personally took up the matter when he arrived in New York a few days later. On 14 September he and Boland met with Ambassador Wadsworth, Deputy Representative of the US delegation (later Permanent Representative after Henry Cabot Lodge decided to run on Richard Nixon's ticket in 1960) and several of his colleagues.[40] Referring to speculation that Tibet might be inscribed on the agenda, Wadsworth explained that the United States preferred, 'for obvious reasons', to remain in the background, but they would cosponsor a request if a strong group of uncommitted delegations emerged and wished them to do so. They believed it best to concentrate on the 'human rights and genocide aspects of the matter'. Moreover, suggesting that the

35 DFA 305/134/2, 14 April 1959.
36 DFA PMUN X/92, 14 April 1959.
37 DFA 305/134/2, 17 April 1959.
38 Ibid., 22 June 1959.
39 DFA PMUN X/92, 11 September 1959.
40 DFA 440/15, 15 September 1959.

Americans were behind the rumor that Ireland might cosponsor the move, 'when it came to a question of what uncommitted countries might be prepared to sponsor such a proposal, the name of Ireland naturally occurred to them'. They correctly asserted that Irish 'association with this proposal would greatly add to its weight' and asked if Aiken and Boland would 'like to think the matter over'.

Aiken replied that the idea had come as a complete surprise because he had been under the impression that the United States opposed such a move. He had intended to refer to Tibet during his speech in the General Debate and when explaining his vote on the question of Chinese representation, but he would have to think carefully about this new proposal. To assuage Aiken's misgivings, Wadsworth assured him again that the American delegation would support the 'inscription of an item on the human rights aspect' of the question.

Why was the USA suddenly courting Ireland, especially in view of their acrimonious differences in the past? Actually, once the fallout over Aiken's first China vote in 1957 had settled Irish-American relations steadily improved: the United States realized that Ireland posed no threat to its long-term interests at the UN. A report labeled 'Private and Confidential' that Boland forwarded to Cremin during the Thirteenth Session in 1958, just after Aiken had returned to Dublin from New York, is illustrative. Boland noted that 'relations with the US delegation were much better this time than last year. The Minister got on well with [John Foster] Dulles and established easy personal relations with [Henry] Cabot Lodge and other US delegates ... '[41] In fact, Lodge told Boland that the more he got to know Aiken 'the better he liked him'.

Of more immediate significance to the United States was the tactical support that Ireland could now provide in New York. After close to ten new Afro-Asian members entered the UN between 1955 and 1957 the USA lost the automatic majority it had commanded in the General Assembly since 1945. This development became apparent at the 1958 Emergency Session on the Middle East when the American delegation failed to secure the passage of its own measure. To be sure, the United States remained the most influential member of the Organization, but it could no longer ram a resolution through the Assembly if the Afro-Asian group and its allies (often the Soviet bloc) opposed it. Instead, to garner a plurality on tough issues the American delegation had to resort to deal-making, bargaining, cajoling, even arm-twisting, all of which often involved financial inducements.[42] In these altered circumstances the USA, for the first time, discerned an advantage in Ireland's independent policy. If they could persuade the Irish delegation to back a

41 DFA PS 35/1, 20 November 1958.
42 Cf. Conor Cruise O'Brien, 'Conflicting Concepts of the United Nations', in Conor Cruise O'Brien, *Writers and Politics* (London, 1965), p. 200; Tavares de Sa, *The Play within the Play*, p. 85.

controversial initiative that they themselves supported, other wavering delegations might then follow suit out of respect for Ireland's autonomous identity. Tibet was one such instance.

Yet just as in the summer, other forces still worked against bringing Tibet before the Assembly. For openers, the moderate success of Nikita Khrushchev's recent meeting with Dwight Eisenhower – and its concomitant 'Spirit of Camp David' – had precipitated a brief thaw in the Cold War, and no one wanted to reignite it by discussing such a controversial issue.[43] The Afro-Asian bloc's natural affinity for China also thwarted such a course of action. More pressing for India were its fragile relations with China, worsened not only by border disputes, but by the recent arrival of several thousand Tibetan refugees. South Africa, the United Kingdom, France, and other European colonial powers objected on the grounds that Article 2.7 of the Charter precluded interference in China's internal affairs – an argument they often invoked to forestall debates about their own colonial holdings. (This position later embarrassed these governments due to public outrage over China's action.[44])

Following their meeting with the Americans, the Irish delegation gauged the support in the Assembly for inscribing Tibet on the agenda; Boland reported his findings to Cremin on 18 September.[45] Of the Asian delegations, Malaysia and the Philippines were 'keen to have a separate item if somebody else took the lead', Nepal was 'positively opposed', and the others were 'hesitant and skeptical'. Unfortunately, the majority found it 'unpalatable to be faced with an issue involving China similar to others on which they had not hesitated to condemn their traditional imperialist adversaries such as Britain, France, and Belgium'.[46] The final position for many in this group depended on the attitude of India, whose response was cryptic. They did not favor inscription, nor would they vote against it; Boland concluded that this was not a position of 'positive opposition'.[47]

Dag Hammarskjold opposed the idea, 'his main fear being that if an item were inscribed it would inevitably lead to a profitless Cold War discussion'. All those approached, including the United States, agreed that should the item go forward it had to be confined to the human rights dimension of the issue: 'Anything which appeared to deny or challenge communist China's suzerainty over Tibet would entail endless Assembly wrangling, and would be unlikely to win general acceptance.'

The Irish delegation, discouraged by its research, told the Americans 'that there seemed to be a general lack of enthusiasm' for the move. More impor-

43   S 16051/B, 20 October 1960.
44   S 16051/B, 20 October 1960; DFA PMUN X/92, 12 October 1959.
45   DFA 440/15, 18 September 1959.
46   S 16051/B, 20 October 1960.
47   DFA 440/15, 18 September 1959.

tant, echoing a familiar Irish concern, they doubted 'whether there was a sufficient body of positive support available to ensure that any resolution put
down would be an impressive demonstration of the moral opinion of the
United Nations on the Tibetan issue'. The American diplomats countered
with the plausible argument that others were waiting for a delegation 'to take
the lead, and once the lead were taken and an appropriate resolution put
down few members of the Assembly would find it possible to vote against it'.
They also reiterated Ambassador Wadsworth's earlier assertion 'that Ireland
was the ideal country' to do so.

Then on 18 September, according to a report Boland sent to Cremin,
Aiken proposed a compromise that the United States welcomed. To test the
waters he would announce, when explaining his China vote, 'that the feeling
of reprobation aroused by events in Tibet should find expression in a resolution of the Assembly'.[48] Such a statement would 'serve to focus the question
whether a special item on Tibet should be put down or not'. Meanwhile, the
Irish delegation, assuming that other delegations would want to know 'what
kind of resolution they had in mind', had submitted a draft text to the
American delegation 'in strict confidence' for their views. Boland included
two copies of the draft with his report – one for Cremin and a second one for
the information of Sean Lemass. He reminded Cremin that 'this does not
mean that a special item on Tibet is certain to be inscribed'; what it did mean
was 'that Ireland has taken the lead' on this issue.

* * *

The delegation refined its strategy during meetings on 19 and 20 September.
They decided to circulate copies of the Irish draft resolution after Aiken's
remarks on Chinese representation. If the reaction was positive they intended
to inscribe the item after a 24 hour wait, but Boland convinced them to line
up potential cosponsors first.[49] Aiken preferred a country near Tibet, so long
as it was not a member of SEATO, the American-led anti-communist alliance
in Southeast Asia.[50] If no partners could be found they courageously agreed
to 'go ahead alone on inscription'.[51]

On 21 September Aiken explained to the Assembly Ireland's third straight
vote in favor of a discussion of the representation of China. After reiterating
his reasons for doing so he noted, because it had 'an obvious bearing' on the
question, 'the feelings of abhorrence and reprobation which the actions of the
Peking government in Tibet have aroused in my country'.[52] True, the Irish
admired the Chinese and 'their ancient culture ... and have always sym-

48 Ibid.
49 DFA 313/36/2, 19, 20 September 1959.
50 S 16051/B, 20 October 1960.
51 DFA 313/36/2, 19 September 1959.
52 Aiken, *Ireland* (1959), pp. 3–7.

pathized with their sufferings at the hands of foreign powers', but they could not accept 'the brutal crushing of Tibetan autonomy, the expulsion of the religious leaders of the Tibetan people, or the use of force on the Indian border'. Ireland, and countries like it devoted to 'liquidating the last remnants of imperialism and upholding the rights of small and defenseless peoples to liberty and peaceful settlements of disputes, must condemn these actions of the Peking government'. More so, 'these views should find expression in an appropriate resolution at this session of the Assembly'.

Boland summarized the reaction for Con Cremin. The Soviet bloc criticized Aiken's speech. Expectedly, it 'received a good deal of favorable comment ... from western delegations'.[53] It 'gave great pleasure to the Americans. The new Secretary of State, Christian Herter, asked to see the Minister to thank him'; Ambassador Wadsworth said there was 'a good deal of red meat in it'. The leader of the Nationalist Chinese delegation respected its 'honesty'. Sticking to its narrow interpretation of Article 2.7 of the Charter, the United Kingdom was unenthusiastic. Other responses were lukewarm. Ominously, India, Nepal, and Burma remained opposed; Krishna Menon told Aiken that the inscription of the item would be 'an embarrassment to the Indian government'. The stand of these latter three countries continued to have 'a dampening effect' on the Afro-Asian bloc, who feared that stirring up the Cold War would stifle the progress of their own agenda. Despite this inauspicious forecast, Boland averred that it would be difficult for the Assembly to remain quiet and he concurred with the American claim that once a leader emerged with a viable resolution other countries would fall in line. Aiken agreed, and following a lengthy meeting on 26 September the delegation 'decided to continue with the proposal pending discussions with other delegations, particularly Afro-Asian and Latin American delegations, regarding its prospects in the General Committee and in Plenary'.[54]

The subsequent canvassing, complicated by fears of stoking the Cold War, concern over Article 2.7, and apprehension over India's role, proved 'painstaking'.[55] Yet the Malaysian delegation – Asian, non-SEATO, eminently suitable – offered to help; their government had instructed them to cosponsor 'any move to put the Tibetan item on the agenda provided that it was able to do so in suitable company'.[56] Aiken gladly accepted their support. An External Affairs summary later noted that they proved 'a most useful associate' throughout the entire debate.[57]

53 313/36/2, 25 September 1959.
54 Ibid., 26 September 1959.
55 S 16057/E, 6 October 1959.
56 S 16051/B, 20 October 1960.
57 The Malaysians had the same high regard for Ireland. While on an official trip to the Netherlands Tunku Abdul Rahman, the Malaysian Premier, told Mr Brian Gallagher, the Irish Ambassador to Holland, that he 'was very pleased' with Irish-Malaysian cooperation at the UN. Being associated with Ireland 'had given them a complete

On 28 September Ireland and Malaysia requested that the 'Question of Tibet' be added to Assembly's slate. To avoid distracting debates over the precise international status of Tibet and Article 2.7, the explanatory memorandum confined itself to the human rights aspect of the issue.[58] It called attention to the '*prima facie* evidence of [the] attempt to destroy [the] traditional way of life of [the] Tibetan people and the religious and cultural autonomy long recognized to them'. It also declared that the UN had a moral obligation, and a legal right, to call for the restoration of religious and civil liberties in Tibet.

Interestingly, Sean Lemass shared Boland's view that the Irish delegation's association with the Tibetan question would deflect criticism of its China vote and thereby reinforce Ireland's anti-communist credentials with the west. On 29 September Cremin sent Boland a 'Very Confidential' letter thanking him for his recent updates on the situation.[59] He said that he had, 'of course, been keeping the Taoiseach informed generally of developments at the UN in relation to matters of particular concern to us', including Tibet.[60] When speaking with him earlier that day Lemass had 'expressed his keen satisfaction at the Minister's intention to sponsor a resolution on Tibet – on the ground that this would dispose effectively of certain of the charges directed against us because of our attitude on the question of Chinese representation'.

The Irish and Malaysian request came before the General Steering Committee on 9 October. Aiken addressed it that day, but on 7 October he refuted charges made during the Assembly's General Debate by Vasily Kuznetsov, the Soviet Deputy Foreign Minister, that the Irish delegation was acting at the behest of the United States. Aiken said he had ignored the comment at first, but then decided that 'to remain silent might be open to misinterpretation as a tacit acceptance of the Soviet delegation's allegations'.[61] The reason Ireland and Malaysia had acted was 'quite simple. We believe that the fundamental rights, and even the very existence of a small nation, and of a small people – the people of Tibet – are threatened.' And whenever the liberties of weaker peoples were violated:

defense against communist-inspired criticism of their action on the matter of Tibet. Nobody would believe for a moment that Ireland was actuated by imperialist sentiments': DFA 305/134/2/II, 30 May 1960.

58 S 16057/E, 6 October 1959.

59 Ibid., 29 September 1959.

60 Earlier Cremin had sent Lemass a copy of Boland's summary of his 14 September meeting with the American delegation. He next forwarded copies of the minutes of the delegation's meetings wherein they planned their strategy, saying that the 'Taoiseach may be interested in these papers.' Two days later Maurice Moynihan noted that they were 'Seen by the Taoiseach'. Cremin later forwarded to Moynihan one of Boland's comprehensive reports, dated 6 October, for the information of Lemass who, he was sure, would 'be interested in reading it': DFA 440/15 18 September 1959; DFA 313/36/2, 26, 28 September 1959; S 16057/E, 10 October 1959.

61 Aiken, *Ireland* (1959), pp. 21–2.

the representatives of other small peoples in this Assembly have the duty to speak out. If we fail to do so in ... a case like that of Tibet, then in our view we would be weakening what is in the long run the only defense of small peoples everywhere – the moral force of public opinion upholding the rights of our Charter.

Ireland's Assembly record in similar cases spoke for itself. It had always been 'governed by adherence not to any bloc, but to the principles of the Charter and to the evolution of the rule of law'.

Aiken reiterated these themes when he addressed the Steering Committee on 9 October.[62] Boland observed, in a minute to Cremin, that the Minister adopted a moderate tone to 'disarm the feeling which we knew existed among quite a number of delegations that the raising of the Tibetan question would defeat current endeavors to thaw out the Cold War', and in contrast to Kuznetsov, whose only aim 'seemed to be to make the discussion as acrimonious as possible'.[63] Aiken was effective, for the Committee decided 11 to 5, with 4 abstentions, to inscribe the 'Question of Tibet' on the agenda and sent the item directly to the Plenary without reference to a Committee.[64] This outcome was better than the delegation 'had thought likely a few days previously. Prospects brightened considerably within the day or two before the meeting.'[65]

On 12 October the Assembly adopted the Steering Committee's recommendation by a vote of 43 to 11, with 25 abstentions. The Soviet bloc, Yugoslavia, and Indonesia voted against it. As anticipated, several Afro-Asian and European delegations abstained, the latter still citing Article 2.7 of the Charter as their reason for doing so despite the emphasis on the human rights aspect of the question. Aiken had originally planned to move right to a debate after this vote, but others persuaded him to delay it so that Ireland and Malaysia could build solid support within the Assembly.[66]

* * *

The Dalai Lama and his brother, Gyalo Thondup, welcomed Ireland's efforts to raise Tibet at the UN. On his way to New York in early October, Thondup called on Hugh McCann, the Irish Ambassador in London, to express his 'deep appreciation'.[67] He boldly suggested that the Irish delegation explicitly mention Tibetan 'independence' in their draft resolution. McCann made no commitment on behalf of the Irish government and forwarded a transcript of his

62 Ibid., pp. 23–8.
63 DFA 313/36/2, 27 October 1959.
64 Aiken, *Ireland* (1959), p. 35.
65 DFA 313/36/2, 27 October 1959.
66 Ibid.
67 DFA 440/15, 1 October 1959.

conversation to Boland. Boland hastily wired Cremin in Dublin, asking him to have McCann immediately inform Thondup, at Aiken's wish, that because the situation was 'extremely delicate' he should 'avoid all statements on possibilities of UN action, especially on [his] arrival in New York, until he has had [an] opportunity of discussing' the situation with Aiken and Dato Ismail, the Malaysian Foreign Minister.[68] McCann contacted Thondup, who 'thoroughly agreed with the Minister's advice'.[69] At the request of the American delegation Aiken and Ismail met with Thondup when he arrived in New York, explained the status of current negotiations, and urged him to refrain from public announcements that might compromise their subtle diplomatic efforts.[70] Thondup promised to be discreet and thanked Aiken and Ismail for 'their championship' of Tibet's cause. The Dalai Lama expressed his gratitude in a separate cable to de Valera.[71]

In the interim between the Assembly's inscription of Tibet and its consideration of the matter the Irish delegation carried out a 'good deal of hard canvassing, not all of which was successful, but some of which bore fruit': Liberia and Peru decided to back the Tibetan initiative.[72] They coordinated debate procedure with sympathetic members, particularly New Zealand and Argentina. Working closely with the Malaysians and several other delegations, Irish diplomats also revised their draft resolution.[73] Because they wanted to secure as large a vote for as strong a resolution as possible it was necessary to moderate its language; it did not refer to the People's Republic if China, nor did it include any of Gaylo Thondup's stronger suggestions.

At last, on 20 October, the Assembly took up a measure cosponsored by Ireland and Malaysia. It affirmed that 'respect for the principles of the Charter of the United Nations and of the Universal Declaration of Human Rights is essential for the evolution of a peaceful world order based on the rule of law', and called for 'respect for the fundamental human rights of the Tibetan people and for their distinctive cultural and religious life'.[74] After Ismail introduced it, Aiken seconded it. Still sensitive to claims that Ireland was 'not acting as an independent agent in this matter', he recalled his state-

---

68 Ibid., 3 October 1959.
69 Ibid., 4 October 1959.
70 S 16057/E, 6 October 1959.
71 On 10 October the Dalai Lama informed Eamon de Valera by telegram that the Tibetan people were 'most grateful and appreciate your government's kind act of sponsoring and supporting my appeal to the United Nations Organization. Kindly continue your interest on the Tibetan problem with the same enthusiasm': DFA 440/15, 10 October 1959. De Valera acknowledged the cable on 21 October.
72 DFA 313/36/2, 27 October 1959. The Irish delegation convinced several Afro-Asian countries to support the initiative by pointing out that if they failed to back Tibet in this case their own credibility would be called into question and similar claims of their own would be weakened: Conor Cruise O'Brien, Personal Interview, 5 August 1993.
73 S 16051/B, 20 October 1960.
74 GA/RES 1353 (XIV).

ment in Dundalk six months previously and asserted that the Irish delegation was not responding to 'any outside suggestion – for there was none – but to the feelings which are invariably aroused in Irishmen by news of the oppression of a small people'.[75] Aiken then refuted the arguments against the resolution. Regarding Article 2.7, he said that the Irish delegation had always adhered to 'the more liberal interpretation ... to the effect that it does not debar us from discussing wholesale violations of human rights wherever they arise'.

The remainder of the debate on 20 October, Boland later reported, 'proceeded more or less in accordance with our hopes and expectations'.[76] On the following day, however, the likelihood of a procedural motion arose that the Irish delegation 'had feared from the beginning'. Before the Steering Committee's debate Anthony Moore, a British delegate, had asked Boland if Ireland would be content to discuss the issue in the Assembly, but not press it to a vote; his request underlined the United Kingdom's preoccupation with their own claims relevant to Article 2.7. Boland firmly replied that Ireland 'would be opposed to any such arrangements which ... would be impossible to explain to public opinion'. The British proposal 'continued to circulate, however, and for a few days we went around making it known that we were entirely opposed to it'. The idea eventually faded, but Aiken resolved to counter 'it strongly if it were put forward in the Assembly debate'.

The Irish delegation sensed its reappearance on the morning of 21 October when they discovered that the British speaker had rescheduled his morning intervention for the afternoon, and the Nepalese delegate, who opposed Ireland's stance, was penciled in to speak a second time. Just after lunch the Hungarian representative referred to the procedural move in his speech, and a British spokesman 'expressed support for the idea without, however, making it the subject of a formal proposal'. When the United Kingdom, the USSR, Nepal, India, and Afghanistan met for consultations in the corridor, the American and Irish delegations concluded that a move to adjourn the debate was imminent and they agreed that Aiken, supported by Lodge, would go to the rostrum to oppose it. When an Irish diplomat confronted the British they admitted that Nepal was about to make the suggestion and that they were going to back it. The Irish envoy made it quite clear that his delegation would fight it and then suggested to the United States that they should lean on the British. They did so, and the procedural effort disintegrated. Boland admitted that if 'Nepal had made the proposal we might well have been beaten on the vote'; even the Scandinavian countries backed it. Soon thereafter, the Assembly carried the Irish and Malaysian motion by a vote of 45 to 9, with 26 abstentions.[77] The USA, New Zealand, Australia, the Netherlands, Pakistan, Brazil,

75 Aiken, *Ireland* (1959), pp. 36–48. Freddy Boland's call for an early statement on Tibet had paid off.
76 DFA 313/36/2, 27 October 1959.
77 GA/RES 1353 (XIV).

Ecuador, Cuba, Venezuela, and others supported it. The Soviet bloc opposed the measure. Those abstaining included the UK, France, Belgium, Spain, Portugal, Finland, South Africa, the Dominican Republic, India, Nepal, Yugoslavia, and Indonesia.

* * *

Several countries lauded Ireland's handling of the Tibetan initiative. The American delegation 'was particularly pleased with the vote'; Henry Cabot Lodge warmly congratulated Aiken, 'expressing the view that the whole operation had been splendidly handled from first to last'.[78] Boland told Cremin that despite the early resistance, 'the prevailing feeling afterwards seemed to be that, on the whole, it was better to have had the matter raised and disposed of', otherwise the UN 'would have been in a weak position if it had simply swept the question of Tibet under the rug'.

In a 'Confidential' minute to Boland, Cremin informed him that Lemass had 'expressed his great pleasure at the result of the vote and his satisfaction with the nature and quality of the Minister's interventions'.[79] The Taoiseach felt that there 'were considerable advantages in the Minister's taking the course he did, and that our stand on this particular issue can do nothing but good'. Cremin added that Lemass' sense of satisfaction was widespread. At a recent luncheon hosted by the Irish Tourist Association several people had 'expressed congratulations at the result of the vote'. During a state dinner in Áras an Uachtaráin honoring Archbishop Antonio Riberi, the Papal Nuncio, de Valera, recently elected President, said that he was delighted Aiken 'had raised the question, had dealt with it in such a comprehensive and able manner, and had secured such a striking vote in favor of our resolution'. In a private conversation with Cremin, Father O'Neill, a Columban missionary and trenchant critic of Ireland's China policy, offered abundant praise and, like Boland and Lemass, recognized that Ireland's stand would 'dispose of much of the misunderstanding' arising from the vote on China.[80] In early December the Dalai Lama, 'on behalf of the people and government of Tibet', thanked de Valera for the Irish delegation's efforts, 'not only in sponsoring the "Question of Tibet", but also for arousing the interest of all peace-loving nations of the world in the tragic situation the Tibetan people are facing today'.[81]

---

78 DFA 313/36/2, 27 October 1959.
79 DFA 440/15, 24 October 1959.
80 Ibid., 27 October 1959. Likewise, a few weeks later Reverend Patrick Joy, S.J., told a public meeting that 'Mr Aiken had now made clear the situation on his stand on the admission of China and, if there has been any doubt, Mr Aiken's magnificent speech on the Tibetan question has put us clearly on the map as the friends of freedom': quoted in *Eire-Ireland: Bulletin of the Department of Foreign Affairs*, No. 459 (16 November 1959).
81 DFA 440/15, 6 December 1959.

The foregoing exploration of Ireland's support for Tibet highlights several important points. Underpinning the United States' early courtship of the Irish delegation was their desire to harness its independent reputation to the realization of their own objective: a UN condemnation of communist China. Frank Aiken was well aware of this dynamic; Freddy Boland and Sean Lemass welcomed it. Yet Irish-American cooperation signaled that the bitterness over the China vote had evaporated. The United States recognized that Ireland really was part of the west and that they could work together on matters of mutual interest.

What's more, the American delegation was crucial to the success of Ireland's initiative: their behind-the-scenes encouragement and promise of steady support in September convinced the Irish delegation to proceed; they prevented its collapse by leaning on Great Britain on 21 October. Their intervention, therefore, makes it clear that while Ireland was highly respected at the UN, its influence was limited. Acting alone, it could not husband a resolution through the Assembly in the face of serious opposition. At the same time, few, if any, nations were capable of doing so; multilateral diplomacy at the UN then and now demands compromise, *ad hoc* alliances, consultation. Indeed, the Irish delegation proved itself adept at working the wheels of UN diplomacy; Ireland was a competent actor in the UN arena.

From Ireland's perspective, why did it shoulder what was, according to a final report prepared by the Department of External Affairs, 'probably the most formidable task undertaken to date by the Irish delegation at the United Nations'?[82] Several factors spurred Aiken into action: China's violation of the Tibetans' human rights; its invasion of a small neighbor; its disregard for international law. Defending Tibet was, for Aiken, a natural Irish reflex. These considerations likewise inspired Boland and Lemass, but their desire to ameliorate the fallout from the China vote cannot be discounted.

To Ireland's great credit, irrespective of the United States' role, it took charge in the Assembly, generated support for the Tibetan cause therein, and faced down opponents of the initiative. The final resolution eventually met with approval precisely because Ireland sponsored it. Few other delegations could have engineered such a diplomatic coup. Further, Ireland did not abandon the Tibetan question after the Fourteenth Assembly, but pursued it at the Sixteenth Session, where it cosponsored a motion that affirmed the right of the Tibetan people to self-determination.[83] Writing on behalf of the Dalai

---

82 S 16051/B, 20 October 1960.

83 GA/RES 1723 (XVI). It passed by the comfortable margin of 56 to 11, with 29 abstentions. At the Fifteenth General Assembly in 1960 Ireland had agreed, with Malaysia, Thailand and El Salvador, to cosponsor a resolution similar to the one passed in 1959, but due to the Assembly's sudden consideration of the Bay of Pigs invasion time simply ran out. Lemass and Aiken stayed in close contact with the Dalai Lama throughout 1960 and 1961: DFA PMUN J/37/60, 2 March 1961, 23 June 1960; DFA PMUN J/37/61, 11 September 1961; DFA 440/15, 26 July, 10 August 1960,

Lama, Gaylo Thondup thanked Aiken for piloting this last resolution 'so eloquently in the Plenary' and contended that it would not only strengthen the
Tibetan people, but serve notice to the Chinese 'that their aggression and their
oppression has not gone unchallenged before the conscience of the world'.[84]

APARTHEID IN SOUTH AFRICA

At the Eleventh Assembly Ireland voted in favor of a resolution mildly repri-
manding South Africa for its practice of apartheid and another one requesting the country to report on its treatment of people of Indian origin, but the
delegation did not play a leading part in the debates.[85] At the Twelfth Session
the delegation abandoned this passive approach and, guided by Conor O'Brien,
emerged as a leading western opponent of apartheid. Not only Aiken's activism,
but Ireland's historical experience, suited it for this role. O'Brien once likened
apartheid to the Penal Laws, which were 'very similar in conception to the
apartheid system, with the distinction that religion and not color provided the
line between conqueror and helot'.[86] This parallel accounted for the 'sense of
outrage' most Irishmen felt when confronted by it.

The injustice of apartheid naturally dismayed Aiken and de Valera, who
had personally fought for Ireland's independence. Yet their ire was sometimes
muted because they had to balance several competing interests, especially
Ireland's close relations with South Africa. Empathy for the Afrikaners had
abounded at home since the Boer War. Afterwards, the two countries secured
the passage of the Statute of Westminster, which broadened the definition of
Dominion status within the Commonwealth. The presence of so many of its
missionaries and emigrants there, and mutual trade, also linked Ireland with
South Africa.[87]

This affinity partially explains de Valera's response to a letter he received
in August 1957 from 'The American Committee on Africa', an anti-apartheid
group headed by Eleanor Roosevelt and Martin Luther King, Jr. It asked him
to back a 'Day of Protest' in Ireland on 10 December (International Human
Rights Day) and requested him to sign an enclosed 'Declaration of Conscience'
acknowledging his support.[88] De Valera, who discussed the letter with Maurice

---

27 February 1961. For Aiken's interventions in 1961, see Aiken, *Ireland* (1961), pp. 23–6,
29–33. At the Twentieth Assembly in 1965 Ireland again cosponsored a resolution
deploring the violation of human rights in Tibet: GA/RES 2079 (XX).

84 DFA 440/15, 21 December 1961.

85 GA/RES 1015 (XI); GA/RES 1016 (XI).

86 O'Brien, *Katanga*, pp. 30–1.

87 Cf. Harkness, *Restless Dominion, passim*; Brigid Laffan, *Ireland and South Africa: Irish
Government Policy in the 1980s* (Dublin, 1988), p. 25; Keogh, *Ireland*, pp. 51, 235.

88 S 11115/A, 15 August 1957.

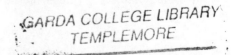

Moynihan, Secretary of the Department of the Taoiseach, said that 'the lines on which he should reply to the letter will require very careful considera-tion ... '[89] He thought a response might be based on 'a statement of adher-ence to the general principles of non-discrimination and respect for human rights', but minus any 'condemnation of the policies of the South African government'. De Valera wished to consult Iveagh House first, so Moynihan dispatched a copy to Sean Murphy.[90]

Murphy was away on leave, but John Belton discussed the letter with Aiken. The Minister advised against signing the enclosed card and recommended a reply along the following lines:

> This country has registered its disapproval of the apartheid policies of the government of South Africa in the last session of the General Assembly of the United Nations and will continue to maintain that position in the United Nations. The Taoiseach feels, however, that a campaign to organize a "Day of Protest" is not necessarily the best way to achieve the abolition of these policies. He considers, therefore, that Ireland cannot properly participate in the proposed campaign but her abstention from doing so in no way implies any approval of the prac-tices in question.[91]

De Valera forwarded a letter incorporating these suggestions to Eleanor Roosevelt.[92]

* * *

A few months later the Special Political Committee commenced a debate on apartheid. On 29 October Conor O'Brien spoke at length and with conviction.[93] Since rolling back apartheid would take time, he encouraged the Committee to persevere in trying to convince South Africa 'that its policies are reprobated by the overwhelming majority of mankind, must therefore fail and ought therefore to be changed'. He rejected the spurious argument that Article 2.7 ruled out a discussion of apartheid: its shadow fell 'far beyond the confines of [South Africa]' and it was therefore an international issue. O'Brien added that Ireland, due to historical and blood ties, had no 'unfriendly feelings' towards South Africans of European descent. Still, apartheid was 'degrading and oppressive' for them as well, and 'signs of unrest, of a stirring of liberal opin-ion among the European population' in South Africa attested to this.

89 Ibid., 23 August 1957.
90 DFA 305/94/II, 23 August 1957.
91 Ibid., 24 August 1957.
92 S 11115/A, 5 November 1957. Aiken had approved the final draft: DFA 305/94/II, 28 October.
93 DFA 417/167/8, 29 October 1957.

Several days later thirty countries introduced a draft motion into the Special Committee; Ireland and Greece were the sole European cosponsors.[94] The measure deplored South Africa's failure to respond to the Eleventh Assembly's resolution, reminded the government of it, and appealed to South Africa 'to revise its policy ... and to inform the Secretary General of its response'. On 1 November O'Brien introduced the resolution into the Committee at the request of its sponsors; obviously they admired his eloquence and respected the Irish delegation.[95] He correctly asserted that the resolution was 'moderately worded' and one 'the great majority of members of the Committee ought to be able to support'.[96] He rhetorically added: 'can we in common decency ... say any less about these practices than this resolution proposes to say'?

Later that day the Special Committee adopted the motion by a vote of 59 to 5, with 10 abstentions.[97] The United States abstained on the vote; Australia, Belgium, France, Portugal, and the United Kingdom opposed it. South Africa had boycotted the Committee's proceedings on the grounds that they violated Article 2.7. Other delegations shared this interpretation. O'Brien reported to Sean Murphy that all of those countries that abstained, and four of the delegations that opposed the measure, had stated during the debate that they 'deplored racial discrimination in itself, but felt that the racial policies of the Union of South Africa were essentially within the domestic jurisdiction of the Union'.[98]

O'Brien later informed Boland that due to the overwhelming support the resolution had received in the Committee 'feeling has perceptibly hardened against South Africa in this matter'.[99] He predicted that Ireland would benefit by its intervention and vote. Conversations with various diplomats had left him with the 'distinct impression ... that the line which we adopted ... and the fact of speaking unequivocally on this subject, will do something to strengthen our influence with a number of delegations'. Several African and Asian emissaries had 'made it clear that they would take account, in other proceedings of the Assembly, of the votes and speeches on this very sensitive issue'. The Austrian delegate on the Special Political Committee, Dr Koller, told O'Brien that when seeking instructions from his government he had referred to the Irish delegation's sponsorship of the resolution. Koller 'seemed to think that the fact that Ireland had taken up this position ... had something to do with the change in the Austrian attitude' from abstention to support for the measure.

94 DFA 305/94/II, 6 November 1957. The other cosponsors included several Afro-Asian delegations and four Latin American countries
95 Ibid.
96 DFA 417/167/9, 1 November 1957.
97 *Irish Press*, 2 November 1957.
98 DFA 305/94/II, 6 November 1957.
99 Ibid., 6 December 1957.

On 26 November the General Assembly carried the Special Committee's resolution by a vote of 59 to 6, with 14 abstentions.[100] The Soviet Union joined Ireland in voting for it; once more the United States abstained. That same day Ireland supported an Assembly motion on 'The Treatment of People of Indian Origin in South Africa', which requested South Africa to discuss this issue with India and Pakistan.[101] Likewise, in mid-October Ireland had voted for a compromise resolution establishing a 'Good Offices Committee' to investigate conditions in South West Africa, a South African-controlled territory not part of the UN's Trusteeship System, where numerous human rights abuses had been reported.[102]

An exchange of letters between de Valera and Mr Scott-Hayward, a racist Irishman in living in South Africa, casts more light on the government's opposition to apartheid. Scott-Hayward had been involved in the Irish independence movement and knew de Valera personally.[103] His screed to de Valera, barely worth mentioning, criticized O'Brien's public remarks at the UN.[104] Maurice Moynihan forwarded a copy of it to Iveagh House for their opinion.[105] Several weeks later External Affairs returned a draft for de Valera to send. Approved by Aiken, it set out 'the position from the point of view of our Permanent Delegation in New York, as supported by the opinion of this Department'.[106] Foremost, UN membership and adherence to the Charter had determined the Irish delegation's policy. Of equal consequence, the South African Catholic hierarchy, the World Council of Churches, and the Commission of the Churches on International Affairs had all condemned apartheid. Finally, the Irish government was:

> far too keenly aware, from our history, of the meaning of class segregation and the supremacy of one race over another, not to feel sympathy for those who are now treated as "second-class" citizens in their own country. It would have been contrary to our traditions, to our sense of moral values, to our belief in human rights, liberty and dignity, to our international obligations and to our Christian faith to have adopted any other policy.

* * *

100 GA/RES 1178 (XII).
101 GA/RES 1179 (XII).
102 GA/RES 1143 (XII). Ireland also voted for other resolutions designed to encourage South Africa to place South West Africa under the Trusteeship System: GA/RES 1138 (XII)–1142 (XII). See also Solomon Slonim, *South West Africa and the United Nations: An International Mandate in Dispute* (Baltimore, 1973).
103 DFA 305/94/III, 28 November 1959.
104 DFA 305/94/II, 4 November 1957.
105 Ibid., 12 November 1957.
106 Ibid., 9 December 1957.

At the Thirteenth Session in 1958 the Irish delegation assumed a more visible profile. This process began in mid-July when the Indian delegation asked Ireland to cosponsor a request for the inscription of the item 'Race Conflict in South Africa' on the Assembly's agenda. The leading role Ireland had taken on the South African issue at the Twelfth Session and its independent posture had obviously caught the attention of the Afro-Asian bloc; O'Brien's prediction to this effect had come true.

When seeking instructions from Cremin on how to respond to the Indian invitation Eamon Kennedy argued that despite the failure of other moderate countries like Norway, Austria, and Malaysia to sponsor the move, his 'own reaction to the request would be to support it'.[107] He reminded the Secretary of the leading role taken the previous year by Conor O'Brien. He had given 'voice to the natural reaction of Irishmen to the unchristian policies of apartheid ... and his arguments echoed the statements on the subject of the Christian churches, both Catholic and Protestant'. Moreover:

> In the light of our own history and of the policies of successive Irish governments, apartheid is, we submit, particularly deplorable, and as the annual resolution on the subject is supported by the vast majority of the Assembly, the Indian request would appear to us to be the kind of *demarche* we could logically support in the light of our own policies and position in the Organization.

Kennedy's minute sparked off an interesting exchange in Iveagh House. In a minute to O'Brien, Dr MacWhite agreed with Kennedy's recommendation 'insofar as the inscription on the agenda is concerned'.[108] Sounding somewhat cautious, though, he advised that the Permanent Mission 'should make it clear that we do not wish at this stage to appear as sponsors of any resolution on this question'; this tactic would provide 'far better scope for maneuvering and of playing, as far as one can, a conciliatory role on this matter'.

Reflecting on the two submissions in his own minute to John Belton, dated 24 July, O'Brien reminded the Assistant Secretary that Ireland was one of 'the sponsors of the anti-apartheid resolution in the relevant committee last year'.[109] Because this position was 'taken on the Minister's instructions', there was 'no question of it being changed this year ... ' He cautioned that should Ireland demonstrate a lack of continuity on this question its influence with the Afro-Asian group would be 'adversely affected – and perhaps very seriously so – by what they would regard as a tendency to evasion on this issue'. These and Kennedy's arguments appealed to Belton. After summarizing them in his

107 Ibid., 11 July 1958.
108 Ibid., 17 July 1958.
109 Ibid., 24 July 1958.

own minute to Cremin he recommended that Ireland accede 'to the Indian request'.[110]

Concurrently, Boland weighed in from New York with his own assessment. Despite the fact that several of the countries sponsoring the item were ' "left-wing" members of the Afro-Asian bloc', and the move was 'not exactly a friendly gesture towards South Africa', Boland advised Cremin that Ireland 'should join in cosponsoring the proposal'.[111] The condemnatory 'attitude which the authorities of the Catholic Church take on the issue of apartheid', and the several occasions whereby clerics who were critical of Ireland's vote on the representation of China had 'warmly approved the attitude we took on the apartheid issue last year', had inspired his counsel. Aside 'from the religious and theological considerations', Boland professed that 'surely this is a case in which we should be guided by our own history'. The Afrikaners were 'giving the colored peoples in South Africa the kind of treatment Cromwell gave the Irish – and with the same kind of fanatical Calvinist fervor!'

Interestingly enough, Boland, Kennedy, and O'Brien had arrived at the same conclusion, but for different reasons; this underscores previously exposed differences in their viewpoints. Opposition to apartheid on moral and historical grounds was unanimous. Kennedy and Boland, however, based a large part of their argument on religious grounds, while sounding uncomfortable about a tactical alliance with the Afro-Asian group. Contrariwise, O'Brien argued that only by supporting India's request, and thereby demonstrating consistency and credibility, could Ireland attain the objective he sought: influence with the Afro-Asian bloc. He had adjudged close relations with this group a priority; Boland and Kennedy were less enthusiastic.

On 31 July Cremin met with Aiken to discuss the Indian offer.[112] O'Brien's reaction to Boland's report, scrawled across the top – 'I agree with Mr Boland's view. A decision is needed fairly soon I think ... at least delay is open to be misconstrued' – probably encouraged him.[113] During their meeting Cremin laid out for Aiken the arguments for and against acceding to the Indian request, drawing from his colleagues' submissions and adding his own views. A slight over-emphasis on the negative aspects of the question hints that Cremin was skeptical about Irish involvement at this stage. Unsettling Cremin, in addition to the South African government's certain displeasure, its recent decision to participate fully in the deliberations of the UN, and protests received after the Twelfth Session from Irishmen living in South Africa, was the ominous prospect that it might react against Ireland 'in some

110 Ibid., 25 July 1958. Belton also noted that 'South Africa will probably resent this action, but we have no special obligation to them. The most we can lose is their single vote in future UN elections.'
111 Ibid., 23 July 1958.
112 Ibid., 1 August 1958.
113 Ibid., (nd) July 1958.

other contexts which are important, e.g. – and although this is very speculative – in connection with the proceedings at the forthcoming [British] Commonwealth Economic Conference'. In addition, only one European country, Greece, had 'so far agreed to cosponsor' the motion; two others with independent reputations – Austria and Norway – had declined.

Aiken hardly needed convincing on this issue, nor would he have been swayed by a pessimistic Cremin. His instinctual response was to support the request, and after hearing the pros and cons he concluded that 'the weight of argument would seem to be in favor of our agreeing to cosponsor the inscription of the item on the agenda'. He promised to discuss the matter with de Valera and one week later agreed to India's request. Cremin immediately informed Boland in New York.[114]

In the light of Ireland's support, the Afro-Asian bloc asked it to cosponsor a moderate motion that they introduced into the Special Political Committee in mid-October.[115] The delegation originally considered it 'unlikely' that they would be called on to speak during the debate,[116] but on 14 October Eamon Kennedy appeared before the Committee. His speech combined respect for South Africa with a firm statement of Irish principles and echoed the arguments he, Boland, and O'Brien had put forth in July in favor of Irish sponsorship of the inscription of the item on the Assembly's agenda.[117]

Two days after Kennedy's intervention the Committee approved the resolution,[118] and on 30 October the General Assembly passed it by a vote of 70 to 5, with 4 abstentions. Australia, Belgium, France, Portugal, and the United Kingdom voted against it on the grounds of Article 2.7; the South African delegation boycotted the meeting. The huge margin of passage underscored not only the nearly universal rejection of apartheid, but the relatively equable tone of the resolution itself; anything stronger would not have garnered such widespread support.

* * *

Ireland's reaction to apartheid remained unchanged at the Fourteenth Assembly in 1959. In early July the Irish Permanent Mission informed Iveagh House that India had once again requested it to cosponsor the inscription of

114 Ibid., 6, 8 August 1958.
115 GA/RES 1248 (XIII). The resolution affirmed that policies 'designed to perpetuate or increase discrimination are inconsistent' with the Charter, called upon all Member States to fulfill their Charter obligations, and regretted that South Africa had 'not responded to appeals of the Assembly' to revoke apartheid. The relevant article of the Charter, Article 55, section (c), reads: 'The United Nations shall promote 'universal respect for, and observance of, human rights and fundamental freedoms for all without distinction as to race, sex, language, or religion.'
116 DFA 417/178, 29 August 1958.
117 S 16057/C, 14 October 1958.
118 *Irish Times*, 17 October 1958.

the item 'Race Conflict in South Africa' on the agenda.[119] Boland recommended that Ireland 'should accede to the Indian request, and as the situation in South Africa has not improved since, it would be difficult to justify any other action'. John Belton echoed Boland's conclusion in a minute to Aiken, who readily agreed. Iveagh House immediately instructed the Mission to cosponsor the inscription. On this occasion Ireland was the only European country to do so.[120]

In early November the Irish delegation and thirty four others introduced a motion into the Special Political Committee mirroring the one approved by the Thirteenth Assembly, with an added appeal 'to all Member States to use their best endeavors, as appropriate, to achieve the purposes of the present resolution'.[121] On 4 November Boland spoke on its behalf in the Committee. The following day the Special Political Committee carried the resolution 67 to 3, with 7 abstentions,[122] and on 17 November the Assembly resoundingly approved it. The UK, France, and Portugal opposed it; Belgium, Canada, the Dominican Republic, Finland, the Netherlands, Luxembourg, and Italy abstained.

The fallout from Ireland's censure of apartheid at the Fourteenth Assembly was more pronounced than the year before, with those living in South Africa asserting that Ireland had gone too far, and some at home claiming that Ireland had not gone far enough. Speaking on 10 November upon his return from New York Eric Louw, the South African Minister for External Affairs, remarked that there 'had been evidence of a much more friendly attitude towards South Africa at the United Nations, but that Ireland was an exception'.[123] Louw erroneously, if not risibly, alleged that the delegation wanted to counteract South Africa's invocation of Article 2.7 because, according to 'an official Irish source', they intended to bring 'the Northern Ireland issue to the United Nations'. Actually, Louw had misinterpreted Eamon Kennedy's public comments defending the Committee on South West Africa's annual report, which he had co-authored, following Louw's severe criticism of it. Louw had assumed that Kennedy was speaking for Ireland, but he was speaking on behalf of the Committee, to which Ireland had recently been appointed.[124]

Nevertheless, having received publicity in Ireland, Louw's comments prompted Daniel Desmond, a Labour TD from Cork, to ask if the Minister for External Affairs would 'clarify the situation regarding Ireland's general attitude towards South Africa'?[125] Lemass, replying for Aiken, who was in New York, assured the Dáil 'that the government entertain nothing but friendly sentiments for South Africa'; relations between the two states have 'always

119 DFA 305/94/II, 3 July 1959.
120 Ibid., 16 July 1959.
121 GA/RES 1375 (XIV).
122 *Irish Times*, 6 November 1959.
123 Ibid., 11 November 1959.
124 DFA 417/135/I, 12 November 1959; DFA 417/135/I, 10 March 1960.
125 DD 178, 28-9, 18 November 1959.

been marked by mutual sympathy'.[126] Concurrently, 'when certain policies of the South African government with serious moral implications have come under discussion in the United Nations our delegation has consistently felt obliged to record its dissent from these policies'. Aiken resounded this view when he returned to Dublin a few days later and added: 'We are not antagonistic to South Africa. We have nothing but goodwill for the people of South Africa.'[127]

If Daniel Desmond worried that Ireland's stand on apartheid might undermine its relations with South Africa, Noel Browne challenged the government to do more. A few days earlier he had submitted a Dáil question inquiring of Aiken 'whether, in order to reinforce the fine sentiments recently expressed' by the Irish Permanent Representative to the UN, the Minister:

> will use whatever powers are at the disposal of the government to ensure a progressively expanding boycott of the importation of South African produce, as advocated by the African National Congress, the largest political group representing the people in South Africa?[128]

A preparatory memorandum for reply to Browne's query, compiled by T.J. Horan, Assistant Secretary in External Affairs, noted that to date 'no country had imposed a boycott on imports from South Africa' and refuted Dr Browne's proposal on several grounds.[129] A boycott, 'were it imposed by us ... would imply a certain degree of dependence by South Africa on her exports to this country', which was not so. From 1954 to 1958 the yearly average of South African exports to Ireland was £735,128, equal to 'only 0.18% of the average annual value (£406,000,000) of South African exports (including exports from South West Africa) in the same period'. Although the bulk of imports from South Africa consisted of nonessential goods such as fresh fruit, they were 'nonetheless commodities that it would be difficult to justify our doing without them or having to pay more for them'. Plus, 'we must assume that the imposition by us of a boycott of South African produce would provoke retaliatory measures'. Irish exports to South Africa, which comprised textiles, vegetable oils, rubber manufactures, dressed leather, medical and pharmaceutical products, and race horses were 'not great, certainly, but they are not without importance in our economy', averaging £72,725 per year. If South Africa imposed a ban on Irish products Irish manufacturers 'would be faced with the prospect of seeking alternative markets at a time when we are engaged in a maximum export drive to develop existing markets and obtain new ones'. Horan's conclusion, therefore, was unequivocal:

126 Ibid.
127 *Sunday Independent*, 22 November 1959.
128 DD 177, 891, 11 November 1959.
129 DFA 305/94/II, 11 November 1959.

Were we to take the initiative in acting on the recommendation of the African National Congress and imposing a ban on imports from South Africa, it is difficult to see ... that anyone would be the losers but ourselves, without having had any effect on the apartheid policy of the Union government.

Horan's memorandum was also effective. In reply to Dr Browne's call for an Irish boycott of South African goods Sean Lemass, speaking on behalf of Aiken, who was in New York, said that the 'answer is in the negative ... In connection with these matters we propose to continue to work within the ambit of the United Nations.'[130]

* * *

The Irish government conspicuously reaffirmed its disavowal of a boycott four months later in the wake of the Sharpville massacre. On 21 March 1960 the South African police killed 69 native South Africans who were peacefully demonstrating against the country's notorious pass laws. World-wide reaction was strong and swift. Meeting in an emergency session at the request of the Afro-Asian bloc, the Security Council adopted a resolution that deplored South Africa's racial policies, called for their repeal, and requested the Secretary General to consult with the government of South Africa.[131] In Ireland Aiken issued a statement mourning the tragedy.[132] Yet when Noel Browne asked him if Ireland would now consider a boycott Aiken said that it would not have the desired effect of ensuring the 'fundamental human rights' of all the people of South Africa.[133]

* * *

Dag Hammarskjold's ensuing failure to persuade South African to moderate its racial policies guaranteed that the issue would arise at the Fifteenth Assembly. On 20 July 1960 the Permanent Mission notified Iveagh House that once more India had requested Ireland to cosponsor the inscription of apartheid on the agenda along with thirty two other countries, including Norway, Sweden, four Latin American delegations, and the entire Afro-Asian bloc.[134] The delegation sought an immediate reply because the deadline was approaching. After unsuccessfully trying to contact Aiken, O'Brien gave the go-ahead, and the Irish Mission added its name to the list of sponsors.[135]

130 DD 177, 891–2, 11 November 1959.
131 SC/RES 134 (1960).
132 *Irish Times*, 24 March 1960.
133 DD 180, 2066–7, 7 April 1960.
134 DFA 305/94/III, 20, 21 July 1960.
135 Ibid., 21 July 1960.

A draft 'Memorandum for the Government' prepared in late August by Paul Keating, First Secretary in the United Nations Section, surveyed the position Ireland was likely to adopt at the upcoming Session.[136] Keating's views were not definitive, but the memorandum closely reflected the Department of External Affairs' philosophy, and it is likely that he spoke with Aiken before completing the piece. After reviewing the course of the debate at previous sessions, and the deteriorating conditions in South Africa in the wake of the Sharpville massacre, Keating correctly predicted that the Afro-Asian nations would take a harder line. Following the failure of the recent British Commonwealth Prime Ministers Conference to influence South Africa's racial policies, Malaysia and Ghana had already decided to boycott South African goods. Thus, the Afro-Asian bloc would probably introduce a resolution recommending 'a boycott or some other form of sanctions directed against the Union in the hope that this will prove successful where other courses of action have failed'. (Such a measure would be non-binding, since only the Security Council could impose punitive measures against a Member State.) The Afro-Asian group was pressing Ireland to back such a move, and 'an element of domestic pressure' had 'found expression in Dáil Éireann where Dr Browne has advocated such a boycott'.

Still, the government did not intend to modify its policy. Aiken, according to the memorandum, remained convinced that it was:

> impossible to maintain an effective system of economic sanctions as was instanced by the failure of the League of Nations in its attempt to enforce them against Italy at the time of the Abyssinian crisis. Moreover, it is felt that even were such sanctions enforced to such an extent as to cripple the South African economy this still would not result in any retreat by the government or any improvement in the condition of those now oppressed by apartheid.

The Minister, therefore, proposed 'to vote against any resolution recommending a boycott or similar sanctions'. The Irish delegation would 'continue to condemn the South African racial system and to call upon the South African government to abandon its policies in this regard'.

Conor O'Brien, recently appointed Assistant Secretary in charge of United Nations and Political Affairs,[137] reviewed Keating's draft memorandum before handing it up for final approval. He disagreed with its wording in one crucial respect and, ultimately, with its entire thrust; his interpretation reveals that he was far ahead of prevailing western opinion with regard to sanctions, but also at odds with his Iveagh House colleagues. In place of Keating's phrase that 'the Minister proposes *to vote against* any resolution recommending a

---

136 Ibid. (nd) August 1960.
137 Akenson, *Conor*, p. 167.

boycott', O'Brien urged, in a minute to Cremin, that the sentence read 'the Minister proposes *not to support* any resolution recommending a boycott'.[138] While not explicitly stating so, O'Brien favored this wording because it would leave the Irish delegation with the option of abstaining on an Afro-Asian resolution calling for sanctions, a move he would then fight for if the opportunity presented itself during the Assembly's deliberations.

O'Brien wanted this phrase inserted because he felt that it was 'unnecessary and undesirable for us to run directly counter to the sense of African and Asian opinion on this matter'. It was unnecessary because, regardless of what the Assembly decided, it was likely that 'only those states which, like Ghana, are already applying, or intend to apply a boycott, will implement the recommendation'. It was undesirable because 'it would seem inconsistent for a government, which in principle is opposed to apartheid, to vote against an attempt to make the Assembly's resolutions more effective', especially when such measures were advocated by the victims of discrimination in South Africa. 'In short, if the people primarily concerned think a boycott resolution may do some good ... we ought not to vote against them.' O'Brien incorrectly speculated that this 'would also be the attitude of the Scandinavian countries, while some Latin American countries, such as Uruguay, would probably go so far as to support the resolution'.

The final memorandum, presented to the government in early September, did adhere to O'Brien's editing suggestion, but ignored his other substantive amendments; save for the replacement of the words *to vote against* with the phrase *not to support*, the final submission was a carbon copy of Keating's draft.[139] Unlike Keating, O'Brien had failed to show how his recommendations were in Ireland's interests. His reaction to their disavowal was not recorded, but his waning influence presaged the shift in Ireland's overall policy the following year.

* * *

When the Special Political Committee finally took up apartheid in April 1961 two draft resolutions, as predicted, were introduced. The Committee adopted a moderate resolution modeled on the Assembly's earlier measures, with an added call for members 'to consider taking such separate and collective' action that might bring about the end of apartheid; Ireland voted for this resolution.[140] Although the Committee approved it, the Irish delegation did not vote for an Afro-Asian motion recommending that Member States impose trade sanctions against South Africa and break off their diplomatic relations with the country.[141]

138 DFA 305/94/III, 30 August 1960.
139 S 16051/A, 7 September 1960.
140 GA/RES 1598 (XV); DD 188, 178, 12 April 1961.
141 DD 188, 178, 12 April 1961.

In the Assembly Ireland once again supported the mild resolution, which passed by a wide margin.[142] The Afro-Asian measure failed to secure the required two-thirds majority. Ireland voted against it and was joined by the United States, Canada, New Zealand, and all of the western European delegations, including Norway and Sweden. By voting against sanctions Ireland thus split with the Afro-Asian bloc on this issue. Whereas earlier the Irish delegation had spearheaded the Assembly's efforts to condemn apartheid by being one of only two European nations to cosponsor the inscription of the item on the agenda, by 1961 it had aligned itself with the western European approach, which condemned apartheid in principle, but opposed the imposition of punitive measures against South Africa.

Noel Browne, still opposed to the government's policy, asked Aiken after the vote in the Special Political Committee if he agreed that when deciding matters such as 'trade sanctions and the withdrawal of diplomatic services', the Minister would 'be in better company voting with the Afro-Asian countries than with the Americans and British as he appears to have been in this connection'?[143] Aiken, no doubt frustrated by Browne's repeated attacks, reminded him that Ireland was not a member of the Afro-Asian bloc, nor 'any other bloc, and as an independent member of the United Nations it is our duty as well as our right to make an independent judgment on these matters'.[144] The delegation tried to give 'to these various complicated and difficult matters as much attention as we can in order to arrive at a conclusion which will help towards a solution and not make the situation worse'.

* * *

An important element underlying the government's opposition to sanctions that Aiken did not refer to in his response to Dr Browne was the impending visit of a South African trade delegation to Dublin. In January Con Cremin had received an inquiry from Mr W.A. Horrocks, South Africa's Senior Trade Commissioner in London, 'as to whether the government would be prepared to receive a special South African trade mission' that was traveling to Britain in the spring.[145] Cremin immediately forwarded the request to the Taoiseach's office, and at a meeting on 26 January the government 'informally agreed that the mission should be received'.[146] That same day Cremin notified T.K. Whitaker, Secretary of the Department of Finance, Mr J.C.B. MacCarthy, the Secretary of the Department of Industry and Commerce, and Mr J.C. Nagle, the Secretary of the Department of Agriculture, of the decision and

---

142 GA/RES 1598 (XV). The vote was 95 to 1, with 0 abstentions.
143 DD 188, 177, 12 April 1961.
144 Ibid.
145 S 14851/A, 26 January 1961.
146 Ibid., 26 January 1961; S 14851/B, 26 January 1961.

suggested that the inter-departmental Foreign Trade Committee undertake a review of Ireland's commercial relations with South Africa.[147]

In early February Mr Horrocks traveled to Dublin to discuss details of the trade delegation's visit with Iveagh House officials.[148] Horrocks confirmed that the mission would be headed by Dr J.E. Holloway, previously Secretary of the South African Treasury, a former South African High Commissioner in London, and one of 60 signatories of a recent anti-apartheid petition. The South Africans hoped to discuss with both government officials and leading businessmen 'the prospects of increasing the volume of trade between both countries' and the desire of several South African industrialists to establish branch operations in Ireland. Both Horrocks and External Affairs officials indicated that there was no interest in amending their mutual trade agreements. The meeting was tentatively scheduled for late April.

In March plans for the trade meeting were mildly disrupted by the sudden announcement that South Africa, due to criticism of apartheid from African and Asian members, would withdraw from the British Commonwealth on 31 May. In an internal Iveagh House memorandum Cremin reviewed the possible implications of this development for Irish-South African relations, since they were based upon South Africa's membership in, and Ireland's close links with, the Commonwealth.[149] Cremin assumed that 'if it is possible to do so, we on our side will wish to maintain the status quo … The question will arise, however, as to whether it will be possible to proceed.' He was especially interested in maintaining the 'free access to the territory of the one country by the nationals of the other'. The 'presence in South Africa, and, I believe, the continued movement to that country, of Irish priests and nuns' had motivated him. Casting light on his unease with Ireland's anti-apartheid stance, he feared that one day, due to 'the rigors of the apartheid policy', South Africa might 'try to restrict the functioning and the recruitment possibilities of the Christian churches in South Africa', which 'would be a serious blow for the Catholic Church there if Irish nationals were not able to enter freely'.

In short, Cremin feared that whereas South Africa's Commonwealth membership had prevented it from unilaterally erecting barriers to the free flow of labor, after leaving it might do so as a retaliatory move against Commonwealth members critical of apartheid. Cremin forwarded a copy of his memorandum to Lemass with the added note that the 'question of nationals may be possibly more difficult and it is bound, I feel, to be very important'.[150] That

147 S 14851/B, 26 January 1961.
148 Ibid., 1 February 1961.
149 S 16057/G, 23 March 1961. Despite leaving the Commonwealth after becoming a republic in 1948, Ireland had secured Commonwealth privileges in subsequent negotiations with the British: Ian McCabe, *A Diplomatic History of Ireland* (Dublin, 1991), pp. 134–5.
150 S 16057/G, 25 March 1961.

morning he had received a call from Father Cormac Daly, OFM, 'about a letter he has received from the Most Rev. Dr MacBride, Bishop of Kokstad, expressing serious anxiety as to the situation which may develop'.

In early April Cremin notified the Departments of Finance, Industry and Commerce, and Agriculture that his Department had completed an examination of the effects of South Africa's departure from the Commonwealth on trade between the two countries.[151] After analyzing Ireland's bilateral and Commonwealth trade agreements with South Africa Cremin concluded that 'unless the preferential treatment we accord to South African imports constitutes a real handicap for us, we should be prepared to contemplate its continuance'. Still, he solicited each Department's 'views on our existing trade relationship with South Africa and the desirability or otherwise of maintaining it'. Subsequently, there was widespread agreement that Ireland's economic relationship with South Africa should not be disturbed. At a meeting on 14 April the Foreign Trade Committee adjudged, 'subject to further consideration of the matter, that there would be no objection to continuing such preferences'.[152]

If Cremin was concerned with the effect Ireland's opposition to apartheid might have on the prospects for Irish Catholic missionaries there and the free movement of Irish labor, Lemass was determined that it would not interfere with the success of the South African trade mission to Dublin. On 2 May Lemass, who had been kept apprised of plans for the meeting, now scheduled for June, requested his new Secretary, Dr Nicholas Nolan, to ask Cremin 'to consider the desirability of having all officials who may meet with the delegation briefed on the line taken in discussions particularly with regard to South African racial policy'.[153] Later that same day Daniel O'Sullivan, Assistant Secretary in the Department of the Taoiseach, informed Nolan that Cremin would 'ensure that officials meeting the South African team will be fully briefed on the line to take in regard to the South African racial policy', and Nolan relayed the message to Lemass.[154]

Cremin followed up his guarantee by circulating a memorandum, entitled 'Apartheid', to all Irish officials due to participate in the trade talks.[155] He

151 S 14851/B, 11 April 1961.
152 Ibid., 14 April 1961. This decision was reconfirmed in letters to Cremin from the Department of Agriculture on 2 May and the Department of Industry and Commerce on 5 May. In March 1962 the Minister for Finance requested the government to utilize the powers granted to it by the Finance Act, 1961 regarding 'a country which ceases to belong to the Commonwealth ... to authorize the Revenue Commissioners ... to continue to grant to South Africa the preferential tariffs accorded to her immediately before 31 May 1961'. On 13 March 1962 the government formally authorized the Revenue Commissioners to maintain the preferential treatment accorded to South African imports: S 14851B, 12 March 1962; GC 3/28, 13 March 1962.
153 S 14851B/61, 2 May 1961.
154 Ibid.
155 Ibid., 31 May 1961.

also sent several copies to Nolan.[156] He first summarized Ireland's policy: apartheid was intrinsically evil and the Irish delegation had consistently opposed it at the UN. He added, however, that it could not be abolished 'easily or speedily'; a peaceful solution could be found 'only as a result of a relatively prolonged evolutionary process'. Hence, the Irish delegation had opposed 'the imposition of sanctions on the Union or the rupture of diplomatic relations'. Furthermore, and with particular relevance for officials greeting the trade mission, the Irish government was 'anxious to maintain friendly relations with South Africa, with which it has many ties, and to which many Irish nationals, including in particular missionaries, have emigrated'. It would, of course, welcome a signal from South Africa that it was 'prepared to revise its racial policies and concede elementary justice to its colored citizens'.

The Irish team was thus forewarned to handle the question of apartheid with delicacy when meeting the South African delegation. Due to other commitments the trade mission's visit to Dublin on 15 June was cut short, so the conference with Irish officials was brief.[157] Various trade issues were raised during an amicable, but inconclusive, discussion. Dr Holloway, the Chairman of the South African delegation, referred to Ireland's interest in 'attracting industry' and expanding the export of Irish glass and textile products to South Africa. The Chairman of the Foreign Trade Committee, Mr T.J. Cahill of the Department of Industry and Commerce, mentioned South African import restrictions and was pleased to hear that they would be eased once the country's foreign currency reserves were replenished. No arrangements were made for a further meeting in Dublin, but Dr Holloway suggested that the Irish government send a trade delegation of their own to South Africa for more formal talks. Apartheid did not arise, but a member of the South African delegation alluded to it during a private discussion with Cremin at a luncheon in honor of the mission.[158]

After reading press reports of the meeting Brendan Corish of the Labour Party asked Aiken to explain how expanding trade contacts with South Africa could be reconciled with Ireland's stand on apartheid at the UN and whether they might 'prejudice Ireland's position of influence in the UN *vis-à-vis* the uncommitted countries and the Afro-Asians'.[159] Aiken dismissed Corish's

156 Ibid., 2 June 1961.
157 Ibid., 15 June 1961.
158 Mr La Grange, a South African diplomat in London, questioned Cremin about Irish attitudes towards apartheid, implying 'that the people generally are not well-informed on the subject and, in particular, do not realize either the serious problem which the mass of Africans create for the white population of South Africa, or all that the government of the Republic has done for their material betterment'. Cremin told him of Irish feelings of sympathy for South Africa, but said that it was 'improbable that anyone in Ireland would be prepared to accept apartheid in the form in which it was presented': ibid., 16 June 1961.
159 DD 190, 1097, 28 June 1961.

implied charge of inconsistency by stressing the non-committal nature of the trade talks and asserting that they would not compromise Ireland's relationship with the Afro-Asian group.[160] Nonetheless, certain questions do arise. Was Ireland's refusal to support economic sanctions against South Africa inconsistent with its opposition to apartheid on moral grounds and its wider UN policy? More so, given the relatively minor contribution of South African trade to the overall Irish economy, would it not have been more appropriate for the Irish delegation to heed the Afro-Asian bloc's call for a boycott?

Several factors suggest that the reply to both questions is no. The government, led by Lemass, had previously deemed the expansion of Ireland's economy a national priority. In this context, Ireland's minimal commercial contacts with South Africa were not a marginal fact of Irish economic activity, but a starting point, a beachhead, for developing future trading relations with the country. Also, the government's attempt to broaden trade with South Africa was one element of a larger strategy designed to attract foreign capital and to pry open export markets that was industriously pursued along a wide front. To postpone the pursuit of economic opportunities in the case of South Africa ran completely against the grain of national policy and was therefore an option never seriously considered.[161]

Simultaneously, Ireland's top policy makers – Lemass, Aiken, Cremin, Boland – were unanimous in their conclusion that economic sanctions simply would not work. They were convinced, by analysis and experience, not merely selfish interests nor Ireland's close ties to South Africa, that the imposition of a boycott would not force South Africa to alter its racial policies; it might, in fact, harden the country's resistance to change. Iveagh House was also consistent on this score: it opposed Assembly resolutions calling for the imposition of economic sanctions against Portugal when it would not modify its colonial policies.[162] (Ireland did comply with an arms embargo leveled against Southern Rhodesia in 1965 by the Security Council because its recommendations were actually mandatory under the Charter.)

Ireland's reluctance to back sanctions against South Africa, and its concomitant tilt toward western Europe, were probably regretted by prominent Afro-Asian delegations, but they were unlikely to erode its reputation within this group in the short run. After all, the Irish delegation's record apropos of apartheid was beyond reproach. It regularly condemned the odious practice and annually sponsored the inscription of the item on the Assembly's agenda. It voted for resolutions calling on South Africa to end discrimination against

---

160 Ibid.
161 The Irish government's pursuit of South African investment in Ireland was successful. In the early 1960s the South African industrial giants DeBeers and Boart Hardmetals established plants at Shannon Industrial Estate which, by the 1980s, collectively employed close to 1,000 people: Laffan, *Ireland and South Africa*, p. 83.
162 GA/RES 2107 (XX).

people of Indian origin every year.[163] Likewise, it made an invaluable contribution to the Committee on South West Africa. Ireland served a three year
term on this body, and Eamon Kennedy performed outstanding work as rapporteur of the Committee in 1959.[164] At the Sixteenth Assembly the Irish
delegation once again cosponsored the inscription of the question of race relations in South Africa on the agenda. Although it parted company with the
Nordic countries by joining with other western nations to defeat a measure
recommending sanctions and abstained when the Assembly censured Eric
Louw, the South African Minister, for his specious comments about race
relations at home, it voted in favor of a successful resolution reiterating the
Assembly's right to call the attention of the Security Council to situations
likely to endanger international peace, and again calling on members to take
'separate and collective action' to end apartheid.[165]

In sum, economic expansion, the desire to promote trade with South Africa,
serious doubts about the efficacy of a boycott, and the Irish delegation's
unequivocal repudiation of apartheid illumine the Irish government's decision
not to endorse sanctions. It was not a topic of heated debate, nor did it provoke much soul-searching within official circles. The policy was straight-
forward and swiftly adopted. It also remained in force for the rest of the decade,
even though the Assembly approved – starting in 1962, and all by a wide
margin – numerous resolutions calling for the imposition of sanctions against
South Africa.[166]

CONCLUSION

It is now clear that during the transitional stage of his supervision of UN pol-
icy Sean Lemass sustained the autonomous, activist identity established by
Eamon de Valera and Frank Aiken at the Twelfth and Thirteenth Assemblies.
By its Tibetan initiative and its censure of South Africa's racial policies, the
Irish delegation reaffirmed its abhorrence of human rights violations anywhere
and its resistance to the invasion of small nations by great powers everywhere.
Ireland's sponsorship of resolutions on Tibet and the annual request for the
inscription of apartheid on the Assembly's agenda were vibrant reminders
that the delegation remained committed to an independent posture.

---

163 GA/RES 1302 (XIII); GA/RES 1460 (XIV); GA/RES 1597 (XV); GA/RES 1662
     (XVI).
164 DFA 417/135/I, 10 December 1958, 23 January 1959. Ireland also voted for several
     resolutions regarding the territory: GA/RES 1247 (XIII); GA/RES 1361 (XIV);
     GA/RES 1360 (XIV); GA/RES 1702 (XVI).
165 DFA PMUN C/22, 19 July, 29 November 1961; GA/RES 1663 (XVI).
166 For the evolution of Ireland's apartheid policy throughout the 1970s and the 1980s,
     see Laffan, *Ireland and South Africa*.

An article published in a respected British weekly following the adjournment of the Fourteenth Assembly in December 1959 captured the essence of
Ireland's independent, energetic profile at the United Nations during Lemass'
years of transition. The author observed that in 'the second row of this year's
Assembly sat the Irish, whose quite different exuberance' had infused the
recently ended session.[167] Ireland's participation at the Council of Europe had
'misled some observers into expecting endless variations on the theme of partition. Instead, the Irish have startled the Assembly by providing it with a
flow of stimulating initiatives on almost every other subject.' Freddy Boland
had won 'such widespread respect, in spite of the irritation that the recent
Irish moves have caused to all the great powers in turn', that he was considered a leading candidate for the presidency of the next Assembly. Indeed:

> The small, young, and bouncy Irish delegation has shown how much
> impact can be achieved by a UN member which cannot be branded as
> a mere tool of one of the big blocks if it sets out not to gain some nar-
> row sectional interest, but to stir up the general conscience of the
> Assembly on broad issues ... Perhaps the Assembly needs a few more
> Ireland's of this kind.

Concurrently, Ireland's independent activities during this period call for
several important refinements. Underlying the Irish delegation's outstanding
defense of the rights of the Tibetan people was Boland's and Lemass' realization that it would assuage critics of Ireland's China vote. On the question of
apartheid, Ireland cooperated with the Afro-Asian bloc by agreeing to cosponsor the inscription of the item on the Assembly's agenda, but they sided with
their European allies by opposing economic sanctions.

Lemass was more intimately involved with the design and execution of
Ireland's UN policy than has heretofore been recognized. He was certainly a
champion of the Irish delegation's autonomous identity, especially when it
fostered responsible initiatives. The record reveals, however, that he intervened at decisive moments in order to temper the delegation's enthusiasm.
What's more, on several occasions he guided Irish policy in a new direction,
away from its bold, independent stance. These moments, critical to understanding the evolution of Ireland's UN role, are explored in the next chapter.

---

167 *Economist*, 19 December 1959. One year later another British commentator noted that
Ireland had 'emerged as a positive, sometimes a nearly decisive, force at the UN':
Daily Herald, 24 October 1960.

CHAPTER 5

The Lemass Era Consolidated: Ireland at the General Assembly, 1961–2

INTRODUCTION

At the Sixteenth Session in 1961 the transitional stage of Sean Lemass' oversight of UN diplomacy gave way to the unfettered Lemass Era. This consolidation denoted the second fundamental shift in Ireland's policy. At this juncture of its United Nations membership Ireland started to act – not always, but in some important cases – less like an independent, or Scandinavian delegation, as it had since the opening of the Twelfth Assembly in 1957. For instance, on European-related matters a hint of caution crept into the delegation's stance. Even more telling was the turn of the compass bearing on straight Cold War issues: Ireland consistently pointed west. This process gathered steam at the Seventeenth Session in 1962 and persisted throughout the remainder of the decade. Its onset and early dynamics are fully explored in this chapter.

A matrix of factors generated this transformation. Underlying all of them was the tectonic shift within the Irish establishment away from the protectionist modalities of the 1930s and 1940s and towards a more open society. In this regard, the economic objectives that had been gaining ground for several years eclipsed lingering aspirations of acting as an autonomous agent in New York. The government resolved that its UN policy should not unduly hamper growth, now adjudged the nation's highest priority. A more specific catalyst was Ireland's application for admission into the European Economic Community, lodged in Brussels on 31 July 1961. But it was not the sole cause of change. Of equal importance was the government's foreign investment drive, which really took off in the early 1960s. Likewise Lemass' international predisposition. Unlike de Valera and Aiken, he was an Atlanticist, sympathized more with the west, and wanted to fix Ireland squarely within it. During the transitional period this inclination was muted; in the Lemass Era it grew more pronounced. So did the Taoiseach's personal intervention in UN affairs. Lemass therefore stamped his personality on Irish policy, just like Eamon de Valera and John Costello before him.

Yet the definitive feature of the Lemass Era from 1961 onwards – the shift from an autonomous to a western orientation – must be qualified, as was the continuity of the transitional years. For starters, the change in policy was neither abrupt nor sudden, but subtle and nuanced, and it originated in the transitional stage. The Irish delegation refused to join the western or any other voting caucus in the Assembly. The rise of the Afro-Asian bloc in the 1960s circumscribed Ireland's distinctive role. Aiken himself put a cap on the delegation's responsibilities after a visit to the Congo in 1961.

Most important, at Lemass' insistence Ireland stubbornly guarded its sovereignty within the international arena. His government judged each issue on its merits. Ireland's support for the west was never reflexive; it was proffered only when doing so was in the nation's interests.[1] (Lemass' more selective approach thus distinguished him from John Costello, whose pro-western rhetoric he echoed, but whose support for the west was doctrinal.) Ireland, accordingly, adhered to its first principles: it remained committed to the UN and a peaceful international order throughout the 1960s and beyond. These commendable accomplishments are explored in later chapters.

UNITED NATIONS POLICY AND THE EEC APPLICATION:
THE EUROPEAN CONTEXT

Ireland's EEC application was not the only reason for its Assembly realignment, but it was important nonetheless. Indeed, exactly how the bid acted on UN policy has remained elusive until now. Central to comprehending this process is a familiarity with the public debate, private negotiations, and diplomatic activity that accompanied the application. A comprehensive review of this milieu is beyond the scope of this study, but a brief synopsis of its European and American dimensions will prove useful.

Most relevant to Ireland's evolving UN posture, from a European perspective, was the Community's growing interest in political cooperation. This aspiration philosophically underpinned the Treaty of Rome, but it remained undefined in the document itself.[2] Therefore, while Iveagh House officials had at first suspected that Ireland's military neutrality might derail its application, they eventually concluded that non-membership in NATO did not disqualify them, even though each member of the EEC – West Germany, France, Italy, the Netherlands, Belgium, Luxembourg – belonged to the military alliance.[3] Remarks by Dr Heinrich von Brentano, the Foreign Minister of the Federal Republic of Germany, during an official visit to Dublin in late May 1961 reinforced this judgment; he said that 'neutral countries would not have to join NATO to secure full membership in the European Economic Community'.[4]

1 Future research into aspects of Irish foreign policy other than the UN General Assembly will reinforce this conclusion.
2 Cf. Maher, *Path*, p. 127.
3 Ibid., p. 140.
4 *Irish Times*, 1 June 1961.

The Bonn Declaration, however, altered the calculus. Announced on 18 July 1961, it revived the concept of political integration by entrusting the Fouchet Committee (comprised of representatives from each of the six EEC members and led by a distinguished French diplomat) to draw up proposals for the statutory implementation of closer political union.[5] A further complication arose in September when Professor Ludwig Erhard, President of the EEC Council, sent letters to Denmark, the United Kingdom, and Ireland acknowledging their respective applications; Erhard's reply to the first two was more encouraging than his reply to Ireland. Immediately thereafter the government received word through diplomatic channels that not only strict economic issues but Ireland's absence from NATO accounted for the difference; doubts had arisen in some capitals about Irish support for European political cooperation.[6]

If these questions persisted, Ireland's application would fail. Determined to prevent this, Irish government officials launched an initiative highlighting Ireland's support for European political cooperation. They aimed it at two audiences. Domestically, they wanted to inform and advise the Irish public of possible changes in the country's relations with its European neighbors. More critical was the external audience: the government resolved to counter the skepticism about Ireland's application circulating within the EEC. They set out to convince its members that although Ireland was the only neutral country to apply for membership, its neutrality 'did not correspond to those of Sweden, Switzerland, and Austria in that its non-involvement in military alliances did not preclude full commitment to the political aims of the Community'.[7]

In September Con Cremin and T.K. Whitaker traveled to the capitals of the six EEC members to clarify various aspects of Ireland's application. They addressed economic and agricultural problems, but focused more on Ireland's empathy for European political cooperation. According to an early report Whitaker sent to Dr James Ryan, the Minister for Finance, they asserted on numerous occasions that the Irish government, 'and the country generally, are very attracted by the idea of greater European unity'.[8] A 58-page summary reviewing every detail of their journey demonstrates that Whitaker and Cremin held fast to these points. They explained to every official in every capital that Ireland welcomed greater political collaboration in Europe.[9]

---

5 Maher, *Path*, pp. 132–4, 149.
6 On 1 September Francis Biggar, the Irish Ambassador in Brussels, phoned Cremin after speaking with M. de Schacht, an assistant to the Secretary General of the EEC, who informed him that 'the difference between the [letters] … is "intentional and significant"'. Certain EEC members were not convinced 'that Ireland had either the economic capacity to become members of the Community or that we fully accept the political implications'. Biggar added that de Schacht 'wondered, for instance, how we felt about closer political cooperation, and he remarked also that our foreign policy tends to diverge in some significant respects than that of the "Six"': S 16877/P, 1 September 1961.
7 Maher, *Path*, p. 141.
8 S 16877/P, 7 September 1961.
9 S 16877/Q, 26 September 1961.

Yet because doubts persisted within EEC circles,[10] Sean Lemass took to the airwaves. He amplified his assertions of the previous two years that Ireland backed the west by affirming the government's commitment to the specific, if as yet loosely-defined, goal of European political cooperation; in retrospect his earlier speeches had prepared Fianna Fáil for this moment. For instance, on 18 January 1962 he told the EEC's Council of Ministers in Brussels that the Irish viewed 'with keen and sympathetic interest every genuine effort to bring the peoples of Europe closer together so as to strengthen the foundations of our common civilization'.[11] Ireland welcomed the Treaty of Rome and the Bonn Declaration, which had reaffirmed the Community's 'resolve to develop their political cooperation'. Squarely facing up to the NATO issue, Lemass said that 'While Ireland did not accede to the North Atlantic Treaty, we have always agreed with the general aims of that treaty.'[12]

How did all of this play out at the United Nations? During their diplomatic mission to the continent Cremin and Whitaker realized that UN policy, while not insignificant, was secondary to the concerns EEC members had about Irish, Danish, and British support for political cooperation. During their discussions there was just one general reference to the UN and no specific comments about Irish policy there.[13] Nonetheless, Ireland's EEC application and the Irish government's public and private efforts to persuade the 'Six' of its commitment to political integration had important implications for Ireland's posture in the General Assembly. The government was willing, in principle, to abandon its independent identity if the future course of European political cooperation required it to do so. Equally significant, Lemass resolved that Ireland's UN activities would not throw up an unnecessary hurdle during the sensitive EEC negotiations set to commence in early 1962. The Irish delegation started paying more attention to European considerations at the UN. It did not automatically side with EEC members, but European susceptibilities became an important factor in the equation of variables that determined several votes. In some instances where Ireland's ballot did not change the delegation went to great lengths to publicly express its sympathy for the European point of view. If an issue was particularly sensitive Ireland considered not taking a forward role so that its actions would not be misconstrued. As a result, on certain European-oriented matters – Bizerte, Algeria, South Tyrol – circumspection eroded Ireland's independent posture. These issues are examined following a review of the American context of the EEC application.

10 Maher, *Path*, pp. 141–4.
11 DFA 305/57/363/28, 18 January 1962.
12 One month later Lemass counseled Dáil colleagues who were critical of his pro-NATO comments that it would 'be highly undesirable that remarks made here should give the impression in Europe that there is a public opinion in this country which regards membership of NATO as something discreditable ... Although we are not members of NATO, we are in full agreement with its aims': DD 193, 6–7, 14 February 1962.
13 S 16877/Q, 23 September 1961. The reference was to the UN Special Session on Bizerte in August 1961, which is explored below.

UNITED NATIONS POLICY AND THE EEC APPLICATION:
THE AMERICAN CONTEXT

The United States was not a member of the European Economic Community, but American opinion was an important element of Ireland's bid to join it. The Irish government hoped to swing the United States' immense influence in Europe behind its EEC application. To accomplish this it was first necessary to generate a positive assessment of Ireland within official American circles, which would not be easy.

Irish officials were long aware of American misgivings about Ireland's application because of its non-membership in NATO.[14] The starting point for their efforts to harness the United States' prestige to their own ends, however, was a 'Secret' report entitled 'Ireland and the State Department' that Thomas J. Kiernan, Ireland's Ambassador to the United States, forwarded to Cremin in late October 1961.[15] Kiernan opened with a brief review of the State Department's assessment of the American Ambassador to Ireland, Grant Stockdale, who was President Kennedy's recent political appointment. Career Foreign Service officials were unenthusiastic about his talents. The same did not apply, though, to Secretary of State Dean Rusk, 'since he has no interest in Ireland and so is not concerned'. His attitude and that of 'the other Rhodes Scholars at the head of the State Department is the obvious one: the British view, as against any Irish view, is all important'. To counter these Anglophile tendencies and the ineffectiveness of the American Embassy in Dublin, Kiernan argued that greater priority should be assigned to direct communications between the Irish Embassy in Washington and the State Department, particularly with regard to the EEC application. His motive was straightforward: 'Although the US is not a member of the EEC, Washington can exert considerable influence.'

On 6 November Sheila Murphy, Assistant Secretary, sent her own 'Secret' minute to Washington in reply to Kiernan's report, which Aiken had initialed.[16] She told Kiernan that 'As a preliminary response' he would soon receive both a copy of the report Whitaker and Cremin had composed following their European journey and another summary 'evaluating the present position of our application'. Murphy added that 'We fully agree as to the importance of seeking the goodwill of the US authorities for our application';

---

14 While visiting the capitals of the 'Six' in September Con Cremin had a conversation with Mr L. Homan, the Dutch Ambassador to the EEC, who told Cremin that in 'his view membership of NATO is not an issue' with regard to Ireland's EEC application, but 'the Americans are inclined to adopt a very "simplistic" attitude in this regard and to classify European countries as "NATO" or "non-NATO" ': S 16877/Q, 26 September 1961.

15 DFA P 12/6/A, 31 October 1961.

16 DFA CM/3, 6 November 1961.

Iveagh House had only been awaiting the completion of the second report 'before briefing you on the matter'.

Meanwhile, the Irish Embassy started to expand its contacts at State. In early November Kevin Rush, Chargé d'Affaires in the Washington Mission, discussed Ireland's EEC bid with Mr Joseph Sweeney, the Irish desk officer. Sweeney, who was sympathetic to Ireland, assumed that the Irish government was 'very concerned about the fate of the application' and promised to assess the attitude of his superiors.[17]

As a follow-up, T.J. Kiernan met with Sweeney on 13 November. He forwarded a detailed summary of their off-the-record conversation to Cremin.[18] Sweeney's forecast was inauspicious: 'The present prospect, as seen by the State Department, is that Ireland's application will be rejected.' Under-Secretary of State George Ball, who was responsible for American policy, believed in 'a greater Atlantic Alliance', envisioned the EEC as ' "taking in" NATO', and did not favor 'neutrals, like Sweden and Ireland, as associate members'. The crux of the matter, Sweeney added, was Ireland's 'refusal to join NATO in the first instance, and our policy of neutrality at the UN'. It therefore had to convince American officials that it was 'prepared to accept the responsibilities of future developments of the EEC', including political and military cooperation.

In the interim Aiken had scheduled a meeting with George Ball on the margins of an upcoming OECD conference in Paris; Iveagh House officials had concluded that this might be an opportune time to discuss OECD matters of mutual interest as well as the EEC. On 17 November a more open, but still skeptical, Ball called on the Irish Embassy in Paris.[19] After discussing the OECD and bilateral trade issues Ball, not Aiken, broached Ireland's EEC application.[20] Aiken proceeded to lay out his case. Ireland was confident it 'could fulfill the obligations called for by membership', including opening up the Irish market to industrial competition. Sounding a familiar Irish theme, he said that Ireland's hesitation concerning NATO was 'well known and related to the partition problem'. Nevertheless, his government believed that if Britain and Ireland entered the EEC as full members the 'tariff problem between the north and the south would tend to disappear, with a corresponding trend towards unity of political aims ... ' Aiken did not explicitly request American support; he had wisely concluded that doing so 'might lead to embarrassment'. Off-the-cuff, Ball claimed that he was 'prepared to take a very large bet that the British application would succeed', but he did not

17 Ibid., 4 November 1961.
18 Kiernan's report was entitled 'The US State Department and Ireland's Application for Membership of the EEC': ibid, 14 November 1961.
19 On 14 November Joseph Sweeney had argued Ireland's case before Ball, who 'had moved from a closed to an open mind', but still had an 'unsympathetic' view of Ireland's EEC application: ibid, 28 November 1961.
20 Ibid., 17 November 1961.

allude to Ireland's prospects in front of Aiken. Later, he mentioned to Dennis MacDonald, the Irish Ambassador to France who was present at the meeting, that 'he was very glad we had applied for full membership'. This was an encouraging, but certainly not conclusive, reply.

After this high-level meeting in Paris Cremin advised Kiernan to ease his courting of American officials because it 'might create an impression of undue anxiety on our part if we were to keep up a more or less continuous approach among the "foothills"' of the State Department, especially since Aiken had just met with Under-Secretary Ball.[21] Cremin did urge Kiernan to contact Ball as 'a follow-up on the Minister's talk with him', but there is no record of a their meeting.

The Washington Embassy's efforts to impress the United States through the lower echelons of the State Department may have been put on hold, but Ireland's desire to secure American support for its EEC application had important consequences for its UN policy. Knowing that American influence might enhance the application's prospects, Lemass surely would not have wanted to offend their sensibilities. More so, having been fully apprised of the State Department's lukewarm opinion of Ireland's bid and its independent role at the UN,[22] Lemass realized that convincing the United States of Ireland's *bona fides* would be an uphill struggle. Therefore, when straight east-west issues thrown up by the Cold War arose in the Assembly Ireland demonstrated its solidarity with the west by casting its votes accordingly. This process transformed the Irish delegation's China vote, which is explored following a review of how Ireland's EEC bid influenced its response to several European issues.

BIZERTE

The challenge that Ireland's European aspirations posed to its independence at the UN cropped up less than one month after it applied for EEC membership. When Tunisia gained its independence in 1956 it permitted France to maintain several military bases in the country on the understanding that an orderly withdraw would follow in due course.[23] By the summer of 1961 France had complied, except in the case of Bizerte, which they were reluctant to evacuate owing to the conflict in near-by Algeria. Frustrated by France's intransigence, President Bourguiba called for a boycott of the base. Rioting broke out near the installation in late July, and the French sent in reinforcements. This provocative act sparked off hostilities. French forces occupied territory surrounding Bizerte, and several hundred casualties ensued.

21 Ibid., 30 November 1961.
22 Ibid., 20, 21 November 1961.
23 DFA PMUN J/37/61, 11 September 1961.

After the French brusquely rebuffed Dag Hammarskjold's offer to intercede, the Afro-Asian bloc called for a Special Session of the Assembly, which would have ten days to convene.[24] At its behest Hammarskjold asked several of the middle powers, including Ireland, to support this move.[25] On 9 August Aiken, Boland, Cremin, and Sean Ronan, First Secretary in the Political and United Nations Section, discussed the Secretary General's request. Aiken was hesitant despite Tunisian pressure.[26] A Special Session, he believed, 'should only be convened if the case was really overwhelming and an immediate danger of significant conflict existed', which presently did not apply.[27] Instead, 'the important objective should be to get talks started between the two parties after a cooling-off period'. All four men also thought that it would difficult to obtain the required two-thirds majority for a resolution favorable to Tunisia at a Special Session. They decided, therefore, to first establish 'how certain other countries such as Venezuela, Mexico, and the Nordic group proposed to reply to the request and that, in any event, Ireland should not provide the majority'.

Within days Argentina, Venezuela, and Uruguay had acceded to Hammarskjold's solicitation, and 'concurrences by Sweden, Finland, and Mexico followed'. The Canadian, Danish, and Norwegian delegations advised their governments not to follow suit because it 'would have a demonstrative rather than a constructive character at that stage'. Aiken concluded likewise: he instructed the Permanent Mission 'not to reply to the request conveyed by the Secretary General but, if approached by other delegations, to explain our position to them'. Ultimately, Aiken's desire to maintain the UN's moral force by avoiding superfluous Assembly sessions made sense. In the light of Ireland's recently submitted EEC application, however, Lemass may have urged caution to sidestep treading on French sensibilities.[28]

* * *

24 DFA 417/230/6, 14 August 1961. Their move to convene an Emergency Session of the Assembly (which would open within 24 hours) was defeated.
25 DFA 305/185/A, 4, 5 August 1961.
26 DFA 417/230/6, 6 September 1961. Mongi Slim, Tunisia's Permanent Representative to the UN, urged the Irish delegation to concur, adding 'that he hoped that countries with traditions such as ours would come to the aid of another small nation threatened by a larger neighbor'.
27 Ibid., 14 August 1961.
28 The insight of Zouhir Chelli, Counsellor in the Tunisian Permanent Mission to the UN, into Ireland's refusal to back the Special Session was very perceptive in this regard. According to an internal Iveagh House summary, he expressed 'himself with some force on the subject, suggesting that there must be some significance in "Ireland's silence", and that if we failed to support the request for the Session it would be the first time that Ireland came down on the wrong side on a colonial issue': ibid., 6 September 1961.

The Special Session convened on 21 August. France boycotted it on the grounds that bilateral talks with Tunisia, not UN intervention, were the best means of resolving the crisis.[29] Three days beforehand the Afro-Asians had circulated a moderate draft resolution; the bloc's more equable members had persuaded the extremists to compromise for the sake of unity.[30] The fourth preambular paragraph, which later provoked some consternation, expressed the Assembly's conviction 'that the presence of French armed forces in Tunisian territory against the express will of the Tunisian government and people constitutes a violation of Tunisia's sovereignty, is a permanent source of international friction, and endangers international peace and security'. The operative paragraphs recognized Tunisia's right 'to call for the withdrawal of all French armed forces present on its territory without its consent' and called for immediate bilateral negotiations to achieve this. Cremin, who headed the Irish delegation since Boland had been elected President of the Special Session,[31] reported to Aiken that due to 'widespread sympathy for [the] Tunisian position' the resolution was assured an 'ample majority'.[32] Those countries with certain reservations, including the United States, had indicated that they would abstain rather than vote against it.

How would Ireland cast its ballot? Before deciding, the Department of External Affairs first had to resolve a conflict – not wrenching, but nonetheless real. On the one hand, several factors augured that the Irish delegation would vote for the Afro-Asian resolution. After all, Ireland enjoyed close relations with the Tunisian delegation, which performed a critical role at the UN similar to its own. Writing in May 1961, Conor O'Brien noted that Tunisia:

> played an important, moderate and constructive part in the United Nations. Its voting position on many issues resembles that of such countries as the Scandinavians, Canada, Mexico, and ourselves, although, of course, its position as a member of the Afro-Asian group sometimes induces it to take up more rigorously anti-colonial stands than any European delegation is likely to do.[33] .

Its UN delegation was led by Mongi Slim, 'an extremely able diplomat ... expected to be the next President of the General Assembly, and whom Ireland has promised to support for that office'. Slim was 'well-known to, and highly thought of, by both the Minister and Mr Boland'.[34] O'Brien added

---

29 Ibid.
30 Ibid., 18, 28 August 1961.
31 Ibid., 15, 18 August 1961. Technically, the Special Session was an extension of the Fifteenth General Assembly, which had elected Boland as its President.
32 Ibid., 21 August 1961.
33 DFA 305/185/A, 11 May 1961. The excerpt was from a general background note on Tunisia.
34 Aiken's and Boland's high regard for Slim was reciprocal. After a talk with Slim in

that 'cordial relations exist between the Tunisian and Irish delegations on the various committees'. A memorandum reviewing the Sixteenth Assembly's agenda, penned two weeks after the Special Session had adjourned but before France had withdrawn from Bizerte, recorded that should Tunisia be 'forced by French intransigence to take a less constructive role it will be a setback for the United Nations.[35]

Even more considerations encouraged External Affairs to adopt a pro-Tunisian stand. Quite compelling was Ireland's national interest. The memorandum quoted above argued that should the question of Bizerte arise at the Sixteenth Session:

> As a small country it is ... in Ireland's interest to curb coercion of the lesser nations by the great powers. It is therefore necessary to maintain the right of the United Nations to intervene in matters such as this to vindicate Tunisia's sovereignty.

Ireland's traditional anti-colonial posture was also persuasive. In a draft he had composed 'for guidance' before departing for the Special Session, Cremin averred that Irish sympathy for Tunisia was 'natural' considering that only recently it had achieved 'a measure of territorial independence' and had rid itself of foreign military bases.[36] Finally, as Boland later reported, Hammarskjold supported the draft.[37] The Secretary General did not determine Ireland's votes, of course, but neither were his sentiments ignored.

Simultaneously, other factors tilted in favor of Ireland adopting a pro-French position by abstaining on the motion (voting against it was out of the question). Ireland's long-standing ties with France carried great weight. Cremin referred to them in his draft speech, and so did an External Affairs memorandum addressing France's deteriorating relationship with the United Nations: Afro-Asian criticism of French policy in North Africa was justified, but 'at the same time [Ireland] has traditionally friendly relations with France and so has no desire to see it publicly vilified'.[38]

Washington T.J. Kiernan, the Irish Ambassador, reported to O'Brien that 'He has, as I am sure you know, a high appreciation of Ireland's moral value to the newly-freed peoples and a high appreciation of the Minister's and the delegation's work at the UN': ibid., 14 February 1961.

35 DFA PMUN J/37/61, 11 September 1961.
36 DFA 417/230/6, 17 August 1961. Cremin's draft was initialed by Aiken, but never delivered at the Special Session. It was primarily an explanation of why Ireland had not supported the calling of the Special Session. Informed by Cremin's awareness of the auspicious relations between the two countries, and perhaps a lingering sense of regret, the speech went out of its way to express Irish sympathy for the Tunisian position.
37 Ibid., 28 August 1961.
38 DFA PMUN J/37/61, 11 September 1961. Boland's remark in an informal report on the question of Bizerte sent to Cremin in late August – the Afro-Asian draft resolution

More pressing, according to a final report by Tadhg O'Sullivan, who had replaced Eamon Kennedy as Counsellor in the Permanent Mission, was 'concern about the negotiations which would follow Ireland's application for membership of the European Economic Community'.[39] Ireland was wary of offending France, one of the EEC's most influential members, by casting a vote in favor of the motion; this line of thinking most likely originated in Iveagh House, and Cremin transmitted it to the delegation upon his arrival in New York. We have seen how this apprehension may have prevented Ireland from backing the Special Session; it may also account for Ireland's subsequent rejection of a Tunisian request to cosponsor the Afro-Asian resolution.[40] The Irish delegation was not alone, however; Denmark, another EEC applicant, shared its concerns on this score. At one point the Danish diplomats suggested to the Irish delegation:

> that no doubt we were as preoccupied as they were with "our mutual interest in another matter", and they revealed that they were pressing hard for Scandinavian solidarity in abstaining on the resolution – the clear implication being that they would like our support in this also.[41]

The Danish reference to Nordic unity highlighted another reason why the Irish delegation was inclined to take up a pro-French line. There were early indications that not only the Scandinavian countries, but all of the western European delegations, might abstain on the Afro-Asian measure.[42] If this prediction held, Ireland would not want to be the only European delegation to vote for it. Such a move would not only draw unwonted attention toward itself, but France would interpret it unfavorably.

* * *

'had seemed to us in Dublin very much slanted against France' – further underscores the empathy for France in official Irish circles: DFA 417/230/6, 28 August 1961.

39 DFA 417/230/6 6 September 1961.

40 Ibid., 18 August 1961.

41 Ibid., 6 September 1961. A conversation on 25 August between Frank Biggar, the Irish Ambassador in Brussels, and Paul-Henri Spaak, the Belgian Foreign Minister, sheds light on Irish concerns about their EEC application. In regard to Bizerte, Spaak 'referred to the difficulties which the French are going to make about the negotiations with the British and said he thought that they would be even more difficult if any of the applicants for admission to the Common Market should vote in favor of the resolution. Mr Spaak suggested that we should give consideration to following the line which the British and the Italians had both taken, namely, to abstain.' Later that night Biggar phoned Iveagh House with news of Spaak's remarks so that Irish officials 'would be prepared, in the event our voting in favor of the UN resolution, for even greater difficulties in our negotiations with the French with regard to the Common Market': ibid., 25 August 1961.

42 Ibid., 24 August 1961.

During the afternoon of 23 August the Irish delegation cabled an update to Iveagh House. The Afro-Asian bloc opposed any amendments to its resolution, which was likely to receive more than 60 votes.[43] Few, if any, countries were expected to vote against it. Those likely to abstain, in addition to the western Europeans and the United States, included the Scandinavians, the old Commonwealth, most Latin American delegations, the Philippines, Japan, and perhaps some of the Brazzaville group (the francophone nations of Africa). A few hours later Freddy Boland reported that after assessing all of the evidence the Mission was leaning toward abstention.[44] Since Aiken had assumed the reins of UN policy, this was a first: Ireland hesitated to back a smaller nation invaded by a larger foe. What a contrast with its quick defense of Hungary, Tibet, and Algeria; new factors were obviously at work.

Concurrently, Boland reminded Iveagh House that if the evolution of the debate altered 'our assumptions substantially, and in particular if [the] text submitted to [a] vote is modified, or [the] pattern of European abstentions changes significantly, we would seek further instructions'. Sensing the latent support for the resolution amid those delegations on the fence, the Mission was reserving the option to change its vote. Alive to this phenomenon, Tunisia appealed to Ireland and similar moderates in the Assembly,[45] and several of those who planned to abstain fell in behind the measure. Indeed, the prevailing Nordic inclination to abstain transmuted into unanimous backing for Tunisia. Irish officials, particularly Sean Lemass, carefully monitored this diplomatic chess match; they were anxious to make just the right move in the light of the EEC application. Then, on the evening of 24 August Aiken ordered the delegation to vote for the resolution; Tunisian diplomacy, restored Scandinavian unity, Ireland's traditions, and Lemass' conclusion that the EEC bid would not be affected all played a part in this decision.[46]

On 25 August the Assembly adopted the Afro-Asian motion by a margin of 66 to 0, with 30 abstentions.[47] Those voting in favor included forty-three Afro-Asian delegations, six Latin American delegations, the Soviet bloc, and seven western European countries: Austria, Denmark, Finland, Iceland, Norway, Sweden, and Ireland. Fourteen Latin American nations, the old Commonwealth, eight western European delegations (Belgium, Greece, Italy, Luxembourg, the Netherlands, Portugal, Spain, the United Kingdom), and

---

43 DFA PMUN X/62, 23 August 1961.
44 Ibid. In his final report, Tadhg O'Sullivan added that 'the same reasons which had determined our attitude to the convening of the session' were also a factor encouraging abstention at that time: DFA 417/230/6, 6 September 1961.
45 On 24 August Taieb Slim, the Tunisian Ambassador in London, personally outlined his country's case to Aiken during a special visit to Iveagh House: DFA 417/230/6, 24 August 1961.
46 Ibid., 24 August 1961, 6 September 1961.
47 GA/RES 1622 (SS–III); S 16057/G, 28 August 1961. Aiken forwarded a report of the voting to Lemass, who reviewed it on 28 August.

the United States abstained. In his final report Tadhg O'Sullivan noted that the result:

> was hailed as a Tunisian diplomatic victory and a blow to French polit-
> ical prestige, but there are grounds for the view that if this was the
> case, it was – especially in the light of the voting – predictable, and that
> nothing transpired during the session which, of itself, would force
> France to abandon the position she has chosen to take up.[48]

With regard to Ireland's stand Boland asserted, in a minute to Cremin, that 'I believe that, in all the circumstances, we were absolutely right to vote as we did'.[49] The ballot was appropriate in the light of Ireland's history and its UN role, but it also had a salutary effect. Continued French intransigence might 'provoke a demand for further action against her at the coming regular Session, perhaps even a proposal that some form of sanctions should be taken against her'. Should this scenario unfold, Ireland's 'vote in favor of the draft resolution puts us in a position to exert a positive, and possibly useful, role in restraint of any such extreme proposals'.

Because the Irish vote did not engender any negative fallout Boland's inter-pretation – that it was correctly cast – was accurate. The Tunisians were extremely pleased.[50] EEC members were unruffled. On 22 September the French Ambassador, Jacques Paris, called on Cremin not for any specific pur-pose, but 'solely for an exchange of views'.[51] When the Session on Bizerte arose Paris 'expressed no opinion on the way' Ireland had voted. He person-ally believed 'that France had, perhaps, made a mistake in being absent'. Cremin agreed, adding that 'there were certain things which could have been said in favor of the French position, but which only France could have said'.

Similarly, there were no repercussions elsewhere in Europe. During his tour of the capitals of the 'Six', Cremin had a conversation on the evening of 12 September with S. Cattani, the Secretary General of the Italian Foreign Ministry, who referred to Denmark's vote on Bizerte, adding that 'the voting had been closely scrutinized ... '[52] Cattani, however, made no reference to Ireland's vote. Neither did he raise it, nor the United Nations, during the

---

48 DFA 417/230/6, 6 September 1961. O'Sullivan's remark about French intransigence
     was accurate: France did not evacuate the military base at Bizerte until October 1963.
49 Ibid., 28 August 1961.
50 On 30 August Habib Bourguiba, the son of the Tunisian President and the newly-
     appointed Permanent Representative of Tunisia to the United Nations, wrote to
     Freddy Boland expressing his 'deepest appreciation and warmest thanks for the unflag-
     ging support you so efficiently gave to the Tunisian cause, regardless of any geograph-
     ical or ideological consideration'. This last reference is interesting; even the Tunisians
     were aware of Ireland's European interests: DFA PMUN X/62, 30 August 1961.
51 S 16877Q/61, 23 September 1961.
52 Ibid.

official talks between the Irish and Italian teams the next day; European political cooperation and NATO were the primary topics of discussion. Moreover, Cattani's comment, according to Cremin, was 'the only reference we heard throughout our tour to the United Nations'. As of mid-September 1961, then, Ireland's UN policy had not thrown up a barrier to its EEC application. In the coming months Sean Lemass took steps to maintain this favorable status quo.

ALGERIA

Despite the General Assembly's best efforts since 1956, the Franco-Algerian conflict still seethed in the autumn of 1961. Suggesting that a settlement might be within reach, French and FLN officials had finally opened direct talks at Evian in May, but they collapsed when France refused to acknowledge that the Sahara region, with its valuable oil reserves, was an integral part of Algeria. Frustrated, the FLN replaced its moderate president, Mr Ferhat Abbas, with the more extreme Ben Kheddah.[53] The atmosphere remained strained when the Sixteenth Session convened in September, so the Afro-Asian bloc once again placed Algeria on the agenda.

Within months of the Special Session on Bizerte, therefore, Ireland again had to take a stand on French colonial policy in North Africa. The same interests collided: Ireland's traditional support for self-determination in Africa; its close relations with France; its desire to prevent France from turning against the UN; its EEC application. The Irish delegation's final position also depended on several particulars: the progress, if any, of future negotiations; the political situation in France and Algeria; the text of any resolution. To its credit, the delegation successfully negotiated these diplomatic rapids, as it had during previous Assemblies. It endorsed Algerian self-rule in principle; qualified its support in a manner sympathetic to France; and effusively praised the courage of General de Gaulle, whose opinion with regard to Ireland's EEC aspirations was of great consequence.

Central to the Irish government's stance in 1961 was its response to the seminal events of 1958–9. In May 1958, with France on the brink of civil war, Charles de Gaulle dramatically returned from his self-imposed exile to lead the Fifth Republic. More astounding, he declared, in his historic speech on 16 September 1959, that the only solution to the Algerian crisis lay in the 'free choice which the Algerians will make for their future'.[54] He did qualify this remarkable *volte face*. In a referendum four years after the territory had been pacified the Algerians would be offered three choices: secession, which might entail the *regroupment* of French citizens and French control of Saharan oil;

---

53 Talbott, *War without a Name*, p. 221.
54 *Irish Times*, 17 September 1959.

complete integration with France; or, a form of local home rule. Significantly, de Gaulle rejected out of hand international (or UN) supervision of the referendum, negotiations with the FLN (which France did not recognize), or talks on any topic other than a cease-fire.

On the afternoon of 24 September 1959 Con Cremin met with Lemass, who outlined both his general views of de Gaulle's speech and 'its relevance to our attitude towards the Algerian problem' in the General Assembly.[55] At the Taoiseach's urging, Cremin penned a summary of Lemass' assessment, submitted it to him for approval, and forwarded it to Aiken, who was in New York.[56] This extraordinary memorandum illuminates Lemass' thinking. Hinting that the Irish rhetoric of previous years should be toned down, and highlighting his own priorities, Lemass said that:

> when a problem, such as that in Algeria, arises, one cannot reasonably ask more than the *bona fide* application of the principle of self-determination; and, while we should maintain the position that we are among the strongest opponents within the United Nations of colonialism, this should not involve our not accepting at face value an offer for Algeria of self-determination, like that made by General de Gaulle, or standing on the anti-colonialist principle to such an extent as to lead to our condemning European countries generally trying to "decolonize" themselves, with which we have friendly relations, and with which we trade.

The Taoiseach then pondered 'whether we might not take an opportunity of an early intervention to express a welcome for the de Gaulle declaration, while not retreating from our fundamental position'.

Freddy Boland carried out this task a few months later in a speech at the UN,[57] but at the Sixteenth Session the task fell to Frank Aiken. On 15 December 1961 thirty-one Afro-Asian delegations introduced a draft resolution into the First Committee. Its sole operative paragraph called upon France and the Algerian representatives 'to resume negotiations with a view to implementing the right of the Algerian people to self-determination and independence [while] respecting the unity and territorial integrity of Algeria'.[58]

Aiken addressed the Assembly on 20 December. Owing to Lemass' influence (especially his concern over the EEC bid), Aiken's speech was much more sympathetic to de Gaulle than his effort the year before.[59] While the Irish delegation intended to vote for the Afro-Asian measure, it was 'by no means an adequate or even an accurate reflection of our point of view on the

55 S 16057/E, 25 September 1959.
56 Ibid.
57 *Irish Times*, 13 December 1959.
58 GA/RES 1724 (XVI).
59 Aiken, *Ireland* (1960), pp. 54–7.

problem of Algeria as it stands at present'.[60] Aiken wished that the resolution, 'instead of simply endorsing one point of view', had shown a greater 'spirit of mutual tolerance and understanding'. For example, the preamble recalled an earlier Assembly resolution demanding an end to colonialism in Algeria,[61] but the measure:

> rather ungenerously, we think, makes no reference at all to General de Gaulle's speech of 16 September 1959, in which he specifically conceded Algeria's right to self-determination – a speech which we in the Irish delegation regard as a truly historic milestone in the history of Algerian freedom.

Moreover, Aiken credited de Gaulle with the 'most significant and encouraging development in connection with the Algerian problem within the last twelve months': the establishment of direct contact between French officials and representatives of the FLN. He bemoaned the resolution's failure to recognize this fact as well, particularly because only bilateral negotiations could lead to 'the establishment of lasting peace and fruitful cooperation'.

The sixth preambular paragraph disheartened the delegation, not because it regretted the suspension of negotiations, but due to its explicit reference to 'the Provisional Government of the Algerian Republic', namely, the FLN, which France refused to formally recognize even though it had commenced negotiations with this group.[62] This sentiment mirrored Ireland's stand at the Fourteenth Session in 1959 and its policy since then;[63] emphasizing it at the UN in 1961 was another means of expressing solidarity with France. Aiken stressed that if the Afro-Asian resolution was 'voted on paragraph by paragraph, my delegation will feel obliged to abstain in the vote on the sixth paragraph of the preamble'.[64] Ireland hoped that a free government of Algeria would soon be 'recognized *de jure* by all the other governments of the world', but since it had not recognized any provisional government the Irish delegation could not vote for a paragraph implying such.

On 20 December the Assembly adopted the Afro-Asian motion, 62 (including Ireland and the Scandinavian countries) to 0, with 33 abstentions (the

60 Aiken, Ireland (1961), pp. 34–6.
61 The second preambular paragraph recalled the Assembly's 'resolution 1514 (XV) of 14 December 1960 in which it proclaimed the necessity of bringing to a speedy and unconditional end colonialism in all its forms and manifestations'.
62 In its entirety the paragraph regretted 'the suspension of the negotiations entered into by the Government of France and the Provisional Government of the Algerian Republic'.
63 In response to a Dáil question in May 1959, Frank Aiken said that the recognition of the Provisional Government would 'hinder rather than help the application of the principle of self-determination to the people of Algeria': DD 174, 1748 6 May 1959.
64 Aiken, *Ireland* (1961), pp. 34–6.

United States, Canada, and the rest of western Europe).[65] The paragraphs were not voted on separately. The Franco-Algerian conflict did not come before the Assembly again. In March 1962 France and the FLN signed a cease-fire accord; in July Algeria received its independence. When Algeria's application for admission into the UN came before the Security Council in October 1962 Frank Aiken, appropriately, spoke on its behalf.[66] Until then the Irish government had stood squarely behind France. When the cease-fire was reached Lemass issued a statement effusively praising de Gaulle. It also recognized 'the very heavy sacrifices made by the Algerian people' but, so as not to offend French sensibilities, did not refer to the Provisional Government of the Algerian Republic.[67] Jacques Paris, the French Ambassador, told Cremin that the statement was 'very good'.[68]

SOUTH TYROL

Also known as Bozen or Bolzano, South Tyrol, an alpine region straddling the Austrian-Italian border, was part of the Austro-Hungarian Empire until the end of World War I, when the Treaty of St. Germain ceded it to Italy.[69] During the inter-war years the government's language policy discriminated against the German-speaking majority in the province, but after World War II the 1947 Peace Treaty of Paris confirmed Italy's jurisdiction. One year earlier the Gruber-de Gasperi Agreement, signed by the Austrian and Italian foreign ministers, recognized the right of the Austrian inhabitants in Bozen and the bilingual border towns of the neighboring Trentino province to local autonomy. But in the late 1950s Austria charged that by uniting the provinces of Bolzano and Trentino into a new area, the Alto Adige, Italy had gerrymandered a new region with an artificial Italian majority. It also claimed that widespread discrimination in education, housing, and government appointments had led to the rise of a violent Austrian nationalist movement along the border.

Insisting that negotiations with Italy were leading nowhere, Austria inscribed the item on the agenda of the Fifteenth Assembly, which convened in September 1960. Ireland thus faced an acute dilemma: this dispute involved two countries with which it had excellent relations; and, the issue touched upon its own interests. According to a memorandum Aiken submitted to the

---

65 GA/RES 1724 (XVI).
66 Aiken, *Ireland* (1962), pp. 15–17. At that time Ireland was serving a one-year term on the Council.
67 *Irish Times*, 22 March 1962; DFA 305/281/E, 20, 21 March 1962.
68 S 16410/B, 22 March 1962.
69 For a detailed historical and diplomatic review of this issue, see Antony Alcock, *The History of the South Tyrol Question* (London, 1970); Mario Toscano, *Alto Adige-South Tyrol: Italy's Frontier with the German World* (London, 1975).

government, Iveagh House preferred that the case be settled in a regional forum. Failing this, the right policy, 'both on general grounds and by reference to the potential implications of the problem for partition, would appear to be to work for a settlement ... in accordance with the principles of the Charter and in a spirit of mutual tolerance and respect for the rights of the individual ... '[70] If a vote were taken Ireland would abstain.

The Special Political Committee took up the question of South Tyrol in late October. On 25 October two draft resolutions surfaced. Italy welcomed a Latin American-sponsored measure, Austria submitted its own text, but neither was acceptable to both parties.[71] By the following day it became apparent that the Italian delegation was about to 'secure a complete and humiliating defeat of the Austrian proposal'.[72] Hoping to avoid this outcome, which would 'lead to nothing but an intensification of the bitterness between the two countries, and an increase in physical force activities by the South Tyrolese',[73] Ireland, Denmark, and other middle powers set out to devise an agreed formula. In the corridors Italy had sharp words for these delegations. In fact, on 27 October the Italian Ambassador in Dublin, E.I. Martino, complained to Sean Lemass about undue Irish meddling.[74]

Still, the Irish delegation, at Aiken's insistence, and despite possible Italian objections, initiated further discussions that produced a compromise resolution.[75] This measure, sponsored by Ireland and sixteen other delegations, recommended that Italy and Austria continue their bilateral negotiations and, if these failed, advised that they consider 'seeking a solution of their difficulties by any means included in the Charter, including recourse to the International Court of Justice or any other peaceful means of their own choice'.[76] The Special Political Committee adopted it unanimously on 27 October, as did the Assembly the following day.

Austria and Italy publicly lauded the motion's sponsors.[77] The Austrians welcomed the compromise because it spared them an ignominious defeat. In private the Italians were less sanguine. According to O'Brien, who played a crucial role in drafting the final agreement and later sent a complete report to

70 S 16051/A, 7 September 1960.
71 DFA PMUN X/44, 28 October 1960. The differences in the texts were very technical, but centered on Italy's desire that the issue remain juridical and Austria's hope that it could be brought within the ambit of the General Assembly.
72 S 16051/C, 11 September 1961.
73 Ibid.
74 DFA PMUN X/44, 28 October 1960.
75 Ibid. The deliberations were quite involved and are beyond the scope of this current review. The delegation's participation in this issue, however, refutes the view that 'the Irish have never been active mediators' at the UN: Salmon, *Ireland*, p. 233.
76 GA/RES 1690 (XV) – where marked.
77 DFA PMUN X/44, 28 October 1960.

Cremin, they would have preferred a voting victory.[78] He predicted that this sentiment would soon evaporate. He seems to have been correct in the short term. On 29 October Ambassador Martino called on Cremin 'to express the thanks of his government for the attitude of our delegation in connection with this resolution'; Cremin informed Lemass of the Italian's new-found appreciation.[79] O'Brien, however, might not have been accurate in the long run. During a conversation with Cremin on 23 March 1961, Martino mentioned that Denmark's role in cosponsoring the South Tyrolian compromise resolution had perturbed Rome.[80] The Italian government had expected more support from a fellow NATO member, and they had spoken to Denmark on the subject. Apart from a brief reference to Ireland's cosponsorship of the motion Martino made no direct comment on Ireland's involvement in this issue, although he may have been dropping a subtle hint.

* * *

Following the failure of talks with Italy and further outbreaks of violence in Bolzano, and despite the Italian government's establishment of a commission to investigate the situation, Austria requested that South Tyrol be inscribed on the Sixteenth Assembly's agenda.[81] On 11 September 1961 Arthur E. Zidek, the Press Attaché in the Austrian Legation at Paris, called on Aiken at Iveagh House. He sought the Irish delegation's support at the UN, but Aiken doubted whether Austrian 'interests would be served by the tabling of another resolution on South Tyrol'.[82] Not only would there be other large and important issues before the Assembly but, as Aiken wisely pointed out, 'it would be difficult to get a resolution tabled or passed as good as the resolution that was passed on this subject last year'. He recommended instead that the Austrian delegation 'ask a number of people like ourselves to mention the matter in our speeches'.

Aiken proffered this sound diplomatic counsel not only with Austria's interests in mind, but Ireland's as well. When forwarding a summary of Aiken's meeting to Boland, Sean Ronan noted, in his covering minute, that Aiken believed that the 'tabling of a resolution on this item during the coming session would be likely to stir up a lot of emotion and create difficulties for states friendly to both parties'.[83] Ireland was just such a country.

On the same day that he had spoken with Zidek, Aiken circulated to the cabinet a memorandum on the Sixteenth Assembly's agenda with a section on South Tyrol. It stated that the Irish delegation's 'attitude will be that of pre-

78 Ibid.
79 S 4831/B, 31 October, 1 November 1960. In mid-November Cremin ran into Martino at Dublin Airport and once again Martino 'gave no hint of any feeling of dissatisfaction' with Ireland's role: DFA PMUN X/44 14 November 1960.
80 S 4831/B, 23 March 1961.
81 S 16051/C, 11 September 1961.
82 DFA PMUN X/44, 13 September 1961.
83 Ibid.

vious years'.[84] It would vote 'for the admission of the item to the agenda' and then would 'persuade both countries to reconcile their differences in a friendly and constructive agreement which will have due regard to the basic rights and interests of the people of South Tyrol'. The advice Aiken gave to Zidek strongly suggests that he did not want the issue to arise at the UN; the contents of the memorandum indicate that if it did Ireland was again prepared to play a conciliatory role.

Like Aiken, Lemass was unenthusiastic about the prospect of Irish intervention in the South Tyrol dispute. After reading his colleague's memorandum on the UN's slate the Taoiseach requested Aiken 'to give some further consideration' to several issues.[85] Apropos of South Tyrol, Lemass did 'not think it wise to take any initiative on this subject'. He conceded that the concerned parties had drawn parallels to the partition of Ireland: the Italians claimed that they were 'dealing with a residual effect of foreign occupation of Italian soil, just as we are in the north-east'; and, 'the Austrians have argued that there is also a similarity, on other grounds' – namely, the rights of minorities. Yet Lemass thought it best for Ireland to maintain a low profile at the UN. Explaining why, he told Aiken that 'having regard to our vital interests in retaining Italian goodwill during the EEC negotiations, it is very important that we should not come into any conflict with them on the Tyrol question at this time'.

Lemass was not over-reacting, he was just being sensible. He was well aware of Italian feelings on this issue: he undoubtedly recalled the Italian Ambassador's visit the previous year when Ireland was trying to forge a compromise resolution; he had also read a report of Cremin's late-March meeting with Martino wherein the Italian envoy had expressed his consternation over the UN's intervention in the South Tyrol issue.[86] Likewise, on 23 September S. Russo, the Italian Under-Secretary of Foreign Affairs, told Thomas V. Commins, the Irish Ambassador in Rome, that if the Alto Adige question arose at the UN he trusted 'that the Irish government's attitude toward the Italian position would not be negative', because this 'would hardly be consistent with what he hoped would be our friendly association with the Common Market'.[87] Lemass' cabinet reinforced his cautious approach. After finally considering Aiken's agenda memorandum on 24 October the government 'informally agreed that we should keep out of the discussion on the question of South Tyrol'.[88] A consensus had emerged in the highest official circles against taking any unnecessary chances with the EEC application on the line.

---

84 S 16051/C, 11 September 1961.
85 Ibid., 13 September 1961.
86 S 4831/B, 27 March, 1961.
87 DFA 313/8/F, 28 September 1961. Commins sent a 'Confidential' report of his meeting with Russo to Con Cremin, who passed it up to Frank Aiken and forwarded a copy to the Irish UN Mission.
88 S 16051/C, 24 October 1961.

When the Assembly took up the question of South Tyrol in late November discussions between Italy and Austria stalled. At this point the Italian Foreign Minister, Antonio Segni, of all people, personally requested the Irish delegation to forge a settlement. He was cognizant of the delegation's mediation the previous year, its unbiased position, and the Irish government's desire to evince its goodwill towards Italy during the EEC negotiations.[89] Accordingly, Ireland and several other delegations drafted a compromise resolution calling 'for further efforts between the two parties concerned to find a solution to the problem', which the Assembly unanimously adopted.[90]

This turn of events was certainly ironic. Whereas Lemass had first advised against entanglement in the dispute out of fear of upsetting Italy, the Italians, seizing on Ireland's wish to demonstrate its *bona fides*, encouraged them to intervene in a friendly manner. Indeed, the Italians were quite pleased with Ireland's contribution. On 5 December Vittorio Winspeare, the new Italian Ambassador, called on Aiken in Iveagh House 'to express the appreciation of his government for the attitude we had taken on the Alto Adige problem'.[91] Officials in Rome were 'very happy with the outcome, and grateful for the way in which [Ireland] had helped to prevent the item being treated in a contentious manner and generating unnecessary "heat"'. Lemass surely welcomed the Italian envoy's remarks when informed of them the following day.[92]

THE REPRESENTATION OF CHINA

The approach to the representation of China that Lemass embraced soon after becoming Taoiseach presaged Ireland's shift on this question at the Sixteenth Session in 1961. We have already seen how he welcomed Ireland's Tibetan initiative in October 1959 because of the strong message it sent to critics of Ireland's China vote. At the Fianna Fáil *Ard Feis* in mid-November of that year Lemass went even further, stating that the Irish government would not support the admission of Peking into the UN:

> unless very specific safeguards were forthcoming in relation to the restoration of the rights of the Chinese people, particularly in regard to religious freedom, and unless there were assurances as to the observance by China of the rule of law in international relations.[93]

Lemass reiterated this stand in an interview published in *Hibernia* just before the Irish delegation's final vote in favor of a discussion of the repre-

89 DFA 428/14/II, 15, 21, 23 November 1961.
90 GA/RES 1661 (XVI); S 16051/C, 10 September 1962.
91 S 4831/B, 5 December 1961.
92 S 16137/K, 6 December 1961.
93 *Irish Times*, 11 November 1959.

sentation of China in September 1960.[94] His qualifications not only went further than de Valera ever had while Taoiseach but, interestingly enough,
Lemass' conditions surfaced in Aiken's explanation of the delegation's vote in
favor of a discussion of the representation of China on 21 September 1959.[95]
This was a new development, for Aiken had not spoken in these terms when
clarifying the same ballot in 1957 or in 1958.[96] More important, he had always
gone to great lengths to discourage speculation on Ireland's position should a
vote on the actual representation of China come before the Assembly.

Several factors account for this departure. The conditions Lemass laid out
for an Irish vote in favor of China's entry into the UN were consistent with
his simultaneous declarations of Irish solidarity with the west; in being so
they underscore his pro-western bias. Lemass was also distancing himself from
an aspect of de Valera's and Aiken's independent policy he found disconcert-
ing and establishing a basis for voting against communist China should the
substantive question ever arise. Correspondingly, he was probably behind the
inclusion of conditions in Aiken's explanation of Ireland's China vote in
1959.[97] Last, Lemass' commentary was a successful public relations exercise
designed to calm the domestic furor aroused by Ireland's policy, which was
more an irritant to him than a cause of the later shift in the delegation's vote.
In early November 1959 Cremin sent Boland press clippings of a recent sym-
posium, entitled 'Red China and Ourselves (Ireland's Vote in the UN)', sponsored by the Dublin Institute of Catholic Sociology. In a concomitant minute
Cremin stressed that the conference was, 'on the whole, calm and reasonable,
and that it has not resulted in any of the kind of publicity to which we were

94 Lemass asserted that the 'benefit to mankind would be incalculable' if the leaders of
    communist China could be 'induced to commit themselves to world peace, and the
    growth of the rule of law in world affairs, and accept an obligation to guarantee fun-
    damental human rights' to the Chinese people. Ireland's 'support for the admission of
    Red China to the United Nations would be conditional on the acceptance by its rulers
    of these obligations': *Hibernia*, 23 September 1960. See also DD 176, 662, 7 July 1959;
    DD 187, 861–2, 21 March 1961.
95 Aiken said that the 'Irish government has taken no decision on the question of the
    representation of China – which is not before us – but ... If a proposal were before
    the Assembly at this moment to accept the Peking government as representing China,
    my delegation would advocate that, before any substantive decision were taken, a United
    Nations effort should be made through negotiation to secure from the Peking govern-
    ment an undertaking to refrain from using force against any of their neighbors, to give
    religious freedom to the Chinese people and to allow the people of all Korea to decide
    their destiny in an internationally supervised election': Aiken, Ireland (1959), pp. 3–7.
96 Cf. Aiken, *Ireland* (1958), pp. 26–8.
97 Quite telling in this regard was Lemass' handling of a report handed to him on 20
    July 1959 by Father Timothy Connolly, the Superior General of the Society of St.
    Columban (an Irish missionary order working in China), which argued that the Peking
    regime would not alter its reprehensible policies if admitted into the UN. On 24 July
    Lemass instructed Aiken to circulate it to the government, which he did: S 16057/D,
    20, 24 July, 1 September 1959.

accustomed last year', especially in the wake of Ireland's Tibetan initiative.[98] He added that Lemass had:

> expressed his satisfaction, on the basis of the press reports, with the position. He went on to say that he feels that the outcry about our vote on the China issue is more or less "dead" and that it will probably receive the *coup de grace* when the Americans announce their support for your candidature for the next session of the Assembly.[99]

* * *

The Irish rhetoric of 1959 became a reality in 1961 when the United States agreed to discuss the representation of China. They still opposed the entry of communist China into the UN, but the recent entry of several Afro-Asian nations into the Assembly meant that they could no longer forestall a debate on the subject. Still, the United States intended to engineer a favorable outcome.

On 7 September the United States Embassy in Dublin forwarded an *aide-memoire* to the Department of External Affairs expanding upon Frank Aiken's recent meeting with Grant Stockdale, the American Ambassador, during which they discussed 'the tactics to be used at the Sixteenth Session' relative to the China question.[100] The United States government, according to the *aide-memoire*, now believed that the best way to raise the issue was 'under a non-contentious title such as the "Question of Chinese Representation"'. Hoping that this topic would be introduced 'by a country or countries friendly to the United States', and recalling the American-Irish cooperation that had proved so effective during the Tibetan crisis in 1959, it appealed to Ireland to cosponsor the inscription of the item on the Assembly's agenda; it had also requested Canada, Columbia, Japan, Malaysia, New Zealand, Nigeria, and Norway to do the same. After high-level consultations Iveagh House declined the request, basically, according to Aiken, 'because Ireland had never been in the foreground on this question, and were involved only insofar as we had to take a position on the debating aspect' of it.[101] Nevertheless, the US government's invitation reveals that it now perceived Ireland as trustworthy on a sensitive Cold War issue; it was also trying to hitch Ireland's independent reputation in the Assembly to its own ends.

98 DFA 417/156/4, 10 November 1959.
99 By the same token, two months later Lemass admitted in Cambridge that the Irish delegation's stand on the representation of China had provoked 'controversial debate' at home and 'some misunderstanding of our national position on Cold War issues very far afield', but he was pleased that 'any such misunderstanding has since been almost entirely removed': quoted in *Eire-Ireland: Bulletin of the Department of External Affairs*, No. 468 (1 February 1960).
100 DFA 417/156/7/I, 7 September 1961.
101 DFA PMUN X/58/A, 8 September 1961.

On 14 September Boland informed a meeting of the several delegations that the United States had approached on this matter of the Irish decision.[102] When the Malaysian representative asked Adlai Stevenson, the new American Ambassador to the UN, what his ultimate objectives were, Stevenson said that he hoped the Assembly would appoint a committee to examine the question, especially in relation to the expansion of the Security Council and other bodies – a delaying maneuver, in other words. Stevenson then suggested that a two-thirds majority should be required on all substantive votes. Boland concurred, adding that the Irish government's 'view was likely to be that such a majority was required because of the importance of the matter'. During a meeting two days later, wherein New Zealand emerged as the sole sponsor of the request for inscription, Governor Stevenson dryly noted 'that he would have thought that those who had been in favor of a discussion of this question would now favor inscription of the agenda item'. At this point a US diplomat whispered to Boland: 'You are not going to rise to the bait?'[103] Boland replied 'that of course we favored inscription of the item; our only difficulty lay in cosponsorship'.

* * *

While Iveagh House and the Permanent Mission decided not to cosponsor the American-inspired agenda initiative, Lemass asserted his authority over the Irish delegation's final position on the substantive question of which government, Peking or Taiwan, should represent China in the UN. On 11 September Aiken circulated a memorandum outlining the Assembly's agenda for consideration 'at the government meeting to be held on Friday 15 September'.[104] The section pertaining to the representation of China noted the United States' readiness to discuss the topic and posed the question 'whether the matter will be introduced in the same manner as in previous years'? External Affairs assumed that a formal request 'for the tabling of an item' would be submitted, but because this had not yet taken place the memorandum stated that 'so far no such initiative has occurred'. There was no hint of the Irish delegation's vote on either the procedural motion that might arise or the substantive issue.

Concerned about a few points in the memorandum, Lemass sent Aiken a personal letter on 13 September asking him 'to give some further consideration' to several details.[105] Having underlined the phrase 'so far no initiative has occurred' in the Chinese representation section, Lemass drew Aiken's attention to the memorandum's claim 'that, so far, there has been no initiative to place this item on the agenda'. He reminded Aiken that 'As you know

102 DFA 417/156/B, 14 September 1961.
103 DFA PMUN X/56, 18 September 1961.
104 S 16051/C, 11 September 1961.
105 Ibid., 13 September 1961.

... we have been approached by the US government to cosponsor a motion.'
Consequently, he thought that the cabinet should be 'so informed and, in
view of the certainty that the matter will be discussed in the Assembly, you
should give in the memorandum an indication of the instructions you desire'.

Aiken did not edit the memorandum, nor was it reviewed by the government at their meeting on 15 September, but later that month he indirectly
replied to Lemass' minute. On 27 September his private secretary, Miss R.
Ennis, informed Dr Nolan, Secretary of the Department of the Taoiseach,
that 'With respect to the Taoiseach's letter of the thirteenth instant', Aiken
did 'not propose ... to submit a further memorandum on the matter'. Instead
he had arranged for Con Cremin to 'brief the Ministers before the meeting
on Friday next, on the points arising in [Lemass'] letter'.[106] There was no
indication why Aiken had chosen this course of action; perhaps he planned to
be out of town or maybe he felt that the uncertain situation did not merit
another memorandum.

It is unlikely that Cremin addressed the cabinet then, for the government did
not consider the 11 September memorandum until 24 October. Interestingly
enough, at a meeting that day 'it was arranged' that Aiken 'would submit the
draft heads of the statement to be made on behalf of Ireland when the item
relating to the question of Chinese representation' came up for discussion in
the Assembly.[107] This was a significant move. Lemass was concerned not only
with the final version of Aiken's speech, but with the vote on the substantive
question; in the sensitive times ahead he wanted to ensure that the delegation
adopted a safe position on this controversial issue.

* * *

In mid-October Sean Ronan sent Cremin an update on developments in New
York. He had just spoken with Peter Thacher, a political and security affairs
specialist on the American delegation, about the likely course of the China
debate, which had been inscribed on the Assembly's agenda under two head-
ings: 'Question of the Representation of China', sponsored by New Zealand;
and, 'Restoration of the Lawful Rights of the People's Republic of China in the
United Nations', sponsored by the USSR.[108] Thacher explained that American
policy had shifted from 'a position of "keep Peking out and keep Formosa in"
to one of "keep Formosa in and keep Peking out as long as possible"'.[109] He
also said that 'Apart from strategic considerations and the disruptive effects
which ... the admission of Peking would have on the United Nations', there
was a practical argument to consider: if the Assembly admitted Peking, and

---

106 Ibid., 27 September 1961.
107 Ibid., 24 October 1961.
108 DFA PMUN X/58/A, 22 September 1961.
109 DFA PMUN X/56, 16 October 1961.

expelled Taiwan, 'there was every danger that mainland China would invade Formosa at the earliest opportunity'.

The United States' strategy, according to Thacher, remained unchanged since September. It intended to propose two resolutions: one declaring that the representation of China was an 'important' question and another establishing a review committee. According to US estimates, the vote on the first motion would be close, but they were 'acting on the assumption that Ireland' would support it. Moreover, Thacher said that when Aiken landed in New York Adlai Stevenson would 'contact him with a view to interesting the Minister in taking an initiative in regard to the US draft resolutions'. Ronan was non-committal. Obviously, the American delegation still hoped to harness Ireland's independent reputation to its plan despite Ireland's earlier decision not to cosponsor the agenda inscription.

Ronan's summary of his conversation with Thacher prompted action in Dublin. On 26 October Cremin spoke with Aiken about the China question and followed up this talk four days later with a 'Confidential' minute to the Minister and an attached 'draft of a possible intervention when this matter comes to be debated'.[110] Cremin made it clear that his draft speech was not 'definitive', but meant 'to develop a line of thought'; it succeeded in doing so, for several elements of it were incorporated into Aiken's speech to the Assembly explaining Ireland's China vote. Cremin's conclusion was the most important aspect of his minute. He noted that the draft did not, 'of course, indicate what we will do if the specific question of the representation of Peking were directly put to a vote'. But there were:

> clearly very good arguments in favor of having Peking represented and, in determining our position on such an issue, we could theoretically invoke what [Eamon de Valera] said on 12 September 1934 about the admission of Russia to the League of Nations.

Simultaneously, a solid basis existed for delaying Peking's admission, which Cremin preferred. He was 'inclined to think that from our point of view, there could be much merit in having the debate on this occasion bear on' the American draft resolution appointing a committee. This scenario would provide 'an excellent opportunity for us to repeat the views put forward' by Aiken and Lemass in 1959 wherein they delineated the conditions communist China had to satisfy before entering the UN.

Cremin's recommendation is significant. It reveals that as of 30 October he was unaware of Ireland's vote on the substantive question. Nonetheless, by that stage Lemass had probably advised Aiken to oppose the entry of communist China into the UN. Regardless of any instructions he may have received from Lemass, Aiken still disliked predictions that Ireland would vote

110 DFA 417/156/7/I, 30 October 1961.

against the admission of Peking. For instance, he welcomed Boland's repudiation of an early October *Irish Independent* article claiming that he had labeled
Peking unfit for UN membership.[111]

Within two weeks of Cremin's late-October minute to Aiken the govern-
ment reached a final decision on the China question. It was outlined in an
External Affairs memorandum entitled 'Representation of China in the
United Nations', dated 13 November and reviewed by the government on 14
November.[112] The first part examined the background to the issue and the
American plan to table two separate measures. Then, in keeping with the
arrangements made at the government's meeting on 24 October, the memorandum outlined Aiken's recommendations for the Irish delegation's intervention during the debate. They were inspired by Cremin's late-October draft
speech; Lemass' remarks in the Dáil in July 1959 and his *Hibernia* interview,
both of which stated that China would have to meet several conditions before
Ireland voted for its entry into the UN; and Aiken's matching explanation of
Ireland's 1959 China vote. Subsequently, the memorandum concluded that in
'accordance with the lines suggested for the delegation's intervention on the
subject the delegation would vote in favor of both United States resolutions'.

The matter came before the Assembly in mid-December. Meanwhile, the
United States had withdrawn its draft resolution establishing a review committee after finding little support for it.[113] It retained its measure declaring
that the representation of China was an important question. The Irish delegation did not cosponsor it, even though the American delegation had asked
it to do so in early November; with his independent policy eroding before his
eyes Aiken could hardly have relished the idea, just as earlier he had not
favored cosponsoring the inscription of the item on the Assembly's agenda.[114]
Eventually, the United States, Australia, Columbia, Italy, and Japan cosponsored the procedural motion. When put to a vote on 15 December it passed,
61 to 34, with 7 abstentions.[115] The United States, most western European
delegations, Australia, Canada, New Zealand, and Ireland voted for it; the
Soviet bloc, Ghana, India, Indonesia, and the Nordic countries were among
those opposing it.

The Assembly also rejected a Soviet resolution that by calling for the
removal of Taiwanese representatives from all UN organs and inviting the
Peking government to participate in the work of the UN would, *de facto*,
replace the nationalist with the communist government. The final tally was 36
to 48, with 20 abstentions. Ireland voted against it. The United Kingdom,

111 DFA PMUN X/56, 5, 13 October 1961; *Irish Independent*, 3 October 1961.
112 S 16051/C, 13, 14 November 1961. The memorandum did not call for a government
     decision to be taken. Cremin sent Boland copies of the memorandum and his draft
     speech: DFA 417/156/7/I, 14 November 1956.
113 S 16051/C, 10 September 1962.
114 DFA PMUN X/56, 9 November 1961.
115 Ibid., 15 December 1961.

Denmark, Norway, Sweden, Finland (all of whom recognized the Peking government), most of the Afro-Asian group, and the communist bloc voted for it.[116] Austria, Cyprus, Iceland, the Netherlands, Portugal, and Nigeria were among those abstaining. The Assembly also rejected an amendment to the Russian measure admitting Peking without ejecting Taiwan. Ireland opposed it.[117]

Lemass' long-standing preferences and the External Affairs concerns reviewed above partially account for Ireland's vote. Several of these elements surfaced in Aiken's address to the Assembly on 11 December. Lemass, exercising control yet again, had asked Con Cremin to relay his thoughts on the speech to the delegation a few days earlier and he even suggested a few minor amendments to the final draft early on 11 December.[118] In his speech Aiken admitted that a case could easily 'be made for having the government which is in effective control of the vast majority of the Chinese people represented here in the United Nations'.[119] Still, he recommended that the Peking government's readiness 'to give effective assurances' that they would refrain from using force 'against any of their neighbors' and respect the 'personal rights and liberties of the Chinese people' be fully explored first. The 'nature of these assurances' would determine 'the final decision of the Irish government on the issue before us'. An argument proffered by the American delegation also appealed to Aiken. He argued against taking 'any decision which might be regarded as providing a pretext for the use of force between Peking and Taiwan' and, echoing his earlier proposals for central Europe, Algeria, and the Middle East, called for a comprehensive regional settlement.[120]

Additional factors underpinned Ireland's stand. The strong anti-communist currents swirling at home cannot be discounted. Any Irish government voting for the admission of communist China into the United Nations in 1961 would have been exposed to withering criticism from the press, the public, and the Church.[121] Lemass was aware of this strain of domestic opinion. He also empathized with its general thrust; the UN vote was consistent with the pro-western sympathies he had broadcasted since being named

---

116 The Irish government had been informed in September, through the Irish Embassy in Stockholm, that the Scandinavian countries intended to vote for the admission of Peking. DFA PMUN X/58/A, 9 September 1961.

117 S 16051/C, 10 September 1962.

118 DFA PMUN X/56, 6, 9 December 1961; S16051/C, 11 December 1961.

119 Aiken, *Ireland* (1961), pp. 22–8. Iveagh House circulated a copy of Aiken's speech to all Irish missions abroad: DFA 417/156/7/I, 6 January 1961.

120 At one point Aiken had considered proposing a non-aggression pact between Taiwan and Peking, but was dissuaded by Cremin, who 'pointed out the delicacy of our getting involved, unless we are absolutely sure of our ground', in such a plan: DFA P 12/16/B/II, 30 November 1961.

121 For instance, on 14 December 1961, the day before the vote was cast in the Assembly, the *Irish Independent* stated that 'If Ireland votes for the admission of Communist China to the United Nations this winter, then the government will be guilty of an error for which it will soon not be forgiven.'

Taoiseach. More so, the new policy marked the fruition of his claims that Ireland would not support Peking's entry into the UN unless it satisfied certain preconditions.

The China vote must also be viewed within the context of shifting Irish-American relations in the early 1960s. It is likely that following the election of an Irish Catholic president Ireland hoped to place its relationship with the United States on a sounder footing in order to, among other things, enhance the prospects for American investment in Ireland; T.J. Kiernan alluded to this diplomatic objective in his 'Secret' report of 31 October.[122] The vote in the Assembly sent a clear signal that Ireland was ready to modify the fundamentals guiding its interactions with Washington. Future research will illuminate this significant bilateral dimension of Irish foreign policy.

The Irish government's more immediate goal was to secure American support for its EEC application; this prize was perhaps the overriding motive for the China vote. Lemass undoubtedly grasped from the start the interrelationship between Ireland's role at the UN, the United States' view of its EEC application, and American willingness to back it in European capitals. Perhaps this explains Aiken's meeting with Under-Secretary of State Ball in Paris in mid-November. It almost certainly influenced any private instructions Lemass issued to Aiken on the China vote. If he did not want to provoke French displeasure over Bizerte or Algeria, nor Italian ill-will over South Tyrol, Lemass surely would have avoided generating American fury over China. In fact, it is inconceivable that Lemass would have allowed the Irish delegation to adopt any other position.

This entire approach probably explains Cremin's thinking when John Stone, the newly appointed Counsellor in the American Embassy, paid a courtesy call to Iveagh House on 16 December, the day after the vote.[123] Stone opened the conversation by stating 'that he was glad to note that the Minister had voted with the USA the previous day on the China issue'. Cremin then inquired whether the Mission had received 'much information from Washington about the EEC', particularly any word 'of Mr Ball's thinking on our application'. Stone 'replied that they had not, but believed that Washington welcomed the fact of our application for membership'. While this is what Cremin wanted to hear, later events would prove Stone's forecast somewhat premature.

Whatever the exact alignment of forces that produced the vote, and even though it differed from previous ones by being not just a vote for discussion, but a stand on who should actually represent China in the UN, this moment

---

122 In the context of Ireland's EEC application, Kiernan asserted that it might be time not 'to cash in on the election of Mr Kennedy', but to take advantage of the improved image of Ireland in the American government following the election of America's first Irish Catholic president: DFA P/12/6/A, 31 October 1961.

123 S 16877/W, 18 December 1961.

marks the end of an era. Previously, Ireland's China policy was the hallmark of its independent, energetic role within the Assembly, a magnet for controversy, yet an opportunity for innovation. The 1961 vote represented an unmistakable delimitation of Ireland's autonomous identity. This was especially so considering that Sweden, Norway, and Denmark, other independent-minded middle powers, all backed Peking's entry into the UN. By no means did the Irish delegation completely relinquish its special role, but by design it moved closer to the west. In fact, Ireland voted with the United States on the China question until 1971 (when it joined its soon-to-be partners in the EEC and backed the entry of Peking). It is interesting to speculate how Eamon de Valera would have dealt with this issue if he was still in power. He may have authorized Aiken to abstain on the vote in order to maintain Ireland's activist reputation at the UN, although this is, of course, merely conjecture.

KOREA

At the Sixteenth Session Ireland reinforced its China vote with others amenable to American thinking. In mid-December the First Committee took up the Korean question. Before considering the substantive elements of this protracted issue the Committee first had to resolve a conundrum over North Korea. Mongolia introduced a draft resolution inviting to the Committee's debate 'representatives of both Koreas, in recognition of the fact that there could be no fruitful discussion without the participation of both states'.[124] An American motion proposed to 'invite only the representative of South Korea, and recall that [North Korea] had not unequivocally accepted the competence of the UN' to debate Korean issues. Greece and Thailand then tabled an amendment to the Mongolian resolution retaining the invitations to both Koreas in the original draft, but making the North Korean invitation conditional on an unequivocal declaration of UN authority in this matter.

On 13 December the United States decided to drop its own resolution, support the Greek move and, if it was approved, vote in favor of the Mongolian draft as amended. The amendment passed by a wide margin, 60 to 17, with 22 abstentions. Ireland, casting the first of several votes in unison with western Europe and the United States, voted for the amendment. The communist bloc opposed it, Austria and Sweden abstained. A last-minute Ethiopian amendment recognizing South Korea's acceptance of the UN's competence was also carried, 58 to 1, with 38 abstentions. Ireland, western Europe and the US backed this clause. The amended Mongolian draft was put to a vote in the Committee and passed, 63 to 18 to 19. Once again Ireland and the west supported it, while Austria and Sweden abstained.

124 DFA 417/230/11, 20 June 1962.

Several days later North Korea refused once again to recognize the UN's right to discuss the situation in Korea. On 19 December the United States proposed a motion, which was carried 54 (including Ireland) to 17, with 22 abstentions, asserting that in this light there was no basis for seating a North Korean representative (without voting powers) in the Committee. A draft resolution addressing substantive issues was then introduced into the Committee. It reaffirmed 'the objectives of the United Nations', including the establishment, by peaceful means, 'of a unified, independent and democratic Korea under a representative form of government' and the 'full restoration of peace and security in the area', urged 'continued efforts to these ends', and requested the UN Commission for the Unification and Rehabilitation of Korea 'to continue its work'.[125] On 20 December the Committee, by a total of 55 to 11, with 20 abstentions, recommended it to the Assembly, where it was adopted that evening; Ireland voted for it on both occasions.[126]

THE CUBAN MISSILE CRISIS

In early 1962 Sean Lemass underscored Ireland's westward drift with specific reminders that entry into the EEC would affect its United Nations policy; he aimed these remarks at an external audience, but they reflected realities on the ground. After asserting once more, in a speech before the Fianna Fáil *Ard Feis* in mid-January 1962, that Ireland welcomed European political cooperation Lemass turned to the UN. He reaffirmed that a small nation's security depended upon peace and the rule of law being 'established between nations as between men', and for the past several years Ireland had played its 'part in trying to build up respect and acceptance for [this] concept through the United Nations'.[127] Still, without providing any details, Lemass cautioned that Ireland's 'membership of a European Community may alter in some degree our role in the United Nations ... ' He elaborated upon this claim one month later when Brendan Corish asked him if, in the light of his *Ard Feis* remarks, he would 'outline in what way he considers Ireland's role in the United Nations might be altered ... '[128] Lemass explained that:

To the extent that Ireland's position within the United Nations has been related to the fact that she has not heretofore been a member of any political or economic group it is reasonable to expect that it may be

125 GA/RES 1740 (XVI).
126 DFA 417/230/11, 20 June 1962. On 30 January 1962 Soo Young Lee, the South Korean Ambassador to the United Nations, sent a letter to Freddy Boland thanking him for Ireland's support. DFA PMUN X/55, 30 January 1962.
127 S 13750/D, 16 January 1962.
128 DD 193, 22, 14 February 1962.

affected in some degree following our membership of the European Economic Community ...

Lemass' comments found their mark. On 24 January T.J. Kiernan sent Cremin a report of his recent conversation with William R. Tyler, Assistant Secretary of State for West European Affairs. Tyler noted that Lemass' *Ard Feis* speech had 'made a very favorable impression on the State Department officials immediately concerned with Common Market developments' and it was 'welcomed as the clearest public statement yet made on our attitude to the European Community'.[129] Tyler had 'referred particularly to two passages in the speech': Lemass' standard assertion that with 'regard to those issues which had divided the nations of the world into two camps' the Irish people 'were not, and do not want to be regarded, as indifferent or neutral'; and, his comments on Ireland's United Nations role. These latter references 'defining the nature of our un-allianced [*sic*] foreign affairs policy and referring to the possibility of a remolding of our UN policies in matters of detailed application from time to time' distinguished Ireland from other European neutrals. More favorably, Lemass' speech was 'being made the subject of a brief memorandum for Mr Ball'.

* * *

Consistent with the foregoing predictions, and its new priorities on Cold War issues, Ireland backed the United States to the hilt when the Cuban missile crisis erupted in the autumn of 1962. Earlier in the year, however, the Irish delegation had already aligned its Cuban policy with the west when related items arose in the General Assembly and in the Security Council. In the wake of the Bay of Pigs invasion in April 1961 Czechoslovakia and Romania introduced a resolution into the First Committee in February 1962 (the Sixteenth Assembly was still in session) decrying alleged plans by the United States to invade Cuba.[130] The motion, which amounted to little more than a propaganda exercise, contained two preambular paragraphs: the first 'expressed deep concern over the tense situation in the Caribbean Sea'; the second re-called that the permanent aim of the United Nations was 'to develop friendly relations on the basis of equal rights, self-determination and non-interference in internal affairs'. The operative paragraphs appealed to the United States 'to end its interference in the internal affairs of Cuba' and called upon both states to settle their differences by peaceful means.

---

129 DFA 313/2/I, 24 January 1962.
130 DFA 305/166/II, 16 February 1962. The measure was formally titled: 'Complaint by Cuba of Threats to International Peace and Security arising from New Plans of Aggression and Acts of Intervention being executed by the Government of the United States of America against the Revolutionary Government of Cuba.'

During the debate the American delegation argued against the adoption of a resolution because doing so would lend 'credence' to the unsubstantiated Cuban charge that the United States planned new acts of aggression. Several Latin American countries, determined to block further communist penetration into the region, backed the USA. When the four clauses were put to separate votes, only the second preambular paragraph passed, by a vote of 41 to 0, with 59 abstentions. The Afro-Asian and communist blocs supported it. Ireland, the United States, western Europe and most Latin America delegations abstained; they also opposed the other three clauses.

Because the second preambular paragraph by itself did not constitute a resolution, the First Committee made no recommendation to the Plenary regarding the item. Nonetheless, the Soviet Union and Cuba engineered a debate. Mongolia submitted a draft resolution with an innocuous preamble and an operative clause akin to the second preambular paragraph approved by the First Committee.[131] On 19 February the Permanent Mission informed Iveagh House that the United States was still 'strongly opposed [to the] adoption of any resolution since this would imply some recognition of [the] Cuban charges ... '.[132] It was difficult to judge the course of the debate, but two outcomes seemed likely: a 'procedural tactic to block a vote, such as [an] adjournment of [the] debate'; or, a 'vote on the draft'. If a blocking vote developed, supported by the Latin Americans and western Europeans, the delegation proposed to back it. Because it was 'difficult to assess [the] voting' if the resolution itself were brought forward, the delegation requested 'authority [to] use discretion in order [to] coordinate [its] line of action with other western Europeans and Latins'. On the morning of 20 February Cremin discussed the Mission's recommendation with Aiken. The Minister approved it, and Cremin advised the delegation to proceed accordingly.[133]

Later that day the United States and the Latin delegations, who had dismissed the Mongolian initiative as an attempt to divide them, devised a strategy to defeat the measure. After permitting Mongolia to move the resolution they would request separate votes on the paragraphs, vote in favor of the preamble, abstain on the operative clause, and then oppose the resolution as a whole.[134] They canvassed other western European delegations, the old Commonwealth, a few Afro-Asian members, the Scandinavian countries (except Finland), Austria, and Ireland. After noting the wide-spread support within this group for the American approach the Irish delegation, according to a report by Tadhg O'Sullivan, 'decided to use the discretionary authority which we had sought in order to coordinate our votes with the proposed line of the Latins and western Europeans'.

131 Ibid., 19 February 1962.
132 Ibid.
133 Ibid., 20 February 1962.
134 Ibid.

Just before the vote Sweden 'received instructions to abstain on the text as a whole, but to vote with the Latins on the paragraphs'. Although the Irish Mission 'considered the possibility of joining Sweden and Finland in abstaining', they decided that the reasons for doing so 'did not outweigh the other considerations for maintaining a position in line with Canada, Austria, New Zealand, and all of the Latin bloc'. Subsequently, they 'voted in the same manner as the Latins and the majority of western Europeans': for the preambular clause; in abstention on the operative paragraph; and against the resolution as a whole, which was voted down, 37 to 45, with 18 abstentions.

One week later Ireland joined with several western delegations on the Security Council – to which it had recently been elected for a one-year term – to thwart another Cuban initiative. On 22 February Cuba urgently requested the Council to consider its complaint that the United States, in convincing a recent meeting of the Organization of American States to expel Cuba and to impose an economic boycott against it, had violated the United Nations Charter and, more so, still planned to invade the island. On 27 February Freddy Boland informed Con Cremin that later that afternoon the Security Council, under the aegis of the United States, would reject the Cuban request by ratifying 'a proposal that the agenda should not be adopted'.[135] Boland added that the Latin American members of the Council (Venezuela and Chile) endorsed the move, and the 'United States have asked us to support the proposal also'. He intended to vote for it 'unless I hear from you to the contrary in the meantime'. After discussing the matter with Frank Aiken, who saw 'No point in going into [the] whole Cuban affair again', Cremin instructed Boland to back the USA, and the Cuban initiative collapsed.[136]

* * *

Irish cooperation with the United States over Cuban matters reached its apex during the missile crisis in October 1962. The crisis erupted when the Central Intelligence Agency confirmed that the USSR was installing ballistic missiles in Cuba capable of carrying nuclear warheads, which indeed were already on the island, but not yet operational.[137] On the night of 22 October John F.

135 Ibid., 27 February 1962.
136 Ibid., 28 February 1962. On March 23 Ireland again joined with the United States and its allies on the Security Council (France, the UK, China, Chile, Venezuela) to defeat a Cuban draft resolution requesting the International Court of Justice to review the legality of Cuba's expulsion from the Organization of American States and the economic boycott levied against it: ibid., 23 March 1962.
137 For recent interpretations of the Cuban missile crisis, see James G. Blight and David A. Welch, *On the Brink: Americans and Soviets Reexamine the Cuban Missile Crisis* (New York, 1989); Dino A. Brugioni, *Eyeball to Eyeball* (New York, 1990); Stephen Rabe, 'The Cuban Missile Crisis Revisited', in *Irish Studies in International Affairs*, Vol. 3, No. 3 (1991); Lawrence Chang and Peter Kornbluk, *The Cuban Missile Crisis* (New York, 1992).

Kennedy delivered his now-famous speech revealing the Soviet build-up, announcing a blockade of Cuba, and promising a full retaliatory response should a missile be launched from the island. Beforehand Dean Rusk, the Secretary of State, had briefed T.J. Kiernan and the rest of his colleagues in Washington on the contents of Kennedy's address.[138]

On the morning of 23 October Matthew McCloskey, the American Ambassador, headed to Sean Lemass' office with a personal letter from President Kennedy. Because the Taoiseach was on a state visit to West Germany in order to discuss, *inter alia*, Irish-German trade and the EEC application, Sean MacEntee, the Tánaiste, received McCloskey. MacEntee 'expressed his sympathy with the government and people of the United States on the serious predicament in which they have been placed'.[139] He also promised the American envoy that he would immediately bring the letter to the attention of the Irish cabinet, which he did at a meeting later that morning.

In his letter Kennedy reviewed 'the dangerous developments in Cuba and the actions I have authorized' to date and then informed Lemass that the United States had requested 'an urgent meeting of the United Nations Security Council'.[140] At the meeting Adlai Stevenson, the US representative, intended to present 'a resolution calling for the withdrawal of missile bases and other offensive weapons in Cuba under the supervision of United Nations observers', which 'would make it possible for the United States to lift its quarantine'. Kennedy added: 'I hope you will ask Mr Aiken to work closely with Adlai Stevenson and speak forthrightly in support of the above program in the United Nations.' The State Department, he assured Lemass, 'will keep your Ambassador informed of all developments'.

Lemass immediately backed up Kennedy. In fact, as he later informed the President, right after hearing his speech on the night of 22 October he had telephoned Aiken, who was in New York, and the two agreed that the Minister 'would keep in close touch with Governor Stevenson and that he would speak in favor of and support the draft resolution which you had decided to submit to the Security Council'.[141] On 23 October, after MacEntee had relayed the contents of Kennedy's letter to Lemass, the Taoiseach instructed Irish officials to inform 'the Americans that we are sympathetic'.[142] Moreover, he told Kennedy that 'throughout the succeeding days I followed very closely the evolution of the situation and kept in constant contact with Mr Aiken in New York'.

During a press conference in Bonn on the afternoon of 23 October Lemass advised the public of Ireland's stand. Its UN delegation 'would certainly sup-

138 S 17061/62 23 October 1962.
139 Ibid.
140 Ibid., 22 October 1962.
141 Ibid., 14 November 1962.
142 Ibid., 23 October 1962.

port in the Security Council any proposal calling for the abolition of weapons of aggression in Cuba ... [and] would also favor UN inspection' of missile sites there.[143] Drawing an analogy to Ireland's guarantee to Britain during World War II, he prodded Cuba to promise that its territory would never be used as launching pad for aggressive acts against the United States. Then, with an eye to its still-pending EEC application, as well as the current crisis, Lemass reiterated Ireland's solidarity with the west: 'we are not in NATO, but that does not mean that we should be regarded as neutral. On the contrary, we have emphasized over and over again that we are on the side of the western democracies ... '

At the same press conference Lemass delivered a symbolic *coup de grace* to Ireland's autonomous role at the UN. He announced, in response to a question about the current status of Aiken's troop withdrawal scheme for central Europe, that because 'the idea made little progress' the Irish government did 'not wish to push that suggestion where it does not seem to be acceptable to those directly concerned'. One week later Michael Mullen, an opposition TD, asked Lemass if these remarks foreshadowed the abandonment of Ireland's 'independent position and a close coordination of Irish policy with that of the United States and the NATO powers generally; and whether this country is likely in the future to make any independent proposals in the United Nations for the ... lessening of international tension'?[144] Skirting the issue, Lemass reminded Mullen that he had replied 'to a specific question about a proposal' that the delegation had long ago decided not to pursue, so no 'change of policy was involved'; he also insisted that Ireland would 'continue to support in the United Nations efforts to reduce international tension ... ' Nevertheless, knowing quite well that Aiken's withdrawal plan was not in synch with NATO doctrine, Lemass had deliberately sent a clear signal about Ireland's new priorities to Konrad Adenauer, the German Chancellor, who may have raised the subject during their private discussions.

It is plain to see that Lemass rowed his government in solidly behind the United States. This was to be expected considering his own western proclivity; the government's new direction in foreign policy; the desire to promote American investment in Ireland and to secure its support for the EEC application; and, most important, Lemass' wish to demonstrate Ireland's unqualified support for the United States as it faced its greatest challenge of the Cold War. Further, Lemass' promise of help at the UN was sincere; the Irish delegation had been cooperating with the United States during the Seventeenth Assembly even before the Cuban ordeal broke out. After a conversation on 17 October with Joseph Sweeney, who had transferred from Washington to the American Embassy in Dublin, Con Cremin informed Lemass 'that there has

143 S 16057/G, 23 October 1962. The Department of External Affairs forwarded Lemass' remarks to all Irish missions abroad: DFA 305/166/III, 31 October 1962.
144 DD 197, 20, 30 October 1962.

been close contact between our delegation and that of the USA' on several matters, including China.[145] How the times had changed since the Twelfth Assembly in 1957.

* * *

While President Kennedy's hastily-assembled Executive Committee monitored the crisis from Washington, the Security Council convened in New York. On 23 October Adlai Stevenson introduced an American resolution calling for 'the immediate dismantling and withdrawal' of all offensive weapons from Cuba; authorizing U Thant, the Acting Secretary General, to dispatch UN observers to verify this process; agreeing to lift the naval blockade upon its completion; and recommending that the USA and the USSR confer prompt-ly 'on measures to remove the existing threat to the security of the Western Hemisphere and the peace of the world'.[146] The Soviet Union submitted its own draft condemning the United States' actions; insisting that it end the quarantine and halt all interference in Cuba's internal affairs; and calling for negotiations between the USA, USSR, and Cuba. On the following day the United Arab Republic (UAR) and Ghana submitted an anodyne measure requesting U Thant to sponsor talks.

In their respective interventions the Romanian representative supported the USSR and the Ghanian and UAR spokesmen questioned the wisdom of the American blockade. On 24 October Frank Aiken joined with the other members of the Council – France, the UK, China, Chile, Venezuela – in criti-cizing Russia's blatant threat to international peace. The Irish people, he asserted, could not comprehend:

> the reasons which led the Soviet government, given the present state of tension existing throughout the world, to take such a step which has the effect of upsetting the existing delicate balance of world security, the stability of which it is in the interest of all of us to maintain.[147]

Aiken also reminded the Castro regime that all governments were 'bound to use the powers they derive from their national sovereignty not only in the best interests of their own peoples, but with due regard for the preservation of good relations with their neighbors and for the peace of the world'. He ended with the admonition that the immediate crisis could be dispelled only 'by agreement, and agreement cannot be achieved without discussions and negotiations. Let us hope, therefore, that negotiations will be entered into while there is still time.'

145 S 16057/G, 18 October 1962.
146 S 17061/62, 22 October 1962.
147 Aiken, *Ireland* (1962), pp. 23–30.

On its face, Aiken's appeal for negotiations mitigated his censure of the USSR. Yet it was wholly consistent with the primary foreign policy objective to which he had dedicated his entire tenure as Minister for External Affairs: the reduction of Cold War tensions. It was indeed characteristic of the man that Aiken sought to further this aim during the Cold War's darkest hour, when the risk of nuclear war was never greater. In this respect he later said: 'as I was due to speak the two fleets were getting very close together in the middle of the Atlantic ... so our suggestion was that as the two resolutions, after making their demands, wound up by suggesting negotiations', so should we.[148]

Significantly, since the two had maintained close contact throughout the debate, Lemass surely approved of the gist of Aiken's remarks. And while the various resolutions never came up for a vote, there can be no doubt about where Ireland would have stood: squarely beside the USA. When Declan Costello, a Fine Gael TD, asked Lemass 'whether Ireland was prepared to support the United States, Russia, or Ghana in the Security Council ... during the recent Cuban crisis', the Taoiseach replied that Aiken's address made 'it clear that we supported the United States position on the removal of missiles from Cuba. We advocated immediate negotiations which were finally agreed to, but if the United States resolution had been put to a vote, we would have supported it.'[149] By the same token, the Irish delegation flatly rejected an offer from the non-aligned Afro-Asian bloc to participate in its own efforts to resolve the situation.[150]

After several more gut-wrenching days the missile crisis essentially ended on 28 October when Nikita Khrushchev accepted U Thant's proposal (extended personally to the Soviet Premier three days earlier) that the UN supervise the dismantling of Russian missiles in Cuba. Khrushchev was actually bowing to US pressure, but by replying to Thant instead of Kennedy he was able to preserve a modicum of respect among Kremlin hard-liners. Thus, just as it had facilitated the British and French retreat from the Suez, the UN had again performed one of its small but vital functions in the international system: providing the cover necessary for a leader to save face at home while extracting his country from a situation abroad that had spiraled out of control.[151]

* * *

148 Quoted in Joseph P. O'Grady, 'Ireland, the Cuban Missile Crisis and Civil Aviation: A Study in Applied Neutrality', *Eire-Ireland*, Vol. 30, No. 3 (Fall, 1995), p. 84.
149 DD 197, 409–10, 6 November 1962.
150 DFA 305/166/III, 31 October 1962; DD 197, 409–10, 6 November 1962.
151 Cf. Tavares de Sa, *Play within the Play*, p. 276; O'Brien, 'UN Theater', pp. 280–4.

In Dublin, meanwhile, the Irish government underscored its diplomatic support for the United States in a concrete manner. On 23 October Ambassador McCloskey relayed to Con Cremin a new request from Washington: would Ireland search Cuban-bound Czechoslovakian planes for munitions during their stopovers at Shannon Airport? After a careful review of several factors – the terms of the Convention on International Civil Aviation (signed in 1944 by both Ireland and Czechoslovakia) which authorized contracting parties to prevent foreign aircraft in or above their territories from carrying weapons of war; decisions by Canada and the United Kingdom to search eastern-bloc planes in transit; the wider political implications – the government consented on 1 November. Lemass personally sanctioned the decision. The first search was carried out in Shannon eight days later, and this policy continued in force for several weeks; no arms were found aboard the Czech planes.[152]

The USA greatly appreciated Ireland's cooperation in such a sensitive matter. On 16 November Edward Martin, Assistant Secretary of State for Inter-American Affairs, invited Ambassador Kiernan to his office at Foggy Bottom. Getting right to the point, he expressed to Kiernan, 'and through him to the government of Ireland, the appreciation of the US authorities of the initiative taken by the government of Ireland concerning the [Czech] flights through Shannon to Cuba'.[153] By searching these aircraft 'the Irish authorities had eliminated the possibility of the facilities at Shannon being used to reinforce the Russian build-up in Cuba, or to deliver nuclear warheads for the missiles already there'. Ireland, Martin asserted, 'had thus rendered a valuable service not only to the security of the USA but to that of the entire world'. One year later these sentiments endured at the highest level: during a meeting in the Oval Office on 15 October 1963 President Kennedy thanked Sean Lemass for 'the action taken by the Irish authorities in having searched at Shannon certain aircraft which were enroute to Cuba'.[154]

---

152 For a review of this dimension of the crisis, see O'Grady, 'Ireland, the Cuban Missile Crisis, and Civil Aviation'. This author accurately limns the Irish government's efforts throughout the years preceding the crisis to keep all of its civil aviation options open, and, simultaneously, to foster the development of Shannon Airport as an international transportation hub and domestic economic locomotive (all legitimate national interests). However, his assertion that the government's priority during the Cuban missile crisis was the maintenance of Irish neutrality, *per se*, is incorrect. The opposite was, in fact, the case: Lemass successfully demonstrated – at the UN, in Bonn, and by agreeing to search Czechoslovakian planes at Shannon – that although Ireland was not a member of NATO, it was *not* neutral in the east-west struggle and could be counted on by the west.

153 DFA 313/2/I, 16 November 1962. After reading Kiernan's 'Confidential' report of this meeting, Frank Aiken forwarded a copy of it to all Irish missions abroad.

154 DFA P 333/1/Annex 1, 27 December 1963.

CONCLUSION

Ironically, by the end of 1962 the drive for European political cooperation had stalled,[155] the Department of State had decided, at least temporarily, to take no official position on any of the pending EEC applications,[156] and in early 1963 Ireland withdrew its EEC bid after de Gaulle rejected the United Kingdom's. Yet at the UN Ireland did not reclaim the independent mantle it had donned in the late 1950s. Instead, throughout the remainder of the decade the Irish delegation followed the course fixed in 1961–2: a western predisposition coupled with a commitment to the United Nations Charter, rather than an autonomous identity.

The pursuit of a policy throughout the 1960s tilted toward the west underscores the nature of the change that occurred at the Sixteenth and Seventeenth Assemblies. It was not merely circumstantial, provoked by Ireland's EEC application alone, although this was an important catalyst. The shift that took place in 1961–2 was a fundamental one originating in Dublin under the direction of Sean Lemass. Lemass was thus responsible for not only initiating a well-known revolution in domestic economic policy, but for quietly promoting the evolution of Irish foreign policy so that it served Ireland's changing national interests.

In this respect, there can be no doubt that Lemass improved Ireland's ties with the United States. One need only compare the strained atmosphere of Eamon de Valera's meeting with the American Ambassador, Scott McLeod, just after the first China vote in 1957, with the State Department's positive view of Ireland after the Cuban missile crisis and the breezy air of Lemass' meeting with John F. Kennedy in October 1963. By this latter stage Lemass had removed the thorny issues between the two governments, and they had become partners rather than antagonists. The United States, for example, now welcomed Ireland's constructive role at the UN. During a press conference in Dublin in late 1962 Dean Rusk, the American Secretary of State, remarked that 'the serious, sane, and clear voice of Ireland in the United Nations and the service which she has rendered to the UN ... is one of the great contributions to world peace'.[157] The briefing papers the State Department prepared for President Kennedy before his meeting with Lemass

---

155 Patrick Keatinge, 'Irish Neutrality in the European Community', in Bo Huldt and Atis Lejins (eds.), *Neutrals in Europe: Ireland* (Stockholm, 1990), p. 56.

156 During a brief six-hour stopover in Dublin on 16 December 1962, Dean Rusk, the American Secretary of State, told Sean Lemass that 'the USA was staying out of the EEC negotiations': S 17377/62, 17 December 1962. In October both T.J. Kiernan in Washington and Cremin in Dublin had received an indication – obviously premature – from American officials that the United States would support Ireland's application: DFA 305/57/363/28/III, 2 October 1962; DFA Washington Embassy Series, E/19, 19 October 1962.

157 *Irish Times*, 17 December 1962.

on 15 October 1963 reached the same conclusion.[158] These reports also praised Lemass' economic policy, which was the main topic of conversation between the Taoiseach and the President.[159] On the following day, when Dean Rusk enquired of Lemass 'whether everything was all right as regards relations between the United States and Ireland', the Taoiseach replied that they 'were satisfactory in every respect'.[160] This was not a biased view: American officials concurred with Lemass' assessment.[161]

At the same time, while Lemass went to great lengths to enhance Irish-American relations, he did not compromise Ireland's integrity. Throughout the 1960s the country remained true to its foremost foreign policy objective: the pursuit of a stable international order. The following chapters examine this noteworthy achievement.

158 John F. Kennedy Presidential Library, National Security Files, Box 118, 7, 11 October 1963.
159 DFA P 333/1/Annex 1, 27 December 1963.
160 Ibid.
161 Cf. DFA 313/2/I, 29 January 1962; DFA 305/57/363/III, 18 June 1962, 2 October 1962.

CHAPTER 6

Swords into Plowshares: Ireland's Nuclear Non-proliferation Initiative

INTRODUCTION

It is important to stress, lest the preceding chapter creates a lopsided view, that the emergence of Ireland's western bias on certain issues did not precipitate, in either the near or long term, the wholesale abandonment of its long-standing traditions in foreign affairs. Several loci existed within the realm of UN diplomacy wherein Ireland's new priorities did not override its internationalism, nor was a fiercely autonomous identity a precondition for effective involvement. A UN policy incorporating an energetic approach to world affairs was still feasible.

To pursue this policy the Irish delegation employed a new diplomatic *tactique*. Irish spokesmen recast Ireland's reputation by emphasizing its commitment to the UN Charter while simultaneously soft-pedaling its earlier independent reputation; this approach preserved the Irish delegation's credibility within the Assembly and enabled it to continue with its good work. The country thus remained committed to the spirit and substance of the United Nations. In fact, in several cases Ireland enhanced its activist reputation, notably nuclear non-proliferation and peacekeeping, which are examined here and in the proceeding chapter.

No less a figure than Sean Lemass, the architect of Ireland's foreign policy realignment, supported this trend. He rightly insisted that Ireland preserve its freedom of maneuver insofar as possible – both inside and outside of the UN. While he said in his mid-January 1962 *Ard Feis* speech that Ireland's entry into the EEC might induce some changes in its UN policy, he sincerely affirmed that it would 'not weaken our allegiance to the principles of the UN Charter, which expresses our own hopes and desires for the world'.[1] Moreover, considering that the UN had many enemies, Ireland:

> By our attitude in the United Nations, by our support of the measures which it took to keep peace in some troubled areas of the world ... has

1 S 13750/D, 16 January 1962.

247

given the world an example of how a small country, without great economic wealth or military power, can nevertheless make a useful contribution to the cause of world peace and of the Christian values which should
guide and direct all the affairs of men. We will not change our policy in
this regard, default on obligations which we have freely accepted, or
leave the burden of fulfilling them to others.

Likewise, when a reporter asked nine months later if Ireland's entry into
the Common Market was 'likely to affect its commitment to the United
Nations', Lemass' reply was unequivocal: 'Not in the least degree. Loyalty to
the United Nations and the desire to enhance its influence and prestige are
keystones of our external policy.'[2] He reiterated this theme in a speech before
the General Assembly in 1963, asserting that 'the further strengthening of the
role of the United Nations in international relations is a positive and important
objective' of Irish foreign policy; this was not a 'purely idealistic approach', but
a 'matter of common sense, of political realism, of national interest'.[3]

FRANK AIKEN AND NUCLEAR NON-PROLIFERATION, 1958–9

During the Cold War international arms control talks focused on disarmament across the board as well as its many sub-topics: the testing of atomic
weapons in the atmosphere and underground; anti-ballistic missiles; the reduction of specific types of nuclear arms; the limitation of conventional forces.[4]
At the Eleventh Assembly in 1956 – its first at the UN – Ireland ignored the
issue entirely, a stance that was consistent with the Inter-Party government's
desire to support the west, yet belied the activism of the years ahead. In a
'Confidential' report bringing Iveagh House up to speed Freddy Boland noted
that the delegation's 'present disposition is not to intervene in the disarmament debate at all'.[5] Its major features were 'very complicated', and insofar
'as they relate to nuclear and atomic warfare, they can be of interest only to
the great powers ... ' Ireland's only chance of enhancing the discussion was
to propose a 'very new or striking idea'. Since the delegation had nothing to
offer along these lines, its 'intervention might only too easily make us appear
to be lecturing [the great powers] on matters of more immediate concern to
them than to us'.

Avoiding confrontation with the great powers was not Frank Aiken's
style at all. So at the Twelfth Session in 1957 he spoke in favor of general

2 *Glasgow Herald*, 1 October 1962.
3 Aiken, *Ireland* (1963), pp. 5–16.
4 Cf. *The United Nations and Disarmament* (New York, 1988); Patrick Glynn, *Closing
  Pandora's Box: Arms Races, Arms Control, and the History of the Cold War* (New York,
  1992).
5 DFA 313/36, 14 January 1957.

disarmament.[6] In 1958 he took a keen interest in another of its corollaries: the non-proliferation of nuclear weapons (then labeled non-dissemination). What motivated Aiken? As he reminded the Assembly that year, in the atomic age, 'if general war is brought upon the world for any motive, however good or however bad, it will neither democratize nor communize it; it will annihilate it'.[7] He was also preoccupied, as any leader must be, with his own country's security: limiting the spread of nuclear arms was 'in the interests of the existing members of the so-called nuclear club – the United States, the USSR, Great Britain, France – as well as in all our interests ... ' After all, the danger to humanity did 'not merely increase in direct ratio to the number' of countries possessing them, but 'in geometric progression'. Indeed, while the established nuclear powers, with their urban, industrialized centers, had much to lose from a nuclear exchange, 'sooner or later... [atomic weapons] will pass into the hands of [smaller] states with much less to lose'. Recently Conor Cruise O'Brien has identified one more of Aiken's concerns: 'his worst nightmare was that terrorist organizations would eventually get hold of nuclear weapons, and use them'.[8]

Consequently, from the Thirteenth Session onwards Aiken, with the tireless assistance of the Irish diplomatic corps, pushed nuclear non-proliferation to the top of the UN's agenda. Their commitment to it serves as a powerful testament to Ireland's pursuit of a farsighted policy even after the emergence of a pro-western stance on Cold War issues. Aiken's total dedication to this cause also sheds light upon his efforts to reduce international discord: he grasped that sharpening tensions around the globe could easily lead to nuclear war, and so he worked to lessen them. Equally significant, by championing arms control Ireland demonstrated its faith in the UN Charter, which explicitly assigned this function to the Organization.[9] In this respect the Irish delegation followed the lead of its precursor at the League of Nations, which actively supported that institution's disarmament campaign throughout the 1930s.[10]

* * *

6 Aiken, *Ireland* (1957), pp. 13–17.
7 Aiken, *Ireland* (1958), pp. 17–18, 29.
8 *Irish Independent*, 15 April 1995.
9 Article 11.1 states: 'The General Assembly may consider the general principles of cooperation in the maintenance of international peace and security, including the principles governing disarmament and the regulation of armaments, and may make recommendations with regard to such principles to the Members or to the Security Council or to both.' Article 26 states: 'In order to promote the establishment and maintenance of international peace and security with the least diversion for armaments of the world's human and economic resources, the Security Council shall be responsible for formulating, with the assistance of the Military Staff Committee, plans to be submitted to the Members of the United Nations for the establishment of a system for the regulation of armaments.'
10 Cf. Kennedy, *League*, pp. 121–4, 150–4.

The highest echelons of the Irish government backed Aiken's non-proliferation initiative: on 9 September 1958 Eamon de Valera, who was then Taoiseach, and the rest of the cabinet gave Aiken the go-ahead after they informally discussed it.[11] Ten days later, in order to gauge the reaction of other countries, especially the nuclear powers, Aiken outlined his plan during the Assembly's General Debate. Expressing a refreshing realistic streak, he said that 'while we all wish for complete nuclear disarmament, we must confront the terrible fact that ... it is quite vain to expect it in the immediate future'.[12] Aiken returned to this point often, always stressing that the nuclear powers would never relinquish their atomic weapons until a world authority had evolved. Meanwhile, the 'difficulty of keeping war in check will increase with every addition to the number of nuclear powers'. The Irish delegation believed, therefore, 'that there should be an internationally recognized treaty restricting the nuclear club to its present membership' and stipulating 'that no state outside the club should manufacture or purchase or be supplied with or be in possession of nuclear weapons'. An Assembly measure endorsing these principles would mark the first step along the difficult path to such an accord.

In the following weeks Aiken sounded out the other delegations about his proposal; he was particularly interested in the reactions of the nuclear powers, whose support was the *sine qua non* of a successful resolution. He initially noted that Ambassador Henry Cabot Lodge was sympathetic, but later events proved this forecast to be over-optimistic.[13] The British and Soviets were lukewarm. France was highly suspicious; after all, they were on the verge of successfully test-firing their first nuclear device. Aiken therefore assured the French (and reminded the other delegations) that under his plan they would be included in the nuclear club – another flash of realistic diplomacy on his part. As his blueprint took shape Aiken floated a trial balloon in the American press to elicit further responses.[14] He also kept Eamon de Valera up to date on his activities.[15]

By mid-October Aiken had fashioned his ideas into a draft resolution. According to an internal Iveagh House report, he had revised the motion 'more than once to meet objections or incorporate suggestions' from other countries; he had also consulted 'with disarmament experts in the UN Secretariat'.[16] On 17 October Aiken introduced it into the First Committee's general disarmament debate – interestingly, it was the first time that Ireland had assumed sole sponsorship of a resolution of such political significance. By its two preambular paragraphs the General Assembly recognized that:

11 S 16057/C, 9 September 1958.
12 Aiken, *Ireland* (1958), pp. 16–22.
13 S 16051/A, 20 November 1959.
14 *New York Times*, 7 October 1958. This article was based on an interview with Aiken: DFA 440/8/1, 7 October 1958.
15 DFA 440/8/1, 8 October 1958.
16 S 16051/A, 20 November 1959.

the aim of the United Nations in the field of disarmament is an effective general agreement on the prohibition of atomic, hydrogen and other weapons of mass destruction which will provide for the cessation of the production of such weapons, the destruction of existing stocks and the progressive limitation of conventional armaments; [and, second,] that the danger now exists that an increase in the number of states possessing nuclear weapons may occur, aggravating international tension and the difficulty of maintaining world peace and thus rendering more difficult the attainment of the general disarmament agreement envisaged in paragraph one.[17]

The motion's sole operative clause called for the establishment of 'an *ad hoc* committee to study the dangers inherent in the further dissemination of nuclear weapons and recommend to the Fourteenth Session of the General Assembly appropriate measures for averting these dangers'. At the same time, Aiken suggested amendments to a seventeen-power draft measure on general disarmament (then under consideration by the Committee) that would have had the same effect as his resolution. In his explanatory remarks Aiken stressed the Irish delegation's ultimate aim: that the *ad hoc* committee's investigation into nuclear proliferation 'would lead to a permanent ban on such dissemination'. Indeed, 'both our amendments and our draft resolution, therefore, are conceived as steps towards the restriction of nuclear weapons – a restriction which in its turn would be a step towards their abolition'.

Several non-aligned countries – Mexico, Ceylon, India, the United Arab Republic – reacted positively to Aiken's initiative. So did Sweden, a mid-sized state with the technological capacity to manufacture nuclear weapons if it so desired. Burma offered to cosponsor the Irish draft resolution. Poland privately concurred.

The Soviet Union's response was mixed. Initially, one of its spokesmen declared during a radio interview that Aiken's proposal 'would not only do nothing to remove the threat of the use of nuclear weapons and of the unleashing of an atomic war', but, by condoning the existence of a nuclear club, 'would eventually constitute a legalization of this weapon of mass destruction by the United Nations ... '[18] Contrariwise, at that stage 'the Soviets had not taken any firm declaratory position against proliferation'.[19] Moreover, because Aiken's plan complimented their push for the establishment of atomic-free

---

17 Aiken, *Ireland* (1958), p. 39.
18 S 16051/A, 20 November 1959.
19 Mohamed I. Shaker, *The Nuclear Non-Proliferation Treaty: Origin and Implementation, 1959–79* (New York, 1980), p. 10, quoted in Evgeny M. Chossudovsky, 'The Origins of the Treaty on the Non-Proliferation of Nuclear Weapons: Ireland's Initiative in the United Nations, 1958–61', *Irish Studies in International Affairs*. Vol. 3, No. 2 (1990), p. 114, n. 7. (This interesting article is based on UN public manuscripts and secondary sources.)

zones in central Europe and elsewhere (which were designed to forestall the spread of nuclear weapons to their borders) it was not unimaginable that they would come out in favor of it someday, especially if the west adamantly opposed it.

Like Poland, some members of NATO and SEATO covertly backed Aiken's initiative. Several of them (Norway, Canada, Australia, New Zealand) lent their qualified support during the First Committee's debate. Members of the Canadian delegation, Freddy Boland later reported, discreetly informed him 'that they had advanced inside NATO ideas with the same tendency. They felt that our initiative in the UN was very helpful to them and to what they described as "the more cautious elements" in NATO.'[20]

By this stage, however, the western nuclear powers had rejected the concept outright. France's reasons were obvious: nothing could interfere with the imminent launch of its own *force de frappe*. After consultations with Washington Ambassador Lodge informed Aiken that his proposal was 'unacceptable'. Commander Noble, the British Minister of State for Foreign Affairs, with whom the Minister had spoken on several occasions, took the same line. Their stated objection was straightforward: 'it would be impossible to control any agreement on the subject; more precisely, it would be impossible to keep the Soviet Union from supplying nuclear weapons surreptitiously to the People's Republic of China'. In other words, in the absence of an effective, reliable monitoring system the USSR could not be trusted.[21]

Yet the real driving force behind the American government's antagonism was its planned response to the Soviet Union's recent threats to aim nuclear missiles at European targets, including Berlin, which 'had shaken the confidence of both the United States and western Europe in the effectiveness of the American deterrent system'. The United States intended to stockpile tactical nuclear weapons on the territory of its NATO allies (while maintaining absolute control over their use, in accordance with American law).[22] Aiken's measure 'would have been a psychological barrier to the type of nuclear arrangements the United States was negotiating'. Indeed, the Irish mission in New York informed Iveagh House that the USA was 'inflexible' on this

20 S 16051/A, 20 November 1959.
21 A report by the Irish delegation touched on the Anglo-American preoccupation with control; its analysis also underscores the gulf, at this juncture, between the Irish and NATO approaches to non-proliferation. The report stated: the 'basis of the US-British objections is not perhaps exactly definable. They have at all stages of their disarmament negotiations with the Soviet Union insisted on the necessity for control of any agreement reached. This is indeed an eminently reasonable general principle, but it seems to have produced something in the nature of "control complex" in their minds so far as any agreement with the Soviet Union is concerned. Therefore, the Minister's argument that absence of control would not vitiate his scheme was, it seems, rejected *a priori* rather than as a result of mature consideration': S 16051/A, 20 November 1959.
22 Shaker, loc. cit.

point.[23] They also preferred to utilize existing bodies, like the Disarmament Commission (comprising all 81 members of the UN), rather than establish a new committee to study non-proliferation. By the same token, the United States did not want to undermine the Atoms for Peace program launched by President Eisenhower in 1953. Intended to check expanding Soviet influence in the nuclear field, it authorized the United States to share atomic energy technology with its allies in exchange for the promise not to divert it to military use and the acceptance of supervision by the International Atomic Energy Agency.

When introducing his resolution into the First Committee Aiken had rebutted these and other objections; some of his arguments echoed his belief in the UN's moral force. To charges that it would be impossible to inspect and control compliance with a non-proliferation treaty, especially the transfer of arms, he cited the evident self-interest that dissuaded nuclear states from supplying atomic weapons to their friends – alliances were temporary – and underlined the price of being exposed as a violator of an agreement endorsed by the General Assembly: 'a propaganda defeat of the first magnitude'. To allay the doubts of NATO members, he stressed that his scheme did not bar the deployment of American nuclear forces in Europe since the United States would still maintain complete authority over them. A few experts believed that the successful conclusion of a nuclear test ban treaty would render Aiken's proposal superfluous, but he discounted this view since nations with the scientific resources to build nuclear weapons might do so even without testing them, and any country could 'obtain such weapons from an existing nuclear state without tests'. Several larger states that had not yet developed a nuclear capability, namely India, claimed that the Irish plan established two categories of states, nuclear 'haves' and 'have-nots'. Aiken asserted, though, that he was not establishing a 'principle to the effect that some states shall have the right to these weapons and other states shall not'. A non-dissemination agreement would actually request certain states to voluntarily 'refrain, over a given period, from the exercise of a right which they indubitably possess – the right to manufacture or acquire nuclear weapons'. Nor would an agreement detract from a country's status; on the contrary, prestige would accrue to those nations that 'possess the skill and resources necessary to produce nuclear weapons but that, by deliberate choice, and in the interests of peace, refrain from producing them'.

* * *

Two days after his Committee speech Aiken, ever the optimist, cabled Con Cremin the news that there was a 'reasonable chance for a good vote for [the] resolution'.[24] He was fully aware of the strident opposition to his measure in

23 S 16051/A, 20 November 1959.
24 DFA 440/8/1, 19 October 1958.

western quarters, but thought that the NATO delegations would not vote against it, but abstain, and thereby permit its passage. In a 'Private and Confidential' update to Cremin, Boland ascribed this sunny outlook to Aiken's tendency 'to take references made in goodwill and politeness as amounting to commitments'.[25]

In the end, Aiken's diplomatic efforts and his moral appeals were to no avail. On 27 October, as the First Committee wound up its disarmament debate, France and the United Kingdom announced that they would oppose Ireland's non-proliferation resolution outright. Jules Moch, a French disarmament expert, said that his country would not be excluded from 'the nuclear powers even while others continue to increase their stockpiles and, with them, the dangers of war'.[26] Likewise, on 31 October Henry Cabot Lodge told the First Committee that the American delegation would 'have to vote against the [measure] presented by the Foreign Minister of Ireland'.[27] The US government shared 'his basic objective', but it could not accept any 'obligation the observance of which cannot be verified'. In addition, the creation of 'an *ad hoc* committee ... would but complicate matters and duplicate the work of the Disarmament Commission'. Lodge did not explicitly refer to the more fundamental issue at stake – his country's desire to place its nuclear weapons in western Europe – for doing so would have been impolitic.

The resolution was doomed: the USA would line up a solid majority against it. During a recess after Lodge's speech Aiken discussed the dire situation with a few members of the Irish delegation. He was, Freddy Boland recalled, still 'determined to push his proposal to a vote' – no doubt a measure of his commitment to it. Conor O'Brien argued otherwise, and Aiken correctly decided to withdraw the motion, but only 'at the very last minute ... '[28] On 4 November Aiken was somewhat disingenuous when explaining to the Assembly his reasons for doing so: he wanted to avoid a debate over what machinery should be set up when the new 81-member Disarmament Commission could 'deal as early as possible with the grave danger of nuclear dissemination'; and, the Irish delegation 'realized that most governments had not had time to study the matter since we introduced our proposals'.[29] Nonetheless, several months later Conor O'Brien reminded John J. Hearne, the Irish Ambassador in Washington, that 'Mr Lodge's statement that the United States would vote against the Irish resolution was, of course, the main

25 DFA PS 35/1, 20 November 1958.
26 *Irish Press*, 28 October 1958.
27 DFA 440/8/1, 31 October 1958.
28 DFA PS 35/1, 20 November 1958. The Irish delegation also withdrew its proposed amendments to the seventeen-power draft resolution on general disarmament in order to secure wider support for it; the Assembly adopted it on 4 November, 49–9–22: GA/RES 1252 (XIII).
29 Aiken, *Ireland* (1958), pp. 51–3. See also DD 176, 498–9, 2 July 1959.

reason why' it was withdrawn.[30] O'Brien then instructed Hearne to relay this information to Senator Hubert Humphrey, the Chairman of the Senate's Sub-Committee on Disarmament, who was sponsoring hearings on the subject.[31]

All was not lost, however. Before officially retracting his measure Aiken adroitly requested the First Committee to vote on just the second preambular paragraph, by which the Assembly recognized the danger inherent in the proliferation of nuclear weapons. It passed, 37 to 0, with 44 abstentions.[32] Those casting an affirmative ballot included Finland, Sweden, Iceland, a few Latin American delegations, several Afro-Asians, and the Soviet bloc. The USA, its European allies, the Commonwealth, and most of Latin America abstained. The NATO delegations were able to do so since the second preambular paragraph did not refer to an *ad hoc* committee; it did not, by itself, constitute a resolution; and it therefore implied no action by the Assembly. The Soviet Union's vote was due more to its congenital opposition to the United States rather than its sudden transformation into a champion of non-proliferation.

During the Thirteenth Session Aiken's proposal absorbed his 'energies to the virtual exclusion of everything else', Freddy Boland later recollected.[33] Was it worth it? On its face, the resolution's withdrawal hints that Aiken fell far short of his goal. Indeed, the entire episode was a bald lesson in great power diplomacy. It evinced once more (like Tibet) the limits of Irish influence in the Assembly.

On the other hand, the members of the Irish delegation proved themselves quite adept in the art of statecraft. The judgment to withdraw the measure before the First Committee struck it down – at O'Brien's and Boland's urging – was the right one. It saved Aiken's concept from long-term damage and preserved the option of resurrecting it at a later date. Bolstering this prospect was Aiken's successful request for a ballot on the second preambular paragraph alone. At the time it seemed insignificant, but it was actually a brilliant stroke. As he told the Assembly: 'the primary purpose of our initiative had been attained ... the declaration of principle recognizing the danger of disseminating nuclear weapons' had been placed on the record.[34] Aiken's wisest diplomatic move was his decision to seek a remedy for one specific aspect of general disarmament – non-proliferation – rather than taking on the entire subject. In this regard he eschewed the comprehensive approach of his blue-

30 DFA 440/8/2/1, 20 May 1959.
31 On 16 June 1959 Hearne handed Humphrey a written statement noting that 'Mr Aiken would like to explain to you, Senator, that a main reason for the withdrawal of the operative parts of the resolution was the decision of the United States to vote against the resolution as a whole': ibid., 17 July 1959.
32 Chossudovsky, 'Ireland's Initiative', p.116.
33 DFA PS 35/1, 20 November 1958.
34 Aiken, *Ireland* (1958), p. 51.

prints for central Europe and the Middle East, which, by their nature, were too broad, too ambitious to succeed. Aiken's restrained, but more realistic, strategy for non-proliferation boded well for the future.

* * *

Many of the leading delegates at the UN admired Aiken's persistence in 1958.[35] He put their respect to the test by raising non-proliferation again at the Fourteenth Assembly in 1959. This time, though, several developments portended a more fruitful discussion of the subject. In Geneva the United States, the UK, and the USSR had made some progress towards the suspension of nuclear tests and, with France, they had established a new ten-member Disarmament Committee to resume general disarmament negotiations. Nikita Khrushchev's successful visit to Washington in September 1959 had temporarily improved Soviet-American relations. A Department of External Affairs report noted that these 'circumstances had a moderating effect on the general tone of the First Committee's discussion of disarmament. The customary Cold War aspect of the question was somewhat reduced' because neither NATO nor the Warsaw Pact wished 'to disturb the prospects for successful negotiations outside the UN'.[36] In Britain, meanwhile, the newly-formed Campaign for Nuclear Disarmament had focused international attention on non-proliferation, which subsequently received a great deal of press coverage.

In June Aiken instructed the Irish Mission in New York to request the inscription of the item on the UN's agenda.[37] Iveagh House then set out to generate support for it. Excellent public relations led to sympathetic newspaper articles in Britain and New York throughout the summer.[38] Dublin instructed its Ambassador in Washington, John J. Hearne, to send copies of Aiken's speeches at the Thirteenth Session to George Kennan, who had recently testified about the dangers of nuclear proliferation before the Senate Foreign Relations Committee – part of his running campaign against the militarization of the Cold War. In mid-June Kennan sent a letter to Hearne thanking him for the material. Of Frank Aiken he said: 'I have followed with great sympathy and admiration his valiant effort to combat the spread of nuclear weapons, and feel that he deserves for it the recognition of people everywhere who are aware of the seriousness of this danger.'[39]

Iveagh House also intensified its contacts with foreign countries. Irish embassies abroad were instructed to discuss the non-proliferation initiative with their host governments, and relevant information was passed on to foreign

35 DFA PS 35/1, 20 November 1958.
36 S 16051/B, 20 October 1960.
37 DFA 440/8/4, 15 June 1959.
38 *Manchester Guardian*, 22 June, 25 August, 15 September 1959; *New York Post*, 26 June 1959.
39 DFA 440/8/4, 15 June 1959.

missions in Dublin – all to promote the idea; to allow these governments time to review an issue vitally affecting their security; and to receive feedback on a draft motion.[40] In late June Freddy Boland reported from the UN that the initial reactions were 'quite encouraging ... the feeling within the Secretariat is that the proposal is a good one and that there are considerable advantages to be gained from having the whole question thrashed out in debate in the First Committee ... '[41] A few members of the Soviet bloc called it 'constructive', and 'other delegations, including those of India, Indonesia, etc., have spoken to us appreciatively about the proposal'.

External Affairs focused its greatest effort, by far, on the United States. Its priority was to craft a measure that was true to Aiken's vision and at the same time garnered American support (an abstention would be acceptable, but would carry less moral and political weight). To this end, Irish officials met with their American counterparts at the UN, in Washington, and in Dublin. In late June Freddy Boland told James Barco, a member of the American delegation, that:

> What the Minister was aiming at was a clear acceptance of the general idea that the further dissemination of nuclear weapons should be checked, and a decision by the UN Assembly to take up the question of the best means of giving effect to this idea without delay. We had not put down any resolution and would like to hear the views of other governments, particularly governments already possessing nuclear weapons, before doing so. We would be particularly glad to know the attitude of the government of the United States. I was sure that the Minister would be anxious to take account of the views of the US so far as was consistent with the purpose of his proposal ... [42]

For their part, the Americans respected Ireland's efforts and never doubted Aiken's sincerity. Yet stumbling blocks remained. State Department officials stressed the need for verification and control provisions in any agreement; they also feared that the USSR would seize on a non-proliferation debate at the UN to stall on other aspects of disarmament then being negotiated in Geneva, like nuclear testing.[43] Unmentioned, but still critical, were the agreements the United States had recently concluded with several of its NATO allies to transfer classified information on nuclear weapons and non-nuclear parts of nuclear weapons systems.

After talks with Boland during his annual leave in Dublin Aiken tailored his resolution 'in order to meet the American objections'; it included the

40 Ibid., *passim.*
41 Ibid., 29 June 1959.
42 Ibid., 26 June 1959.
43 Ibid., 10 July 1959.

word 'control', but it did not explicitly mention verification – Aiken felt that this was unnecessary.[44] On 16 July he personally handed a copy to R.E. Ward, Counsellor in the American Embassy, who forwarded it to the State Department.[45] Washington, quite expectedly, was unenthusiastic, so Aiken came up with another version accenting 'the problems of inspection and control involved ... '[46] On 5 August he gave this latest draft to Scott McLeod, the American Ambassador, defended it, and passionately addressed several other tangential issues.[47]

Iveagh House circulated copies to the rest of the embassies in Dublin and to all of the permanent missions at the UN. In early September the French Chargé d'Affaires, Jean Blanchard, apprised Con Cremin that his government, while grateful that the draft took account of French sensitivities by referring to nations 'producing' nuclear weapons, could not support it; the best they could do was abstain.[48] The German envoy, Felician Prill, told Cremin that his government was fearful that the Irish proposal might disrupt NATO; Cremin emphasized that it would not preclude the stationing of nuclear weapons on allied territories so long as the nuclear power retained control of them.[49] Diplomats in the Soviet Mission at the UN were noncommittal.

* * *

On 14 September Boland and Aiken, who had recently arrived in New York, had a friendly discussion about the Irish draft with several members of the American delegation.[50] Of concern to the United States at this point was whether Aiken was calling for a prior commitment, in principle, to a non-proliferation treaty or simply requesting that a study on its feasibility be undertaken by an appropriate international body; if the former was the case, the most the USA could do was to abstain. Aiken said that 'his main purpose was that a serious attempt should be made to reach an agreement' and he promised to 'have another look at the text of the resolution in the light of the view they had expressed'.

On 16 September Aiken defended Ireland's request that non-proliferation be added to the agenda before the General Steering Committee, which duly inscribed it as a sub-heading under general disarmament.[51] Further discussions between the Irish and American delegations ensued, and in mid-November Aiken introduced a well-crafted resolution into the First Committee. Its major

44 Ibid., 17 July 1959.
45 DFA PMUN 334, 16 July 1959.
46 DFA 440/8/4 4 August 1959.
47 Ibid., 10 August 1959.
48 Ibid., 12 September 1959.
49 Ibid., 25 August 1959.
50 DFA 440/15, 15 September 1959.
51 Aiken, *Ireland* (1959), p. 57.

preambular paragraph mirrored the one approved by the First Committee in 1958. By its first operative clause the Assembly suggested:

> that the ten-nation Disarmament Committee,[52] in the course of its deliberations, should consider appropriate means whereby this danger may be averted, including the feasibility of an international agreement, subject to inspection and control, whereby the powers producing nuclear weapons would refrain from handing over the control of such weapons to any nation not possessing them and whereby the powers not possessing such weapons would refrain from manufacturing them.[53]

The second clause invited the Disarmament Committee to pass on the results of its deliberations on these matters to the Disarmament Commission.

In a lengthy address Aiken ardently defended the resolution's merits and refuted the prevailing arguments against concluding a non-proliferation convention.[54] Contrary to the previous year, the motion received widespread support in the First Committee. Most significant, Aiken's attention to American sensibilities had paid off: in late October Henry Cabot Lodge had informed him that his delegation would vote for the resolution.[55] The State Department was pleased that it did not call for a prior commitment to a treaty (only that this option be considered along with other 'appropriate means') and that it explicitly endorsed full inspection and control. US diplomats were also responding to domestic sentiment. Congress, suspecting that the Eisenhower Administration 'had overreacted to Sputnik', was reviewing the Atoms for Peace program; they feared that it 'was actually helping countries to develop at least a threshold nuclear capability'.[56]

The United States' stand cleared the way for many NATO, western, and Latin American delegations to fall in behind the resolution. Their representatives, in general, 'endorsed the purposes of the Irish resolution and expressed appreciation of the Irish delegation's initiative in the matter'.[57] Envoys from the Netherlands and Turkey 'expressed their approval of the procedural aspect of the resolution: it did not prescribe a specific remedy for the problem, but referred it' to the ten-power Committee. The majority of the Afro-Asian bloc backed the motion. India's spokesman cautioned, however, that his delegation's vote did not imply that 'it endorsed the continued manufacture or retention of nuclear weapons by the nuclear powers'.[58] Ceylon raised a

---

52 The Committee comprised France, the USSR, the UK, the USA, Bulgaria, Canada, Czechoslovakia, Italy, Poland, and Romania.
53 GA/RES 1380 (XIV).
54 Aiken, *Ireland* (1959), pp. 60–70.
55 DFA 440/8/4, 29 October 1959.
56 Shaker, op. cit. p. 15.
57 S 16051/B, 20 October 1960.
58 Quoted in Chossudovsky, 'Ireland's Initiative', p. 118.

persistent concern: 'if nuclear weapons were distributed within alliances, other countries might have to resort to producing their own weapons'. Indonesia, on the other hand, held that 'it was up to the non-nuclear nations to refuse to accept nuclear weapons'.

The Soviet bloc abstained, according to several of its delegates, because the resolution was inadequate: it did not 'refer to the basic demand that nuclear weapons should be prohibited and eliminated from the armament of states'; it 'did not advocate 'the establishment of atom-free zones'; nor did it confront the stationing of American atomic weapons in Europe.[59] They believed instead that the Soviet Union's proposal for general and complete disarmament would prevent the spread of nuclear arms. France also abstained despite Aiken's repeated assurances that his resolution acknowledged its pending membership in the nuclear club. On 16 November the First Committee approved the Irish draft resolution by a vote of 66 to 0, with 13 abstentions. Con Cremin informed Sean Lemass, who had been closely following the matter.[60] Four days later the General Assembly adopted it by a similar margin.[61] This was a significant achievement: world opinion had officially recognized nuclear proliferation 'not only as a danger, but as a danger which required consideration and negotiation within the framework' of general disarmament.[62]

NUCLEAR NON-PROLIFERATION, 1960–5

The ten-nation Disarmament Committee convened in the spring of 1960. It failed to consider nuclear proliferation, however, because the Soviet Union walked out of the talks in June.[63] Two months later Frank Aiken, who was disappointed by this development, instructed the Irish delegation to request that non-proliferation be placed on the agenda of the Fifteenth Session.[64] He also made a crucial strategic decision: to promote a measure more assertive than the two previous ones. In mid-September Conor O'Brien forwarded a draft to Freddy Boland, which, he said in a covering minute, 'embodies our present thinking in the Department'.[65] He pointed out 'that it goes considerably further than last year's effort in as much as it makes positive recommendations' regarding a non-proliferation treaty rather than just proffering the idea as one possible solution. O'Brien and Aiken realized 'that this might forfeit for it some of the support we had last year and that we may run into

---

59 S 16051/B, 20 October 1960. Aiken countered these criticisms when speaking in reply to the First Committee's debate. Aiken, *Ireland* (1959), pp. 71–3.
60 DFA 440/8/4, 17 November 1959.
61 GA/RES 1380 (XIV).
62 Chossudovsky, 'Ireland's Initiative', p. 119.
63 S 16051/A, 7 September 1960.
64 DFA PMUN 334, 15 August 1960.
65 Ibid., 12 September 1960.

opposition with it', yet they felt that it would be 'worthwhile to register progress by a stronger resolution this year even if initially we could not muster as much support for it. It would be disappointing to say the least of it to find ourselves merely marking time on the matter.'

O'Brien's forecast was correct: the new motion garnered slightly less backing than the year before. It did, however, attract four new cosponsors (Ghana, Japan, Mexico, Morocco) and on 20 December 1960 the General Assembly adopted the Irish-inspired, five-power resolution, 68 to 0, with 26 abstentions. Its three operative paragraphs called upon 'all governments to make every effort to achieve permanent agreement on the prevention of the dissemination of [nuclear] weapons'; called on the nuclear powers, 'as a temporary and voluntary measure pending the negotiation of such a permanent agreement, to refrain from relinquishing control of such weapons to any nation not possessing them and from transmitting to it the information necessary for their manufacture'; and called upon countries 'not possessing such weapons, on a similar temporary and volunteer basis, to refrain from manufacturing these weapons and from otherwise attempting to acquire them'.

Ironically, the voting tables had turned. Whereas the American delegation had voted for the Irish resolution in 1959, this time it abstained, even though Aiken once again went to great lengths to accommodate its point-of-view.[66] In short, the United States could not abide the motion's call for a treaty as the exclusive means for dealing with non-proliferation because it had not yet adopted this policy, nor did it appreciate the instructions to the nuclear powers, even though they were voluntary. Joining the USA were several of its NATO allies, including the UK, South Africa, the Philippines, China, Australia, a host of Latin American countries, and France, which had recently detonated its first nuclear device in the Sahara. Four members of NATO voted for the measure: Canada, Denmark, Iceland, and Norway. In another reversal so did the Soviet Union, although it was trying to score points in the propaganda war more than anything else.

* * *

The passage of this latest resolution pleased Aiken, but he pursued the issue again at the Sixteenth Session so as to further his ultimate goal: a non-proliferation treaty. In early September, just before the Assembly convened, Aiken aired his views in a respected journal. He pressed for an international convention by invoking national interests and moral arguments. In remarks aimed at the United States (which hardly assuaged their genuine concerns) he downplayed the need for control measures: they might prove to be unnecessary

---

66 For instance, while they were drafting the resolution Aiken told the Irish delegation 'that the official US reaction should be awaited and any suggested amendments from that quarter sympathetically considered': DFA PMUN J/50/60, 8 October 1960.

because adhering to an agreement would 'be so clearly in the interests of all nations'.[67] He reminded NATO once again that the 'proposals of the Irish delegation would not prevent the holding of [atomic] weapons on the territory of the allies of the nuclear nations – so long as the nuclear powers retain control'. Aiken also refuted the complaint that his plan created two categories of states: 'haves' and 'have-nots'. 'Certainly all nations' had the right to produce nuclear weapons, he wrote. 'But any nation which voluntarily foregoes its right to such destructive power in order to get others to do likewise is likely to serve its own vital interests better' than by producing more nuclear arms, which only threatened civilization.

Soon after this article appeared important developments transpired that augured well for Aiken's initiative: the USA and the USSR independently announced that they had officially incorporated the pursuit of a nuclear non-proliferation treaty into their general disarmament programs. President Kennedy enunciated this policy before the General Assembly in September 1961. His administration had resolved many of the stumbling blocks regarding verification and control and had determined that progress on the non-proliferation front would complement efforts to conclude a limited nuclear test ban treaty. The Soviet Union, for its part, had decided (albeit erroneously) that a non-dissemination measure might forestall the spread of nuclear weapons to NATO countries, particularly West Germany.

Iveagh House, meanwhile, had circulated a draft resolution to several foreign governments for their early consideration.[68] Much more assertive than the previous year's, it called for the rapid conclusion of a permanent non-proliferation agreement; outlined some of its specific terms; and dropped all references to temporary and voluntary measures in the interim. Initial reactions were very positive, according to an update Freddy Boland dispatched to Con Cremin in late September. Members of the Canadian delegation, which had parted with the US by voting for Ireland's motion at the Fifteenth Session, 'noted that our preliminary draft this year was stronger than the resolution adopted last year', welcomed this, and suggested that they would 'support our resolution this year'.[69] An American official, Mr Popper, informed Boland that since 'our idea now figured in the US disarmament proposals it followed that this year the United States would support a resolution on the lines of our draft', although a few questions might arise about its wording. Boland reassured Popper that Iveagh House would 'take into account any amendments his delegation wished to make'. He also advised Cremin that 'it is likely that our resolution this year will achieve virtual unanimity'.

Throughout October and November the Irish mission in New York stayed in close touch with all of the key delegations at the UN. It passed on points

67 Frank Aiken, 'Can We Limit the Nuclear Club?', *Bulletin of the Atomic Scientist*, Vol.
    18, No. 7 (September, 1961), pp. 263–6.
68 DFA 440/8/10/I, 17 August 1961.
69 DFA 313/36/4, 30 September 1961.

raised about the Irish draft to the Department of External Affairs in Dublin, which agreed to minor amendments suggested by the USA, the UK, Canada, the Netherlands, even the Soviet Union.[70] In short, to ensure widespread agreement Iveagh House amalgamated the views of other foreign ministries, so long as they did not dilute the fundamental aim of the Irish measure. By mid-November Aiken had settled on a definite formula that approximated to the final resolution.[71] Through Cremin, Sean Lemass stayed abreast of the unfolding deliberations.[72]

On 30 November Aiken introduced the motion into the First Committee; Ireland was its sole sponsor. Its key preambular paragraph noted the need for a non-proliferation convention, 'subject to inspection and control'. Its first operative clause called upon:

> all states, and in particular upon the states at present possessing nuclear weapons, to use their best endeavors to secure the conclusion of an international agreement containing provisions under which the nuclear states would undertake to refrain from relinquishing control of nuclear weapons and from transmitting the information necessary for their manufacture to states not possessing them, and states not possessing nuclear weapons would undertake not to manufacture or otherwise acquire control of such weapons; [the second clause urged] all states to cooperate to those ends.[73]

In his remarks Aiken welcomed the USA's and USSR's recent commitment to non-proliferation and counseled them 'to strike while the iron is hot, to begin at once in the manner which appears to them most appropriate to negotiate' a treaty.[74] During a brief debate the draft underwent only minor revisions, and the Committee unanimously approved it.[75] On 4 December the General Assembly did likewise. Interestingly, Irish diplomats employed some procedural legerdemain to guarantee voting unanimity. To overcome France's dogged determination to abstain they suggested that the measure be adopted by acclamation. 'With some reluctance, the French delegation agreed to this' tactic, which was subsequently employed in both the Committee and in the General Assembly.[76]

---

70 Ibid., 3, 5, 28 October 1961; 7 November 1961.
71 Ibid., 15 November 1961.
72 S 16051/C, 30 November 1961.
73 GA/RES 1665 (XVI).
74 Aiken, *Ireland* (1961), pp. 13–18.
75 DFA 440/8/10/I, 30 November 1961.
76 DFA 313/36/4, 5 December 1961.

CONCLUSION

The passage of this motion marked an important milestone in international affairs: for the first time both nuclear and non-nuclear states committed themselves, in principle, to the speedy negotiation of a non-proliferation agreement. The full story leading to its conclusion is beyond the scope of this study, yet a crucial element of it was Ireland's sponsorship, throughout the rest of the decade, of additional General Assembly non-dissemination measures modeled on the 1961 version – when the pace of the negotiations slowed Ireland utilized world opinion to prod them along.[77] Scholars agree, more so, that Ireland's 1961 resolution served as the 'guiding concept' for the final treaty.[78]

Frank Aiken deserves great credit for his absolute dedication to this cause. William Epstein, a former Director of the UN's Disarmament Division, said that he 'did the nations and peoples of the world a great service'.[79] The international community agreed: when the United States, the UK, the USSR, and many other states signed the Nuclear Non-Proliferation Treaty in Moscow in 1968 they invited Aiken to be its first signatory.[80] Conor Cruise O'Brien, who collaborated so closely with him at the UN, has said: 'That treaty is Frank Aiken's monument.'[81] O'Brien also noted, correctly, that it 'remains Ireland's chief contribution to global security, and not an inconsiderable one'. Monitoring it, he admitted:

> is no easy matter. But neither has the treaty been a negligible factor. It places an international stigma on the acquisition of nuclear weapons, and legitimizes international pressures on governments seeking to acquire such weapons. It is likely that there would be many more nuclear weapons in the world today than there actually are, had it not been for that bold initiative of Frank Aiken's, 27 years ago.

In conclusion, several aspects of Aiken's relentless pursuit of non-proliferation from 1958 to 1968 merit attention. First, the initiative's ultimate success depended upon the commitment of the nuclear powers to a non-proliferation treaty, which transpired in 1961. In addition, Iveagh House constantly took account of the views of the United States and other key countries when drafting its resolutions. These two facts highlight the limits of Ireland's influence in the General Assembly: acting alone, it could not guarantee a motion's survival, as in the case of Tibet, nor could it further those of its proposals rejected

---

77 GA/RES 1911 (XVIII); GA/RES 2028 (XX); GA/RES 2149 (XXI). See also *The United Nations and Nuclear Non-Proliferation* (New York, 1995).
78 Chossudovsky, 'Ireland's Initiative', pp. 127–8.
79 Ibid., p. 112.
80 Keatinge, *A Place*, p. 163.
81 *Irish Independent*, 15 April 1995.

by the great powers: Areas of Law, troop withdrawal from central Europe, peace in the Middle East. Contrariwise, by cooperating with other countries, the Irish delegation achieved its aim – in this case, the passage of viable non-proliferation measures – which underscores its mastery at multilateral diplomacy in the UN. In fact, the Irish delegation's rare combination of principle, skill, and teamwork earned it the respect of its peers. In early December, for instance, the United States inquired whether Ireland would be willing to accept a nomination to the newly-created eighteen-member Disarmament Committee (composed of five western, five communist, and eight neutral countries, it was the latest international body assigned the thankless task of conducting general disarmament talks).[82] Iveagh House turned this offer down owing to staff shortages, but it was a further sign of solid Irish-American relations during the Lemass era. (It was also another indication that Ireland was not as overtly independent as it was in the late 1950s and had shifted toward the west, for otherwise the United States would not have sponsored it for membership on a committee dealing with such a vital aspect of American security policy.)

One of the most interesting features of Aiken's handling of the entire non-proliferation debate was the realistic streak he consistently displayed. When campaigning for a resolution and treaty he periodically appealed to national interests. He included France in the nuclear club even before it exploded its first nuclear warhead. He studiously assured the United States that his proposals did not preclude the stationing of American nuclear weapons on NATO territory. When a few Dáil deputies accused him, in early 1962, of bowing to NATO on this point, Aiken defended his stance. He rightly noted, with the full support of Sean Lemass, that without this understanding the Irish resolution 'would not have been passed unanimously last year. Indeed, it would not have been passed at all.'[83] Finally, Ireland succeeded because it jettisoned a comprehensive approach to general disarmament and concentrated instead on just one of its dimensions: non-proliferation. This wise move paid important dividends: a series of successful resolutions and, eventually, a treaty. All the same, Aiken never converted into a disciple of *realpolitik*: his particular vision of international relations still animated his endeavors. The long-term benefits of non-proliferation were always foremost in his mind. As he told the General Assembly in 1961, the fundamental purpose of a nuclear non-proliferation convention was 'to prevent the danger of nuclear war becoming greater during the period of time it must take to evolve and strengthen a generally accepted system of world security based on international law and law enforcement'.[84] In brief, an agreement would buy time 'for the gradual evolution of a stable world order'.[85]

82 DFA 313/36/4, 9 December 1961.
83 DD 194, 643–6, 28 March 1962; S 16051/C, 21 March 1962.
84 Aiken, *Ireland* (1961), p. 13.
85 Aiken, *Ireland* (1959), p. 76.

CHAPTER 7

Keeping the Peace: Ireland, the UN, and the Congo

INTRODUCTION

Like nuclear non-proliferation, Ireland's conduct during the Congo crisis of the early 1960s demonstrates that despite the Lemass government's tilt to the west on Cold War issues it remained true to vital principles of the nation's UN policy since 1955 and, indeed, its foreign policy since 1922. Throughout the duration of this trying episode Ireland supported the Organization in two ways: diplomatically, after it came under attack from the USSR; and, militarily, by contributing troops to the UN's peacekeeping operation in the Congo (ONUC). The country's peacekeeping role, in fact, underscores several features of its foreign policy during this era: its commitment to *successful* decolonization in Africa, since the fundamental aim of ONUC was to aid the Congo's transition to self-rule; Frank Aiken's desire to ameliorate international tension, specifically by preventing the transformation of central Africa into a Cold War battlefield; Ireland's high profile in the General Assembly; and, how it linked its own security to the efficacy of the UN. Like non-proliferation again, peacekeeping was an area where Irish foreign policy proved effective by pursuing limited, tangible aims rather than comprehensive settlements.

THE ORIGINS OF THE CRISIS

It is not possible to examine Ireland's four-year-long military and diplomatic involvement in the Congo in detail, but its entry into the conflict warrants attention.[1] The Congo crisis had both international and African origins. The

---

1 Actually, both Ireland's military role in the Congo and its broader peacekeeping tradition from the late 1950s to the present day merit their own separate, comprehensive studies based on Irish government sources; these two volumes are now feasible in the light of the opening of the National Archives. Some work based on secondary sources, or on primary materials, in part, has been completed. For a review of Ireland's military contribution to ONUC see: Thomas McCaughren, *The Peacemakers of Niemba* (Dublin, 1966); Nina Heathcote, 'Ireland and the United Nations Operation in the Congo', *International Relations*, Vol. 3, No. 11 (May, 1971); Siobhan Pierce, 'The Irish Army's

thaw in Soviet-American relations precipitated by the Khrushchev-Eisenhower meeting at Camp David in September 1959 failed to hold as the Cold War intensified in 1960. The most vivid symbol of the freeze in east-west relations was the collapse of the May 1960 Big Four Summit in Paris. Shortly thereafter the Soviet Union withdrew from nuclear disarmament talks in Geneva; France's subsequent testing of a nuclear device did little to improve the diplomatic forecast. Meanwhile, Berlin remained a hot spot in the Cold War, and other fronts opened in Laos, Cuba, and even in outer space.

During the second half of 1960 the Cold War also spilled over into central Africa. In July 1960 the Congo (Zaire today) achieved its independence from Belgium, which had given it only five months to prepare for self-rule. Rioting broke out within days when Congolese soldiers mutinied against Belgian officers whom the government had asked to help train the army. Belgium immediately sent troops back into the country to protect Europeans still living there. Fearing a return to colonial rule, the central government of President Joseph Kasavubu and Prime Minister Patrice Lumumba strenuously opposed the move. The leader of the Katanga province, Moise Tshombe, welcomed it and promptly proclaimed the secession and independence of Katanga. For its part, Belgium recognized an opportunity to reestablish its presence in the mineral rich province, home of the Belgian company Union Minière. These developments embittered relations between the Congo and Belgium; led to further bloodshed; provoked a greater European exodus; and pushed the country to the brink of civil war.

Called into action by Dag Hammaraskjold, the Security Council met on 14 and 22 July and established a United Nations peacekeeping force to restore public order in the Congo and to facilitate the withdrawal of the Belgian troops.[2] ONUC was not authorized, however, to use force to expel the Belgian soldiers from the Congo or Katanga and it was prohibited from interfering in the internal affairs of the country.[3]

Participation in the UN's Peace-Making Mission in the Congo, 1960–64' (unpublished M.A. thesis), University College, Dublin, 1993. Commentary on Irish peacekeeping in general is found in: Con Cremin, 'United Nations Peacekeeping Operations: An Irish Initiative, 1961–68', *Irish Studies in International Affairs*, Vol. 1, No. 1 (1979), pp. 79–84; Salmon, *Ireland*, pp. 203–4, 232–3; John Duggan, *A History of the Irish Army* (Dublin, 1991), pp. 249–278; *The Defence Forces: Peacekeepers in the World* (Department of Defence Pamphlet, Dublin, 1995).

2 For a review of events in the Congo preceding the establishment of ONUC, and its subsequent history, see Ernest W. Lefever, *Uncertain Mandate: Politics of the UN Congo Operation* (Baltimore, 1967).

3 One writer accurately notes that 'Hammarskjold's initiative on the Congo question was a logical expression of his deep commitment to decolonization in Africa, his desire to protect the new states and isolate them from the Cold War, his interest in making the United Nations a more effective peacekeeping instrument, and his readiness to strengthen the executive capacity of the Secretary General': ibid., p. 12.

On 16 July Hammarskjold appealed to Sean Lemass for the provision of a light infantry battalion to ONUC.[4] Two days later the Taoiseach discussed the request with several members of the cabinet, including Aiken and Kevin Boland, the Minister for Defense, Freddy Boland (who was in Dublin for annual consultations), and General Sean McKeown, the Army Chief of Staff. Acting swiftly, they arranged for Kevin Boland to draft amendments to the Defense Act, 1954 'so as to enable the government to comply with requests of this nature'; for Aiken to ascertain what other contribution would be acceptable 'if it proved impossible or difficult to provide a battalion'; and for Lemass to discuss with James Dillon and Brendan Corish, the leaders of the opposition, 'the immediate introduction of the legislation that would be required' (this marked the start of full bipartisan cooperation on ONUC).[5]

On 19 July the cabinet formally considered the matter. Sean MacEntee, the Tánaiste and Minister for Health, and James Ryan, the Minister for Finance, were hesitant, but Lemass, with the support of Aiken and Kevin Boland, allayed their apprehensions.[6] The cabinet thus agreed to Hammarskjold's request for a battalion, in principle, and approved Boland's draft legislation, entitled the Defense (Amendment) Bill, 1960.[7] A temporary measure, it authorized Irish troops to serve overseas under UN supervision for a period of six months; restricted them to duties of a police nature; and mandated voluntary participation only. Introduced into the Dáil just hours after the meeting, it passed the next day.[8] Meanwhile, the Army had gotten down to business immediately, and an advance party of officers embarked for the Congo on 22 July; the bulk of the Irish troops followed them five days later. General McKeown aptly labeled their rapid deployment 'a small miracle'.[9]

The government's decision to send Army units to the Congo was truly historic. It reflected Ireland's commitment to international institutions, which it had exhibited since the foundation of the state. In a real sense it marked the fulfillment of Eamon de Valera's pledge to support any collective security action undertaken by the League of Nations (which he effectively rescinded once the League failed to enforce sanctions against Italy in 1936).[10] What's more, it was a concrete expression of faith in the UN, a principle that Ireland had upheld since it entered the Organization. For instance, several years earlier de Valera's cabinet had agreed, in principle, to contribute troops to the UN's Emergency Force in the Suez Canal (UNEF) if the Secretary General called

4   Andrew Cordier Papers, Box 165, 16 July 1960.
5   S 16137/B, 18 July 1960.
6   Brian Farrell, *Sean Lemass* (Dublin, 1983), p. 118.
7   CAB 2/20, 19 July 1960. On 20 July Eamon Kennedy, Counsellor in the Irish Mission, informed Hammarskjold of the government's decision: Andrew Cordier Papers, Box 165, 20 July 1960.
8   DD 183, 1905, 20 July 1960.
9   General Sean McKeown, Military History Society of Ireland Conference, 30 June 1995.
10 Kennedy, *League*, pp. 221–3.

for them (this contingency never arose); the cabinet even approved at that time (but never introduced into the Dáil) amendments to the Defense Act, 1954 that would have made it legally possible to dispatch the soldiers to Egypt.[11] Aiken built on this precedent in a memorandum that he circulated to the government on 19 July. He argued 'that in accordance with the spirit' of Article 25 of the UN Charter ('The Members of the United Nations agree to accept and carry out the decisions of the Security Council in accordance with the present Charter') it was 'incumbent on Ireland to take such steps as it can to comply with the Secretary General's request'.[12] By the same token, when Hammarskjold requested a second battalion in late July Aiken reminded the cabinet, in another submission, that:

> In its intervention in the Congo the United Nations has undertaken a work of the greatest difficulty and importance. If it fails to receive the necessary cooperation, not only may the undertaking fail ... but the value of the Organization as a mediator in disputes may be compromised and the dangers to world peace correspondingly increased.[13]

More specifically, Ireland wished to assist the UN with one of its most important tasks: decolonization in Africa. In the process of knitting ONUC together Dag Hammarskjold sought to balance Afro-Asian troops with European forces; a constructive contribution from the latter might counter Belgium's dismal record in the Congo, improve Afro-European relations, and mitigate the bitter legacy of colonialism. Aiken concurred. In his first memorandum he asserted that it was 'most desirable in the interests of the development along peaceful lines of the emerging states of Africa and the preservation of good relations between Europe and that continent' that European countries be associated with ONUC. In their absence the danger existed 'for increasing the very great racial tensions that exist in Africa', which would 'only damage future relations between the two continents ... '

Ireland was uniquely suited to this task. Hammarskjold's European choices were limited to neutral countries without a history of colonialism, such as Sweden, Yugoslavia, and Ireland. This restriction accounted for his initial request for Irish troops, and he specifically mentioned it in his petition for another Irish battalion.[14] In his second memorandum Aiken stressed this fact when arguing for an affirmative response; in other words, since Ireland satisfied the requirements of this particular mission a responsibility devolved upon it to act accordingly. His arguments were compelling, in the national and international interest, for the government acceded to Hammarskjold's second request in early August.[15]

11 CAB 2/18, 3 September 1957; CAB 2/18, 21 March 1958.
12 S 16137/B, 18 July 1960.
13 Ibid., 2 August 1960.
14 Ibid., 30 July 1960.
15 CAB 2/20, 4 August 1960.

For its part, the Department of Defense wholly endorsed participation in ONUC. After all, it had already authorized Irish officers to serve in non-combative UN observer missions (which required no change to existing law). In the summer of 1958 more than thirty were seconded to the Observer Group in Lebanon (UNOGIL), which moved into the country after American troops withdrew.[16] One year later several officers joined the Truce Supervision Organization along the Israeli-Egyptian border (UNTSO), which the Security Council established in the late 1940s.[17] The Department welcomed the opportunity to join ONUC because it would boost the Army's morale by enabling both officers and enlisted troops to serve abroad; the enthusiastic response from the Irish forces proved this to be so.[18]

Nevertheless, the decision to dispatch combat troops to the Congo was a quantum leap for the government: for the first time it sent Irish forces abroad into a potentially deadly situation. Contemporaries clearly recognized this. One observer noted that the Defense (Amendment) Bill, 1960 proposed 'a fundamental change in Irish law. It authorizes the government to send contingents of the Irish Permanent Defense Force for service outside the state with international forces established' by the United Nations.[19] The decision was also a leap in the dark, for at that time no one foresaw the scope of the Congo operation, the demands it would entail, or just how long it would last.

KHRUSHCHEV'S RESPONSE

The Fifteenth Assembly, which convened in September 1960, presented Ireland with another opportunity to display its support for the UN when shockwaves from the Congo rocked the Organization. The session opened with good news for Ireland, however: Freddy Boland was elected President of the General Assembly – quite an honor for a nation that had entered the UN only five years earlier. The entire election process cannot be recounted in detail, but several points deserve mention. First of all, Boland, the western-sponsored candidate, enjoyed the full diplomatic backing of the United States.[20] Thus, delegations from most of western Europe, NATO, the old Commonwealth, Latin America, and the moderate wing of the Afro-Asian bloc voted for him. He defeated Thor Thors of Iceland, the Nordic candidate, and Ambassador Nosek of Czechoslovakia, the Soviet bloc nominee. The US delegation's support for Boland serves as another reminder, like Tibet and nuclear non-

16 S 16137/A, 29 July, 20 August, 19 September 1958.
17 *Irish Press*, 16 December 1959.
18 General Sean McKeown, Military History Society of Ireland Conference, 30 June 1995.
19 *Irish Times*, 20 July 1960.
20 O'Brien, *Katanga*, p. 46; S 13750/C, *passim*; 417/215/1, *passim*.

proliferation, that Irish-American relations had been placed on a much stronger footing after the China vote. Yet Sean Lemass' insistence that Boland's name not go forward until the United States publicly endorsed his candidacy recalls, again like Tibet and non-proliferation, the Irish delegation's limited sway within the Assembly; acting alone it could not guarantee Boland's victory. Concurrently, the Irish government's electoral alliance with America in 1960 portended its shift to the west on Cold War issues in 1961. Boland's presidency, which by its very nature demanded decorum, protocol, and tact, hastened this change. As one commentator put it just before the election: 'it will be difficult for Ireland to be unorthodox when, as is now almost certain, the Assembly will have an Irish president in the person of F.H. Boland'.[21] By no means, though, was Boland's victory simply the result of American patronage. It was due in most part to the enormous respect he had won from his diplomatic peers across the board and the esteem the Irish delegation had earned by acting so constructively at the UN.

* * *

Boland's inauguration coincided with the outbreak of a serious diplomatic crisis. The Soviet Union, which had originally supported the establishment of ONUC, soon became disenchanted with Hammarskjold's handling of the operation. It claimed that by refusing to prevent the secession of Katanga he was overly sympathetic to European imperial interests and the west generally. Russia then broke with the UN by providing transport planes to Prime Minister Lumumba, who used them in an unsuccessful attempt to invade the province. When the Fifteenth Session (better known as the Summit Assembly because so many world leaders were present) opened, the USSR launched a malicious attack against Dag Hammarskjold and the UN Secretariat. Khrushchev led the assault in several speeches to the Assembly. On 23 September he called for the replacement of the post of Secretary General with a tripartite executive – his infamous troika proposal.[22]

On 24 September the Irish delegation, according to the minutes of its meeting that day, resolved to defend Hammarskjold. It agreed that coordination between the 'moderate elements in the Assembly would be necessary to smooth over the present difficult situation'.[23] The 'Belgrade-Cairo-New Delhi group' was deeply concerned, yet the delegation concluded that 'the efforts of this "left-of-center" group should be supplemented by "right-of-center" elements such as Sweden, Norway, Canada, Tunisia, Mexico, Burma, Ceylon, Venezuela, New Zealand, Japan, and Ireland' – an accurate flash of self-description indeed. Aiken instructed his colleagues to carry out 'informal

21 *Irish Times*, 6 September 1960.
22 For a comprehensive review of this period, see Claude, *Swords into Plowshares*, pp. 285–303.
23 DFA PMUN J/50/60, 24 September 1960.

consultations' with Norway, Sweden, and Canada about how 'to defend the United Nations and the Secretary General against the attacks now being leveled against them'.

Meanwhile, Aiken personally intervened on Hammarskjold's behalf. As he later explained to Con Cremin, Khrushchev's 23 September outburst had provoked such 'uneasiness among the middle-roaders' that Jawaharlal Nehru, the Indian Prime Minister, 'was thinking of suggesting, in his General Debate speech ... that Hammarskjold should appoint three deputy Secretaries General' as advisers.[24] Since this scheme sounded too much like Khrushchev's troika, Aiken passed the word along to the Indian delegation that to propose it 'would be disastrous ... it would undermine the morale' of UN forces in the Congo. After hearing that the Norwegian delegation held the same view Aiken spoke to Nehru 'strongly along these lines'. Earlier, Harold Macmillan, the British Prime Minister, had delivered the same message. These behind-the-scenes overtures proved decisive: Nehru dropped the proposal from his speech.[25]

It was a fortunate decision. During another diatribe on 3 October Khrushchev demanded that Hammarskjold resign. In a masterly reply the Secretary General told the Assembly later that day:

> It is not the Soviet Union or, indeed, any other big powers who need the United Nations for their protection; it is all the others. In this sense the Organization is first of all *their* Organization, and ... I shall remain in my post ... in the interests of all those other nations, as long as *they* wish me to do so.[26]

In his report to Cremin, Aiken noted just how beneficial it was that Nehru had discarded his proposal. Otherwise, when Khrushchev called for the Secretary General to step down 'Hammarskjold would not have been in a position to say, as he did, that he would remain as long as he had the support of the small power countries'.[27]

At the Irish delegation's late September meeting Aiken had decided that his General Debate speech would be primarily 'a defense of the United Nations itself and of the Secretary General's efforts to remain independent of the opposing forces in the Cold War'. On 6 October he followed through on this promise, delivering one of his longest speeches at the UN. In short, Aiken appealed to the middle powers and the newly-independent nations 'to discipline ourselves as loyal and practical supporters' of the UN.[28] He reminded them that:

24 DFA 313/36/3, 13 October 1960.
25 Freddy Boland and Walter Nash, the Prime Minister of New Zealand, also worked hard to dissuade Nehru: Urquhart, *Hammarskjold*, p. 462.
26 Quoted in ibid., p. 464.
27 DFA 313/36/3, 13 October 1960.
28 Aiken, *Ireland* (1960), pp. 6–22.

It is both our duty and our interest to rally to its defense when it is attacked. If smaller powers are to be effective in building a better world order, they must, at whatever short-term inconvenience to themselves, support the [UN] Charter and the Universal Declaration of Human Rights, no matter where or by whom they may be violated.

Aiken resoundingly endorsed the office of the Secretary General, in principle, and Dag Hammarskjold, in particular, whom 'by his wisdom, impartiality, devotion to duty, and loyalty to the principles of the Charter has earned the confidence of the overwhelming majority' of UN members 'and has deserved the confidence of all'.

In the short run Aiken's address did not placate the Soviet Union. In fact, on 12 October one of the most infamous episodes in Assembly diplomacy occurred: Freddy Boland shattered the presidential gavel while calling to order a rambunctious Nikita Khrushchev, who earlier had demonstrated his displeasure with the Assembly's debate by banging his shoe on the table. In a 'Personal and Confidential' report to Cremin several days later Boland called the Soviet Premier 'the personification of elemental violence ... power-drunk, and a doctrinaire'.[29] In his own update to Cremin one day after the debacle Aiken noted that 'Freddy has earned great praise for his handling of the debates so far.'[30] He had prevented 'the Assembly from becoming a bear-garden until yesterday', but everyone expected the situation to improve once Khrushchev returned to Moscow later that evening.

* * *

The UN fared better in the long run. In December the Fifteenth Assembly adjourned for a break. Before it reconvened in March 1961 Boland dispatched an update to Cremin. Although not an item on the resumed Session's formal agenda, one of the principal issues was 'likely to be the future of the United Nations itself', owing to Soviet Union's violent campaign against it.[31] Hammarskjold was convinced that the best means of defeating it was 'an unambiguous demonstration by the uncommitted and independent members' of their determination 'to stand by the Organization in all circumstances'. Boland concurred. He called for 'a positive counter-offensive, a series of firm, decisive and unambiguous protests by the smaller countries ... ' Aiken's October speech was an excellent example of what he had in mind, and Ireland should 'take the lead' at the resumed Assembly. Moreover, by pursuing 'this matter actively, we will be not only helping to safeguard the future of the UN, but serving our own national interests as well'.[32]

29 DFA PS 35/1, 23 October 1960.
30 DFA 313/36/3, 13 October 1960.
31 DFA PMUN J/37/60, 27 February 1961.
32 Boland's sentiments became official policy when they were incorporated into an External Affairs memorandum for the government reviewing the resumed Session's agenda: ibid., 2 March 1961.

Spurred on by his colleague, Aiken ardently reiterated his support for the UN and the Secretary General before the Assembly on 28 March 1961.[33] He challenged the small and middle powers to do the same, and they responded. Writing to Cremin after the Fifteenth Session had adjourned, Boland said that the second half 'did a good deal to repair some of the damage done to the United Nations by the proceedings during the first part'.[34] Hammarskjold considered it a more 'constructive and useful' meeting. He was especially pleased by Guinea's failed diplomatic ploy to abet the Soviet Union. To undermine Hammarskjold's authority in the Congo, their delegate proposed the deletion of the words 'the Secretary General' from an Assembly resolution on the Congo, but the motion was overwhelmingly defeated, 11 to 83, with 5 abstentions. India, Indonesia, and 'other well-known neutralists were among those who voted against the proposal'; only Guinea and Cuba voted with the Soviet bloc. In his own report Conor O'Brien said that this outcome represented a 'very significant victory for the Secretary General and, indeed, the equivalent of a vote of confidence in him'.[35] The vote essentially conveyed 'the Assembly's desire that he should continue in office. His hand is thus greatly strengthened.'

UN officials welcomed the Irish delegation's comportment. In May 1961 Andrew Cordier, Executive Assistant to Hammarskjold, sent a letter of thanks to Freddy Boland for his work 'as President of the General Assembly during this difficult session. Your masterful handling of the problems of the podium, which combined skill, tact, and firmness, was appreciated by us in the Secretariat', as well as by the Member States. Further, wrote Cordier, those of 'the staff who had the privilege of working with you are grateful for the friendly understanding which you always manifested. You really are a "member of the team" and everyone is happy for the experience of working under your leadership.'[36]

* * *

After this strong start in New York and on the ground in the Congo, Ireland remained dedicated to ONUC until it concluded in 1964. This was true even in the face of serious challenges. Tragedies occurred, like Niemba, where several Irish troops were killed in an ambush; twenty-six Irish soldiers lost their lives overall. Crises erupted, in Katanga for instance, which not only led to the tragic death of Hammarskjold in a plane crash, but involved Irish forces

---

33 Aiken, *Ireland* (1961), pp. 3–12.
34 DFA PMUN J/37/60, 24 April 1961.
35 DFA 305/384/IV, 18 April 1961.
36 Andrew W. Cordier Papers, Chronological File, Box 56, 9 May 1961. The 'team' was Hammarskjold's inner circle of advisers, like Cordier and Ralph Bunche, who were particularly active in organizing peacekeeping operations.

in heavy fighting. The intensification of the Cold War in Berlin and Cuba caused Sean Lemass to wonder whether ONUC had left Ireland vulnerable on the home front.[37] Yet the government never wavered. In fact, besides contributing men and material to ONUC, the Irish delegation spearheaded moves to establish an equitable system of financing for peacekeeping missions. The goal of this initiative was to prevent political forces from hijacking UN operations in the field. While it did not produce a concrete formula, it did keep the financial issue current in the Assembly and evinced Ireland's commitment to a fundamental principle of the UN Charter: universal responsibility for peacekeeping operations.[38]

In retrospect, the impact of Ireland's participation in ONUC on its standing in New York proved to be quite compelling. Without doubt, the Congo era marked the apex of Ireland's high profile within the United Nations system. In terms of ONUC itself, several battalions of the Irish Army deployed to Africa. Ireland was a permanent member of the Secretary General's consultative body, the Congo Advisory Committee. In January 1961 General Sean McKeown replaced General Carl von Horn of Sweden as the commander of ONUC;[39] other Irish officers served on its military staff throughout the operation. In May 1961 Dag Hammarskjold plucked Conor Cruise O'Brien out of the Irish diplomatic corps to act as his personal representative in Katanga.[40] Elsewhere, Irish officers had just returned from Lebanon, several were still in the Sinai, and in 1962 two more joined the UN's Temporary Executive Authority in West Irian (UNTEA). In 1959 Ireland started a three-year stint on the Committee on South West Africa. In 1960 it was elected to serve a one-year term on the Security Council in 1962. Freddy Boland was president of the Assembly in 1960 (two years earlier he was Chairman of the Fourth Committee).

Ironically, certain aspects of these roles diminished Ireland's prominence in the UN. As noted, the inherent nature of Boland's presidency necessitated a sober Irish presence in the Assembly. Events in Katanga had a similar effect. After bitter fighting broke out there in September 1961 wild rumors surfaced in the Irish media about the fate of Irish soldiers engaged in the hostilities.[41] Sean Lemass sent Frank Aiken to the region to assess the situation. He found the media reports farfetched. Still, the experience chastened him. Aiken concluded that Ireland had taken on too much responsibility and should therefore reduce its workload in New York. Among other things, he

---

37 S 16051/C, 13 September 1961; S 16137/J, 13 October 1961; S 16137/M, 5 November 1962.
38 Cf. Cremin, 'Peacekeeping Operations: An Irish Initiative'; Sharp, *Irish Foreign Policy*, pp. 50–65.
39 CAB 2/21, 15 December 1960; Andrew Cordier Papers, Box 162, 28 December 1960.
40 Andrew Cordier Papers, Box 165, 16 May 1961.
41 Cf. *Irish Times*, 15–20 September 1961.

decided that Irish diplomats would no longer accept any committee chair-manships in the Assembly.[42]

In like manner, Ireland's defense of Hammarskjold in the face of the Soviet Union's attack, combined with its participation in ONUC, which the USSR detested, had the unintended, but real, effect of placing it in a more western light despite its independent reputation and the involvement of other middle powers in the mission.[43] Nonetheless, it must be understood that whereas the Lemass government wanted to back the United States and Europe on Cold War issues like China and Cuba, it joined ONUC to assist the United Nations, not the west, regardless of the secondary effect this had on its alignment within the Assembly. The government's original reasons for doing so (reviewed above), and its warnings to the UN Secretariat that it would not permit Irish troops to become entangled in the internal affairs of the Congo,[44] prove this beyond all doubt.

ONUC's record in the Congo itself was mixed at best: after the last UN forces withdrew the country remained unstable for years. The mission also placed great financial and political strain on the United Nations. Yet its inter-national impact was much more significant, if often overlooked: it prevented a great power clash in central Africa. One year after ONUC ended Conor O'Brien noted that 'by sending troops to the Congo in 1960, the United Nations averted, or helped the major powers to avert, an occasion of interna-tional war'.[45] This was no small achievement, for the outbreak of Soviet-American hostilities anywhere during the Cold War, even in the Congo, could have set off a nuclear exchange everywhere. Thus, by supporting ONUC Ireland helped reduce international friction, which was Frank Aiken's primary foreign policy objective.

At home, membership in ONUC had a very important consequence: it established an Irish peacekeeping tradition that thrives to this day. For instance, just as ONUC was ending in June 1964, Irish troops shipped out to the UN Force in Cyprus (UNFICYP), where they still remain. Irish soldiers have served in Kashmir, Lebanon, the Golan Heights, Afghanistan, Iraq, Namibia, central America, Cambodia, Yugoslavia, and elsewhere. In all, Ireland has participated in more than twenty-five UN missions, not to mention several European Union operations. Through these efforts Ireland has backed up its rhetoric in New York. Indeed, along with nuclear non-proliferation, peace-keeping has been one of Ireland's most significant contributions to the inter-national order.

42 I would like to thank Ambassador Tadhg O'Sullivan for bringing this to my attention: Personal Interview, 15 June 1995.
43 Cf. Salmon, *Ireland*, pp. 203–4.
44 S 16137/B, 9 August 1960; DFA 305/384/II, 11 November 1960; DFA 305/384/III, 7 April 1961.
45 Conor Cruise O'Brien, 'The United Nations, the Congo, and the Tshombe Government', in Conor Cruise O'Brien (ed.), *Writers and Politics* (London, 1965), p. 219.

CONCLUSION

In addition to peacekeeping and non-proliferation, Ireland sustained other well-established features of its UN policy throughout the 1960s despite its slant to the west on Cold War matters. The delegation's advocacy of the right to self-determination, for example, never flagged. When the future of the Belgian colony of Rwanda arose during the Sixteenth Session the Irish delegation played a leading role in drafting a resolution amenable to both the Afro-Asian bloc and Belgium.[46] Several months later the Belgian Foreign Minister, Paul-Henri Spaak, told Cremin that Freddy Boland had been 'extremely helpful' during the deliberations and he 'was very impressed by Mr Boland's standing in New York and his wide and detailed knowledge of United Nations affairs'.[47]

At this juncture the Assembly considered the situation in Rhodesia for the first time. It approved an Afro-Asian resolution recommending that a UN committee should verify if Southern Rhodesia had attained a full measure of self-government.[48] The Afro-Asian group hoped that the committee would conclude that this was not so because the racial policies of the white-ruled Southern Rhodesian government denied the vast majority of the native population the right to vote.[49] The United States, the western Europeans, the Nordic delegations, and the old Commonwealth all voted against the measure. The Irish contingent, however, adopted a conspicuous position by abstaining. In a report to Cremin after the vote the usually cautious Boland defended this move, noting that Ireland occupied a 'special position *vis-à-vis* the Afro-Asian bloc'.

The same line of thinking informed the Irish delegation's stand on Rhodesia at the Seventeenth Session in 1962. The Afro-Asians introduced a motion into the Assembly requesting the government of the United Kingdom to sponsor a new constitution extending basic political rights to the entire population of Rhodesia and asking the Secretary General to lend his good offices to a resolution of the dispute.[50] Claiming that Southern Rhodesia was an independent state, the United Kingdom put great pressure on Ireland to abstain in conjunction with the rest of western Europe (except Norway), the United States, and the old Commonwealth. Rejecting this argument, Sean Lemass instructed the Irish delegation to vote for the resolution,[51] which passed by the overwhelming margin of 81 to 2, with 19 abstentions.

---

46 DFA 305/420, 20, 22 February, 7 March 1962; GA/RES 1743 (XVI).
47 DFA 313/36/E, 24 May 1962. Cremin undoubtedly appreciated hearing this comment from an EEC foreign minister.
48 GA/RES 1745 (XVI).
49 DFA PMUN J/53/1, 26 February 1962.
50 GA/RES 1760 (XVII).
51 S 16057/G, 2 November 1962.

The Irish delegation played an active part in the deliberations preceding the ballot; it suggested an amendment regarding the Secretary General's role that produced a larger vote in favor of the measure, for example. In a summary of the debate Tadhg O'Sullivan, Counsellor in the Permanent Mission, observed that the Afro-Asian bloc 'attached considerable value to the policy adopted by us on this occasion'.[52] They welcomed 'independent policies such as the present one which, they feel, have a strong moral effect when adopted by countries which they regard as being among the friends of the colonial powers'.

Throughout the rest of the decade Ireland advocated the swift introduction of majority rule in Rhodesia. It also supported efforts to end colonialism in Angola, South West Africa (Namibia), Mozambique, and the rest of Africa and Asia. Several studies confirm that Ireland maintained this policy even after joining the EEC in 1973; its high level of commitment to decolonization, in fact, distinguished it from the rest of the Community.[53]

* * *

Frank Aiken's refusal to formally align the delegation with a voting bloc in the Assembly – neither an Afro-Asian-dominated non-aligned coalition nor a European-centered moderate caucus – evinces again how Ireland held fast to its principles (and Aiken's desire to uphold the country's independent reputation). The first opportunity to join such a group arose in mid-June 1961 when press reports hinted that the Non-Aligned Movement was about to invite several European neutral countries to its upcoming conference in Belgrade, Yugoslavia. Cremin notified Boland, by letter, that Aiken's:

> disposition is rather strongly against our accepting an invitation to such a conference if we should receive one – on the ground that the constitution of blocs of this kind could be more harmful than beneficial, and that insofar as we ourselves are concerned, the utility of our role in the United Nations derives from the fact that we are not committed to any group or to the line of conduct advocated by such a group.[54]

Boland agreed. In a reply to Cremin he noted that it was important to 'strengthen our relations with the Afro-Asian bloc', but felt that this could be achieved 'without putting ourselves in an international category to which we do not really belong'.[55] At the end of the month Aiken informed the Dáil that

---

52 DFA PMUN J/53/I, 7 November 1962.
53 Cf. Leon Hurwitz, 'The EEC and Decolonization: The Voting Behavior of the Nine in the UN General Assembly', *Political Studies*, Vol. 24 (1976), pp. 441–2; Rosemary Foot, 'The European Community's Voting Behavior at the United Nations General Assembly', *Journal of Common Market Studies*, Vol. 17, No. 4 (1979), p. 357.
54 DFA 305/429/I, 15 June 1961.
55 Ibid., 20 June 1961.

he would not seek an invitation to the conference; subsequently, neither Ireland nor the other European neutrals received one.[56]

Aiken's stand was not only sound, but consistent: six months later he rejected Irish participation in a liaison of moderate delegations. In mid-January 1962 Boland informed Cremin of the widespread fear that India's recent invasion of Portuguese Goa might provoke further attempts to overthrow colonial administrations 'by the use of force', with the Afro-Asian bloc 'using the Soviet veto in the Security Council and its own blocking third in the Assembly to prevent any strong reaction on the part of the United Nations'.[57] He warned that unless the Afro-Asians were willing to enforce 'the Charter against their own members just as much against any other member of the Organization, the United Nations will cease to be of any value to themselves or anyone else'.

The American and British delegations, he added, believed that the 'only possible means of preventing this danger' lay in 'positive action on the part of the group of middle-of-the-road states', including Ireland. They could:

> instill into the minds of the Afro-Asian countries the simple ideas that we are vitally concerned with the survival of the United Nations Organization itself; that the use by the Afro-Asians (in combination with the Soviet bloc) of their voting strength to force through unrealistic proposals ... can only result in weakening and perhaps destroying the United Nations; and that rather than see that happen, the middle-of-the-road states, instead of voting for or abstaining on Afro-Asian proposals as they have usually done in the past, will in the future vote against them in any case in which positive harm to the United Nations itself seems to them likely to result.

Boland agreed that 'the development of such a *tactique* is necessary' and thought that the Irish delegation should promote it among the middle powers. Evidently, his earlier opposition to similar action – attendance at the Non-Aligned Movement's conference – had eroded under pressure from the Afro-Asian bloc.

Before taking action Boland sought Aiken's view. Cremin soon informed him that Aiken was unenthusiastic: the Minister preferred 'to avoid our either initiating, or being firmly associated with, a move of the kind in question'.[58] Aiken had wisely discerned two weaknesses in the proposal:

> it could imply the constitution of a kind of bloc, however loose; and, it might give the impression of an element of *a priori* reasoning in the adoption by the states concerned of a particular position in relation to a particular problem.

56 DD 190, 1096–7, 28 June 1961.
57 DFA 305/144/B, 18 January 1962.
58 Ibid., 25 January 1962.

He suggested instead that the larger powers should exert more influence in Afro-Asian capitals and the middle powers 'should say more clearly what they think in the debates in New York'; Ireland had done so, but some of the others had not.

* * *

Coherence in so many areas – non-proliferation, peacekeeping, decolonization, voting blocs, and elsewhere – refutes the criticism of Ireland's mid-1960s UN policy leveled by a former member of the delegation. Speaking in Dublin in May 1964 while on leave from the University of Ghana, where he was Chancellor, Conor Cruise O'Brien claimed that Ireland had 'tarnished her image among Afro-Asian countries by too close an alignment with American and western viewpoints in the United Nations'.[59] It had 'always taken a '"moderately western" attitude', but the delegation's recent voting record 'on major east-west issues has revealed an obedience to the US and Common Market pressures which has deprived Ireland of the confidence' of the Afro-Asian bloc; O'Brien specifically mentioned China. Four years later he again decried Ireland's westward inclination, particularly its silence over Vietnam.[60]

O'Brien's remarks do underscore the country's shift on Cold War issues. Yet had he remained a member of the Irish delegation he would have been unable to forestall this change; witness his 1960 failure to persuade Aiken and Lemass to back sanctions against South Africa. By this stage his superiors differed with him about Ireland's priorities. As a contemporary rejoinder put it, O'Brien's critical viewpoint did not do justice to 'what is presumably the basic reason for our government's general position on foreign policy in recent years, viz., that policy should be harmonized as much as possible with what the government sees as the country's vital economic interests'.[61] O'Brien's strictures were also exaggerated and inaccurate; Iveagh House's own analysis of the Irish delegation's voting record bears this out.[62] O'Brien's ultimate aim was to carve out his own political identity: when canvassing for a Labour seat in the Dáil in 1969 he advocated a more independent UN policy; after being elected he repeated this call while in opposition.[63]

* * *

59 *Guardian*, 21 May 1964.
60 *Irish Times*, 3, 4 June 1968. On this occasion O'Brien reviewed two booklets of Aiken's speeches at the UN in 1966 and 1967. He was equally critical in another article written the following year: O'Brien, 'Ireland', pp. 131, 133.
61 *Leader*, 17 August 1967. The same source agreed that 'on questions of fundamental human rights our attitude should not be decided by economic self-interest, [nonetheless] our government's difficulty in combining adherence to principle on these questions with what it considers to be desirable for the safeguarding of the vital economic interests of our people should at least be appreciated'.
62 DFA 305/384/42, 18 October, 7 November 1967.
63 Cf. Keatinge, *Formulation*, p. 257; DD 241, 1929, 28 October 1969.

In addition to the subtle westernizing effect of Freddy Boland's presidency and Irish participation in ONUC, a shifting institutional context that gained momentum in the 1960s – the rapid growth and radicalization of the Afro-Asian bloc – also eroded Ireland's independent position within the General Assembly. The Irish delegation started tracking this trend in the late 1950s and accurately predicted its implications.[64] We have already seen how it forced the United States into a tactical alliance with Ireland over Tibet at the Fourteenth Session. In 1970 Con Cremin, who had replaced Freddy Boland as Permanent Representative to the UN in 1964 and therefore witnessed much of this process first-hand, described its further evolution.[65] In the late 1950s the balance of power in the Assembly still rested with the west. By December 1960, however, 'the pattern had already radically changed' owing to the recent entry of many newly-independent Afro-Asian nations, including seventeen in that month alone. Two years later UN membership reached 110. In 1970 it stood at 126, with the 41 African members commanding 'great power'. They did not 'all profess the same policies, but nevertheless those who take a particular line, often extreme, are sufficiently numerous to carry' the rest of the African and Asian delegations with them.

Other developments throughout the 1960s bolstered the Afro-Asian bloc's influence. In 1963 the Organization of African Unity was established 'to exert maximum diplomatic pressure within the UN system, and the world community, in areas that affect the political, economic, social, and cultural interests of the people of Africa'.[66] Its leaders believed that the OAU could also expedite 'the rapid decolonization of Africa'. In the wake of the 1967 Six Day War most of the Arab nations rallied to the Afro-Asian cause. The emergence of the Third World, which comprised over 90 Member States in 1970, attracted Latin American support.

The Afro-Asian bloc's extremism unnerved some Irish officials; Boland, unsurprisingly, was one of them. In mid-January 1962 he informed Cremin that Indonesia's threatening posture in its dispute with the Netherlands over West Irian, and Afro-Asian support for it, were 'causing grave concern to the western powers and to the middle-of-the-road delegations in the United Nations such as ours'.[67] The following month he spoke of the 'growing feeling here at the United Nations that unless the activities of the powerful Afro-Asian bloc can somehow or other be kept within the bounds of reason,

---

64 S 16051/A, 20 November 1959; S 16051/B, 20 October 1960; DFA 305/166/II, 8 May 1961; DFA 313/36/C, 26 April 1960.
65 DFA 417/220 7 September 1970. Cremin's effort was part of a memorandum he had penned for a proposed, but never completed or published, External Affairs booklet commemorating the United Nation's twenty-fifth anniversary. See also Claude, *Swords into Plowshares*, pp. 447–8.
66 Wellington W. Nyangoni, *Africa in the United Nations System* (Rutherford, 1985), p. 193.
67 DFA 305/144/B, 18 January 1962.

serious harm to the United Nations may result'.[68] Writing in the early 1970s
Sean Lemass admitted that the increase in Afro-Asian membership was positive in one sense: the UN had become 'a congress of nation states – most of
them small states – which on a global basis is more representative of the whole
of mankind than ever before in history'.[69] On the other hand, the Afro-Asian
bloc often proposed 'unrealistic resolutions', which, because they could not be
implemented, tended 'to erode and weaken the authority of the Assembly
itself'.

More significant was the decline of the fire brigade, the group of middle
powers that often negotiated disputes between the Afro-Asian delegations and
the European colonial powers. Ireland was a well-known member of this centrist group, and its prized reputation owed much to its tireless mediation of
conflicts. Yet in his report Cremin noted that these arbiters had become obso-
lete. The voting majority the Afro-Asians controlled enabled them:

> to secure approval for a particular text – and if necessary to insist on
> occasion that only a simple majority is required – to such an extent that
> they are indifferent to more moderate counsels, and the intermediaries
> (the fire brigade of the Hammarskjold days) are no longer used – or
> indeed heeded.

In this new diplomatic environment Ireland's progressive reputation faded.
The Afro-Asian bloc's rise overshadowed the Irish delegation's high profile. So
did another outcome of the Afro-Asian capture of the Assembly: an American-
led western retreat to the Security Council, where the USA, the UK, and
France retained their vetoes.[70] This gradual shift erased one of the conditions
that had catapulted Ireland to the apex of UN diplomacy: the centrality of
the General Assembly within the UN system. Indeed, today the Assembly
attracts little international attention compared with the Security Council and
UN-sponsored international conferences on the law of the sea, the environment, the status of women, population control, and economic development.

Still, most interpretations of Ireland's declining visibility in the Assembly
are over-simplified.[71] Not only do they exaggerate it, but by ascribing this
transformation solely to institutional dynamics (the rise of the Afro-Asian
group) they overlook and underestimate the Lemass government's control of
its own destiny. They neglect how it deliberately remolded its policy on Cold
War matters. Frank Aiken's curtailment of the delegation's responsibilities
after his trip to the Congo is ignored. Likewise, they give short shrift to

---

68 DFA PMUN J/53/1, 26 February 1962.
69 Lemass, 'Small States', p. 118.
70 Stanley Meisler, *United Nations: The First Fifty Years* (New York, 1995), p. x–xi.
71 Cf. Patrick Keatinge, 'Ireland and the World, 1957–82', in F. Litton (ed.), *Unequal
    Achievement* (Dublin, 1982), p. 227; Salmon, *Ireland*, pp. 227–8.

Ireland's consistency in several areas, including decolonization, which, ironically, was so important to the Afro-Asian bloc.

The Lemass government, like all Irish administrations before it, deftly navigated the changing currents of international affairs in pursuit of the nation's interests. By the middle of the 1960s it had established a firm course – sympathy for the west on Cold War issues combined with a dedication to the international order – that it steadily pursued for the rest of the decade. The compass bearing then shifted somewhat in the early 1970s when the outbreak of hostilities in Ulster, Ireland's entry into the EEC, Fianna Fáil's replacement by a coalition government in 1973, and Garrett Fitzgerald's subsequent appointment as Minister for Foreign Affairs marked the opening of another era in Irish foreign policy.

Conclusion

Irish diplomacy at the United Nations General Assembly constitutes a compelling chapter in the history of Irish foreign policy. It is now clear that the pursuit of national interests guided it. The governments of John Costello, Eamon de Valera, and Sean Lemass consistently advocated common Irish objectives. Nevertheless, each administration defined, in turn, the primary aim pursued under its tutelage.

The identification of distinct interests by separate administrations illumines an important, often underestimated, fact: despite their shared goals, Fine Gael and Fianna Fáil often endorsed divergent foreign policies before the 1960s. Fine Gael was avidly pro-western, stridently anti-communist. This orientation's roots extended back to the 1920s and 1930s. It reached its zenith in 1956 when, in the midst of the Cold War, the Inter-Party government transformed Ireland's UN delegation into a model ally of the west. After being ousted from power in 1957 Fine Gael spokesmen trenchantly criticized Fianna Fáil for abandoning this course.

Fianna Fáil did so because it preferred an activist, independent style. Eamon de Valera initiated this policy at the League of Nations and cemented it during World War II. Frank Aiken continued this trend at the United Nations, where Ireland's autonomous approach crested during the Twelfth Assembly in 1957 and the Thirteenth in 1958. With the ascendancy of Lemass in 1959 Fianna Fáil's and Fine Gael's differences gradually faded. During the 1960s Fine Gael even found aspects of Fianna Fáil's modified UN stance praiseworthy.[1] In the early 1970s their foreign policies converged, at least with regard to the most important issue of the period: EEC membership.[2] Still, the Labour Party opposed entry into the EEC,[3] and partisan differences persist to this day on sensitive topics like Northern Ireland, neutrality, European political cooperation, and Irish membership in NATO.

1 DD 191, 551, 11 July 1961; DD 194, 1324–6, 4 April 1962; DD 208, 881–2, 12 March 1964. The speaker on these occasions was Declan Costello.
2 The results of the 1972 referendum on EEC membership, in which 83% of the electorate voted in favor, reflected both Fianna Fáil's and Fine Gael's support for EEC membership: Keatinge, 'Europeanization of Irish Foreign Policy', p. 41.
3 Maher, *Path*, p. 342.

Despite Fianna Fáil's and Fine Gael's differing interpretations of UN policy in the late 1950s, it was never an issue during a general election.[4] Both parties, however, were accountable to the electorate, which raises an interesting question: what impact did domestic opinion have on Ireland's UN policy? In retrospect, it never determined a specific vote; in no instance did Irish statesmen adopt a position solely because of the possible reaction at home. Perhaps that was because no lobby ever coalesced around a foreign policy issue other than the EEC during the late 1950s and early 1960s. (An anti-apartheid movement did gather momentum in the 1970s.) The only issue that generated real opposition was Aiken's China vote. It was, however, neither organized nor overwhelming, and was at most a secondary cause of the changed vote in 1961. It is thus tempting to conclude that policy makers operated in a vacuum, uninfluenced by an electorate that never expressed 'consistent or profound interest in foreign policy'.[5]

Nevertheless, domestic sentiment was quite influential. It established broad parameters that Iveagh House officials respected, especially in those cases recalling Ireland's historical experience: the invasions of Hungary, Suez, and Tibet; decolonization; apartheid in South Africa.[6] Indeed, Ireland's UN posture successfully captured the public mood. Otherwise, Irish voters, who were well aware of the country's UN policy because the media covered it extensively, would have made it a matter for public debate, if not an election issue.

What about neutrality, one aspect of Ireland's foreign policy that the electorate paid closer heed to? Generally, it had the same effect on UN policy as domestic opinion: it never determined a vote; rather, its influence was indirect. Fine Gael welcomed 'the possibilities the UN offered of compensating for the "accident" of formal neutrality', and so backed the west.[7] For de Valera and Aiken, neutrality entailed important responsibilities: to propose solutions to international problems that the great powers could not; and, to contribute to peacekeeping operations. Lemass soft-pedaled it, both rhetorically and by a UN voting pattern that did not call attention to Ireland's status.

* * *

4 Cf. Keatinge, 'Europeanization of Irish Foreign Policy', p. 37; Lee, *Ireland*, pp. 327–8, 365. The UN did crop up during a by-election in November 1957 when Fine Gael criticized Fianna Fáil's policy, but this tactic failed: Frank Sherwin, an independent candidate, won; Fianna Fáil's nominee was second; Fine Gael's was last. One commentator noted: 'If the by-election proves anything, it is that the electorate ... are not interested in party politics at the present time. The poll of less than 46% was a reflection of the apathy that existed in the constituency. That may have been due, in some measure, to the fact that there was no major political issue before the voters': *Irish Times*, 16 November 1957.
5 Keatinge, *Formulation*, p. 174.
6 Likewise, with regard to foreign policy in general, one scholar has alluded to 'those boundaries formed by the prevailing political culture, beyond which the policy maker will hesitate to venture': Keatinge, *Formulation*, p. 173.
7 MacQueen, 'Aiken', p. 229.

Although Ireland was militarily neutral, it was neither neutralist nor non-aligned. The appellation middle power best describes it during the 1950s and 1960s. Even more specific, Ireland was center-right. The delegation used this label themselves in September 1960 when they decided to rally other like-minded states (Sweden, Norway, Canada, Tunisia, etc.) to Hammarskjold's defense. In January 1962 Freddy Boland included Ireland in this same group when he proposed the formation of a middle-of-the-road bloc to counter the growing extremism of the Afro-Asian group. Moreover, six months earlier he and Aiken had rejected Irish attendance at the Non-Aligned Movement conference in Belgrade. Ireland had far more in common with other European neutrals – Sweden, Switzerland, Finland, Austria – than with those nations that gathered in Yugoslavia.

The reaction of an Iveagh House official to criticism of the delegation's independent policy underscores Ireland's European sensibilities and its centrist position within the Assembly. In an October 1961 *Irish Times* article entitled 'Ireland and Europe: Our Will to Integrate', Garrett Fitzgerald, who was then a strong advocate of EEC membership, erroneously apportioned some of the blame for the delay in the Community's consideration of Ireland's application to its United Nations 'policy of "non-alignment", which has at times provoked irritation in western circles, and especially in continental Europe'.[8] Fitzgerald admitted that 'Few people in Ireland would question certain features' of it, like peacekeeping and support for self-determination, but he argued that Ireland's disagreements with its European neighbors:

> might have provoked less irritation ... if they had been presented as the reluctant inability of a close friend to support a colleague in an unreasonable attitude, rather than as a slightly self-righteous approach by a European country which through no fault of its own missed the tide of imperialism ...

Paul Keating, First Secretary in the Political and United Nations Section, immediately brought Fitzgerald's article to Con Cremin's attention. The future Taoiseach's misguided 'remarks on our "self-righteous" policy of "non-alignment"' had irked him.[9] Keating correctly asserted that it was 'contrary to fact to suggest that when we disagreed with any of the European

---

8 *Irish Times*, 18 October 1961. Fitzgerald's analysis was incorrect because Ireland's UN policy had not provoked undue consternation in Europe.

9 DFA 305/57/363/28/I, 18 October 1961. Máire MacEntee repeated Keating's arguments in her own minute to Cremin, and suggested that Fitzgerald's views be corrected. Cremin replied that he would speak to Fitzgerald: DFA 305/57/363/28/I, 18, 23 October 1961. Although there is no record of a conversation between the two, a later article by Fitzgerald on the subject that does not refer to Ireland's UN policy suggests that Cremin persuaded him to tone down his stance: Garrett Fitzgerald, 'The Political Implications of EEC Membership', *Studies*, Vol. 51 (1962).

powers on colonial matters we did so as other than a close friend who felt a reluctant inability to support an unreasonable attitude'. For instance, Ireland had supported the Netherlands over West New Guinea. During debates about Algeria, the delegation had consistently expressed its 'respect for France in our interventions, and indeed by our attitude have to some extent modified criticism of France and proved a constructive rather than a destructive critic'. And it would 'be going far to say that our attitude on the Congo is contrary to EEC policy', as Fitzgerald claimed. Keating's interpretation was accurate. Ireland often disagreed with its European neighbors, but it never adopted an unfriendly attitude towards them. It was simultaneously independent and centrist, but never neutralist. In fact, Ireland's relations with the members of the EEC, the Nordic countries, NATO, and the rest of Europe were excellent.

* * *

Keating's defense of Ireland's policy is a reminder that talented, committed individuals, from top to bottom, contributed to its success. In all three cases the Taoiseach's role was decisive. John Costello was the first to grasp that the nation could play a serious role at the United Nations. He then translated this vision into reality and in the process defined Ireland's participation in the Assembly. Eamon de Valera, no stranger to international affairs, built on Costello's success. Despite his age, and contrary to common assumptions, he stayed abreast of UN proceedings and intervened at key moments. He did not grant his Minister for External Affairs complete freedom, but in what was perhaps his wisest move gave Aiken wide latitude so that he could carve out a unique place for Ireland in the UN.

Sean Lemass played the most active part of all. He frequently tracked the formulation of policy from its inception until its conclusion, especially in those cases where Ireland's relations with the west or its trading partners were at stake: South Tyrol, Algeria, South Africa, China, Cuba. This process began in 1959 when Lemass started reorienting Fianna Fáil's foreign policy toward the west. By 1961 he had harmonized the country's UN posture with the government's economic program. Moreover, he ensured that henceforth Ireland's foreign policy focused on the future, rather than the past.

Liam Cosgrave, the Inter-Party government's Minister for External Affairs, whose best-known contribution to Irish policy was his three-principles Dáil speech, delivered a more important one at the Eleventh Assembly; by all accounts it was an excellent effort. Like de Valera, Cosgrave prudently allowed his subordinate wide discretion: in this case it was Freddy Boland. Cosgrave's impact on Ireland's role at the UN was moderate, but only because he presided over just one session of the Assembly.

On the other hand, Frank Aiken's tenure as Minister for External Affairs lasted for twelve years, during which he attended an equal number of Assembly sessions; his influence on policy, therefore, was profound. He was fired by the conviction that Ireland could help the United Nations 'become really effective for the benefit of mankind and for the promotion of permanent world peace'.[10] To achieve this aim he transformed the Irish delegation into an independent actor within the General Assembly. This mode reached its peak during the Twelfth and Thirteenth Sessions, when Aiken's *tactique* enjoyed de Valera's full blessing. Although Lemass subsequently remolded Ireland's policy, Aiken continued to play a vigorous, leading role throughout the 1960s by rechanneling his own, and the delegation's, energies into new areas. Ultimately, Aiken's stewardship of Ireland's policy must be remembered for its most abiding legacy: under his guidance Ireland fulfilled its potential for meaningful action within the United Nations system. For this he deserves commendation.

Dedicated professionals in the Department of External Affairs assisted these elected officials. The two Secretaries of the Department, Sean Murphy and Con Cremin, made significant contributions to the design and implementation of policy. So too did the rest of the Iveagh House staff and those assigned to the Permanent Mission in New York. Freddy Boland's role was unparalleled, Conor Cruise O'Brien's skills were unequaled, and the efforts of their colleagues – Máire MacEntee, Eamon Kennedy, Tadhg O'Sullivan, Eoin MacWhite, Paul Keating, Robert McDonagh, Sean Ronan – were unmatched.

The interplay of the Taoisigh, their ministers, and the Irish diplomatic corps highlights two points. Contrary to what is commonly assumed, the Irish government did not pursue separate economic and foreign policies. Even though his plan was misguided, Costello thought that Ireland's UN role might attract foreign investment. De Valera did not let Goa disrupt trade with Portugal. Lemass kept a tight rein on UN policy so that it did not interfere with foreign investment, nor Ireland's EEC bid. The closest link between economic priorities and foreign affairs occurred under his supervision. This is ironic; most scholars have concluded that the Lemass era was the period of greatest fragmentation.

The tension that existed between the Aiken-Cruise O'Brien axis and the Cosgrave-Boland axis was a positive force. One who experienced it first-hand has accurately noted that it 'increased the effectiveness of the delegation'.[11] It encouraged the Irish team to hone their interventions on troop withdrawal from Europe, the Middle East, and Algeria. It brought out the best in Boland; his resilience revealed him to be the consummate diplomat. Likewise, Aiken was open-minded; Eamon Kennedy was courteous; Conor O'Brien was forthright. Disagreements were professionally and promptly resolved.

* * *

10 DD 159, 152, 3 July 1956.
11 O'Brien, 'Ireland', p. 130.

It is now possible to account for one of the salient features of Ireland's participation at the UN: its high profile within the General Assembly. The confluence of several factors generated it. These included the Assembly's primacy over the Security Council within the UN system; an international order divided into east and west, north and south; tactics designed to prevent global tensions from paralyzing the Assembly (middle powers, the fire brigade, peacekeeping); inherent characteristics that qualified Ireland for these roles (neutral, European, a history of foreign rule); the decision of Irish statesmen to assume these duties, wedded to their outstanding ability to perform them; and, Ireland's own initiatives, which raised its standing in the Assembly.

Nonetheless, if the conflux of various forces produced Ireland's high profile, the converse must be true: their disintegration weakened it. This transpired throughout the 1960s, and Ireland's visibility dimmed. Domestic economic priorities overtook Aiken's independent stance; the Lemass government sided with Europe and the United States on Cold War issues; Freddy Boland's presidency of the General Assembly and Irish participation in ONUC colored Ireland's identity with a western tint; after his journey to the Congo in 1961, Frank Aiken instructed the delegation to shed some of its Assembly duties; the emergence of a confident Afro-Asian bloc obviated the need for a fire brigade; it also initiated a shift away from the Assembly and back to the Security Council; in the 1970s Irish foreign policy concentrated on the European Economic Community.

Ireland's record, however, was more important than its reputation. To be sure, Ireland did not achieve all of its objectives. In the short term, Aiken failed to secure his foremost aim: the relaxation of international discord. Cold War tensions actually peaked in 1962 when the Berlin and Cuban missile crises pushed the world to the brink of nuclear Armageddon. India and Pakistan clashed over Kashmir, despite Aiken's mediation in the Security Council in 1962. Within years the United States was fighting an all-out war against communists in Vietnam. 1967 witnessed the Six Day War in the Middle East. One year later the Soviet Union brutally quelled the Prague Spring in Czechoslovakia. Throughout the decade the atomic powers produced thousands of nuclear warheads, notwithstanding the signing of several accords. It is clear, therefore, that Ireland – except in the Congo – was incapable of assuaging superpower conflicts despite Aiken's fierce desire to do so.

Nor has the UN evolved into the major international force that Aiken envisioned. Throughout the Cold War, according to one critic, 'the United Nations proved equally ineffective in every case involving great power aggression', just like the League of Nations in the 1930s.[12] It did not roll back Soviet oppression in Hungary, for example. Nor did it forestall the inevitable outbreak of hostilities in the Middle East. Despite the Assembly's condemnation of it in the late 1950s, China refused to relax its grip on Tibet; since

12 Kissinger, *Diplomacy*, pp. 249–50.

then it has tightened the screws to such an extent that Tibetan culture now faces extinction. Parts of Africa, like Rwanda, are mired in poverty, political instability, and ethnic conflict. South Africa languished for decades before ending apartheid. In the post-Cold War era the UN has 'failed to fulfill the underlying premise of collective security – the prevention of war and collective resistance to aggression' – in the Balkans, the Horn of Africa, and in other regions around the world.[13]

On its face, therefore, the inclination of Irish statesmen to stress the moral dimension of international relations might seem superfluous. Despite their emphasis on the moral force of decisions taken by the General Assembly – the 'moral conscience of mankind' – its ability to modify the behavior of other states was limited. So too was Ireland's. Its high profile at the UN did not translate into real power in the international system. Like its peers in the Assembly – Sweden, Norway, Tunisia – Ireland remained a secondary actor on the world stage.

All the same, during its brief tenure at the UN the Costello government realized its primary interest by actively supporting the west at every opportunity (regardless of the fact that its contribution to western security was minimal). Likewise, Sean Lemass successfully promoted Ireland's international interests at the UN without damaging its economic interests at home. And in truth, the United Nations has contributed to global stability, notwithstanding its skeptics. Away from the glare of the international spotlight its specialized agencies (WHO, ILO, UNESCO, UNICEF) have quietly administered economic, technical, educational, refugee, health, and cultural programs that have improved the lives of millions of people. By the same token, George Ball, who was Under-Secretary of State in the Kennedy and Johnson administrations and the American Ambassador to the UN in 1968, said that the UN's:

> most important achievement has been to serve as a kind of midwife, bringing into existence so many new nations; in other words, it has been the instrument to manage, to stimulate, and, at the same time, to prevent major breakage from, the movement of a billion people from colonial dependency to some kind of independence. That enormous change in the political structure of the world could never have been accomplished if the UN had not been available to play its role, and I think it played it extremely well.[14]

On a political level, the last word on the UN belongs to Conor Cruise O'Brien, whose experiences there sustain his acute insights. In one of his

13 Ibid.
14 Quoted in Linda M. Fasulo, *Representing America: Experiences of US Diplomats at the United Nations* (New York, 1984), p. 123.

many essays on the subject, he responds to the question: if so many 'millions of people are estimated to have died in wars since 1945, the year the United Nations was born', why did it 'not *do* something'?[15] His answer: 'The question is misconceived. The United Nations cannot do anything, and never could. It is not an animate entity or agent. It is a place, a stage, a forum ... ' More to the point, the UN 'has developed a set of rituals' that assist international diplomacy in subtle ways. It is a place where it is 'possible for powerful people who have made fools of themselves to climb down and not look quite as foolish as they deserve to look': Suez in 1956, Cuba in 1962. The UN is also valuable owing to 'its proven capacity to fail, and to be seen to fail'. When statesmen are faced with an insurmountable challenge they can assign the thankless task to the UN, thereby reducing the pressure on them to act: Hungary, Somalia, Rwanda, Bosnia. These functions seem marginal. Yet during the Cold War they meant the difference between peace and nuclear holocaust. The UN, therefore, 'has probably helped others – perhaps millions of others – to survive'.

For its part, by acting through the UN Ireland did reduce international tension – in the long run. Its own initiatives and the Organization's efforts laid the groundwork for future breakthroughs. Ireland's commitment to nuclear non-proliferation focused attention on the issue until the international community was ready to conclude a treaty. Today Irish and UN soldiers monitor cease-fire lines and human rights in Cyprus, Lebanon, Kashmir, Bosnia, Rwanda, and elsewhere. Under constant international pressure South Africa eventually abandoned apartheid. The UN, with the assistance of Irish personnel, ushered in Namibian independence. Ireland and the UN still advocate the rule of law in foreign affairs and universal respect for human rights.

In sum, and contrary to reports at the time, Ireland did not bestride the world like a Colossus. It did not even bestride the UN. But it did stand shoulder to shoulder with other states in the General Assembly, especially the middle powers: Sweden, Norway, Denmark, Canada, Malaysia, Tunisia. Ireland's contribution to the international order was modest. But it was also real. Ireland acted not only as peacekeeper, but as a peacemaker – a record of substance indeed.

15 O'Brien, 'UN Theater', pp. 280–4.

The United Nations System, 1961

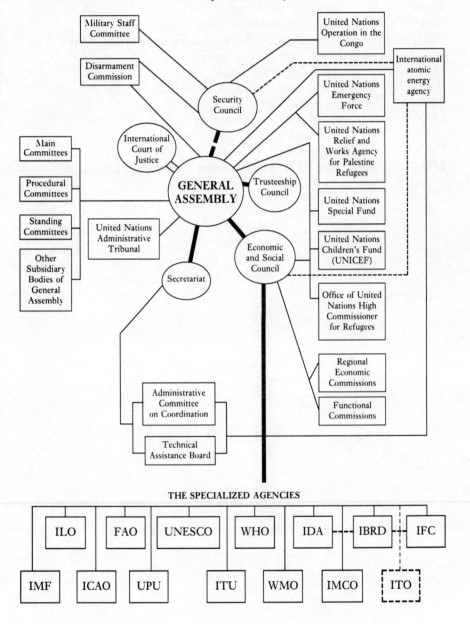

THE SPECIALIZED AGENCIES

Legend

ILO	International Labour Organisation
FAO	Food and Agriculture Organization of the United Nations
UNESCO	United Nations Educational, Scientific and Cultural Organization
WHO	World Health Organization
IDA	International Development Association
IBRD	International Bank for Reconstruction and Development
IFC	International Finance Corporation
IMF	International Monetary Fund
ICAO	International Civil Aviation Organization
UPU	Universal Postal Union
ITU	International Telecommunication Union
WMO	World Meteorological Organization
IMCO	Inter-Governmental Maritime Consultative Organization
ITO	International Trade Organization (General Agreement on Tariffs and Trade)

The General Assembly, 1961

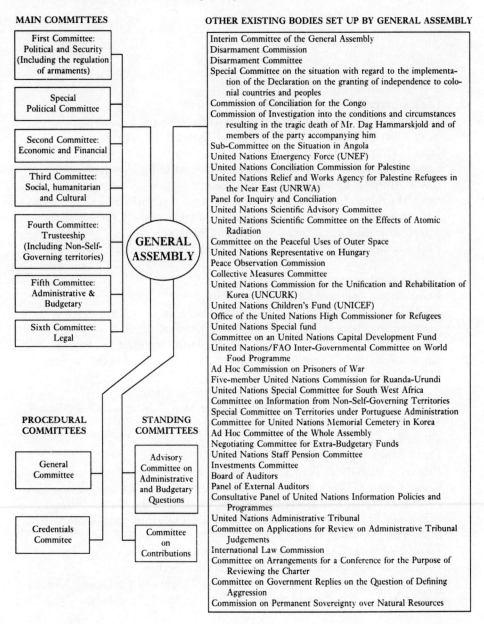

MAIN COMMITTEES

First Committee:
Political and Security
(Including the regulation
of armaments)

Special
Political Committee

Second Committee:
Economic and Financial

Third Committee:
Social, humanitarian
and Cultural

Fourth Committee:
Trusteeship
(Including Non-Self-
Governing territories)

Fifth Committee:
Administrative &
Budgetary

Sixth Committee:
Legal

**GENERAL
ASSEMBLY**

**PROCEDURAL
COMMITTEES**

General
Committee

Credentials
Commitee

**STANDING
COMMITTEES**

Advisory
Committee on
Administrative
and Budgetary
Questions

Committee
on
Contributions

OTHER EXISTING BODIES SET UP BY GENERAL ASSEMBLY

Interim Committee of the General Assembly
Disarmament Commission
Disarmament Committee
Special Committee on the situation with regard to the implementa-
tion of the Declaration on the granting of independence to colo-
nial countries and peoples
Commission of Conciliation for the Congo
Commission of Investigation into the conditions and circumstances
resulting in the tragic death of Mr. Dag Hammarskjold and of
members of the party accompanying him
Sub-Committee on the Situation in Angola
United Nations Emergency Force (UNEF)
United Nations Conciliation Commission for Palestine
United Nations Relief and Works Agency for Palestine Refugees in
the Near East (UNRWA)
Panel for Inquiry and Conciliation
United Nations Scientific Advisory Committee
United Nations Scientific Committee on the Effects of Atomic
Radiation
Committee on the Peaceful Uses of Outer Space
United Nations Representative on Hungary
Peace Observation Commission
Collective Measures Committee
United Nations Commission for the Unification and Rehabilitation of
Korea (UNCURK)
United Nations Children's Fund (UNICEF)
Office of the United Nations High Commissioner for Refugees
United Nations Special fund
Committee on an United Nations Capital Development Fund
United Nations/FAO Inter-Governmental Committee on World
Food Programme
Ad Hoc Commission on Prisoners of War
Five-member United Nations Commission for Ruanda-Urundi
United Nations Special Committee for South West Africa
Committee on Information from Non-Self-Governing Territories
Special Committee on Territories under Portuguese Administration
Committee for United Nations Memorial Cemetery in Korea
Ad Hoc Committee of the Whole Assembly
Negotiating Committee for Extra-Budgetary Funds
United Nations Staff Pension Committee
Investments Committee
Board of Auditors
Panel of External Auditors
Consultative Panel of United Nations Information Policies and
Programmes
United Nations Administrative Tribunal
Committee on Applications for Review on Administrative Tribunal
Judgements
International Law Commission
Committee on Arrangements for a Conference for the Purpose of
Reviewing the Charter
Committee on Government Replies on the Question of Defining
Aggression
Commission on Permanent Sovereignty over Natural Resources

Delegation Personnel, 1956–65

Eleventh General Assembly, 1956
Liam Cosgrave, Minister for External Affairs
Frederick H. Boland, Permanent Representative to the United Nations
Sean Murphy, Secretary, Department of External Affairs
John J. Hearne, Ambassador to the United States
Conor Cruise O'Brien, Counsellor, International Organizations Section
Sheila Murphy, Counsellor, Political Section
Sean Morrissey, Legal Adviser, Department of External Affairs
Eamon Kennedy, Counsellor, Permanent Mission to the United Nations
Joseph Shields, Counsellor, Washington Embassy
Paul Keating, Second Secretary, Permanent Mission to the United Nations

Twelfth General Assembly, 1957
Frank Aiken, Minister for External Affairs,
Frederick H. Boland, Permanent Representative to the United Nations
Sean Nunan, Ambassador, Department of External Affairs
Conor Cruise O'Brien: Counsellor, International Organizations Section
Eamon Kennedy, Counsellor, Permanent Mission to the United Nations
Máire MacEntee, First Secretary, International Organizations Section
Aedan O'Bierne, Second Secretary, Washington Embassy
Paul Keating, Second Secretary, Permanent Mission to the United Nations

Thirteenth General Assembly, 1958
Frank Aiken, Minister for External Affairs.
Frederick H. Boland, Permanent Representative to the United Nations
Conor Cruise O'Brien, Counsellor, International Organizations Section
Eamon Kennedy, Counsellor, Permanent Mission to the United Nations
Máire MacEntee, First Secretary, International Organizations Section
Sean Ronan, Consul, Chicago
Eoin MacWhite, First Secretary, Political Section
Patrick Power, First Secretary, Administration Section
Paul Keating, Second Secretary, Permanent Mission to the United Nations
Robert McDonagh, Second Secretary, Irish Embassy, Stockholm

Fourteenth General Assembly, 1959
Frank Aiken, Minister for External Affairs
Frederick H. Boland, Permanent Representative to the United Nations
Conor Cruise O'Brien, Counsellor, International Organizations Section
Eamon Kennedy, Counsellor, Permanent Mission to the United Nations
Joseph F. Shields, Counsellor, Washington Embassy
Sean Ronan, Consul, Chicago
Eoin MacWhite, First Secretary, Political Section
Máire MacEntee, First Secretary, International Organizations Section
Robert McDonagh, Second Secretary, Political Section
Brendan Nolan, Second Secretary, Permanent Mission to the United Nations

Fifteenth General Assembly, 1960
Frank Aiken, Minister for External Affairs
Frederick H. Boland, Permanent Representative to the United Nations
Conor Cruise O'Brien, Counsellor, Political and United Nations Section
Eamon Kennedy, Counsellor, Permanent Mission to the United Nations
Máire MacEntee, First Secretary, International Organizations Section
Paul Keating, Second Secretary, Political and United Nations Section
Robert McDonagh, Second Secretary, Political and United Nations Section
Dennis Holmes, First Secretary, Bonn Embassy
Brendan Nolan, First Secretary, Permanent Mission to the United Nations
Joseph Shields, Counsellor, Washington Embassy

Sixteenth General Assembly, 1961
Frank Aiken, Minister for External Affairs
Frederick H. Boland, Permanent Representative to the United Nations
Sean Morrissey, Legal Advisor, Department of External Affairs
Sean Ronan, Counsellor, Political and United Nations Section
Gerard Woods, Consul-General, Boston
Frank Coffey, First Secretary, London Embassy
Tadhg O'Sullivan, Counsellor, Permanent Mission to the United Nations
James Kirwan, Vice-Consul, New York
Sean Ó hÉideáin, Consul-General, Chicago
Noel Dorr, Third Secretary, Information Section
Brendan Nolan, First Secretary, Permanent Mission to the United Nations

Seventeenth General Assembly, 1962
Frank Aiken, Minister for External Affairs
Frederick H. Boland, Permanent Representative to the United Nations
Tadhg O'Sullivan, Counsellor, Permanent Mission to the United Nations
J.G. Molloy, Assistant Secretary, Department of External Affairs
T.J. Horan, Ambassador, Madrid Embassy
Sean Morrisey, Legal Adviser, Department of External Affairs

James Kirwan, First Secretary, Political and UN Section
Brendan Nolan, First Secretary, Permanent Mission to the United Nations
Louis Cullen, Third Secretary, Rome Embassy
Eamonn Ó Tuathail, First Secretary, Washington Embassy

Eighteenth General Assembly, 1963
Frank Aiken, Minister for External Affairs
Frederick H. Boland, Permanent Representative to the United Nations
Tadhg O'Sullivan, Counsellor: Permanent Mission to the United Nations
Hugh McCann, Secretary, Department of External Affairs
T.J. Horan, Ambassador. Madrid Embassy
Joseph Shields, Ambassador, Rome Embassy
Denis Holmes, First Secretary, Bonn Embassy
Aedan O'Beirne, First Secretary, Information Section
Brendan Nolan, First Secretary, Permanent Mission to the United Nations
Patrick Campbell, First Secretary, Vatican Embassy

Nineteenth General Assembly, 1964
Frank Aiken, Minister for External Affairs
Cornelius Cremin, Permanent Representative to the United Nations
Tadhg O'Sullivan, Counsellor, Permanent Mission to the United Nations
Brian Gallagher, Department of External Affairs
Patrick Power, Department of External Affairs
Edward Brennan, Consul-General, Hamburg
Denis Holmes, First Secretary, Bonn Embassy
Brendan Nolan, First Secretary, Department of External Affairs
John Burke, Vice-Consul, New York
Patrick Campbell, First Secretary, Vatican Embassy

Twentieth General Assembly, 1965
Frank Aiken, Minister for External Affairs
Cornelius Cremin, Permanent Representative to the United Nations
Tadhg O'Sullivan, Counsellor, Permanent Mission to the United Nations
T.J. Horan, Ambassador, Madrid Embassy
Sean Ronan, Assistant Secretary, Department of External Affairs
Sean Ó hÉideáin, Counsellor, Economic Section
James Kirwan, Consul-General, San Francisco
Gearóid Ó Clérigh, Consul-General, Boston
Brendan Nolan, First Secretary, Political and United Nations Section
John Burke, First Secretary, Permanent Mission to the United Nations

Bibliography

PRIMARY SOURCES

National Archives, Dublin
Department of Foreign Affairs
  Common Market Series
  Confidential Reports Series
  Council of Europe and UN Series
  Embassy Series: Berne; Brussels; London; Ottawa; Paris; Permanent Mission to
    the United Nations; Rome; Washington, DC
  Estimates, Administration, and Establishment Series
  Information and Political Series
  International Peace and Atomic Energy Series
  Relief of Distress Series
  Secretary's Series: P, PS, S Files
  United Nations Series
Department of Industry and Commerce
  General Files
Department of the Taoiseach
  Cabinet Minutes
  Government Minutes
  Secretariat Files

United Nations Archives, New York
Secretary General Series
Secretariat Series
Peacekeeping Operations Series

Private Papers
Frederick H. Boland, Manuscripts Department, Trinity College, Dublin
Andrew Cordier, Columbia University, New York
Eamon de Valera, Franciscan Library, Killiney, Co. Dublin
John Foster Dulles, Princeton University, Princeton
John F. Kennedy Presidential Papers, Kennedy Library, Boston
Henry Cabot Lodge, Massachusetts Historical Society, Boston
Conor Cruise O'Brien, University College Dublin Archives
Adlai Stevenson, Princeton University, Princeton
U Thant, United Nations Archives, New York

Personal Interviews
Mr Frank Aiken, Jr, 17 April 1992
Mr Fergal Boland, 12 December 1993
Mr Liam Cosgrave, 2 April 1992
Ambassador Eamon Kennedy, 11 March 1993
Dr Conor Cruise O'Brien, 5 August 1993
Mrs Máire MacEntee O'Brien, 7 June 1996
Ambassador Tadhg O'Sullivan, 15 June 1995
Sir Brian Urquhart, 23 September 1994

Irish Government Publications
Dáil Éireann. Parliamentary Debates, 1922–69
Eire-Ireland: The Bulletin of the Irish Department of External Affairs. Dublin,
    1948–70
Papers Relating to Ireland's Application for Admission into the United Nations.
    Dublin, 1946
Texts Concerning Ireland's Position in Relation to the North Atlantic Treaty. Dublin,
    1950
The Defence Forces: Peacekeepers in the World. Department of Defence Pamphlet,
    1995

United Nations Publications
General Assembly: Official Documents
Security Council: Official Documents
United Nations Chronicle
The United Nations and Apartheid, 1948–94: New York, 1995
*The United Nations and Decolonization: Highlights of Thirty Years of United
    Nations Effort on Behalf of Colonial Countries and Peoples. New York, 1977*
The United Nations and Disarmament. New York, 1988
The United Nations and Nuclear Non-Proliferation. New York, 1995
United Nations Organization Weekly Bulletin
United Nations Yearbook, 1955–65

Newspapers and Magazines

America   *Irish Times*
Daily Herald   *Leader*
Catholic News   *Le Monde*
Economist   *Monitor*
Glasgow Herald   *New York Times*
Guardian   *Observer*
L'Illustré   *Pilot*
Irish Independent   *Tablet*
Irish Press   *The Times*

SECONDARY SOURCES

Aiken, Frank. *Ireland and the United Nations*. Dublin, 1957–68.

—— 'Can We Limit the Nuclear Club?' *Bulletin of the Atomic Scientist*, Vol. 17, No. 7 (September, 1961).

Akenson, Donald Harman. *The United States and Ireland*. Cambridge, 1973.

—— Conor: *A Biography of Conor Cruise O'Brien*. Two Vols. Montreal, 1994.

Alcock, Antony. *The History of the South Tyrol Question*. London, 1970.

Asmal, Kader. *Irish Opposition to Apartheid*. New York, 1971.

Barcroft, Stephen. 'Irish Foreign Policy at the League of Nations, 1929–1936'. *Irish Studies in International Affairs*, Vol. 1, No. 1 (1979).

Birnbaum, Karl E. and Neubold, Hanspeter, eds. *Neutrality and Non-alignment in Europe*. Vienna, 1981.

Blight, James G. and Welch, David A. *On the Brink: Americans and Soviets Reexamine the Cuban Missile Crisis*. New York, 1989.

Browne, Noel. *Against the Tide*. Dublin, 1986.

Brugioni, Dino A. *Eyeball to Eyeball*. New York, 1990.

Burns, Arthur Lee and Heathcote, Nina. *Peacekeeping by UN Forces*. New York, 1963.

Buckley, Timothy K. 'Attitudes toward the United Nations Peacekeeping Role in the Congo, 1960–64'. Unpublished M.A. Thesis, University College, Cork. 1986.

Chossudovsky, Evgeny. 'The Origins of the Treaty on the Non-Proliferation of Nuclear Weapons: Ireland's Initiative in the United Nations, 1958–61'. *Irish Studies in International Affairs*, Vol. 3, No. 2 (1990).

Chubb, Basil. *The Government and Politics of Ireland*. London, 1970.

Claude, Inis L. *Swords into Plowshares: The Problems and Progress of International Organizations*. London, 1965.

Conrad, John P. and van den Haag, Ernest. *The UN: In or Out?* New York, 1987.

Cordier, Andrew, and Foote, Wilder, and Harrelson, Max (eds.). *Public Papers of the Secretaries-General of the United Nations*. Seven Vols. New York, 1969–76.

Costello, John A. *Ireland in International Affairs*. Dublin, 1948.

Cremin, Cornelius. 'United Nations Peacekeeping Operations: An Irish Initiative, 1961–68'. *Irish Studies in International Affairs*, Vol. 1, No. 4 (1984).

Cronin, Sean. 'The Making of NATO and the Partition of Ireland'. *Eire-Ireland*, Vol. 20, No. 2 (1985).

—— *Washington's Irish Policy, 1916–1986: Independence, Partition, and Neutrality*. Dublin, 1987.

Daly, Mary. *Industrial Development and Irish National Identity, 1922–39* Dublin, 1992.

Djonovich, Dusan, J. *United Nations Resolutions: Series I: Resolutions Adopted by the General Assembly*. Twenty Four Vols. Dobbs Ferry, 1973–88.

—— *United Nations Resolutions: Series II: Resolutions and Decisions of the Security Council*. Eleven Vols. Dobbs Ferry. 1988–92.

Driscoll, Dennis. 'Is Ireland Really Neutral?' *Irish Studies in International Affairs*, Vol. 1, No. 3 (1982).

Drudy, P.J. and McAleese, D., eds. *Ireland and the European Community*. Cambridge, 1983.

——, ed. *The Irish in America: Emigration, Assimilation, and Impact.* Cambridge, 1985.

——, ed. *Ireland and Britain since 1922.* Cambridge, 1986.

Duggan, John. *A History of the Irish Army.* Dublin, 1991.

Dwyer, T. Ryle. *Irish Neutrality and the USA.* Dublin, 1977.

—— *Strained Relations: Ireland at Peace and the USA at War, 1941–45.* Dublin, 1988.

Edwards, Owen Dudley, ed. *Conor Cruise O'Brien Introduces Ireland.* Dublin, 1969.

Epstein, William. *The Last Chance: Nuclear Non-Proliferation and Arms Control.* New York, 1976.

Fanning, Ronan. *The Irish Department of Finance, 1922–58.* Dublin, 1978.

—— 'The United States and Irish Participation in NATO: The Debate of 1950'. *Irish Studies in International Affairs,* Vol. 1, No. 1 (1979).

—— 'London and Belfast's Response to the Declaration of the Republic of Ireland'. *International Affairs,* Vol. 58, No. 1 (1982).

—— 'Irish Neutrality – an Historical Perspective'. *Irish Studies in International Affairs,* Vol. 1, No. 3 (1982).

—— *Independent Ireland.* Dublin, 1983.

—— 'The Life and Times of Alexis Fitzgerald'. *Magill,* Vol. 8, No. 18 (September, 1985).

—— 'The Anglo-American Alliance and the Irish application for membership in the United Nations'. *Irish Studies in International Affairs,* Vol. 2, No. 2 (1986).

—— 'Irish Neutrality'. Bo Huldt and Atis Lejins, eds. *Neutrals in Europe: Ireland.* Stockholm, 1990.

—— 'Charles de Gaulle, 1946–58 – From Resignation to Return: The Irish Diplomatic Perspective'. Joannon, Pierre, ed. *De Gaulle and Ireland.* Dublin, 1991.

Farrell, Brian. *Chairman or Chief? The Role of the Taoiseach in Irish Government.* Dublin, 1971.

—— *Sean Lemass.* Dublin, 1983.

Fasulo, Linda M. *Representing America: Experiences of US Diplomats at the UN.* New York, 1984.

Fitzgerald, Garrett. 'Political Implications of Irish Membership in the EEC'. *Studies,* Vol. 51 (1962).

Fitzgerald, William. *Irish Unification and NATO.* Dublin, 1982.

Foot, Rosemary. 'The European Community's Voting Behavior at the United Nations General Assembly'. *Journal of Common Market Studies,* Vol. 17, No. 4 (1979).

Foster, Roy. *Modern Ireland, 1600–1972.* London, 1988.

Freiberger, Steven Z. *Dawn Over Suez: the Rise of American Power in the Middle East, 1953–57.* Chicago, 1992.

Fry, M., Keatinge, P. and Rotblat, J., eds. *Nuclear Non-Proliferation and the Non-Proliferation Treaty.* Berlin, 1990.

Glynn, Patrick. *Closing Pandora's Box: Arms Races, Arms Control, and the History of the Cold War.* New York, 1992.

Gordenker, L. 'Conor Cruise O'Brien and the Truth About the United Nations'. *International Organizations,* Vol. 23, No. 4 (1969).

Harkness, David. *The Restless Dominion.* London, 1969.

Hayes-McCoy, G.A. 'Irish Defense Policy, 1938–51'. *Ireland in the War Years and After*. Nowlan, K.B. and Williams, T.D., eds. Dublin, 1969.

Heathcote, Nina. 'Ireland and the United Nations Operation in the Congo'. *International Relations*, Vol. 3, No. 11 (May 1971).

Hederman, Miriam. *The Road to Europe: Irish Attitudes, 1948–61*. Dublin, 1983.

Higgins, Rosalyn. *United Nations Peacekeeping, 1946–67*. Four Vols. Oxford, 1979–81.

Hill, Ronald J. and O'Corcora, Micheal. 'The Soviet Union in Irish Foreign Policy'. *International Affairs*, Vol. 58, No. 2 (1982).

Hixson, Walter, L. *George F. Kennan: Cold War Iconoclast*. New York, 1989.

Horne, Alistair. *A Savage War of Peace: Algeria, 1954–62*. London, 1977.

Huldt, Bo. *Sweden, the UN, and Decolonization*. Stockholm, 1974.

―― and Lejins, Atis, eds. *Neutrals in Europe: Ireland*. Stockholm, 1990.

Hurwitz, Leon. 'The EEC and Decolonization: The Voting Behavior of the Nine in the UN General Assembly'. *Political Studies*, Vol. 24 (1976).

James, Alan. *The Politics of Peacekeeping*. London, 1969.

Keatinge, Patrick. 'Ireland and the League of Nations'. *Studies*, Vol. 59 (1970).

―― *The Formulation of Irish Foreign Policy*. Dublin, 1973.

―― *A Place Among the Nations: Issues of Irish Foreign Policy*. Dublin, 1978.

―― 'Ireland and the World, 1957–82'. Litton, F., ed. *Unequal Achievement*. Dublin, 1982.

―― 'The Europeanization of Irish Foreign Policy'. Drudy, P.J. and McAleese, Dermot, eds. *Ireland and the European Community*. Cambridge, 1983.

―― *A Singular Stance: Irish Neutrality in the 1980s*. Dublin, 1984.

―― 'Irish Neutrality and the European Community'. McSweeney, Bill, ed. *Ireland and the Threat of Nuclear War*. Dublin, 1985.

Kelleher, John, V. 'Ireland … Where Does She Stand?' *Foreign Affairs*, Vol. 35, No. 3 (1957).

Kennedy, Michael. 'The Irish Free State and the League of Nations, 1922–32'. *Irish Studies in International Affairs*, Vol. 3, No. 4 (1992).

―― *Ireland and the League of Nations, 1919–46: International Relations, Diplomacy and Politics*. Dublin, 1996.

Keogh, Dermot. 'History of the Irish Department of External Affairs'. Steiner, Z., ed. *The Times Survey of Foreign Offices Around the World*. London, 1982.

―― *Ireland and Europe, 1919–48*. Dublin, 1988.

―― 'Profile of Joseph Walshe, Secretary of the Department of Foreign Affairs, 1922–46'. *Irish Studies in International Affairs*, Vol. 3, No. 2 (1990).

―― 'Ireland, the Vatican and the Cold War: the Case of Italy, 1948'. *Irish Studies in International Affairs*, Vol. 3, No. 3 (1991).

―― *Twentieth-Century Ireland: Nation and State*. Dublin, 1994.

―― *Ireland and the Vatican: Politics and Diplomacy of Church-State Relations, 1922–60*. Cork, 1995.

Kissinger, Henry. *Diplomacy*. New York, 1994.

Kyle, Keith. *Suez*. New York, 1991.

Laffan, Brigid. *Ireland and South Africa: Irish Government Policy in the 1980s*. Dublin, 1988.

Lee, Joseph, ed. *Ireland, 1945–70*. Dublin, 1979.

―― *Ireland, 1912–85: Politics and Society*. Cambridge, 1989.

Lefever, Ernest W. *Uncertain Mandate: Politics of the UN Congo Operation.* Baltimore, 1967.

Lemass, Sean. 'Small States in International Organizations'. Schou, A. and Brundtland, A.O., eds. *Small States in International Relations.* Uppsala, 1971.

Luard, Evan. *A History of the United Nations.* Two Vols. London, 1982 & 1989.

Lustick, Ian. *Unsettled States, Disputed Lands: Britain and Ireland; France and Algeria; Israel and the West Bank-Gaza.* Ithaca, 1993.

Lyons, F.S.L. *Ireland since the Famine.* London, 1973.

MacDonagh, Michael. 'Ireland's Attitude to External Affairs'. *Studies*, Vol. 48 (1959).

MacQueen, Norman. 'Ireland's Entry into the United Nations, 1946–56.' Gallagher, Thomas and O'Connell, James, eds. *Irish Contemporary Studies.* Manchester, 1983.

——— 'Frank Aiken and Irish Activism at the United Nations'. *International History Review*, Vol. 6, No. 2 (May, 1984).

Maguire, Maria. *A Bibliography of Published Works on Irish Foreign Relations, 1921–78.* Dublin, 1981.

Maher, Denis. *The Tortuous Path: The Course of Ireland's Entry into the EEC, 1948–73.* Dublin, 1986.

Manning, Maurice. *The Blueshirts.* Dublin, 1970.

Mansergh, Nicholas. 'Irish Foreign Policy, 1945–55'. Nowlan, K.B. and Williams, T.D., eds. *Ireland in the War Years and After.* Dublin, 1969.

McCabe, Ian. *A Diplomatic History of Ireland.* Dublin, 1991.

McCarthy, John F. *Planning Ireland's Future – The Legacy of T.K. Whitaker.* Dublin, 1990.

McCaughren, Thomas. *The Peacemakers of Niemba.* Dublin, 1966.

McMahon, Deirdre. *Republicans and Imperialists: Anglo-Irish Relations in the 1930s.* London, 1984.

McSweeney, Bill, ed. *Ireland and the Threat of Nuclear War.* Dublin, 1985.

Meisler, Stanley. *United Nations: the First Fifty Years.* New York, 1995.

Millar, T.B. *The Commonwealth and the United Nations.* Sydney, 1967.

Moynihan, Maurice, ed. *Speeches and Statements of Eamon de Valera, 1917–73.* Dublin, 1980.

Mulkeen, Thomas. 'Ireland at the UN'. *Eire-Ireland*, Vol. 8, No. 1 (1973).

Neuhold, Hanspeter. 'Permanent Neutrality in Contemporary International Relations: A Comparative Perspective'. *Irish Studies in International Affairs*, Vol. 1, No. 3 (1982).

Nowlan, K.B. and Williams, T.D. *Ireland in the War Years and After.* Dublin, 1969.

Nyangoni, Wellington W. *Africa and the United Nations System.* Rutherford, 1985.

O'Brien, Conor Cruise. *To Katanga and Back: A UN Case Study.* London, 1962.

——— *Writers and Politics.* London, 1965.

——— *Ireland, the United Nations, and Southern Africa.* Dublin, 1967.

——— *United Nations: Sacred Drama.* London, 1968.

——— 'Ireland in International Affairs'. Edwards, Owen Dudley, ed. *Conor Cruise O'Brien Introduces Ireland.* Dublin, 1969.

O'Connor, Brian. *Ireland and the United Nations.* Tuarim pamphlet. Dublin, 1961.

Ó Drisceoil, Donal. *Censorship in Ireland, 1939–45: Neutrality, Politics and Society*. Cork, 1996.

O'Halpin, Eunan. 'Intelligence and Security in Ireland, 1922–45'. *Intelligence and National Security*, Vol. 5, No. 1 (1990).

O'Grady, Joseph. 'Ireland, the Cuban Missile Crisis, and Civil Aviation: A Study in Applied Neutrality'. *Eire-Ireland*, Vol. 30, No. 3 (Fall, 1995).

Ozgur, Ozdemir. *Apartheid: The United Nations and Peaceful Change in South Africa*. Dobbs Ferry, 1982.

Pierce, Siobhan. 'The Irish Army's Participation in the UN's Peace-Making Mission in the Congo, 1960–64'. Unpublished M.A. Thesis, University College Dublin, 1993.

Prill, Felician. 'Sean Lester'. *Studies*, Vol. 49 (1960).

Rabe, Stephen. 'The Cuban Missile Crisis Revisited'. *Irish Studies in International Affairs*, Vol. 3, No. 3 (1991).

Raymond, Raymond J. 'Irish Neutrality: Ideology or Pragmatism?' *International Affairs*, Vol. 60 (1984).

—— 'Ireland's 1949 NATO Decision: A Reassessment'. *Eire-Ireland*, Vol. 20, No. 3 (1985).

—— The Marshall Plan and Ireland'. Drudy, P.J. *The Irish In America: Emigration, Assimilation, and Impact*. Cambridge, 1985.

—— 'David Gray, the Aiken Mission and Irish Neutrality'. *Diplomatic History*, Vol. 9 (1985).

Rosenberg, Joseph. 'The 1941 Mission of Frank Aiken to the United States: an American Perspective'. *Irish Historical Studies*, Vol. 22 (1980).

Russell, Ruth B. *The United Nations and United States Security Policy*. Washington, 1968.

Salmon, Trevor. 'The Changing Nature of Irish Defense Policy'. *The World Today*, Vol. 35, No. 11 (1979).

—— 'Ireland: A Neutral in the Community?' *Journal of Common Market Studies*, Vol. 20, No. 3 (1982).

—— *Unneutral Ireland*. Oxford, 1989.

Schou, A. and Brundtland, A.O., eds. *Small States in International Relations*. Uppsala, 1971.

Shannon, William. *The American Irish*. Amherst, 1966.

Shaker, Mohamed I. *The Nuclear Non-Proliferation Treaty: Origin and Implementation, 1959–79*. New York, 1980.

Sharp, Paul. *Irish Foreign Policy and the European Community*. Aldershot, 1990.

Singer, Marshall. *Weak States in a World of Powers: The Dynamics of International Relationships*. New York, 1972.

Skinner, Liam. *Politicians by Accident*. Dublin, 1946.

Slonim, Solomon. *South West Africa and the United Nations: An International Mandate in Dispute*. Baltimore, 1973.

Smith, Raymond. *The Fighting Irish in the Congo*. Dublin, 1962.

—— *Under the Blue Flag*. Dublin, 1980.

Skelly, Joseph Morrison. 'Ireland, the Department of External Relations, and the United Nations, 1946–55: a New Look'. *Irish Studies in International Affairs*, Vol. 7 (1996).

Smylie, R.M. 'Unneutral Neutral Eire'. *Foreign Affairs*, Vol. 24 (1946).

Steiner, Z. ed. *The Times Survey of Foreign Offices Around the World*. London, 1982.

Sureda, A. Rigo. *The Evolution of the Right to Self-Determination: A Study of United Nations Practice*. Leiden, 1973.

Talbott, John. *The War Without a Name: France in Algeria, 1954–62*. London, 1981.

Tavares de Sa, Hernane. *The Play within the Play: The Inside Story of the UN*. New York, 1966.

Toscano, Mario. *Alto Adige-South Tyrol: Italy's Frontier with the German World*. London, 1975.

Urquhart, Brian. *Hammarskjold*. New York, 1972.

—— *A Life in Peace and War*. New York, 1987.

—— *Ralph Bunche: An American Life*. New York, 1993.

Whelan, Anthony. 'Self-Determination and Decolonization: Foundations for the Future'. *Irish Studies in International Affairs*, Vol. 3, No. 4 (1992).

Whelan, Bernadette. "Ireland and the Marshall Plan'. *Irish Economic and Social History*, Vol. 19 (1993).

Willets, Peter. *The Non-Aligned Movement*. London, 1978.

Williams, T.D. 'Ireland and the War'. Nowlan, K.B. and Williams, T.D., eds. *Ireland in the War Years and After*. Dublin, 1969.

—— 'Conclusion'. Nowlan, K.B. and Williams, T.D., eds. *Ireland in the War Years and After*. Dublin, 1969.

—— 'Irish Foreign Policy, 1949–69'. Lee, Joseph, ed. *Ireland, 1945–70*. Dublin, 1979.

Young, John, N. *Erskine H. Childers, President of Ireland: A Biography*. Gerrards Cross, 1985.

Zacher, Mark W. *Dag Hammarskjold's United Nations*. New York, 1970.

Index